Insurgencies

Edited by

Sandra Buckley

Michael Hardt

Brian Massumi

THEORY OUT OF BOUNDS

15 Insurgencies: Constituent Power and the Modern State Antonio Negri

14 When Pain Strikes Bill Burns, Cathy Busby, and Kim Sawchuk, Eds.

13 Critical Environments: Postmodern Theory and the Pragmatics of the "Outside" Cary Wolfe

12 Metamorphosis of the Body José Gil

11 The New Spinoza Warren Montag and Ted Stolze, Eds.

10 Power and Invention: Situating Science Isabelle Stengers

9 Arrow of Chaos: Romanticism and Postmodernity Ira Livingston

8 Becoming-Woman Camilla Griggers

7 A Potential Politics: Radical Thought in Italy Paolo Virno and Michael Hardt, Eds.

6 Capital Times: Tales from the Conquest of Time Éric Alliez

5 The Year of Passages Réda Bensmaïa

4 Labor of Dionysus: A Critique of the State-Form Michael Hardt and Antonio Negri

3 Bad Aboriginal Art: Tradition, Media, and Technological Horizons Eric Michaels

2 The Cinematic Body Steven Shaviro

1 The Coming Community Giorgio Agamben

Insurgencies

Constituent Power and the Modern State

Antonio Negri

Translated by Maurizia Boscagli

Theory Out of Bounds *Volume 15*

University of Minnesota Press

Minneapolis • London

The University of Minnesota Press gratefully acknowledges financial assistance provided for the translation of this book by the McKnight Foundation.

The University of Minnesota Press gratefully acknowledges the contribution of Michael Hardt and Timothy Murphy to the publication of this book; they provided invaluable assistance in translating certain sections of the manuscript and in editing the translation.

Published by the University of Minnesota Press
111 Third Avenue South, Suite 290
Minneapolis, MN 55401-2520
http://www.upress.umn.edu
Printed in the United States of America on acid-free paper

LIBRARY OF CONGRESS CATALOGING-IN-PUBLICATION DATA
Negri, Antonio, 1933–
[Potere costituente. English]
Insurgencies : constituent power and the modern state / Antonio Negri ; translated by Maurizia Boscagli.
p. cm. — (Theory out of bounds ; v. 15)
Includes bibliographical references and index.
ISBN 0-8166-2274-4 (hc). — ISBN 0-8166-2275-2 (pb)
1. Constitutional law—Philosophy. 2. Constituent power.
3. Revolutions. I. Title. II. Series.
K3165.N4413 1999
342'.001—dc21
99-30982

The University of Minnesota
is an equal-opportunity educator and employer.

11 10 09 08 07 06 05 04 03 02 10 9 8 7 6 5 4 3 2

Contents

Foreword

THE HISTORY of modern Euro-American revolutions has often been read by scholars as a series of contrasts or alternatives. The dynamics of the American Revolution are opposed to the French, or perhaps both are contrasted to the Russian experience. Such studies end up by posing the different modern revolutions as emblems of opposing ideological positions—liberal, bourgeois, totalitarian, and so forth. Antonio Negri proposes, rather, that we trace the common thread that links these modern revolutions and read them as the progressive development and expression of one and the same concept, *constituent power*. Constituent power is the active, operative element common to all modern revolutions and the conceptual key to understanding them.

One can approach the concept of constituent power through the democratic practices of modern revolutions and begin by looking at the popular organizational frameworks that are its expressions in the different revolutionary experiences, such as the constituent assemblies in the American and French revolutions or the soviets in the Russian. Here we find that constituent power is an expression of the popular will, or, better, it is the power of the multitude. Democracy itself is thus inseparable from the concept and practice of constituent power.

Throughout the modern era, however, constituent power has been in conflict with *constituted power*, the fixed power of formal constitutions and central authority. Whereas constituent power opens each revolutionary process, throwing open the doors to the forces of change and the myriad desires of the multitude, constituted power closes down the revolution and brings it back to order. In each of the modern revolutions, the State rose up in opposition to the democratic and revolutionary forces and imposes a return to a constituted order, a new Thermidore, which either recuperated or repressed the constituent impulses. The conflict between active constituent power and reactive constituted power is what characterizes these revolutionary experiences. After the defeat of each revolution, constituent desires disappeared but did not die. They burrowed underground in wait for a new time and a new place to spring forth again in revolution. This is the story Negri tells as he traces the movements of constituent power and its revolutions from Machiavelli's Florence to the English Revolution, and from the American, to the French and Russian revolutions. Each time constituent power springs forth and each time it is beaten back by constituted power and its forces of order. How can we make a revolution, Negri asks continually throughout his study, that is never closed down? How can we create a constituent power that is never reined in and defeated by a new constituted power? How can we finally realize democracy?

We should situate Negri's conception of constituent power alongside the other attempts to understand the centrality of the political in modern thought and society, such as Michel Foucault's theory of power and Hannah Arendt's notion of politics and action. The primary contribution of Negri's work is his articulation of a distinction within power between constituent power and constituted power. This distinction provides him both an analytical and an evaluative criterion that differentiates power. Negri thus forces us to refuse any unitary conception of power and recognize, rather, two fundamental powers that conflict continually throughout modernity. Similarly, modernity and its development cannot be captured in any unitary conception or teleological development; modernity is instead characterized by the antagonistic play between constituent power and constituted power, and its development is determined by their relative advances and declines. The two powers can thus serve as emblems for the fundamental alternatives within modernity and the two competing notions of the political that characterize it.

Negri's book opens in an intellectual field in which constituent power has been recognized but continually negated—the field of constitutional and legal theory. Legal theorists, particularly continental legal theorists, are among the scholars who have devoted the most attention to the concept of constituent power, but as Negri shows they have distorted it and taken away its revolutionary character, twisting it finally into a support of rather than a threat to constituted power. This conceptual defeat at the hands of legal theorists serves as an introduction to all the theoretical and practical defeats that constituent power has suffered throughout modernity. From Florence to Philadelphia and St. Petersburg, the revolutionary forces of constituent power were defeated—but only to rise again in another form and another place. Constituent power remains the positive alternative of modernity that points still toward a future revolutionary expression.

Theory Out of Bounds Series Editors

O N E

Constituent Power: The Concept of a Crisis

On the Juridical Concept of Constituent Power

TO SPEAK of constituent power is to speak of democracy. In the modern age the two concepts have often been related, and as part of a process that has intensified during the twentieth century, they have become more and more superimposed. In other words, constituent power has been considered not only as an all-powerful and expansive principle capable of producing the constitutional norms of any juridical system, but also as the subject of this production—an activity equally all-powerful and expansive. From this standpoint, constituent power tends to become identified with the very concept of politics as it concept is understood in a democratic society. To acknowledge constituent power as a constitutional and juridical principle, we must see it not simply as producing constitutional norms and structuring constituted powers but primarily as a subject that regulates democratic politics.

Yet this is not a simple matter. In fact, constituent power resists being constitutionalized: "Studying constituent power from the juridical perspective presents an exceptional difficulty given the hybrid nature of this power.... The strength hidden in constituent power refuses to be fully integrated in a hierarchical system of norms and competencies.... constituent power always remains alien to the law."[1] The question becomes even more difficult because democracy, too, resists being constitutionalized: democracy is in fact a theory of absolute government, while constitutionalism is a theory of limited government and therefore a practice that limits democracy.[2] Our aim then will be to find a definition of constituent power within the boundaries of this crisis that characterizes it. We will try to understand the radical character of the foundations of the concept of constituent power, and the extent of its effects, from democracy to sovereignty, from politics to the State, from power [*potere*] to strength [*potenza*].[3] In short, we will try to understand the concept of constituent power exactly insofar as it is the concept of a crisis.

Therefore let's first consider the articulations of the juridical definition of constituent power: they will allow us to get immediately to the core of the argument. Afterward, we will consider the problem of constituent power from the standpoint of constitutionalism.

What is constituent power from the perspective of juridical theory? It is the source of production of constitutional norms—that is, the power to make a constitution and therefore to dictate the fundamental norms that organize the powers of the State. In other words, it is the power to establish a new juridical arrangement, to regulate juridical relationships within a new community.[4] "Constituent power is an imperative act of nation, rising from nowhere and organizing the hierarchy of powers."[5] This is an extremely paradoxical definition: a power rising from nowhere organizes law. This paradox is unsustainable precisely because it is so extreme. Indeed, never as clearly as in the case of constituent power has juridical theory been caught in the game of affirming and denying, absolutizing and limiting that is characteristic of its logic (as Marx continually affirms).

Even though constituent power is all-powerful, it nonetheless has to be limited temporally, defined, and deployed as an extraordinary power. The time of constituent power, a time characterized by a formidable capacity of acceleration—the time of the event and of the generalization of singularity—has to be closed, treated, reduced in juridical categories, and restrained in the administrative routine. Perhaps this imperative to transform constituent power into extraordinary power, to crush it against the event, to shut it in a factuality revealed only by the law, was never as anxiously felt as during the French Revolution. Constituent power as all-embracing power is in fact the revolution itself. "Citizens, the revolution is determined by the principles that began it. The constitution is founded on the sacred rights of property, equality, freedom [*liberté*]. The revolution is over," proclaimed Napoleon with inimitable, ironic arrogance,[6] because to claim that constituent power is over is pure logical nonsense. It is clear, however, that that revolution and that constituent power could be made legal only in the form of the Thermidor.

The problem of French liberalism, throughout the first half of the nineteenth century, was that of bringing the revolution to a conclusion.[7] But constituent power is not only all-powerful; it is also expansive: its unlimited quality is not only temporal, but also spatial. However, this latter characteristic will also have to be reduced—spatially reduced and regulated. Constituent power must itself be reduced to the norm of the production of law; it must be incorporated into the established power. Its expansiveness is only shown as an interpretative norm, as a form of control of the State's constitutionality, as an activity of constitutional revision. Eventually, a pale reproduction of constituent power can be seen at work in referendums, regulatory activities, and so on, operating intermittently within well-defined limits and procedures.[8] All this from an objective perspective: an extremely strong set of juridical tools covers over and alters the nature of constituent power, defining the concept of constituent power as an insoluble essence.

If we regard the question from a subjective perspective, the crisis becomes even more evident. After being objectively perverted, constituent power becomes, so to speak, subjectively desiccated. First of all the singular characteristics of its originary and inalienable nature vanish, and the nexus that historically links constituent power to the right of resistance (and that defines, in a sense, the active character of the former) is erased.[9] What is left then undergoes every type of distortion. Certainly, once situated within the concept of the nation, constituent power seems to maintain some of its originary aspects, but it is well known that this is a sophism, and that the notion of constituent power is more suffocated than developed by the concept of nation.[10]

Not even this reduction suffices, however, and the beast seems not yet to be tamed. Thus the action of the scissors of logic is added to the ideological sophism, and juridical theory celebrates one of its masterpieces. The paradigm is split: to originary, commissionary constituent power is opposed constituent power proper, in its assembly form; finally, constituted power is opposed to both.[11] In this way, constituent power is absorbed into the mechanism of representation.[12] The boundlessness of constituent expression is limited in its genesis because it is subjected to the rules and relative extension of suffrage; in its functioning because it is subjected to the rules of assembly; and in the period during which it is in force (which is considered delimited in its functions, assuming more the form of classic "dictatorship" than referring to the idea and practices of democracy).[13] Finally, and on the whole, the idea of constituent power is juridically preformed, whereas it was claimed that it would generate the law; it is in fact absorbed in the notion of political representation, whereas it was supposed to legitimize this notion. Thus constituent power, as an element connected to representation (and incapable of expressing itself except through representation), becomes part of the great design of the social division of labor.[14] This is how the juridical theory of constituent power solves the allegedly vicious circle of the reality of constituent power. But isn't closing constituent power within representation—where the latter is merely a cog in the social machinery of the division of labor—nothing but the negation of the reality of constituent power, its congealment in a static system, the restoration of traditional sovereignty against democratic innovation?[15]

This solution is too easy. In spite of everything, the problem cannot be abolished, erased, dismissed. It remains as a problem, and the interpreters of the law are left to their Sisyphean labor. How then can we avoid a theoretical path that eliminates, together with the vicious circle, the very reality of the contradiction between constituent power and juridical arrangement, between the all-powerful and expansive effectiveness of the source and the system of positive law, of constituted normativity? How can we keep open the source of the vitality of the system while controlling it? Constituent power must somehow be maintained in order to avoid the possibility that its elimination might nullify the very meaning of the juridical system and the democratic relation that must characterize its horizon. Constituent power and its effects exist: how and where should they operate? How might one understand constituent power in a juridical apparatus? This is the whole problem: to maintain the irreducibility of the constituent fact, its effects, and the values it expresses. Three solutions have then been proposed. According to some, constituent power is transcendent with respect to the system of constituted power: its dynamics are imposed on the system from outside. According to another group of jurists, that power is instead immanent, its presence is implicit, and it operates as a foundation. A third group of jurists, finally, considers the source—constituent power—as neither transcendent nor immanent but, rather, integrated into, coextensive, and synchronic with the positive constitutional system. Let's examine these positions one by one and emphasize their internal articulation. It seems that in each case the transcendence, immanence, or integration and coexistence can be present to a greater or lesser degree, thus determining singular and diverse juridical and constitutional effects.

This is the case for the first group of authors, those who consider constituent power as a transcendent source. Here constituent power is assumed to be a fact that first precedes the constitutional arrangement but then is opposed to it, in the sense that it remains historically external and can be defined only by constituted power. This is actually the traditional position, but it is revised insofar as the contradiction is avoided through a dislocation of planes. Whereas the order of the constituted power is that of the *Sollen* (what ought to be), the order of constituent power is that of *Sein* (what is). The first belongs to juridical theory, the second to history or sociology. There is no intersection between norm and fact, validity and effectiveness, what ought be and the ontological horizon. The second is the foundation of the first but through a causal link that is immediately broken, so that the constituted juridical system is absolutely autonomous.

The great school of German public law, in the second half of the nineteenth century and at the beginning of the twentieth, has by and large identified itself with this position. According to Georg Jellinek, constituent power is exogenous with respect to the constitution and derives from the empirical-factual sphere as normative production.[16] This normative production is limited, or, better, it contains its own limitation because the empirical-factual is that historical and ethical reality that à la Kant—if the law allows it—limits the extension of the principle outside of the law. Constituent power, if the law and the constitution allow it, wants nothing but the regulation and therefore the self-limitation of its own force.[17] In this sense the transcendence of the factual with respect to the law can be considered a difference of minimal degree. It is interesting to notice how Jellinek's school (particularly when faced with the effects of the revolutionary council movement in post–First World War Germany) does not hesitate to reduce the gap that divides the source from the juridical arrangement, thus accepting the need to include within this space revolutionary productions and ensuing unforeseen institutional effects that certainly exceed the fundamental norm of the constitution of the *Reich*.[18]

This is what Hans Kelsen refuses. For him transcendence is utmost and absolute. The characteristic of the law is to regulate its own production. Only a norm can determine, and does determine, the procedure through which another norm is produced. The norm regulating the production of another norm and the norm produced according to this prescription (representable through the spatial image of superordination and subordination) have nothing to do with constituent power. Norms follow the rules of the juridical form, and constituent power has nothing to do with the formal process of the production of norms. Constituent power is itself, at the limit, defined by the system in its entirety. Its factual reality, omnipotence, and expansiveness are implied in that point of the system where the formal strength [*potenza*] of the law is itself omnipotent and expansive: the basic norm [*Grundnorm*].[19] And the fact that in Kelsen's final writings the entire factual, jurisprudential, and institutional life of the law appears to be absorbed in the normative process does not change the situation much. The new dynamic is never dialectical;

at most, it is a tracing of the real, and in any case the system never loses its absolute autonomy. As far as constituent power is concerned, we witness the paradox of being able to consider it as active for its whole constitutional life, but never capable of being a source of definition or principle of movement for any aspect of the system.[20] How can we comment on this scenario? Little or nothing remains of constituent power through and after this operation of the formal founding of the law, and therefore of the ethical (as in Jellinek) or sociological (as in Kelsen) reduction of its concept. Again, the point of view of sovereignty imposes itself against that of democracy; the transcendence of constituent power is its negation.

The result does not seem much different when constituent power is considered as immanent to the constitutional and juridical system. Here we are not confronted by the articulation of a set of positions pertaining to any one school, but by a variety of positions typical of various theoretical tendencies. In this case, the historical density of constituent power is not a priori excluded from theoretical investigation; but the way in which juridical theory relates to it is no less problematic. Indeed, even though constituent power becomes a real motor of constitutional dynamism (and juridical theory accepts its presence), at the same time several neutralizing operations are put into action. These are operations of transcendental abstraction or temporal concentration, so that, in the first case, the inherence of fact to law may be diluted in, we could say, a providential horizon; or, in the second case, it may solidify in a sudden and isolated action of innovation. The minimum and the maximum degrees of immanence are measured here with respect to the decreased reach of the effects, or to the irrational and immediate intensity of the cause. If the effectiveness of the constituent principle is given, it is with the aim of restraining it and regulating it. The position of minimum incidence of the constituent principle, as immanent principle of the juridical system, can be typically studied in John Rawls's work.[21] He considers constituent power as the second part of a sequence, following an originary stage during which the contractual agreement on the principles of justice has been made, and before third and fourth stages that center, respectively, on law-making mechanisms and hierarchies, and the execution of the law. Constituent power is reabsorbed into constituted law through a multistaged mechanism that, by making constituent power immanent to the system, deprives it of its creative originality. Furthermore, political justice or, really, the justice of the constitution (that produced by constituent power) always represents a case of imperfect procedural justice. In other words, in the calculus of probabilities the organization of political consensus is always relatively indeterminate. To the limit that constituent power encounters in the contractual mechanism must be added an overdetermined ethico-political limit, which is the (Kantian) condition of the constitution of the transcendental. Immanence is weak, of minimal degree, even though effective.[22]

Let's now consider some theoretical positions in which the degree of immanence is greater. Once again we need to shift our attention, after this brief excursus into the Anglo-Saxon world, to the juridical theory and also the political theory of the German *Reich*. Ferdinand Lassalle claims that the normative validity of the juridical-formal constitution depends on the material and formal (that is, sociological and juridical) degree of adaptation of the orders of reality that has been posed by constituent power. This is an actual formative power. Its extraordinariness is preformative, and its intensity radiates as an implicit project onto the system as a whole. Keeping in mind the resistance of the real conditions and the reach shown by constituent power, the constitutional process can be imagined and studied as an intermediate determination between two orders of reality.[23] Hermann Heller, another critic gravitating in the orbit of those juridical tendencies close to the workers' movement, brings to completion Lassalle's vision. Here the process of constituent power becomes endogenous, internal to constitutional development. Initially, constituent power infuses its dynamism into the constitutional system and then is itself reformed by the constitution.[24] We are not far from the moment when Rudolf Smend can call the constitution "the dynamic principle of the State's becoming."[25] How can the origins of constituent power be, at the end of the analytical process, completely absorbed by the State? How is it possible that the mediation of different orders of reality ends with a dynamism centered, or better, made its own, as an intimate essence, by the State? Once again, what is going on here is a neutralization of constituent power. And although these authors deny it, claiming rather that the evolution of the State also implies the progressive realization of a set of constituent norms, the determination that these norms assume in the real movement becomes totally uncertain. The immanence of constituent power is shown by the State to be a form of natural evolution.

Can constitutional history be a natural history? Two major twentieth-century scholars answer this question: Max Weber and Carl Schmitt. With an acute perception Weber understood that the naturalist criterion is insufficient to make constituent power immanent to constituted power. Instead, Weber insistently pushes constituent power to confront historicosocial reality.[26] Throughout the core of his political sociology where he defines the theory of the types of legitimacy, it is clear that for Weber constituent power is situated between charismatic and rational power. Constituent power derives from the first the violence of innovation, and from the second its constitutive instrumentality. It suddenly forms positive law according to an innovative project that grounds a paradigm of rationality.

Weber develops this German casuistry with his study of the Russian revolutions of 1905 and 1917, which were contemporary to his work.[27] He perfectly grasps the complexity of the relationships between irrationality and rationality, and between the collective and the individual, that run throughout the constituent phase. That said, his sociological formalism does not seem to lead to results any more valid than juridical formalism. Linking charismatic legitimation to rational legitimation is not enough to allow Weber to articulate an original phenomenology of constituent power. The attempt fails because Weber's methodology remains, despite every effort to the contrary, founded on a fixed typology, a typology not so much of the form of production as of the figures of consistency of law and the State. This is a unique case of myopia, as if in order to define constituent power, one had to discuss the projections of constituted power, or worse, the consequences, the perverse effects of constituent power. Constituent power, as much as charismatic power, must be judged as a category of its own. They do not have the same kind of historical consistency as other types of legitimacy. They are defined by changing practices (albeit extremely important ones) rather than concrete determinations. They are ideal types that pervade the entire juridical arrangement, immanent but in the end esoteric, strange, and extraordinary. Hence Carl Schmitt's position, which claims to grasp the concreteness of this limit: concretizing the formal means making it into the absolute principle of the constitution.[28]

The "decision" that Carl Schmitt sees as marking the very possibility of law, the identification and conflict of friend and enemy, and that he sees as running through the whole system, shaping it and overdetermining it—this act of war represents the maximum of factuality, cast as absolute immanence in the juridical system.[29] This immanence is so profound that at first sight the distinction between constituent and constituted power fades, so that constituent power appears according to its nature as originary power or counterpower, as historically determined strength, as a set of needs, desires, and singular determinations.[30] In fact, however, the existential matrix through which constituent power is defined is stripped away from the beginning, brought back to the abstract determinations of violence, of pure event as voluntary occurrence of power. The absolute tendency of the foundation of constituent power becomes a cynical claim; after coming very close to a material definition of constituent power, Schmitt gets entrapped in the irrational overdetermination of the conception of sovereignty, no longer of a pure concept of strength [*potenza*], but of power [*potere*].

We are now approaching the last of the positions that we set to examine: the one that considers constituent power as integrated, constitutive, coextensive, and coexistent with constituted law. This is obviously the perspective supported by the great twentieth-century institutionalist schools.[31] Later, juridical dogmatics adopted this position in a generalized manner. What then is the theoretical thesis that, albeit with many variations, these authors have sustained? They all consider the historical institutional element as a vital principle; far from being purely factual, however, this element is prefigured, and recognized as originary, as implicitly constituted by legality (that is, the legality of positive law). The normative fact is torn away from its inessentiality and from the customary and organic characteristics that tradition had attributed to it, to be understood instead in terms that—in different degrees—depict it as an activity from whose development the system itself issues.[32] The minimum degree of this dynamic integration can be found in the work of Santi Romano,[33] and probably also Schmitt the theorizer of "dilatory compromises."[34]

In French institutionalist writing we find instead an extremely high degree of interpenetration of the different elements of institutional production. This interpenetration, however, seems to be on the one hand too limited by the positivity of public law and on the other often disturbed by the infiltration of impromptu ideologies.[35] It is in authors such as Rudolf Smend, Ernst Forsthoff, and Costantino Mortati that we can observe the formation of a thoughtful theoretical equilibrium within the institutionalist current. In Mortati the juridical constitution is grafted onto the social constitution, which is formed by a set of groups and forces: "Every society from which a particular State formation emerges and to which it is connected possesses its own intrinsic normativity, which is indeed produced by its own organization around political forces or political ends."[36] The formal constitution will thus be interpreted, revised, and possibly changed on the basis of the "material constitution." The limit of the formal constitution's flexibility stretches among the forces that constitute society politically and that form the material constitution by the means of continual institutional compromises. What stands as the foundation of the constitution and determines its dynamic apparatus is not a basic norm but a ceaseless movement.[37]

Once we are confronted by this weighty figure of the play of political forces as the material basis of the constitution, where has the originary and liberatory quality of constituent power gone? Couldn't this play of forces produce, as it has in fact produced, sinister figures of totalitarian power? Where has that intimate and continuous allusion of constituent power to democracy and to a politics that takes shape in the scenario of the multitude's strength gone? Where is its creative and irresistible character? Certainly the jurists wanted to tame this wild beast, but here we have before us an already domesticated animal—even worse, one reduced to mechanical behaviors and to the inert repetition of a preconstituted social base. Whether it is transcendent, immanent, or coextensive, the relationship that juridical theory (and through it the constituted arrangement) wants to impose on constituent power works in the direction of neutralization, mystification, or, really, the attribution of senselessness.

What if there were no other way? What if the very condition for maintaining and developing the juridical system were to eliminate constituent power? Given the impossibility of solving the problem of constituent power from the point of view of public law, we should examine this problem from the perspective of constitutionalism. Here things are easier. From the point of view of constitutionalist and liberal ideology, constituent power is in fact subjected to the fire of critique and to institutional limitation through an analysis that works to unmask (or so it claims) any sovereign demand of the community. Constitutionalism poses itself as the theory and practice of limited government: limited by the jurisdictional control of administrative acts and, above all, limited through the organization of constituent power by the law.[38]

> *Even revolutions must bow to the supremacy of law.... Constituent power, as the ultimate power, must legitimize itself by finding expression through legal procedure; this originary historical fact is not justified by mere obedience, but by the juridical mode in which it is expressed, a mode that, with its formalization, guarantees the people's constituent power. Thus all of the constituent process is regulated by law; and there exist neither normative facts nor a constituent power that, based on the form, manages to command obedience; nor is there a material constitution realized through the praxis of the political class. This is because the constitution is not an act of government, but the act of the people.*[39]

This sophism, this Oedipal consequence of the parable of Menenius Agrippa itself eliminates, within the sphere of constitutionalist thought, the possibility of proceeding in the determination of constituent power. It is just as well, then, to use this opposition to recognize in constituent power (insofar as this power is the opposite of the constitutionalist idea of checks and balances) the mark of a radical expression of democratic will. In effect, the praxis of constituent power has been the door through which the multitude's democratic will (and consequently the social question) has entered the political system—destroying constitutionalism or in any case significantly weakening it. Constitutionalism defines the social and political order as the articulated set of either different social orders or different juridical and political powers.

The constitutionalist paradigm always refers to the "mixed constitution," the mediation of inequality, and therefore it is a nondemocratic paradigm.

In contrast, the paradigm of constituent power is that of a force that bursts apart, breaks, interrupts, unhinges any preexisting equilibrium and any possible continuity. Constituent power is tied to the notion of democracy as absolute power. Thus, as a violent and expansive force, constituent power is a concept connected to the social preconstitution of the democratic totality. This preformative and imaginary dimension clashes with constitutionalism in a sharp, strong, and lasting manner. In this case, history does not dispense with the contradictions of the present; in fact, this mortal struggle between democracy and constitutionalism, between constituent power and the theory and praxis of the limits of democracy, becomes more and more prominent the further history advances.[40] In the concept of constituent power is thus implicit the idea that the past no longer explains the present, and that only the future will be able to do so. As Alexis de Tocqueville writes, "The past has ceased to throw its light upon the future, and the mind of man wanders in obscurity."[41] Paradoxically, this negative idea, more than a thousand other motivations, explains the birth of "democracy in America." This is why constituent power produces and reproduces itself everywhere and continually. Constitutionalism's claim of regulating constituent power juridically is nonsense not only because it wants to divide this power but also because it seeks to block its constitutive temporality. Constitutionalism is a juridical doctrine that knows only the past: it is continually referring to time past, to consolidated strengths and to their inertia, to the tamed spirit. In contrast, constituent power always refers to the future.

Constituent power has always a singular relationship to time. Indeed, constituent power is on the one hand an absolute will determining its own temporality. In other words, it represents an essential moment in the secularization of power and politics. Power becomes an immanent dimension of history, an actual temporal horizon. The break with the theological tradition is complete.[42] But this is not enough: constituent power, on the other hand, also represents an extraordinary acceleration of time. History becomes concentrated in a present that develops impetuously, and its possibilities condense into a very strong nucleus of immediate production. From this perspective constituent power is closely connected to the concept of revolution.[43] And since it is already linked to the concept of democracy, now it positions itself as the motor or cardinal expression of democratic revolution. And we see it taking part in all the mechanisms—at times, extremely violent—that pulsate in the democratic revolution, vibrating between the one and the many, between power and multitude, in a very fast, often spasmodic rhythm. What could this rhythm of constituent power share with the inert and traditional time of constitutionalism?[44]

It is not the constitutionalist approach, therefore, that can help us solve the problem of the crisis of the concept of constituent power.[45] At this point, however, we must ask ourselves: given the deep ambiguity that this theory (both the juridical and political-constitutional one) casts on the concept of constituent power without being able to resolve it, wouldn't this concept effectively be the concept of a crisis? So that, instead of attempting a solution, wouldn't the attempt to better identify its critical characteristics, its negative content, and its unsolvable essence be more in accordance with the truth? Here we have probably reached the real object of our investigation: to examine, first of all, what is the real nature of constituent power. If this nature is in crisis (as our analysis of the attempts of juridical or constitutionalist reduction has indicated), then we should consider in the second place what is the site or limit on which this crisis takes shape. Third, we should investigate if the limit (that is, the present conditions of the crisis, unsurpassed and at the moment unsurpassable) can somehow be overcome. In short, if in the history of democracy and democratic constitutions the dualism between constituent power and constituted power has never produced a synthesis, we must focus precisely on this negativity, on this lack of synthesis, in order to try to understand constituent power.

Before concentrating on this issue, allow me one final observation about the concept of representation, which since the beginning we have considered as one of the fundamental juridical-constitutional instruments for controlling and segmenting constituent power. Now, even at the end of this excursus, the mystifying figure of representation recurs in the context of the development of constituent power.[46] Perhaps the concept of democratic representation is intrinsically related to constitutionalism in such a way that fundamental functions of the latter persist in the former.[47] From this perspective the crisis of the concept of constituent power will not reside only in its relationship to constituted power, constitutionalism, or any juridical refinement of the notion of sovereignty. This crisis will also concern the concept of representation because, at least from the theoretical point of view, a primary and essential denaturalizing and disempowering of constituent power takes place on this theoretical-practical node.

Absolute Procedure, Constitution, Revolution

Confronted by the crisis of the concept of constituent power as a juridical category, we must ask ourselves whether—instead of trying to overcome the crisis, as juridical thought does to no avail—we should, rather, accept it, in order to grasp better the nature of the concept. To accept this crisis means, first of all, to refuse the notion that the concept of constituent power may somehow be founded by something else—taken away, that is, from its own nature as foundation. This attempt surfaces, as we have seen, whenever constituent power is subordinated to representation or to the principle of sovereignty, but it already starts operating when the omnipotence and expansiveness of constituent power are limited or made subject to constitutionalist aims. Constituent power, they say and decree, can only be defined as extraordinary (in time) and it can only be fixed (in space) by a singular determination: it is considered either as a normative fact that is deemed preexistent or as a material constitution that develops in tandem with it! But all this is absurd: how can a normative fact validated by custom do justice to innovation? How can a preconstituted "political class" be the guarantor of a new constitution?[48] Already the effort of enclosing constituent power in a cage of spatiotemporal limitation was unsustainable, but any attempt to block it by giving it finality becomes downright inconceivable. One can try to minimize the impact of the event, but certainly it is not possible to define its innovative singularity in advance.[49] These logical skirmishes, carried on to the verge of nonsense, in fact constitute the mystification that juridical theory and practice take care to collect and rearticulate into the theories of sovereignty and representation. Constituent power, limited and finalized in such a way, is thus held back within the hierarchical routines of successive production and representation, and conceptually reconstructed not as the system's cause but as its result. The foundation is inverted, and sovereignty as *suprema potestas* is reconstructed as the foundation itself. But it is a foundation contrary to constituent power; it is a summit, whereas constituent power is a basis. It is an accomplished finality, whereas constituent power is unfinalized; it implies a limited time and space, whereas constituent power implies a multidirectional plurality of times and spaces; it is a rigidified formal constitution, whereas constituent power is absolute process. Everything, in sum, sets constituent power and sovereignty in opposition, even the absolute character that both categories lay claim to: the absoluteness of sovereignty is a totalitarian concept, whereas that of constituent power is the absoluteness of democratic government.

In this way, thus, by insisting on the concept of constituent power as an absolute process—all-powerful and expansive, unlimited and unfinalized—we can begin to appreciate the originality of its structure. But we must immediately face an objection: what else can absoluteness given in this form be but the absoluteness of an absence, an infinite void of possibilities, or, really, the presence of negative possibilities? It seems to me that in this objection the misunderstanding of absence is exacerbated by the misapprehension of the concept of possibility. This objection can be refuted. If the concept of constituent power is the concept of an absence, why should this absence result in an absence of possibilities or the presence of negative possibilities? In fact, here we are touching a crucial point in the metaphysical debate, the debate centering on the question of strength [*potenza*] and its relation to power [*potere*]. The metaphysical alternative in the definition of strength that runs from Aristotle to the Renaissance and from Schelling to Nietzsche is precisely an alternative between absence and power, between desire and possession, between refusal and domination.[50] Sometimes this alternative is closed, as it is when power is considered from its origin as preexisting physical fact, as finalized order, or as dialectical result. In other cases the alternative is open. A great current of modern political thought, from Machiavelli to Spinoza to Marx, has developed around this open alternative, which is the ground of democratic thought.[51] In this tradition, the absence of preconstituted and finalized principles is combined with the subjective strength of the multitude, thus constituting the social in the aleatory materiality of a universal relationship, in the possibility of freedom.

The constitution of the social is a strength founded on absence—that is, on desire—and desire unceasingly feeds the movement of strength. Human strength produces a continual dislocation of desire and accentuates the absence on which the innovative event is produced. The expansiveness of strength and its productivity are grounded in the void of limitations, in the absence of positive determinations, in this fullness of absence. Constituent power is defined emerging from the vortex of the void, from the abyss of the absence of determinations, as a totally open need. This is why constitutive strength never ends up as power, nor does the multitude tend to become a totality but, rather, a set of singularities, an open multiplicity. Constituent power is this force that, on the absence of finalities, is projected out as an all-powerful and always more expansive tendency. Lack of preconstituted assumptions and fullness of strength: this is a truly positive concept of freedom. Omnipotence and expansiveness also characterize democracy, since they define constituent power. Democracy is both absolute process and absolute government. Thus, the effort to keep open what juridical thought wants to close, to get to know more deeply the crisis of its scientific lexicon, does not simply make available to us the concept of constituent power but makes it available to us as the matrix of democratic thought and praxis. Absence, void, and desire are the motor of the politicodemocratic dynamic as such. It is a disutopia—that is, the sense of an overflowing constitutive activity, as intense as a utopia but without its illusion, and fully material.[52]

Hannah Arendt well understood this truth about constituent power.[53] She arrives at it by an oblique path, by counterposing the American to the French Revolution, but it is no less effective a path, rather so much stronger for being paradoxical. The thesis about the two revolutions has a long history. It was elaborated by Friedrich von Gentz in his introduction to the German translation of Edmund Burke's *Reflections on the French Revolution*,[54] but it was above all popularized by John Adams's supporters against Jefferson during the presidential campaign of 1800.[55] The American Revolution and Constitution, founded on the respect and development of freedom, stands against the horrid Jacobins, against the revolution as an abstract and ideological force. Arendt takes up the same notion, shifting however its central axis, which is no longer the opposition between the concrete and the abstract but between political and social revolution. Political revolution transcends the social without annihilating it but, rather, by producing a higher level of understanding, equilibrium, and cooperation, a public space of freedom. Social revolution, instead, and the French Revolution in particular, nullifies the political by subordinating it to the social. The social, in turn, left to itself, spins emptily in a search for freedom that becomes increasingly blind and insane. Whenever the political does not allow society to understand itself, to articulate itself in understanding, folly and terror will triumph. Hence totalitarianism cannot but be established. Later and more than once we will have to go back to this thesis of the two revolutions to evaluate it from different points of view. For the time being let's leave aside the historical judgment and consider instead how the principle of freedom takes shape in Arendt's theory, because it is precisely through this concept, and by refusing tradition, that she deeply renews political theory. Certainly, revolution is a beginning, but modern history begins only when the constituent principle is removed from violence and war. Only then is the constituent principle freedom: "Crucial, then, to any understanding of revolutions in the modern age is that the idea of freedom and the experience of a new beginning should coincide."[56]

But what does this freedom become? It becomes public space, constituting a communicative relation, its own conditions of possibility, and therefore its own strength. It is the polis. Freedom is a beginning that poses its own conditions. The right of community predominates over all others, over the right to life, over the very specifications of the right to property, so that it is both a constituent and constituted principle. "Independent government and the foundation of a new body politic"—this is what it means "to be free." Freedom cannot be reduced; neither does it come after liberation: freedom means to "be already free"; it is political constitution, an absolute process (Arendt, 26 ff). As far as we are concerned, then, following our argument, we want to stress how this new definition of the constituent principle is grounded on nothing more than its own beginning and takes place through nothing but its own expression. The radical quality of the constituent principle is absolute. It comes from a void and constitutes everything. It is not by chance that, at this point, Arendt takes stock and, through a very rich and fierce phenomenological exercise, begins demolishing any heteronomous (and in particular social) content of public space, both its constitutive process and the constituent actors. The problem lies in posing the social as a priori, as preceding the constitutive event, and in characterizing the social as a preconstituted political question (53 ff). This is the case not only for historical reasons: "Nothing... could be more obsolete than to attempt to liberate mankind from poverty by political means; nothing could be more futile and more dangerous" (110). Not only because this is a pure and catastrophic illusion:

> *The masses of the poor, this enormous majority of all men, whom the French Revolution called* les malhereux, *whom it turned into* les enragés, *only to desert them and let them fall back into the state of* les miserables, *as the nineteenth century called them, carried with them necessity, to which they had been subject as long as memory reaches, together with the violence that had always been used to overcome necessity. Both together, necessity and violence, made them appear irresistible:* la puissance de la terre. *(110)*

The reason for this situation is theoretical and deeper. Only the political reconstruction of reality, the constitution of public space, allows for the revolutionary rebirth—that is, it makes the search for happiness a possibility: "The central idea of [the American] revolution... is the foundation of freedom, that is, the foundation of a body politic that guarantees the space where freedom can appear" (121). This idea is therefore an ontological institution, an actual fundamental determination of being. The concept of constituent power is the constituent event, the absolute character of what is presupposed, a radical question. And it is exactly on this point, the radical fundamentality of political being, that Arendt is strongest. Constituent power, insofar as it constitutes the political from nothingness, is an expansive principle: it allows no room for either resentment or resistance; it is not selfish but supremely generous; it is not need but desire. Arendt's denunciation of "the social question"[57] proceeds as a parallel to an overflowing and expansive notion of the ontological institutionality of political democracy: in all its forms, from the Greek *polis* to the Renaissance city, from the American assemblies to the revolutionary workers' councils of 1919 and 1956.[58]

Why do these strongly made points, so powerfully deployed in the discussion and definition of constituent power by Arendt, leave us in the end unsatisfied, even ill at ease? At the very moment when she illuminates the nature of constituent power, Arendt renders it indifferent in its ideality or equivocal in its historical exemplification. If one teases her writing a little, each of the characteristics attributed to constituent power loses its intensity, becomes pale, and reveals—eclipsed by the brilliance of the exposition—its opposite. Thus, for instance, the constitutive phenomenology of the principle reveals itself as perfectly conservative. The continuous celebration of the fact that freedom preexists liberation and that the revolution is realized in the formation of political space becomes the key to a historicist hermeneutics that systematically flattens down, or deforms, the novelty of the event and limits it to the American example.

The ambiguity of the beginning and the absolute taking root of constituent power (an ambiguity connected to the Heideggerian definition of being and the consequent constitutive alternative of freedom) are resolved by Arendt in formal terms, according to the demands of an idealism content to find a correspondence in institutions. Arendt attacks with fierce determination the categories of pity and compassion as devastating functions of the process that produces the ideology of the "social question." She counterpoises desire to sympathy, truth to theatrics, the mind to the heart, patience to terror, foundation to liberation. Up to this point she upholds the ontological radicality of the constituent principle; but she does not sustain the trajectory that would lead to preserving political space as a terrain of freedom and a horizon of desire, thus denying it as a space dedicated to mediation and the production of power. She does not unmask Rousseau as the theoretician of sovereignty as much as she scorns him as the theoretician of compassion. Arendt wants political emancipation, and she considers it as the accomplishment of the American Revolution: in fact, she conceives this passage only as the realization of a determinate constituent apparatus and exalts it in its crude effectiveness as an ideal paradigm. Rather than being an ontological beginning, political emancipation becomes here a hermeneutic legacy.[59]

Arendt's argument is even more clearly inadequate if we focus on her analysis of the dynamic of constituent power. The choice of taking the American Revolution as an exemplary model not only blocks the ontological process but also cheapens the analysis of the political apparatus. For Arendt the *Constitutio libertatis* is simply and merely identified with the historical events of the American constitution (139–79). All the theoretical problems that the definition of constituent power has raised are resolved by seeking rational alternatives and a political decision founded not on them but on the basis of the solutions imposed on them by the American constitution.

Arendt thus gives us a series of banalities, more appropriate to a neophyte than to a Heideggerian philosopher. For example, she proposes the notion that constituent power is a continual historical process not limited by its immediate determinations but temporally open to interpretation and improvement; or that the constitutional absolute divides into and is justified by the dynamics that generate it, such that constituent power and constituted power do not compose a vicious circle but, rather, are progressively legitimated in a virtuous circle; or finally that constituent power may be creative, but at the same time it has the nature of a pact made by mutual consent: "The grammar of action: that action is the only human faculty that demands a plurality of men; and the syntax of power: that power is the only human attribute that applies solely to the worldly in-between space by which men are mutually related, combine in the act of foundation by virtue of the making and the keeping of promises" (175). To say this means nothing but going back to that Anglo-Saxon sociology that, between Talcott Parson and John Rawls, proposes a "positive sum" political exchange, polite and consensual, and has very little to do with Arendt's intuition of the absolute foundation.[60] In fact, Arendt opens by refusing contractualism and ends by praising it; she begins by grounding her argument in the force of constituent power and concludes by forgetting its radical quality; she starts by foregrounding the reasons for democracy and ends by affirming those of liberalism.

It will not appear strange, then, that even Arendt's definition of the expansiveness of constituent power is marred by contradictions and difficulties. Indeed, this is inevitable: the hermeneutics of the liberal constitutional model presents a linear and not an antagonistic schema for the development of constituent power. It is linear and idyllic if compared to the real problems that the American Revolution had to face since its beginning, problems of class struggle, slavery, and the frontier. It is linear and spontaneist as in the worst versions of sociological institutionalism.[61] The antagonistic event disappears. Thus Arendt's philosophy comes close, without deserving it, to the "weak" versions of Heideggerianism, those versions that produce its most extreme results.[62] Even though sought after and acknowledged, the foundation is abandoned to the version that the real provides of it. This is not realism but, rather, a historicist cynicism: it eclipses the real effort that constituent reflection has developed in the hope of recognizing the fullness of strength in the absolute of the foundation, and the fullness of freedom in the void of the ontological basis.

At this point we can understand how Habermas, although taking his point of departure from a perspective that does not possess the strength and does not accept the risk of Arendt's theory (which is what makes it great),[63] still develops a reasonable and acceptable critique of her positions. Habermas elaborated a theory that can be called "the reversal of the thesis of the two revolutions."[64] In other words, he claims that both the French and the American Revolutions derive from specific interpretations of natural right. The French Revolution takes natural right as an ideal to realize, whereas the American Revolution takes it as a real state that political intervention can only disfigure. The constitutive productivity of the political is thus all on the side of the French Revolution: it is the only modern revolution. The American Revolution is a conservative revolution, whose ideology is premodern and corporative, thus antimodern and antipolitical.

In fact, the revolutions in America and France were quite different. The interpretation of the revolutionary act was different because whereas in one case it was necessary to impose *ex novo* a conception of natural right against a despotic power, in the other what mattered was to liberate the spontaneous forces of self-regulation in order for them to agree with natural right. The relation to the State, too, was different: in America the revolutionaries had to resist a colonial power, whereas in France they had to build a new order. Finally, the political ideology was different, liberal in the first case and democratic in the second: in America the revolution had to set in motion the egoism of natural interests, whereas in France it needed to mobilize moral interests. Consequently, it is not true that in the French Revolution the social subordinated the political—rather, the social was constituted by the political, and herein lies the superiority of the French Revolution. Constitutive is the opposite of conservative. Thus the relationship between society and State, as it is posed in the two natural-right constitutions, is radically different, even divergent. In France and only in France was the constitutive principle affirmed and fully defined: in the *Declaration of the Rights of Man* it immediately became an act of the constitutional foundation of a new society. Should we say, then, that there are two constitutions? Certainly, but the French constitution was the constitution of the future, running throughout the history of the nineteenth century, grafted onto the history of the working class, and still constituting today the principal basis of the judicial arrangement of the welfare state.[65]

What should we say? This Habermasian reversal leaves a bad taste in our mouths because although correct it is ungenerous. Actually, Arendt has given us the clearest image of constituent power in its radicalness and strength. The abbot's frock in which she later dressed up the principle does not take away its lively figure; it simply masks it. The problem is that we demand that the constituent principle be ontologically grounded: it must be defined not by ordered space but open time; it must be the temporal constitution of the existent; it must be crisis. How and where can all this be defined? It is clear that Habermas and his lukewarm philosophy, his slow transcendentalism prove fully inadequate: but how can we grasp, define, and portray the creative richness of the constitutive principle? How can we do so without getting trapped in the delicate nets of the philosophy of communication or without falling prey to a conservative syndrome—while remaining on the terrain of ontology?

Perhaps, in a not unusual coincidence of opposites, the only image that corresponds to Arendt's definition of constituent power is the one articulated by Carl Schmitt. We have already talked about it, but it is worth returning to it, to clarify and explain further. How does Arendt interpret Schmitt's work? Certainly, she does not adopt his reduction of law to the brutality of the originary fact, nor does she consider constituent power as fully and coextensively inherent in the constituted order.[66] Rather, Arendt's interpretation of Schmitt can be seen in the perception of an unexhausted expressive radicalness (which can simultaneously be a subject) that issues from the constitutive source and that is located in the need for the decision and in the identification of friend and enemy. The sovereign is the one who can "suspend" the law,[67] who can thus suspend the law that itself establishes sovereignty, who can make constituent power consist in the principle of its negation.

In an entirely Nietzschean manner, we need to stress that the act of suspending, far from being defined in negative terms, founds and inheres to the possibility of the positive. The more the first decision shows itself to be negative, the more radically it opens a number of grounding, innovative, linguistic, and constitutional possibilities. With this the constitutive act opens positively: the *ursprungliche Wort oder Sprache* is set free,[68] and it is on such creative depth that the sense of community is articulated, both in the extensiveness of the *Gemeinschaft*, so important for Arendt, and in the barbaric manner that Schmitt proposes to his "friends."[69] Here we are neither confusing the two communities nor reproaching Arendt's liberalism for wearing a suit that, albeit vaguely, resembles the equivocal sense of Schmitt's decisional community. In fact, we are merely recognizing in the ontological intensity of Arendt's definition of constituent power a direction that, while distancing her from any transcendental horizon of a formal type (à la Habermas), leads her toward an ontologically pregnant and socially relevant constitutive foundation—a Commonwealth of friends, a counterpower, a powerful social instance.[70]

This distant relationship, which however shows a strong resemblance between Carl Schmitt and Hannah Arendt, can also be verified in different and more indirect ways. When their thought on constituent power is compared to that of another author, perhaps a theoretical precursor and in any case a problematic catalyst of their theories, John Caldwell Calhoun, these resemblances become evident.[71] In Calhoun's thought, too, constituent power is defined as a negative power and opens a singular and extremely radical dialectic. He developed this problematic within the parameters of the constitutional discussion of the American Confederated States before the Civil War. Calhoun's declarations that the government (as constituent agent and expression of community) ontologically precedes the constitution and that the constituent act is defined as the capacity to prescribe the choice between war and peace, to impose possible compromises, and thus to organize confederate public law as a truce are so intense that they can be linked back, as Arendt makes clear,[72] purely and simply to the right of resistance and organized in constitutional procedure. The right of resistance provides us with a basic and fascinating reference point. It is the negative power par excellence, whose prefigurative force can hardly be eliminated from the history of modern constitutionalism. The right of resistance, together with the negative, emerges as the radically founding expression of community. Exactly at this point, whereas Schmitt capitulates to the force of an attraction that is by now devoid of principles, Arendt's thought runs into a sort of insurmountable roadblock when she discovers that "nothing resembles virtue so much as a great crime": nothing resembles constituent power so much as the most radical and deep, most desperate and fierce negation.[73]

Whereas Schmitt can play with this negation and Habermas can make it disappear in the flattest of transcendental horizons, Arendt instead remains both fascinated and repulsed by it. Here probably lie the origins of her (so contradictory!) conversion to classical and conservative constitutionalism. We see how she cannot stand the deeply radical and very powerful principle she discovered. Arendt's march gets bemired. Constitutionalist thought in general and American constitutionalism in particular come to her rescue in her attempt to free herself from the vortex of the crisis, from the definition of constituent power as crisis. The procedure is well-known: one voluntarily makes oneself prisoner of the sophism of sovereignty, subjects oneself to the traditional routine of its definition, and thus creates a situation in which only constituted power can justify constituent power.

But isn't there any other line of thought capable of appreciating the radicalness of constituent power without drowning it in the philistinism of traditional juridical theory? In attempting an answer, we start from a particular conviction (which we will try to confirm historically and construct theoretically throughout this work) that the truth of constituent power is not what can be attributed to it, in any way whatsoever, by the concept of sovereignty. It cannot be so, because constituent power is not only, obviously, an emanation of constituted power, but it is not even the institution of constituted power. It is, rather, an act of choice, the precise determination that opens a horizon, the radical apparatus of something that does not yet exist, and whose conditions of existence imply that the creative act does not lose its characteristics in the act of creating. When constituent power sets in motion the constituent process, every determination is free and remains free. On the contrary, sovereignty presents itself as a fixing of constituent power, and therefore as its termination, as the exhaustion of the freedom that constituent power carries: *oboedientia facit auctoritatem.* No, the phrase "expression of strength" can never mean "institution of power."

But at the very moment when strength gets instituted it ceases being strength and thus declares itself as never having been such. There is only one correct (and paradoxical) condition for a definition of sovereignty linked to that of constituent power: that it exists as the praxis of a constitutive act, renewed in freedom, organized in the continuity of a free praxis. But this contradicts the entire tradition of the concept of sovereignty and all its possible meanings. Consequently, the concept of sovereignty and that of constitutive power stand in absolute opposition. We can thus conclude that if an independent way of developing the concept of constituent power exists, it has excluded any reference to the concept of sovereignty. It relies, rather, on the basis of constituent power itself and tries to unravel from this and nothing else every constitutional consequence.

Let's try once again to measure the density of the concept by comparing it to other theoretical positions. We can begin with a crucial and irreducible claim: when strength is institutionalized, it is necessarily negated. By this claim we open a polemic with institutionalism, and in particular with the most sophisticated forms it has assumed in recent times.[74] Breaking with Arendt's Heideggerian ambiguities, the institutionalism of the contemporary supporters of the "invention of the social" or of the "model of the polis" does not come closer but, rather, grows more distant from the radicalness of the concept. Indeed, the organic continuity of the institutional process in this case relies on a purely ideological basis—as if the most sacred principles and fundamental rights could lay claim to historical causality and ontological effectiveness and were not instead made real by the same crisis that, by embodying them, makes them great and important. This, however, is not the point. We must instead make clear that constituent power, from the perspective of its originary radicalness, cannot be conceived satisfactorily as a formal process of the constitution of freedom. It is not an élan vital that realizes itself in institutionality;[75] it is not an act that, by determining itself, becomes more and more actual;[76] neither is it a fusion of wills that like a superheated metal congeals in a constitutional figure.[77] In other words, beyond the apologetic banalities of contemporary institutionalism, any philosophy that even heroically has an institutionalist outcome must be refused if we want to grasp the strength of the constituent principle. This is because in the constitutive act there is never any vertical and totalitarian dimension. The active elements are, rather, resistance and desire, an ethical impulse and a constructive passion, an articulation of the sense of the insufficiency of existence and a deeply vigorous reaction to an unbearable absence of being.

In these elements strength takes shape as constituent power: not to seek institutionality but to construct more being—ethical being, social being, community.[78] Once again we discover the extremely close and profound link between constituent power and democracy. The desire for community is the spirit and soul of constituent power—the desire for a community that is as thoroughly real as it is absent, the trajectory and motor of a movement whose essential determination is the demand of being, repeated, pressing on an absence.[79] "What is potent can be and not be."[80]

Here we have rediscovered the relation between constituent power and absolute procedure. Rediscovering this relationship, after considering how many substantial offenses and mystifications have been imposed on it, allows us to reflect with new eyes on the originary radicalness of the concept. What does constituent power mean if its essence cannot be reduced to constituted power but must, rather, be grasped in its originary productivity? It means, first of all, the establishment of a continuous relationship between constituent power and revolution, an intimate and circular relation such that where there is constituent power there is also revolution. Neither constituent power nor revolution has ever come to an end when they have been internally connected. This notion takes us back to the historical origins of the concept of constituent power. The term was probably introduced for the first time during the American Revolution,[81] but it belongs to the development of Renaissance political thought from the fifteenth to the eighteenth centuries as an ontological notion of the formative capacity of historical movement.[82] Even when the idea of revolution appears to be subjected to the power of the stars or to the necessity of the Polybian cycle of political regimes—"I have seen in the revolution a circular motion"[83]—even then it constitutes "le fond mobile de la science humaine," the foundation of the new science that constitutes history.[84]

After 1789, revolution and constituent power step on to the great stage of history and modern thought as indissoluble characteristics of transformative human activity. When we speak of revolution, we speak of constituent power.

Figures of rebellion, resistance, transformation, creation, the construction of time (accelerated, programmed, extended time), and the invention of law are bound together in this synthesis. Revolution is necessary, as necessary as the human need to be moral, to constitute oneself ethically, to free body and mind from slavery, and constituent power is the means toward this end.[85]

From this point of view the relation between revolution and law, between revolution and constitution becomes a continuum on which what exceeds the rational is represented by revolution. The law and the constitution follow constituent power: constituent power gives rationality and substance to the law.[86] Constituent power stands as a revolutionary extension of the human capacity to construct history, as a fundamental act of innovation, and therefore as absolute procedure. The process started by constituent power never stops. The question is not to limit constituent power, but to make it unlimited. The only possible concept of constitution is that of revolution: precisely, constituent power as absolute and unlimited procedure. Condorcet comes near this concept when, in 1793, he defines the "loi révolutionnaire" as "that law that starts, accelerates, and rules the course of the revolution," thus understanding that the law gives shape to the temporal flux of the revolution and actively designs itself on its modality.[87] The *Declaration of the Rights of Man of 1793* repeats this concept when it regards citizens' rights as active in the constitutional schema and recognizes in this activity the motor of social democracy.[88] The Marquis de Sade is in perfect agreement when, with far-sighted cruelty, he incites his readers to that "necessary insurrection in which the republican constantly holds the government of which he is member."[89] In this context it is not surprising that in 1789, in the midst of the counterrevolutionary campaign, Immanuel Kant proposed considering the revolution as an educational process and as a cultural action with extensive and profound effects on the whole human environment, a process that constitutes the "commonality of ends."[90]

A web of a thousand threads defines the originary radicalness of constituent power. The coherence of the weave, however, is always in danger. Perverse institutional or formal determinations are superimposed on the concept and, as in Arendt's case, deprive it of that radical ontological opening that gives it shape. How can this radicalness be conceived? How can it be recognized in history and law, avoiding any false path? Carl Schmitt, who, notwithstanding the folly of the results, has posed this question with extraordinary intensity, refers us to Spinoza.[91] I, too, am convinced that Spinoza's philosophy allows us to construct a first schema of the concept of constituent power and to guard it from misunderstandings and mystifications. The effort to theorize "a causality that accounts for the effectiveness of the All upon its parts and the action of the parts upon the All" makes Spinoza "the only or almost the only witness" of a theory of a totality without closure,[92] a constituent power without limitations.

From Structure to the Subject

Up to this point we have accumulated a series of problems. We have before us a productive source of rights and juridical arrangement that refuses to close and stubbornly repeats its claims in the face of juridical theory's and political philosophy's attempts to fix it in a final form. It seems that the issues on the table cannot be addressed except through the intervention of a force capable of mediating the radicalness of constituent power. This force must be able to interpret the structure when this structure is presented as absolute procedure, as continually reactualized strength, but nonetheless positively grounded in reality. An adequate answer to the question that motivates my investigation will be found by identifying a strength adequate to structure, and a subject adequate to absolute procedure. The problem of constituent power thus becomes a question about the construction of a constitutional model capable of keeping the formative capacity of constituent power itself in motion: it is a question of identifying a subjective strength adequate to this task.

If this subject is the subject of an absolute procedure, then it is not enough to pose the question of the subject raised by constituent power. In juridical theory this question arises whenever the voluntary nature of law is affirmed and the subject of this will must be discovered.[93] Posed in these terms the search is too generic because it does not insist on the logically adequate relationship between subject and structure. The history of juridical thought, however, does provides a series of examples that come close to this objective. We should examine them more closely.

The first hypothesis: the subject in question is the nation.[94] This concept seems to be, at first sight, particularly appropriate to that of absolute procedure, except that, on the one hand, it is a generic concept, real only in the imaginary (and therefore indefinitely manipulable); on the other, it is a concept that is historically determined at different times, often with the function of breaking and limiting the constituent process. The generic conception of the nation (resulting from an intricate play of ethnic determinism, historical judgments, political necessities, juridical demands, but above all a strong naturalistic overdetermination) produces a polysemy that allows for sophistic interpretations of the concept and instrumental uses of it in practice.[95] The latter conception, which refers to historical determinations, sets in motion a constitutional dynamic that, far from procedurally reopening the relationship between the subject and the constitutional structure, hypostatizes and blocks it.[96]

A second hypothesis aimed at posing an adequate relationship between subject and structure (in the dynamic sense) sees the subject as the people.[97] The concept of "people," however, is no less generic than that of "nation." This definition also soon falls prey to the juridical mechanism of qualification. The generic essence of the concept is reread in a constitutional key: if the "people" is the subject of constituent power, it can be so only insofar as it first undergoes an organizational process capable of expressing its essence. Indeed, to imagine and above all to assume as scientific subject "an ordering force that can be ordered by a multitude without order" would represent a contradiction in terms.[98] This conception does go beyond the limitations and the naturalistic and organicist mystifications of the idea of constituent power as an attribute of the nation. The theoretical desire to clear away the ambiguity of the nation is clear. Equally clear, however, is the will to break the expansive force of the concept of constituent power.[99] The fact that any definition of the constituent subject in terms of the people boils down to a normativist conception and a celebration of the constituted law is not an accident but a necessity.[100] This normative conception confuses constituent power with one of the internal sources of law and with the dynamics of its revision, its constitutional self-renovation. Briefly stated, constituent power is the people only in the context of representation.

A third hypothesis: constituent power as subject is already materially defined by juridical mechanisms inherent in its composition, and constituent power is itself a multiplicity of juridical powers set in a singular relationship—such that elements of juridical mediation are always necessarily presupposed.[101] From this point of view, which is eclectic but still effective, the possibility that constituent power is represented as absolute procedure is taken away or transfigured from the beginning. The point here is not to insist on the singularity of the historical definition of every emergence of constituent power, but to pose this determination as an unsurpassable limit, as materially determined self-limitation. Juridical theory has become clever. It does not deny constituent strength but affirms its singularity. It does not, however, consider constituent power a process and a precarious ontological insistence but, rather, a limit. Limitation is posed à la Hegel as determination.[102] Mediation and compromise are assumed within constituent power as the subject that founds the material constitution—not outside but within it: this is the effectiveness of mystification. This is in fact a matter of mystification because the problem of constituent power cannot be solved by making singularity the limit of its absolute character—a temporal, spatial, and procedural limit. The fact that the absolute character of constituent power lies in its singularity is perfectly evident, but this, and not something else, is the problem.

At this point we could examine other theories that try to connect constituent power to absolute procedure in order to domesticate the former, but they would really tell us nothing new. It is more interesting to notice that the negation in absolute terms of the adequate relationship between subject and procedure is the figure of a metaphysical negation—that is, a negation of the fact that multiplicity can be represented as a collective singularity, that the multitude can become a unitary and ordering force, that this relationship (open and impossible to bring to a conclusion) between subject and procedure can be real and effectively constitute a real temporality. On the contrary, any formation of power must be constituted outside this human context—by the divinity or some other ideal overdetermination, in transcendence or transcendentality. The negation of an adequate relationship between subject and structure is thus always embedded in an external and hypostatic figure for the justification of power. The radicalness of constituent power cannot be negated in reality, but here it is simply denied in principle.

It is not enough, however, to expose and denounce the metaphysical partiality of the positions that relativize constituent power in a transcendental manner in order to resolve our problem, the problem of its absolute character. Denunciation cannot take the place of a constructive argument. Thus we must pose once again the problem of the adequate relationship between subject and absolute procedure.

Michel Foucault is undoubtedly the one who has made the most substantial progress in defining a concept of power that, in its relationship to the subject, allows for constructive dimensions and absolute openings. In Foucault, humanity appears as a set of resistances that release (outside any finalism that is not an expression of life itself and its reproduction) an absolute capacity for liberation. Life is liberated in humanity and opposes anything that encloses it and imprisons it.[103] What we need to stress here is that the relationship between subject and procedure is free. In other words, after demonstrating how power can subjugate humanity to the point of making it function as a cog of a totalitarian machine (we could accept this specific use of the term *totalitarianism*), Foucault shows instead how the constitutive process running through life, biopolitics and biopower, has an absolute (and not totalitarian) movement. This movement is absolute because it is absolutely free from determinations not internal to the action of liberation, to the vital assemblage [agencement].[104]

Starting from this viewpoint, which permits us to ground the question of the constituent subject, Foucault allows us to go still further. Indeed, he shows us that the subject is, first, strength, production. Certainly, the subject can be reduced to a pure phantom, a residue of the totality of the system of repression. But how productive it remains, even in this reductive horizon and imprisoned within these mechanisms! It is productive because on this limit the subject goes back into itself and rediscovers there the vital principle. Second, besides being strength, the subject is also action, a time of action and freedom, an assemblage—open because no teleology conditions or prefigures it. Foucault critically performs a process of disarticulation of the real and then, constructively, reopens a process that assumes the disarticulation as a positive condition. What was a path through necessity opens the way for a process of freedom.[105] This is essentially the same process we find in Spinoza.[106] Third, Foucault develops the paradigm of subjectivity as the place of the recomposition of resistance and public space.[107] Here we are confronted by a figure of the subject that formally and methodologically has characteristics adequate to absolute procedure. In effect this subject is strength, time, and constitution: it is the strength of producing constitutive trajectories; it is time that is in no way predetermined; and it is thus a singular constitution. When this critique has destroyed the prisons of constituted power, it identifies itself as ontological strength, constituent power capable of producing absolute events. The political is here production, production *par excellence*, collective and non-teleological. Innovation constitutes the political; constitution cannot but be constant innovation. What Arendt tried to articulate in terms of the inessentiality of liberal politics as alternative to a Heideggerian void of being Foucault constructs in the fullness of being, as an apparatus of positive freedom. The social, negated by Arendt as the suffocation of the political, reveals itself as the space of biopolitics—of that human radicalness of the political that constituent power reveals in its absoluteness.[108]

Absoluteness is under no circumstance totalitarianism. The latter is not a necessary corollary of the former, but this accusation springs up whenever the sacred principles of liberalism are not glorified and thus demands our attention.[109] If our "adequate subject" is in no way tied to liberal principles, or, rather, if in some ways it contradicts them, it need not for this reason be totalitarian. The equation "refusal of liberal principles equals totalitarianism" is reductive and mystifying. It is founded on a tradition of modern thought that presumes to found human rights on contractualism. Contractualism, however, cannot be the ground for human rights, cannot give them that material and immanent basis, that worldly absoluteness that is the only guarantee of the rights themselves. The perspective of constituent power puts the contractualist position under attack and recognizes in it the inevitable deferral to transcendence, to constituted power and its apology. This is indeed the outcome of contractualism, the logical demand that it claims it cannot resist, whether expressed by Hobbes as a God that transforms the association of individuals into sovereignty and the *contractum unionis* into *contractum subjectionis*, or by Rousseau as the "will of all" that is sublimated in a "general will," or by idealist transcendentalism as the process of the economic and the ethical that leads the contingent and the singular to the totality of the spirit and its State configurations.[110]

On the other hand, another tradition of modern metaphysics, from Machiavelli and Spinoza to Marx, sees the development of the dynamic of constituent power as absolute, but here that absoluteness never becomes totalitarian. In Machiavelli and Spinoza strength is expressed and nourished by discord and struggle; in both authors the process extends between singularity and multitude, and the construction of the political is the product of permanent innovation. What in Machiavelli is involved in the analysis of popular movements and the conflictuality of republics, in Spinoza develops in a high metaphysics. And it is precisely when we compare it to Spinoza's metaphysical absolute that the claim of pushing constituent power, its procedure, and its subject toward totalitarianism (even as a hypothesis) becomes ridiculous. There does indeed exist a totalitarianism in which the enigma of constituent power is not revealed, where its powerful effectiveness is denied or mystified in constituted power, and where the radicalness of its metaphysical strength and collective desire [*cupiditas*] is refused. In the lack of desire, the political becomes disciplinary totality, totalitarianism. Neither in Machiavelli nor in Spinoza, however, does the revolutionary process that embodies and establishes the constitution present itself as closure; rather, it is always open, both temporally and spatially. It flows as potently as freedom. It is at the same time resistance to oppression and construction of community; it is political discussion and tolerance; it is popular armament and the affirmation of principles through democratic invention. The constituent absolute and the democratic absolute have nothing to do with the totalitarian conception of life and politics. This absolute that builds the social and the political together has nothing to do with totalitarianism. Once again, then, political philosophy finds its dignity and its primary distinctions in metaphysics—on the one hand, the idealist metaphysics that, from Hobbes to Hegel, produces a transcendental concept of sovereignty; on the other, the historical materialism that develops a radical concept of democracy from Machiavelli to Spinoza to Marx. In this framework it is evident that the opposite of democracy is not totalitarianism but the concept of sovereignty itself, and it is now clear that the concept of democracy is not a subspecies of liberalism or subcategory of constitutionalism but a "form of governability"[111] that tends to destroy constituted power, a process of transition that frees constituent power, a process of rationalization that provides "the solution to the *riddle* of every constitution."[112]

We thus reach a turning point where we can verify what we have been arguing until now—that is, where we can verify our claim of having identified, at least formally, an image of the subject that allows us to sustain adequately the concept of constitution as absolute procedure. It seems to me that this formal figure must now be confronted with reality, with the history of subjects and constitutions, with life and politics. This is an open subject, projected into a totality without closure. To begin, let's again consider a characteristic, between the formal and the material, already attributed to our subject: that of temporality. Our subject is, and cannot but be, a temporal subject, a temporal constitutive strength. That said, once again two paths open in front of us. On the one hand, temporality is brought back to and confused in being, emptied of the elements that constitute it and therefore reduced to mysticism—in short, necessarily rooted in a firm principle that is the relation of being with itself.[113] On the other hand, temporality can be grounded in human productive capacity, in the ontology of its becoming—an open, absolutely constitutive temporality that does not disclose Being but instead produces beings.

A rereading of Marx's thought in this context can allow us to make progress in the definition of a materially adequate relationship between the constituent subject and absolute procedure. Marx's metaphysics of time is much more radical than Heidegger's.[114] Time is for both a matter of beings. Social time is the apparatus through which the world is quantified and qualified. But here we are once again, always at the same point: Marx frees what Heidegger imprisons. Marx illuminates with praxis what Heidegger reduces to mysticism. Heideggerian time is the form of being, the indistinctness of an absolute foundation. Marxian time is the production of being and thus the form of an absolute procedure. Marxian temporality represents the means by which a subject formally predisposed to being adequate to an absolute procedure becomes a subject materially capable of becoming part of this process, of being defined as constituent power.[115] Clearly, it is not only by comparison with the Heideggerian conception of time that this characteristic of Marxian temporality becomes clear, and from now on we will go along Marx's independent path. It is useful, however, to keep in mind this clash of perspectives because some crucial showdowns over it take place in contemporary philosophy: between Benjamin and Arendt, between Sartre and Foucault and Deleuze. Through the same clash, one might say, the whole political-constitutional debate of our times takes place as well.

Let's thus focus on Marx, on the crucial point where the critique of power and the critique of labor intersect, because this is what we are talking about, and it is on this crux that the contradictions of the history of constituent power develop. The definition of constituent power, when we move from the concept to the real, is decided on this problem. Naturally, Marx's path is a long one. From the critique of ideology to the critique of power to the critique of labor, an extraordinary accumulation of theoretical initiatives unravels.

We begin with *The Holy Family* and "On the Jewish Question" of 1844. Marx's demystification of the concept of equality here leads to a critique of labor, or, better, the proclamation of human rights leads to the discovery of the universality of exploitation and private appropriation, to the denunciation of individualism and the exaltation of the community of workers.[116] Political emancipation is nothing but the attempt to displace the meaning of the impulse to revolt, the juridical hypostasis of the social status quo. Human rights and all the constituent propositions of the bourgeoisie represent neither productive forces nor utopia. They are nothing but mystifications and celebrations of the status quo. So-called political emancipation celebrates the force of the constituted while pretending to exalt the constituent.[117]

In *The German Ideology* of 1845–46 constituent power is defined twice. In its bourgeois formulation it is immediately class consciousness, a universal that through its affirmation adjusts the State constitution to the demands of bourgeois rule and the productive necessities of the division of labor. Constituent power is also expressed as communism: "Communism is for us not a *state of affairs* that is to be established, an *ideal* to which reality [will] have to adjust itself. We call communism the *real* movement that abolishes the present state of things. The conditions of this movement result from the premises now in existence."[118] This defining process results in a further development: "Thus things have now come to such a pass that the individuals must appropriate the existing totality of productive forces, not only to achieve self-activity, but, also, merely to safeguard their very existence. This appropriation is first determined by the object to be appropriated, the productive forces, which have been developed to a totality and which only exist within a universal intercourse"; and "the appropriation of these forces is itself nothing more than the development of the individual capacities corresponding to the material instruments of production. The appropriation of a totality of instruments of production is, for this very reason, the development of a totality of capacities in the individuals." Further: "Only the proletarians of the present day, who are completely shut off from all self-activity, are in a position to achieve a complete and no longer restricted self-activity, which consists in the appropriation of a totality of productive forces and in the thus postulated development of a totality of capacities." Finally, "All earlier revolutionary appropriations were restricted.... In all expropriations up to now, a mass of individuals remained subservient to a single instrument of production; in the appropriation by the proletarians, a mass of instruments of production must be made subject to each individual, and property to all. Modern universal intercourse can be controlled by individuals, therefore, only when controlled by all."[119]

The idealist residues that so heavily resound in these pages have to be dispelled, and they are defused in Marx's later historical writings. In his writings of 1851–52 on revolution and counterrevolution in Germany the opposition between "universal class" and "real movement" is brought back to the model of constituent power—an open constituent power that takes the form of a permanent revolution, in other words, a process in which the subject's independence is affirmed at the moment when it continually rolls back the enemy's oppression and simultaneously expresses, accumulates, and organizes its own power.[120] Here, therefore, constitutive temporality is foregrounded and defined as the continuity of the process and a dimension of ontological accumulation.

In Marx's writings on the Paris Commune of 1871, constituent power emerges finally as a perfect synthesis of a historical subject, the Parisian proletariat in arms, and an absolute process. The proletarian Commune itself is "essentially a working class government, the product of the struggle of the producing against the appropriating class, the political form at last discovered under which to work out the economical emancipation of labor." Further: "The working class did not expect miracles from the Commune. They have no ready-made utopias to introduce *par decret du peuple*.... They have no ideals to realize, but to set free the elements of the new society with which old collapsing bourgeois society itself is pregnant." Finally: "The great social measure of the Commune was its own working existence. Its special measures could but betoken the tendency of a government of the people by the people."[121] This is where the concept of constituent power reaches its highest poignancy in Marx, when the project of the abolition of the State is not subordinated to anarchist spontaneity but focused on the nexus (dynamic and expansive, and yet precise) between political movement and political power.[122] If there were in English the terminological distinction that many languages mark between two kinds of power—*potestas* and *potentia* in Latin, *pouvoir* and *puissance* in French, *potere* and *potenza* in Italian, *Macht* and *Vermögen* in German (which we have been marking as *power* and *strength* in this translation)—it would reside in this distinction between political movement and political power. Indeed, Marx translates strength [*potenza*] as "political movement," that constituent force of a radical democracy in which the critique of power is combined with the emancipation of labor, the "real movement."

But this is not enough. As long as we follow the political Marx, political revolution and social emancipation are two historical matrices that intersect on the same terrain—the constitutional terrain—but still in an external manner, without a metaphysical logic of this intersection being given. There must be something deeper and more urgent that demonstrates that this encounter is in no way accidental and makes necessary the materialist rule according to which political liberation and economic emancipation are one and the same thing. This necessity resides at the core of Marx's theory of capital, where living labor appears as the foundation and the motor of all production, development, and innovation. This essential source also animates the center of our investigation. Living labor against dead labor, constituent power against constituted power: this single polarity runs through the whole schema of Marxist analysis and resolves it in an entirely original theoretical-practical totality.[123] The basis of Marxian discourse in the passage from the critique of power to the critique of labor and vice versa therefore consists in the deployment of the concept of living labor as an instrument that, while destroying the equivocal quality of the bourgeois theory of labor (consolidated, accumulated, dead labor set against the creativity of living labor), shows the bourgeois theory of power itself to be an overdetermination of living labor by dead labor.

Living labor, instead, embodies constituent power and offers it general social conditions through which it can be expressed: constituent power is established politically on that social cooperation that is congenital in living labor, thus interpreting its productivity or, better, its creativity. In the immediacy, the creative spontaneity of living labor, constituent power finds its own capacity for innovation; in the cooperative immediacy of living labor, constituent power finds its creative massification.[124] One must look carefully at this nucleus of living labor, this creative tension that is at the same time political and economic, productive of civil, social, and political structures—in a word, constituent. Cooperative living labor produces a social ontology that is constitutive and innovative, a weaving of forms that touch the economic and the political; living labor produces an indistinct mixture of the political and economic that has a creative figure.[125]

More than a century has passed since Marx elaborated this theory of constituent power, identifying the proletariat as its historical carrier. Doubtless, this theory has had wide effect, even though, like other theories, it has by now reached its historical limit.[126] What remains of it is not so much the effort to identify the proletariat as the agent of a permanent revolution and thus the adequate subject of an absolute constitutional procedure, as much as the terrific metaphysical effort to propose constituent power as the general genealogical apparatus of the sociopolitical determinations that form the horizon of human history. This problematic is more contemporary than ever; and in the conclusion of this book we will certainly have to take into account the answer to the Marxian question about what the nexus between constituent power and that word *communism* might be—the nexus on which Marx synthesized the entire historical process. In any case, here we must keep in mind for the next stage of our inquiry some relations that Marx, above all, in concluding the materialist tradition of the definition of democracy as expression of strength, has helped to identify. In particular I am thinking of the relation that attaches the constitutive temporality of constituent power to an adequate subject and the one that poses the absoluteness of the nexus of subject and structure at the center of the creative process of the political.

One last reflection. Our argument will trace the conceptual formation of constituent power from a historical point of view, but it will not follow a continuous process: rather, it will move among various hypotheses. In each of the next five chapters we will analyze a particular figure of the formulation of the concept of constituent power and its singular destiny. In Machiavelli constituent power opens toward a strong dialectic between virtue and fortune—a dialectic that sets in play the revolutionary adventure of the Renaissance. In the English Revolution we will focus on Harrington's thought and his reading of the concept of constitution, but also the blockage of the constitution or, better, that "reversed" revolution that after 1688 fixed the constitutional conditions of the affirmation of the gentry and capitalist accumulation. The American Revolution and the clash of constituent positions among Adams, Jefferson, and the authors of *The Federalist* will illustrate how the ideology of freedom was made the constituent principle of a dynamic constitution of space, where democracy and imperialism confront each other.

The French Revolution poses for the first time the constituent principle as the principle of an absolute procedure, which is recognized in the movement of the popular classes against the bourgeois demand to restore the principle of sovereignty. In the Russian Revolution, finally, constituent power concretely measures itself with a utopian conception of time and tries to embody an absolute procedure. The tragedy of the Russian Revolution, in its greatness and misery, relates directly to the core of our investigation. Therefore, we are not proposing a genealogy of the concept: concepts have no history except in the materiality of the history of humans and societies. Rather, we will try to define through the alternatives of constituent power the differentiated set of its possibilities: not a set of different expressions united by the custom of linguistic usage, but an expressive potential (of desires, wills, constructive experiences) accumulated inside our fundamental being from past experiences.

We are not interested in the archaeology of constituent power; we are interested in a hermeneutics that, beyond words and through them, can grasp the life, the alternatives, the crisis and the recomposition, the construction and the creation of a faculty of humankind: a faculty to construct a political arrangement. Therefore, what does the virtue [virtus] of Machiavelli's people in arms and the discovery of the material determinations of the relations of power in Harrington have in common? And how does the American renovation of classical constitutionalism overlap with the French ideology of social emancipation? How does the egalitarian impulse of communism dramatically coexist with the enterprising spirit of the Bolsheviks? It is clear that each of these enterprises will discover its meaning within the set of events that shapes them individually. But it is also true that the meaning of these events is inscribed in the consciousness of us all and etched in our being because it has somehow determined it. These events have for us a meaning worth investigating because they have constructed new horizons of reason and have proposed new dimensions of historical being. The journey we propose will be neither concluded by ideological syntheses nor contented with tracing the evolution of the concept; instead, it will try to lead us to the analysis of the strength of contemporary humanity. To understand our desire through the thousand stratifications that underlie it is the only path if we want to understand the concept.[127]

The concept of constituent power is the core of political ontology. Thus, it is evident that the conclusion of the journey that we are now beginning will involve confronting the contemporary crisis of constitutionalism and asking ourselves what subject today is adequate to sustain an absolute constitutional procedure capable of opposing the concept of sovereignty. At the same time we will attempt to determine where the living labor of strength resides, how it is represented, how it operates today.

T W O

Virtue and Fortune: The Machiavellian Paradigm

The Logic of Time and the Prince's Indecision

> The swift sun over the surface of our world had run full a thousand,
> four hundred ninety-four courses
> after the time when Jesus first visited our cities and, with the blood he
> spent, quenched the sparks of devilish fire,
> when discordant Italy opened into herself a passage for the Gauls and
> suffered barbarian peoples to trample her down.[1]

THIS POEM by Machiavelli although unremarkable does mark a beginning, the beginning of a new historical era, and it reveals a problem, the problem of "mutation." This is the initial dimension of Machiavelli's thought. The *First Decennale* is dated "Ides of November 1504," and therefore it was composed ten years after Charles VIII's descent to Italy. It goes back to that fatal date and dramatizes it in the light of the events of the entire decade and in particular of those of the previous year, 1503, which had witnessed Julius II's succession and the beginning of Valentino's disgrace.

In the sky appeared "the soul of splendid Alexander, that it might have rest, departed to the blessed spirits; / his sacred footsteps were followed by his three dear and intimate handmaids: Luxury, Simony, Cruelty."[2] Irony does not take anything away from "mutation." In fact, the irony allows Machiavelli to express the invective and the curse, which would otherwise be inappropriate in the public writing of a diplomat. In his personal writings of the same period Machiavelli is more explicit. To Giovanni Ridolfi he intensely writes of the "mutation" that manifests itself in those years; what he witnesses is an unceasing movement, an absolute acceleration of history.[3] A couple of years later, writing again to Ridolfi, Machiavelli once again insists on the radicalness of the ongoing "mutation" and on the absolute contingency and precariousness of its senses and meanings.[4] There is mutation, "and it is reason that wants it. Because France's fortune is weary, above all in Italy, given the recent events; and the Emperor's fortune is new." Theory must move among the events, writes Machiavelli to Soderini (winter 1503–1504), in a familiar tone.[5] We can and must look things in the face, perceive all their articulations, and hold on to the "true." The "true" that reason grasps is "mutation."

The first structure of truth is therefore "mutation." The logic of historical time is entirely structured by mutation, but is the "true" merely the recognition of this logic? Is mutation something irresistible and uncontainable? Or, rather, is there a second definition of truth that reveals it as the possibility of modifying this logic? This second definition does exist, and it resides in force, or better, in the synthesis of prudence and arms. *Words to Be Spoken on the Law for Appropriating Money, after Giving a Little Introduction and an Excuse* expresses the new definition: "All the cities ... ruled by an absolute prince, by aristocracies, or by the people ... have had for their protection force combined with prudence, because the latter is not enough alone, and the first either does not produce things, or, when they are produced does not maintain them."[6] Arms and judgment thus constitute together the means of the existence of power and the effectiveness of the system, the authority of the Signoria. "The mutations of the kingdoms, the ruin of the provinces and the cities" depend on this relation. Thus the Florentine Signoria must provide to these necessities, and since judgment abounds, it must pay urgent attention to the question of arms. The Signoria must learn from what happened in the previous years in Arezzo and Valdichiana. The Republic must not rely on others' armies, the armies of the Valentino or the King of France, but, rather, directly provide its own army. And the citizens must themselves contribute if they want freedom. Already at the beginning of the mutation of 1494 we saw that we could resist and reverse the cycle. When the Italians temporarily set aside their differences and armed themselves, "the truth was known / That the French can be defeated." And for the Signoria, clamoring between fear and hope, suffering all the uncertainty of navigating the insidious sea of the Italian "mutation," "the way would be easy and short / If you'd once again open Mars' temple."[7]

Truth and arms, then: on one hand, the true as reflection on the mutation and, on the other, the true as action on the mutation. (Others would say, "the arms of critique and the critique of arms.") But not even this is enough. The concept of mutation is more complex. It establishes the logic of time on an ontological horizon of dense, multidirectional, and changing materiality. If the concept of mutation that we are subjected to is inscribed in a naturalist logic, then the mutation on which we act will also be so. Vice versa: if we change the point of view and give the mutation on which we act a humanistic connotation, also the mutation that dominates us must have the same meaning. In other words, nature and praxis move one within the other and together constitute the world of life and the object of science.[8] In this perspective the logic of time manifests its polyvalence, versatility, and freedom. We move within this wholeness and live the dynamics of this totality. This is the third determination of the "true."

There are numerous terrific examples of Machiavelli's theoretical-practical perspective, looking both inside and outside his own contemporary history. Let's examine his analysis of how the mutation comes about in *Legation to the Emperor Maximilian.*[9] Machiavelli follows Maximilian's court throughout the Austrian, Swiss, and Italian Alps. He observes and describes the Swiss form of democratic organization and above all their military equipment. Then he deals with Maximilian and how his project is taking shape. This is the genesis of the mutation—but how complex it is! Semifeudal imperial traditions and very modern forms of armament combine in the most different ways. The democratic Swiss constitutions carve a space for themselves in the Empire and represent, nonetheless, the core of the Emperor's army. Mutation and the new traverse, recuperate, and transform nature and history. When the mutation is profound, it appears as an original praxis that renews and changes tradition.

Another example on a less exotic and more familiar terrain can be found in the *Discourse on Remodeling the Government of Florence, upon Request of Pope Leo X,* written in 1520 in the mature stage of Machiavelli's thought.[10] Here the reflection on mutation occupies center stage. The instability of Florentine institutions during the entire fifteenth century was due to the fact that a choice between a princedom and a republic was never made. The fact that this indecision did not lead to ruin and catastrophe is due to external dangers that periodically strengthened the institutions. But at that time the political situation was different from the present one. Florence was *prima inter pares* in an independent national context, and the unique constitution of the Medici Signoria could only survive in that extremely peculiar situation. After 1494 nothing can ever repeat itself. The mutation marks the impossibility of taking up once again the old Medici formulas and at the same time the possibility of finally choosing the most modern of the figures of government, the Republic. It would certainly be a republic protected by the Pope and a constitution in which a series of competencies were guaranteed by the Medici, but it would also be a Republic that takes into consideration the universality of the citizens and urges them to participate widely in the government. The great mutation that has taken place can therefore be enacted. A new constitution can renew praxis and make the Republic into the body of a civil experience—an institution that corresponds to the mutation that has taken place. The true is the life of a common body, the life of the Republic.

But this last definition still needs to be developed, and the path of this development is long. In the 1510s Machiavelli poses questions concerning mutation and how to intervene in it. What is mutation? Is it a pure and simple historical condition, as dense as one likes and multidimensional, but substantially something given to us and that we have undergone? If this were the case, the force of mutation and its innovative dimension would be welcomed by indifference. "Tamquam in profundum gurgitem ex improviso delapsus," Machiavelli could anticipate. The naturalism that appeared to have been modified by the vigorous intervention of praxis now seems to have been recomposed, and the objective factors seem to be indifferent. But this is not the direction of Machiavelli's experience and theoretical reflection. The line he draws moves from the naturalistic horizon to a historical structure. Mutation acts on the structure of history and proposes political reality as second nature. The return to equilibrium of the elements shaken by the crisis and now reconfigured in a new pattern takes place according to mechanisms similarly charged with naturalness and historicity and according to determinations marked by popular conflicts, popular unions and disunions, by the accumulations of experience of peoples and princes. Time is therefore the matter of which social relations are constituted. Time is the substance of power. Time is the rhythm on which all the constitutive actions of power are selected and organized.

Machiavelli's chief theoretical operation thus consists of reading mutation as a global structure, traversed throughout by human action. But this action is itself structural. It extends itself to the globality of the historical horizon and grasps and dominates the variations of time, giving them sense and meaning. In other words, Machiavelli constructs a scientific function that wrenches mutation away from destiny and turns it into an element of history; he wrenches history away from the past and considers it as a temporal continuum; he snatches time away from continuity and constructs the possibility of overdetermining destiny. Insofar as Machiavelli's thought definitively overcomes naturalism, it also modifies humanism. This modification consists in the relationship between structure and time that defines mutation: a relationship that is extremely deep, global, and inextricable, but always singular, active, and interrupted. In this insertion of time, humanism becomes tragic, whereas reality presents itself as the highest impulse to innovation and life. The true is measured by these dimensions: the true is constitutive.

In Machiavelli this truth is the product of an *Erlebnis*. Indeed, the years between 1502 and 1504 offer Machiavelli, the young Florentine secretary, an extraordinary experience. Sent to the court of Valentino, he observes the Duke's movements on behalf of the Signoria.[11] His first reports have a cautious tone and mostly deal with Valentino's positions. Valentino claims to have obtained the King of France's and the Pope's unconditioned support (soldiers from the first and money from the second), and thus he asks the Florentines for their friendship and support—that is, their alliance. Machiavelli observes and reports all this. He also notices the ripening of Valentino's revenge on Vitellozzo Vitelli and Oliverotto da Fermo, and its culmination in their execution on New Year's Eve, 1502. Along with the revenge, Machiavelli witnesses Valentino's victories in Urbino, Sinigaglia, and then Perugia, perhaps Siena, in addition to the Romagne. Once Valentino's action develops, Machiavelli's participation becomes more and more explicit. He warns the Signoria that he is yielding to Valentino's passion, but he is yielding in order to be more useful to the Signoria itself.

Really, Machiavelli discovers for the first time the practice of princely power in its immediacy and restlessness: the apparatus begins to become clearer. Already in his previous *Legation to France* Machiavelli had demonstrated his extraordinary analytic abilities,[12] and yet the difference of style between the two *Legations* is extraordinary. Whereas the first focuses on the objective and gothic aspect of power, the second foregrounds its subjective and modern quality. And with such passion! What is, then, the secret of Valentino's success? How can the enigma of the making of power be disclosed? "I temporize, fixing my eyes upon each thing, and wait for my moment" (*Opere*, 2:932). This is a first response: the secret lies in how Valentino valorizes his being in time, his political being.

Yet this is not enough to define the political: the political implies an increase of tension, a suspension that tends toward explosion, a stretching out toward the existence of a powerful overdetermination, toward the breaking of the preexisting orders and symmetries. When Valentino's revenge is put into practice, an innovation of time takes place (*Opere*, 2:932–38): the old time is concluded, new plans for conquest are opened, new coincidences of interests are defined, and therefore new schemata of alliance, new horizons of hostility. On the whole, the new presents itself as a synchronic affirmation that prefigures a new diachronic movement (*Opere*, 2:956). Let's pause a little longer on Machiavelli's reflections. In judging Valentino's adventure, he tells us that "the government of this Lord since I have been here has rested only on his good fortune—the cause of which has been the firm opinion commonly held that the King of France would aid him with soldiers, and the Pope with money; then there is another thing that has worked for him no less than this one, namely the sluggishness of his enemies in pressing him."[13] Now the enemies can no longer do him any harm!

Time is the protagonist in two ways: on the one hand, we have the "delay" of Valentino's enemies, which is to say, the lack of "virtue"; on the other, opposed to the enemies' delay we have the "immediacy" and "punctuality" of Valentino's action. Between these two poles takes shape the definition of "virtue" and "fortune" as different apparatuses for grasping time, as producers of subjectivity on a certain temporal rhythm. The political is configured as a grammar of time.

The *Description of the Method Used by Duke Valentino in Killing Vitellozzo Vitelli and Oliverotto da Fermo, Sir Pagolo and the Duke of Gravina Orsini* is the construction of a grammar of power.[14] How is strength constituted? Through a temporal game that runs through reality and reorganizes it toward normative finalities. The temporal game, on its surface, is made of exemplary fraud, deceit, and violence but actually consists of slowdowns or accelerations of time, or long silences, sinister waitings, savage assaults, fierce surprises, and a frenzy of action. Here is Valentino, betrayed, isolated, gathering and dissimulating his strength, ready however, and able to explode in a sudden revenge. This is the behavior of a cat—albeit sustained by the logic of temporal trajectories that he knows how to negotiate. Here is the Duke once again, alone and hidden. In order to facilitate his resistance and then the reversal of his bad fortune, however, the Duke aids France's effort to take the Romagne away from Venice and the Pope's attempt to reconstruct the Church's territory and reconsolidate his power.

Valentino moves against this background—working on it, resolving its problems, and grasping its possibilities. It is his will to power that gathers this sparse temporality in order to make of it, in reality—later distilled in Machiavelli's political laboratory—an invincible weapon. Machiavelli shows Valentino as the only hero of this story. He is the organizer of the State, the one who overdetermines historical time and reorganizes it. Here begins to take shape an idea of sovereignty that no longer owes anything either to medieval common law or contractualism.[15] As for Valentino's will, it gets abstracted from the objects to which it is applied, and even though traversing them, it detaches itself from any goal other than its own realization as power. Valentino can want anything, so formal is his gaze and so total is his immersion in reality. He is fully at one with the gathering of time that his actions determine.

The whole scenario on which the figure of Valentino is delineated becomes formal, as if absorbed into this very clear light. While in other countries, as Machiavelli tells us, solid old structures persist,[16] here the archaic and medieval elements of political constitutions are overturned by the dynamic of the new power, like a subsumption of the old into the new. This disproportion, this dissymmetry, and even the simple difference between the eras are led back to a new logic, a new plasticity of the image and scientific treatment. Just as in Ariosto the myths and legends of the chivalric era are recomposed in a new fantastic figure that marks an absolute novelty,[17] so too in Machiavelli the time of innovation collects and reshapes the entire political tradition.

It is not by chance, then, that immediately after his experience with Valentino, Machiavelli reflects on his *Erlebnis* and translates it into a model of political action. Indeed, in that same year, 1503, he addresses "the very prudent Lords" who govern the Signoria, offering them his reflections in *On the Method of Dealing with the Rebellious Peoples of the Valdichiana.*[18] What he had learned from Valentino is presented here in normative terms. The normativity of the theoretical argument is, in the humanistic manner, guaranteed by the reference to the ancients, but its goal is purely technical.

In this text Machiavelli transforms political science into political technology in a direct and unmediated way: "I have always heard that history is the teacher of our actions, and above all of the princes, and that the world was similarly inhabited by men who always had the same passions, and there always existed those who served and those who commanded; those who serve willingly and those who serve unwillingly; those who rebel and those who are punished" (*Opere*, 2:676). We should compare, then, taking our cue from the *Discourses on the First Decade of Titus Livius* and from Lucius Camillus's way of governing, the manner in which the Romans acted in order to consolidate their power in territories agitated by innumerable rebellions and the manner in which the Florentine Signoria acted in a similar situation. Nothing is more different and dangerous for the Florentines. "In the past the Romans thought that people who have rebelled must either be aided or repressed, and that any other solution is extremely dangerous" (*Opere*, 2:677), whereas the Signoria neither did nor thought so. Especially with respect to Arezzo, it acted in a confused manner, without any determination. Such behavior is so much more dangerous because Valentino presses now at the gates of Tuscany, so that certain cities that are unsafe for the Signoria can become safe bases for Borgia. Borgia, we must always remember, is a master of "recognizing an occasion," and now he is forced to do so if he wants to take advantage of the power of the Pope, who has only a short time to live. It is therefore "necessary" that the Duke "takes the first chance that presents itself to him, and that he entrusts a good part of his cause to fortune" (*Opere*, 2:679). The Duke seizes "his" time. Now, the political technology that Machiavelli proposes to implement against the rebel cities, the exemplary use of punitive terror, and the extreme passions aroused when there is no other alternative but life or death—well, all these once again are nothing but a technique of time, a way of leaving no room for other uses of time. Valentino is a monster of exceptional ability in the use of time, but the Republic, like the Romans in the past, can make this technology normal, appropriate its apparatus, and enjoy its effects.

At this point it is not surprising to find among the notes and reflections that Machiavelli develops in his reports of the *First Legation to Rome*, between the beginning and the middle of December 1503, the summary of the terrific theoretical experiences he lived (*Opere*, 2:963–1001). The background is described right away. On October 23, 1503, Machiavelli goes to Rome to bring the condolences of the Republic for the death of Pius III, to follow the vicissitudes of the Conclave that should elect della Rovere, Cardinal of San Pietro in Vincoli, to the Cathedral of Saint Peter, and to negotiate a military pact with Giampaolo Baglioni. His military mission lasts until the end of December. As Machiavelli had witnessed Valentino's ascent, now he can watch his rapid, catastrophic fall. His reports begin after the nomination of Julius II. Machiavelli immediately tries to understand the Pope's political position, which emerges gradually. It is a position of territorial restoration of the Church's dominions, relying on the axis of alliances between France and Florence, and that regards the Republic of San Marco as its direct adversary. Indeed, the Venetians had attacked the Romagne and the Marche. The Pope seems to hesitate, but it is evident that he is only biding time to build the conditions for the reconquest. On the other hand, it is not only the dominions of the Church that are at stake. If Venice procedes in its conquest, it will threaten a hegemony over all of Italy. And the other princes cannot accept this.

Valentino's fall takes place against this background. Inexplicably, he has supported the nomination of Julius, who was one of his enemies. Julius begins by treating him well, hoping to send him against the Venetians to reconquer the Romagne. But Valentino clearly understands that this is the Pope's will and not his. He hesitates: "He does not seize the right time," not even to run away, to start marching with his men. His charisma is gone. He trusts that the others are good and honest and denies to others the evil of his own character. A core of naïveté, powerlessness, and foolish ambition begins to appear in his actions.

Machiavelli follows the manifestation of this progressive paralysis of the will and is not at all deterred by the fascination that Valentino continues, nonetheless, to exert upon him. He is irascible and irritated. He speaks too much, curses, and lets time slip out of his hands. Finally, the Pope, after Valentino's men have left, has him arrested. The Florentines stop the rest of Borgia's troops and arrest don Michele, the hired assassin. Fortune has therefore completely turned against Valentino, whom the Pope holds prisoner and alive until the former will return to him the cities that are still faithful to the Church. "I cannot say anything else of his [Valentino's] situation, nor what the outcome will be: we must wait for time, that is the father of truth" (*Opere*, 2:965). "And so it seems that this Duke little by little is sliding into the grave" (*Opere*, 2:998). Time now has slowed: "Little by little," the time of good fortune slipping away, relentless time of strength fading away. The dissymmetry and the overdetermination of power are all against Valentino, who is no longer able to seize the moment and master it for his own advantage.

Now appears a new theoretical passage, after Machiavelli has seen the fatality of mutation become historicity, after defining power as overdetermination, and overdetermination as the ability to innovate during a difficult moment, after considering these movements as figures of time. This is a passage that allows us to gather strength in action, as will, as concentration, and as a subject with a project. To be more clear, the problem is to make historical time internal to anthropological time, to give singularity to the strength that has been revealed. To solve this problem, Machiavelli looks to many different examples. He has lived the experience of Valentino, exceptional but brief. He wants other fields in which to experiment with this problematic. The theme that concerns him is still that of mutation, and the difficulty, already observed since 1494, is to resist it—to build a power capable of confronting the Italian crisis.

The fact of having renovated his methodology does not make the facts to which the methodology must be applied disappear. How can a new power constitute itself in Italy? How can the current mutation be overdetermined and ruled? Valentino's experience must be put to use, but how? The constituent subject must once again be seen in action, but where, in which dimensions? The simplest answer would seem to be the one indicated by the constitution of the great European absolutist states. In particular, the French experience stands at the center of the analysis of Machiavelli, who is a political writer as well as a diplomat. He accomplishes three legations to France, in 1500, in 1504, and 1510.[19] In 1511 he is again on a mission in France. Perhaps in 1510 and perhaps a little later he writes *On French Affairs*, an extremely lucid analysis of the French constitution.[20] Machiavelli describes it with great intensity, as an irreversible fact that forms a very powerful reign. (The French constitution concentrates power patrimonially on the hereditary axis and subjugates the barons, letting them participate in political life and simultaneously disarming them. His notes on the conditions of the people, on the peculiar position of the Church, on the tax system, and so on are all very rich. In sum, this is a brief treatise of political science.) Is this, then, the model of overdetermination that Machiavelli proposes also for Italy? Is this the great constitutive subject in action that must take shape also in Italy? Machiavelli's negative answer to these questions had already been anticipated in the previous *Legations*. Certainly the greatness of the French court is adequate to the force of its kingdom, not only for domestic French matters but also for European affairs: "Here the key questions of the Italian situation are being discussed" (*Opere*, 2:890). When the ambassadors from Genova, Siena, and Lucca flock to offer fresh money to the king, Machiavelli gives us another strongly significant observation: "This is a sign, as the very prudent Your Lordships can see, that each has more fear of this king than trust in the others" (*Opere*, 2:897).

Certainly, France is a great military power, capable of imposing its force everywhere, at least until other powers stop it. That said, however, no analogy or reference can be drawn for the solution of the Italian problem, first, because Italy is more modern than France (this argument appears above all in the *Second Legation to France*).[21] In France the king's power is founded on the old-fashioned feeling of authority that is unknown in Italy. The absolute sovereignty of the monarch is old. Second, because—and here we touch on one of the most significant points of the Machiavellian analysis—the Italian crisis is so profound that constitutive action must reach the most radical level and demonstrate the strength of a creative act.

The *Third Legation* situates us in this perspective. Here Machiavelli portrays the diplomatic negotiations taking place at the European level among the French, the Papacy, and the Empire, as a bellicose crescendo that nobody can control anymore. Florence is by now involved in a situation that is beyond its power. Machiavelli recognizes a growing feeling of absolute impotence, which at times is converted into self-irony. In fact, he sees the inertia of the process as a force that goes against the stream with respect to the givens of political logic. Catastrophe is imminent. Further, since the Italian equilibrium has broken down, that is, since the mutation has taken place, all the games pass over the head of the Italian princes. Only the Papacy is a power that can participate in the great game, but it too is weak and it is even more weakened by the Council called by the very Christian king at Tours. This is a Council that radically challenges, à la Savonarola, the Pope's temporal power.[22] What can be said or done? There is no way out. Only the Emperor or the King of England can now stop the French. Yet whether an agreement is found or war declared, the aim in either case will not be peace but, rather, a more advantageous division of Italy. How can one resist this frightening drift? How can the freedom of the Italian territories be defended in a situation of international subordination?

In this legation Machiavelli poses the problem explicitly. It appears therefore evident that *On French Affairs* does not point to the solution of the Italian problem, which Machiavelli had made consonant with the perception of the mutation. In France the old material constitution, together with the humility and the obedience of the subjects, does not provide for the reopening and the overdetermination of historical time. In France the institutionalization of power is utmost. France is not a model for Italy, because here in Italy power is always republican, because the monarchy requires conditions unthinkable in Italy, because the Italian constitution has always been the constitution of freedom, and because in Italy the mutation has become radical to an extreme degree.

The long detour among the affairs of France takes us back, then, to the core of the problem—that is, where power appears as constitutive subject in action. A second *Erlebnis* furthers Machiavelli's analysis and allows it to become even more radical. It is well known how things went. In August 1512 the Spanish army descends from the Bolognese Apennines. The Signoria and the people refuse to yield to the threats directed against Florence, to give up their alliance with France, and to liquidate Soderini (who is responsible for those policies). The Florentines mount a strategy of defense, and a front, which the Spaniards avoid, is organized at Firenzuola. Then they attack Prato, plunder the city, and kill four thousand people. Terror invades Florence. Soderini is asked to leave.

On September 16, the Medici return to the city, "reinstated with all the honors and ranks of their ancestors. And this city remains very quiet and hopes not to live less honored with their aid than she lived in times gone by when the Magnificent Lorenzo their father, of most happy memory, was ruling."[23] In this situation Machiavelli tries to maintain good relations with both the Palleschi (*Opere*, 2:717–720) and the Medici.[24] But the purge follows and his efforts to save himself do not work. On November 7, Machiavelli is expelled from the administration; on November 10, he is exiled from the city for one year; and on November 17, he is banned from the palace. The investigation on the management of the Florentine army continues until December 10, and Machiavelli is frequently interrogated.[25]

In this period Machiavelli begins writing *On Princedoms*, that is, the first draft of what will later become *Discourses on the First Decade of Titus Livius*.[26] What is the plan of this "book of the Republics" that is presented as a commentary on the *Discourses on the First Decade*? From what we can guess, and this is not much, it is a vindication of the republican form of government, confronted with its present crisis, and with the horizon of mutation. It is a project oscillating between the analysis of free government and the foundation of power, a project that proposes the reading of the reciprocal conditions of power and freedom.[27] But while busy with this elaboration, on February 13, 1513, after the humanist and republican plot of Boscoli is discovered, Machiavelli is arrested and tortured. Freed in March with the amnesty following Leo X's (Giovanni di Medici's) election to Pope, he withdraws in Sant'Andrea in Percussina, near San Casciano.

He starts writing to Francesco Vettori, speaker for the Sovereign Pontiff in Rome.[28] Life begins again: "And so we are lingering upon these universal happinesses, enjoying what is left of life, which seems to me like a dream." Whatever may still happen to him, he will accept everything, "for I was born poor, and I learned earlier to stint myself than to prosper."[29] "So if sometimes I laugh or sing, / I do because I have just this one way / for expressing my anxious sorrow."[30] "It is no wonder that I did not write to you"—he writes to a friend—it is, rather, a miracle that I am alive, because my office has been taken from me and I have been on the point of losing my life.... I have endured all sorts of evils, the prison and others, I have endured.... Physically I am well, but for anything else, bad."[31] "I got used not to desire anything with passion."[32] But is this true? Until his arrest Machiavelli had dealt with the republics. Probably he had got to chapter XVIII of book I of the *Discourses on the First Decade of Titus Livius*, "How Free Government Can Be Maintained in Corrupt Cities, If It Is Already There; and If It Is Not There, How It Can Be Set Up."[33] Now he has nothing else to do but proceed with his work: "Fortune has determined that, since I do not know how to talk about the silk business or the wool business or about profits, I must talk about the government."[34] Indeed, he continues, but instead of writing "of the Republics," he applies himself to "a pamphlet *De Principatibus*." And with such passion! Why?

Let's immediately clarify one point. To be concerned with the "princedom" is not in opposition to being concerned with "the Republics."[35] *Princedom* means neither monarchy nor aristocracy; princedom is neither a category of Polybius's taxonomy nor the Polybian model of the best government, which results from the combination of the one, the few, and the many.[36] Here princedom is simply the relation between power and mutation, strength and mutation, strength and power. It is the historical subject of the overdetermination of mutation. By suspending the writing of the book "of the Republics" and by beginning *The Prince*, Machiavelli privileges the analysis of foundation and condition over that of freedom and expression. "I put on garments regal and courtly"; "I enter in the ancient courts of ancient men"; "I feed on that food that only is mine"; "for four hours I do not feel boredom, I forget every trouble, I do not dread poverty, I am not frightened by death; entirely I give myself over to them"; "And because Dante says it does not produce knowledge when we hear but do not remember, I noted everything in their conversation which has profitted me, and have composed a little work *On Princedoms* where I go as deep as I can into consideration on this subject, debating what a princedom is, of what kinds they are, how they are gained, how they are kept, why they are lost."[37] Princedom is the principle of power; it is strength in action. So much more so the new princedom. Its movement, that is, the principle of overdetermination of mutation, is what interests Machiavelli. Its operation is here purely and simply metaphysical.

Other elements explain this theoretical decision to stop writing the *Discourses* and begin *On Princedoms*. First, the intensity of his political discussion with Vettori. Already in the first letters, when he left prison, Machiavelli had offered himself to Vettori as "slave." He needs to work and to demonstrate his professional capabilities of political analysis, so he sends Vettori letters that are each a little essay. Here we are not so much concerned with the specific content of these letters, which follow one another throughout 1513; they focus repeatedly on his negative view of the crisis of the Italian equilibrium, a crisis raised up to the level of world history, that was already characteristic of the last *Legation* to France.[38] From it follows an entirely pessimistic reflection on the condition of moral and political customs of the Italians ("poor, ambitious, and cowards," so much so that "I want now to begin to lament with you our ruin and servitude").

The extraordinary importance of these letters derives, rather, from the comparison, continually proposed, between the play of the great European states' political-military means and the condition of Italian powerlessness. What is the constitutive principle in this situation? It cannot be hypothesized as quantity of force: the international relationship is by now too disproportioned. Thus it implies a new poltical quality, a qualitative leap. The prince cannot be but a new strength, a new paradigm, an ontological difference. Nothing else. In the poverty of San Casciano, Machiavelli thinks again about the defeat. Already in a letter to Soderini, in September 1512 (immediately after his friend and Lord had left for exile), Machiavelli had focused his reflections on the nexus between individual destinies and "the times and the order of things."[39] Now, this nexus is desperate, the conflict unsolvable, and virtue, if it is born, is the offspring of an avaricious nature. It is the soul folding upon the nothingness of the meanings of history.

Here a sort of Calvinist ascesis of the political takes shape, but grafted on the warp of contingency, which is a materialist and atheistic fabric. Therefore, here the constitutive principle is strength that expresses itself on this criss-crossing of objective limits and subjective, individual desperation. It is a constitutive principle when a foundation is absent, a heroic principle in a world without divinity. If the historical time of mutation is entirely emptied of meaning, at the same time it is made part of the intensity of anthropological time, and on this nexus the possibility of the constitutive hypothesis is posed.

Here is the complex of reasons for which Machiavelli stops writing the *Discourses on the First Decade of Titus Livius*, the book of "the Republics," to work at the "pamphlet" *On Princedoms*. The mutation of world politics, the dislocation of Italy's destiny, his personal desperation, and his metaphysical intuition of the radicalness of the foundation all spur him to look for the definition of strength.[40] What we have here is an extremely profound rupture, taking place not so much within Machiavelli's thought, since he was almost predisposed to produce this theoretical innovation ("for when this thing—*The Prince*—were read, it would become clear that in the fifteen years during which I have studied the art of the State, I have neither slept nor frolicked through them"), as inside the entire theoretical-political tradition of Western thought (*Opere*, 1:919).

We are now ready to read *The Prince*. But in approaching the text we must immediately notice and anticipate a few substantial limits. Perhaps they are inherent to the theoretical and political conditions of the formation of the text, but not for this reason less relevant. What I mean is that, although grasping the urgency of the constitutive principle without foundation can well constitute the basis of this very radical strength and help us toward the definition of the essence of *The Prince*, this cannot hide the aporetic quality of the text. In fact, the movement that leads the constitutive principle toward its unfolding, its spreading, and to its representation in a typical form—in this movement itself the argument develops also toward limits and aporias, toward quarrels and contradictions, toward, it seems to me, a substantial and problematic irresolution. We know that *The Prince* is not a humanistic treatise of good government and even less a Polybian chapter of the theory of State forms—and how welcome this is! But neither is *The Prince* a completed theoretical pamphlet for founding an alternative political project.

To a careful and calm reading it reveals itself a sort of scrapbook, unconcluded and varied, sustained by an external and often casual logic, and relying on uncertain terminology. Why? The constituent principle, once discovered, is entrusted to the crisis; in fact, it is kneaded into the crisis. Let me clarify: here I am not denying the incredible ontological depth of the principle nor do I forget the powerful source of life it reveals in the alternate play of solitude and project.[41] But the ontological innovation is suspended over a void of consequences, over the desperation of an unreachable objective. *The Prince* is a nest of contradictions and the point of departure of interrupted paths. The dynamic point of view, when we try to historicize it, becomes either rhetorical or contradictory. In fact, Machiavelli's constituent principle here is subversive, merely subversive. The course of his thought is antagonistic and not tendential; he is interested in the crisis and not in the solution, and yet he continually looks for this solution even when he knows he cannot find it.

On these premises, let's now move to *The Prince.* The first part, chapters I–IX, presents a sort of digging toward the definition of the constituent principle, toward the configuration of the new prince.[42] The typology of princedoms is ample, and ample also are the number of cases that Machiavelli excludes from scientific consideration. He is not interested in Republics ("I shall omit discussing republics because elsewhere I have discussed them at length"),[43] nor in hereditary princedoms, because they cannot be conquered unless there is "an extraordinary and excessive strength that can take them," or "extraordinary vices of the Prince" that make him hated. Nor will be taken into consideration mixed princedoms, that is, princedoms that have been annexed (chap. III), "members" of other dominions, that is, "misshapen states of language, customs, organization." Finally, two last exclusions, parallel and alternative: that of a centralized, Asiatic state (IV), and that of democratic princedoms. Nothing can be said of the latter other than "in truth there is no certain way for holding such states except destruction" (V:23). And on this point, remembering the Boscoli plot, Machiavelli adds: "Because always a subjected city has as a pretext of rebellion the name of liberty and her old customs. . . . But in Republics there is more life, more hate, greater longing for revenge; they are not permitted to rest — nor can they be — by the recollection of their ancient liberty; so the surest way is to wipe them out or to live among them (V:24).

Thus we come to the new princedoms, the only ones that interest Machiavelli: "De principatibus novis qui armis propriis et virtute aquiruntur" (VI). This princedom resides outside the inertia of the existing orders; it is entirely produced by virtue. And since "all the armed prophets won, and the disarmed ones lost," this virtue is armed. *Ex novo*, from armed virtue, comes the princedom as constituent principle. The perspective from which Machiavelli talks, here, and the nature of his judgments reveal a further operation developing in these chapters: the formation of a scientific subject that looks at the world with the eyes of the new Prince. These judgments are, because of their origin, analytical a posteriori, and because of their form, ethical and prescriptive. This means that the point of science and that of the hero are intimately connected: it is impossible to separate them. The subject is singular and productive, a concrete universal. The judgment can be analytic (and affect the ethical matter) because it is a posteriori—it is founded on strength. The *nosse* is the product of the *posse*; the logical order is that of strength. For this reason the new Prince is not simply the author of the State: he is the author, rather, of logic and language, of ethics and the law. But for the same reason, for this combination of strength and truth, the new Prince is himself a value, a productive strength, a creation ex nihilo. The measure of the production of the State is also the ethical norm; ontological production and ethical overabundance characterize the action of the new Prince. This ontological basis and this ethical overabundance are revealed by the Prince's capacity to affect time, to lengthen or shrink it, to give it a shape, to connect creative and destructive effects to it (VII–XI).

Yet already in this first exploration of the new prince, we begin to find, besides the positive determination, the negative one, which cannot be completed in the process of strength. Fortune is opposed to virtue—the product to the production, the constituted force to the constituent one. In analyzing the figure of Valentino and his deeds, Machiavelli does not want to blame him despite his failure: in fact, he finds it useful "bringing him forward in this way as worthy of imitation by all those who through Fortune and by means of another's forces attain a ruler's position" (VII:36). And the failure? It comes from outside sources: it is caused by the death of his father and by the very bad choice of his successor. The autonomy of the constitutive process is dominated by chance. Nor is another example more felicitous. Discussing "de his qui per scelera ad principatum pervenere," Machiavelli exclaims, "It cannot, however, be called virtue to kill one's fellow citizens, to betray friends, to be without fidelity, without mercy, without religion; such proceedings enable one to gain sovereignty, but not fame" (VIII:36). Once again the ethical autonomy of the new Prince is considered from a heteronomous point of view. Even worse, by distinguishing "the well used cruelties" from those "badly used," Machiavelli nonetheless thinks that the necessary cruelties must be deployed all "at the same time"—and here his thought is cunning, if not cynical. We could go on with exemplifications on these themes, since they are not lacking. On the contrary! But to what end? They would only help stress what we are now beginning to learn, that that remarkable constitutive strength, capable of overdetermining strength and of producing new ontological reality, always runs into an obstacle. Who creates the obstacle we do not know. Machiavelli does not pose the problem; for him it is enough to have shown that formidable radical power that invests the world and builds it again, as if out of nothing.

His only problem is now to develop that radical strength, to further grant the conditions of its force of application. Thus, in a second group of chapters of *The Prince* (XII–XIV) he will be concerned with the relationship between constitutive virtue and armament: "The principal foundations of all states, the new as well as the old and the mixed, are good laws and good armies. And because there cannot be good laws where armies are not good, and where there are good armies there must be good laws, I shall omit talking of laws and shall speak of armies" (XII:47). Also in this case we have a theoretical movement that combines an extreme rigor in deepening and unraveling the theme of strength with a fragmentary and often casual exemplification: the latter produces a horizon antagonistic to the projection of virtue, a sort of irresistible density that opposes it.

Let's follow these two developments and their intersections. Sometimes Machiavelli seems to be talking of constitution rather than of constituent power when he connects laws and arms. This is not when he unites virtue and "one's own arms" (that is, the arms of the people, the armed people): in this case, the third term of the relation is without doubt constituent power. The problem, instead, arises when examining the relation of fortune to arms and mercenaries to slavery ("Italy, slave and vituperated" because it had entrusted itself to mercenary armies), and concluding that "without her own armies no princedom is secure; on the contrary she is entirely dependent on Fortune that in adversity loyally defends her" (XIII:54). Yet he does not draw definitive conclusions from these affirmations.

Certainly, arms are an instrument of constituent power: they are not only its body but also its extensions. Arms are the means of the constitution of the princedom, not only in wartime, but also in time of peace, because they organize the city and dispose it to virtue. And as virtue is an absolute principle, so arms are its absolute figuration.

Yet this reasoning is forced, incapable of sustaining a sufficient level of argumentation. In fact, while defining the principle, Machiavelli denies an answer to the question that now becomes fundamental: for whom are the arms? For the Prince or for the people? How can "one's own arms" not be democratic arms? Here not only the "book of the Republics" is abandoned, but also the possibility of a democratic alternative.

Indeed, Machiavelli is taken by a sort of theoretical exasperation that pushes him continually to maintain his rigid defense of the principle. But in this way the exemplification spoils the principle, instead of bringing to light its soul. We will return to these questions extensively. For the time being let's underline the inadequacy of the demonstration. Yet we must keep in mind, let me repeat it, that in Machiavelli's discussion the inadequacy of the argument does not concern the strength of the principle: it only offers a more violent and fierce illustration of it. If we return to the general development of the "pamphlet," we are in fact facing such a juxtaposition of planes of discourse that it is impossible to find our bearings, unless we keep to the general design: the image of a will to demonstrate that is also a will to strength, a project to assume history from a constitutive, genealogical point of view, and continually to overdetermine it through a sort of *surenchère*, a progressive dislocation, and overloaded by strength. In its confusion each passage is given in a "prolix order," but at the same time it is a step on the path of a further experiment of overdetermination.[44]

And now what? Can armed power close the historical crisis and make mutation positive? No. We need to push forward the attempt at overdetermination. That principle, which has no foundation except in an absolute operation carried out on the alternatives of life and death, cannot but always proceed forward; constituent power is this going beyond any limit, it is a will that does not subside. The time constructed on this rhythm is both overabundant and unconcluded. Won't this definition of constituent power, then, be not only the basis of the concept of the political, but also the cause and the emblem of its crisis? Aren't the dynamics and the crisis of the political founded on the same principle? We have now reached the core of *The Prince*: its theme is the tragedy of constituent power. But it is a necessary tragedy:

> *I have decided that I must concern myself with the truth of the matter as facts show rather than with any fanciful notion. Yet many have fancied for themselves republics and principalities that have never been seen or known to exist in reality. For there is such a difference between how men live and how they ought to live that he who abandons what is done for what ought to be done learns his destruction rather than his preservation, because any man who under all conditions insists on making it his business to be good will surely be destroyed among so many who are not good. Hence a prince, in order to hold his position, must acquire the power to be not good, and understand when to use it and when not to use it, in accord with necessity. (XV:57–58)*

A necessary tragedy because as we have seen, in the production of the State and the development of the constituent principle, the true and the good are tied in a single nexus with strength, so that their horizon is still that of strength, and the division is always a posteriori, while the action is anterior, analytic, free.

Which prince is then worth praising? He who possesses all the moral qualities or, rather, he who is capable of maintaining with any means his State and strength? For the prince

needs to be so prudent that he escapes ill repute for such vices as might take his position away from him, and that he protects himself from such as will not take it away if he can; if he cannot, with little concern he passes over the latter vices. He does not even worry about incurring reproaches for those vices without which he can hardly maintain his position, because when we carefully examine the whole matter, we find some qualities that look like virtues, yet—if the prince practices them—they will bring him safety and well being. (XV:58–59)

The contingency of the action, clashing with the necessity of the conditions, determines the tragedy of the political—the tragedy of an irreducible complexity. In these central chapters of *The Prince* Machiavelli insistently continues to describe these conditions, and to underline their heteronomous and/or perverse effects (XVI). However, as he explains, the problem does not consist so much in the complexity of the result so much as in the complexity of the apparatus, in the fact that the exertion of power always appears as an equation with infinite variables. The political takes shape by situating itself in the midst of the game of these variables, and committing itself to choose one or the other: "de crudelitate et pietate; et an sit melius amari quam timer, vel e contra": "The answer is that it is desirable to be both, but because it is difficult to join them together, it is much safer for a prince to be feared than loved, if he is to fail in one of the two" (XVII:62).

Here we come to the definitive portrait of politics:

You need to know, then, that there are two ways of fighting: one according to the laws, the other with force. The first is suited to man, the other to the animals: but because the first is often not sufficient a prince must resort to the second. Therefore he needs to know well how to put to use the traits of animals and of man. This conduct is taught to princes in allegory by ancient authors, who write that Achilles and many other well-known ancient princes were given for upbringing to Chiron the Centaur, who was to guard and educate them. This does not mean anything else (this having as teacher one who is half animal and half man) than that a prince needs to know how to adopt the nature of either animal or man, for one without the other does not secure him permanence.

Since, then, a prince is necessitated to play the animal well, he chooses among the beasts the fox and the lion, because the lion does not protect himself from the wolves. The prince must be a fox, therefore, to recognize the traps and a lion to frighten the wolves. Those who rely on the lion alone are not perceptive. By no means can a prudent ruler keep his word—and he does not—when to keep it works against himself and when the reasons that made him promise are annulled. If all men were good this maxim were not good, but because they are bad and do not keep their promises to you, you likewise do not have to keep yours to them. Never has a shrewd prince lacked justifying reasons to make his promise-breaking appear honorable. Of this I can give countless modern examples, showing how many treaties of peace and how many promises have been made null and empty through the dishonesty of princes. The one who knows best how to play the fox comes out best, but he must understand well how to disguise the animal's nature and must be a great simulator and dissimulator. So simple-minded are men and so controlled by immediate necessities that a prince who deceives always finds men who let themselves be deceived.

A prince, and above all a prince who is new, cannot practice all those things for which men are considered good, being often forced, in order to keep his position, to act contrary to truth, contrary to charity, contrary to humanity, contrary to religion. Therefore he must have a mind ready to turn in any direction as Fortune's winds and the variability of affairs requires, yet, as I said above, he holds to what is right when he can, but knows how to do wrong when he must. (XVIII:64–65, 65–66)

The prince's strength organizes therefore the logic of time—but it does so without reaching any conclusion. The truth is always and only effectual. The solidity of this truth comes from its being cut out of the totality of being. Each affirmation is negation. But strength consists exactly in going beyond the limit, the closure, the cutting out. The tragedy has by now become a dynamic principle, the concept itself of constituent power. Virtue constructs the world—and also its own limit. The tragedy of the political consists of this. The effectuality of this situation is its unresolvability: there is no way of resolving the political.

Perhaps through myth? Not yet. In fact, Machiavelli could already conclude *The Prince* here; he has already told us everything. He prefers to continue the demonstration, and he does so in a systematic and prolix manner, from the foundation of the political to the definition of the government. In four chapters (XX–XXIII) he reproposes the aporias of the foundation of the political by examining them in the practice of power. But by now the contradiction has become so deep that only the constituent dynamics—this desperate grasping of time that presses and burns any other determination—only the constituent dynamics, therefore, matters. The political eulogy of Ferdinand d'Aragon ("He can be almost called the new prince, because, through fame and glory he has transformed himself from a petty ruler to the foremost king among the Christians") ends precisely in a sort of apology of the overdetermination of time (XXI:81). "These actions have in such a way grown one from another that between one and the next never has he given people any interval of leisure for working against him." Every temporal interstice is closed by the constituent virtue of the new prince.

But, once again, don't precisely this overabundance of life and energy, this undefined pulsation, this continual creation that, at the end of the logical tendency and the ethical tension, make the picture opaque, lead to the inversion of all this? However we approach the text, we always find ourselves caught by these sudden reversals, the text's violent, almost irresistible incoherence—and we do not know yet what causes it, attracted as we are by the force of the constituent principle. Machiavelli is as much a prisoner of this development as is that collective subject that appears in *The Prince* and that Machiavelli identifies with.

The last three chapters of *The Prince* become thus an attempt to avoid the problem that had been constructed. The nonfunctioning of the theory of *The Prince* will be attributed to the personal failure of Italian princes, and the impossibility of resolving the crisis of the concept of the political will be overcome through a dislocation of discourse—by relying on myth. First of all, we have a definitive declaration of contradiction and failure: "Cur Italiae principes regnum amiserunt." The chapter begins with a eulogy of the "new prince," and with a self-praise of the teaching developed, revealed, and applied by Machiavelli: "The things written above, carried out prudently, make a new prince seem an old one, and make him quickly safer and firmer in his position than if he were in it by right of descent" (XXIV:88).

This is the image of the new prince, of the Italian Renaissance lord—but why, then, have these princes failed to find application, and why have these princes undergone mutation and emerged destroyed? Machiavelli's answer is very unsatisfactory: "Therefore these princes of ours, who have been many years in their princedoms, and then have lost them, should not blame Fortune, but their own laziness." What is the meaning of this reference to the lack of personal virtue?

No explanation can be given to it. By wondering about it (strange question after insisting so much on a method that valorizes only effectual reality), Machiavelli tries to circumscribe a sphere of responsibilities in which historical action can be evaluated case by case.

Here is, therefore, the chapter on "free will." "Quantum fortuna in rebus humanis possit, et quomodo illi sit occurrendum" (XXV:90). Once again, various layers of discourse are superimposed. First, we have a pious, or semipious answer, working to preserve free will in this enormous machinery of the world. However, Machiavelli solemnly concluded: "In order not to annul our free will, I judge it true that Fortune may be mistress of one half our actions but even she leaves the other half, or almost, under our control." Very kind, this fortune! Particularly if we consider that it is crazy and capricious as "one of our destructive rivers which, when it is angry, turns the plains into lakes, throws down the trees and the buildings, takes earth from one spot and puts it in another; everyone yields to its fury and nowhere can repel it." Yet Machiavelli, with empty good sense, even after understanding the radicalness of the conflict that agitates and constructs the political, that defines it as crisis, proposes new prescriptions on how fortune can be dominated.

The first method is that, even in front of the very impetuous rivers, in quiet times it is possible to build shelters and embankments, or dig canals to curb the impetus: "The same things happen about Fortune. She shows her power where strength and wisdom do not prepare to resist her." The second is to side with it, as with a young, beautiful, and free woman, in this case standing in front of fortune:

> *I believe this: it is better to be impetuous than cautious, because fortune is a woman, and it is necessary, in order to keep her under, to cuff and maul her. She most often lets herself be overcome by men using such methods than by those who proceed coldly; therefore always, like a woman, she is the friend of young men, because they are less cautious, more spirited, and with more boldness master her. (XXV:90–92)*

This argumentative strategy is invalid—in fact, the relationship between virtue and fortune is not dialectical, reciprocal, or functional. Machiavelli had understood the nature of this relationship more correctly in his pre-Calvinist letter to Soderini: indeed, there is no dialectic between virtue and fortune, he had affirmed in it, nor between freedom and necessity; there is only a strong will to power that explodes forward, radically transforms reality, and sets in motion an irresistible mechanism. An absolute disutopia. An ontology of radical construction. An impulse of being on the verge of nothingness.

After a few chapters in which the argument has been moving to no purpose, now, in the last one (XXVI) the elephant gives birth to the mouse: "Exhortatio ad capessendam Italiam in libertatemque a barbaris vindicandam." It is true that this *Exhortatio* does not seem to have been written together with the rest of the pamphlet but, rather, a couple of years later.[45] This fact, however, does not modify the substance of the matter, because the fall of constitutive reasoning already took place around chapter XVIII of *The Prince*: from this point on, the argument first vacillates and then lets itself be attracted by custom, either banal (XXIV) or fashionable (XXV). When in chapter XXVI myth is introduced to solve the problem of the relationship between virtue and fortune, when, in such a move, the whole methodological structure of *The Prince* is thrown to the dogs, well, then all this might have been written later, in the context, that is, of that stylistic and theoretical decline that begins around chapter XVII.

But let's look closer at the last chapter of *The Prince.* "I believe," writes Machiavelli, "so many things now join together for the advantage of a new prince that I do not know what time could ever be more fit for such a prince to act" (XXVI:93). Will Italian virtue reappear, upon this excess of poverty and corruption? Will Italy rise again, now that it has been enslaved, scattered, without a leader, without order, beaten and stripped of everything, invaded by enemies? The writing becomes prophetic. Certainly, an awakening will become possible if the Italians will take up arms: "And in Italy there is no lack of matter on which to impose any form; there is great power in the limbs, if only it were not wanting in the heads" (XXVI:94). This omen is realizable not only formally, but also materially. There is the possibility, indeed, as Machiavelli adds, to surpass the military organization that has made the Swiss and Spanish infantries so strong, and to constitute new Italian military orders: "A prince that recognizes the defects of both these types of infantry, then, can organize a new one that will repel cavalry and not be afraid of infantry" (XXVI:95–96).[46]

To operate in this way will be the dignity of the new prince, who is expected as a savior: he will be welcomed with love by the people, with desire for revenge against foreigners, with faith, piety, and tears. "To everybody this barbarian domination stinks." "Thus may your illustrious family appropriate." Here utopia falls back down to earth; the contradiction is revealed. Because here the arms are either those that turn virtue into constituent power and therefore are principle and strength, or they are those of the monarch. They cannot be both. Machiavelli had clearly demonstrated this in the middle of his pamphlet—when the overdetermination of time had taken up arms and had constructed a project of freedom. Here the mention of the Medici is false and rhetorical, as much as the *Dedication to the*

Prince, written between September 1515 and September 1516; the two texts recall each other.[47] Here Machiavelli becomes once again a man who needs help and gives up that familiarity with the ancients that has pushed him to investigate the foundation and, rather, dons the clothes of the courtier. The magic of a method that had allowed him to merge the scientific subject with a collective subject, the people with the prince, fades:

No one, I hope, will think that a man of low and humble station is overconfident when he dares to discuss and direct the conduct of princes, because, just as those who draw maps of countries put themselves low down on the plain to observe the nature of mountains and of places high above, and to observe that of low places put themselves high up on mountain tops, so likewise, in order to discern clearly the people's nature, the observer must be a prince, and to discern clearly that of a prince, he must be one of the populace.[48]

This prudence is in opposition to the methodical exaltation of the beginning of *The Prince*, to its introspection into power. "The Biblical phrases, the Petrarchan cry" of the ending, notwithstanding Chabod's opinion,[49] do not show the climax of Machiavelli's pathos but, rather, reveal his weak point, the escape into myth. If there are no doubts that *The Prince* was written in a brief period,[50] it is also certain that it disperses the energy of the initial nucleus by degrading it in the course of the text. From this point of view it does not seem that some interpreters are far from the truth when they tone down Chabod's exclamatory argument.[51]

But let's return to the substance of our discussion and to that of Machiavelli. We have seen how the Machiavellian intuition about a constituent power that founds the State by renewing it (which therefore consists of an external foundation that is a very radical activity without presuppositions) is tied to the biographical experiences of the Florentine secretary in the prehistory of *The Prince*. We have also seen how Machiavelli starts writing the *Discourses on the First Decade of Titus Livius* and, due to the tragedies of his life, feels the urgency to suspend that work and give definitive form to the concept of constituent power. This is, therefore, a concept that is entirely linked to the problematic presuppositions of the *Discourses*: from this perspective *The Prince* is a republican formula: "The new prince makes the republics."[52] But this beginning is wrapped in a series of contradictions—contradictions in the argument that reveal how far the exemplification is in general from the essence of the project, but, above all, contradictions concerning the principle. The principle cannot be restrained. However, it is always confronted by new limits. It is productive, but what it produces is opposed to itself. The relation between virtue and fortune, the way it is structured in *The Prince*, becomes unresolvable. The constituent principle is not a dialectical principle—it cannot be resolved or overcome—but this quality itself keeps it in a terribly precarious state. This is the precariousness of a strength open onto multiple horizons and never coherently articulated: a process that becomes tragic.

Machiavelli is aware of this problem: the constituent principle and strength are in fact absolute, but any actualization opposes them, wants to deny their absoluteness. If the absolute overflows or is dislocated, it finds itself confronted by the rigidity and irrationality of the constituted. This is the problem of constituent power, and this is the problem of the new prince. Every time virtue is realized, it discovers that it is working to accumulate something that, once it becomes strong, is opposed to it. Virtue against fortune: the opposition is still simple, elementary—but the violence it carries is enormous. Within the text the crisis of *The Prince* takes place when Machiavelli, after defining the principle, tries to measure the amplitude of action, the dynamic spectrum. The capability of acting on time from inside time, to constitute it as much as overdetermine it, must be armed: virtue becomes constituent power in this moment because it is on the relationship with arms that virtue forms the social orders. But not even this is enough: the themes of the exercise of power, of government are foregrounded, but here once again is verified the inconclusiveness of the principle, its crisis, and its always unresolved and often perverse dialectic.

All this would be irrelevant if the constituent principle were not the absolute principle. It is as such that it cannot disguise itself, either by assuming the costume of the monarch, or in the figure of myth. When the principle goes into crisis, the unresolved absolute is caricatured by the Medici. Or in the pathos of an unthinkable and literary patriotic utopia. No, this is impossible for *The Prince*. The absoluteness of its principle requires an absolute figuration. Only the absolute is not utopia. The constituent principle is absolutely open, but this opening must not be confused with determinations based on hopes, or worse, on fantasy and dream. Only material and actual reality can nourish the absolute. On the contrary, the only decision of *The Prince* is this clear indecision about the absolute.

Democracy as Absolute Government and the Reform of the Renaissance

When Machiavelli starts working again at "the book of the Republics" (by now it is the *Discourses on the First Decade of Titus Livius* that he will complete between 1515 and 1517), his thought has already taken that qualitative leap that consists in the elaboration of the constituent principle.[53] He can now apply the concept to that general theory of the forms of government that had been developing, on the basis of Polybius, in the eighteen chapters produced before the drafting of *The Prince.*

How is this qualitative improvement made visible? It can be recognized in the fact that, from chapters XVII–XVIII of the *Discourses,* the constituent principle animates the theory of princedoms—the republic becomes the Prince's body, the living matter of constituent power. The crisis of political discourse, which Machiavelli had experienced between 1512 and 1513, both in the writing of *On Princedoms* and in his personal life, is theoretically surpassed.

The interpretation of the relation between *The Prince* and the *Discourses* has always been tormented—not so much for philological reasons as for political motives. The Italian interpretive tradition, by insisting on the synthesis of the two works, on their contributing to one single line of thought, prevailingly tends to affirm the primacy of *The Prince* and to exalt the concept of the autonomy of the political, which, starting from that primacy, could be found in Machiavelli's entire work.[54] On the other hand, the Anglo-Saxon interpretive current, by insisting on the distinction or, better, on the substantial divergence between the two works, tends to privilege the *Discourses* for their republican intonation and for that idea of mixed government that pervades them.[55]

As for *The Prince,* according to this interpretive tendency, it would be an occasional work, when they do not affirm that it is a substantially ambiguous work. It seems to us, contrary to what both interpretive schools sustain, that the very close interdependence of *The Prince* and the *Discourses,* far from determining his waning, implies instead the celebration of the republican prince. The absoluteness of the political, invented in *The Prince,* is made to live in the republic: only the republic, only democracy, is absolute government.[56] The fact that *The Prince* is a circumstantial work, born within an extremely particular experience, does not isolate its central concept but makes its exceptional intensity available for the construction of the theory of the republics: Machiavelli puts the principle at the service of democratic government.

But let's see how the first eigththeen chapters of book I of the *Discourses* develop, and how the constituent principle of *The Prince,* almost as if it had been called by them, precipitates them. Book I opens affirming the necessity to "hunt for seas and lands unknown" in the political universe. How? Through imitation. While in art and medicine one resorts to "the examples of the ancients," this is not done in other spheres: "When I see . . . that the most worthy activities which histories show us, which have been carried on in ancient kingdoms and republics by kings, generals, citizens, lawgivers and others who have labored for their native land, are sooner admired than imitated... I can do no other than, at the same time, marvel and grieve over it."[57] This introduction is not rhetorical, because it immediately refers imitation to nature, and nature to passion—that is, it allows him to project history on the fabric of anthropology, and to affirm since the beginning the emergence of the subject. History must be read not for pleasure but in order to act.[58] The reference is formal for the time being, but it will be no longer as soon as we get into the midst of the discussion. We do so by crossing the Polybian theory of the forms of the State, and through the verification of his method of construction of the Roman model.

In *Discourses*, chapter II of book I is divided in two large parts: the first describes the cycle of the republics—that is, it moves from the Aristotelian definition of the three good forms of government and the three bad ones, and observes their dynamic principle: how we move from the princedom to tyranny, from tyranny to the aristocratic regime, and then to the oligarchy; how, finally, democracy triumphs, which, however, by turning into anarchy, reopens the cycle. These metamorphoses take place through accidental logics, often casual, yet regular: "And this is the circle in which all states revolve as they are governed and govern themselves."[59] This circle can, nonetheless, be broken. In the second part of the chapter Machiavelli applies himself to show how in the Roman mixed constitution, the three good forms of government could be detached from the malice of their opposite and thus stabilized, unified, balanced. Rome is the triumph of the mixed constitution. Certainly, its constitutional history is born only from two actors, as capable of expressing politics as of being subjected to synthesis: consular monarchy and senatorial aristocracy. But the tribunal institution immediately emerges, which imparts perfection to the Roman constitution, insofar as it imposes the presence of the democratic principle in it. So far Machiavelli is absolutely Polybian. But the insertion of the democratic principle—claims Machiavelli against Polybius—is not banal: it is actually a real revolution, so that the constitution "by remaining mixed, made a perfect republic: to which perfection was added through the disunion of the Plebs and the Senate." Cycle of the republics, mixed constitution—and then the hammer blow (what has Polybius to do with it anymore?) of the principle of disunion.

The following chapters, from III to X, are a very high illustration of the democratic model and of the function of disunion in maintaining freedom; from X to XV a vindication of religion as constitutional cement of the city, and its exaltation as a venue from the political to the anthropological, from the rational to the passional, from the analysis to the program.

Let's look at chapters III to X. If all men are evil and can become criminals, says Machiavelli, even more evil are the patricians when their power is not opposed by the power of the people. A "riotous" republic is born from this predicament, certainly, but the riots produce "good order": "Those who will carefully examine the aims of the riots will see that they have produced no exile or violence against the common good, but laws and orders in favor of public freedom" (I.4:203). Machiavelli concludes: "The people, though they are ignorant, can grasp the truth."

How can we comment on this extraordinary affirmation? What happened to Polybius here? Much of his theory is retained, even though the reasoning is beginning to become dislocated. Although it is recognized that the people are capable of producing the truth and are called "the guardian of freedom" (I.5), the schema of mixed government remains, and with it a certain pessimism and naturalism of Polybian origin that prevent the anthropological dimension of the analysis to turn into a support for democracy. In the following chapters, even when the reference to Polybius seems to disappear, the Polybian model of mixed government continues nonetheless to impose itself. The plebeian riot and the popular initiative defend freedom and represent the interpretive key to the progress of the institutions, but they must be read within the sphere of the balancing of powers. We can clearly see that in these chapters the concept of constituent power has not yet been constructed by Machiavelli. And also when Machiavelli dynamizes the Polybian dimension and introduces the famous distinction between quiet republics (as Sparta and Venice) and open and imperial republics (as Rome), he does not renovate radically, but simply improves Polybius's model (I.6). The expansiveness of the model, that is, the analysis of a republic that is open and capable of overthrowing toward the outside its own internal imbalances, does not modify the Polybian conception of the mixed government (I.7–10).

When, after these chapters on disunion, Machiavelli moves to consider ancient religion and its function in the city, he reveals analogous ambiguities in relation to the Polybian text (I.11–15). Religion is first considered as a common element, as a bewitching ether, within which disunion can be given, but it will always be concluded positively exactly through the religious tie: "Religion as something altogether necessary to maintain a well-ordered state." "Hence if there should be a debate on the prince to whom Rome was most under obligation, whether Romulus or Numa, I believe that Numa would sooner get the first place. Because where there is religion it is easy to bring in arms; but where there are arms and not religion, only with difficulty can the latter be brought in" (I.11:224–25). From these observations stems the invective against the Christian religion that is an actual religion of corruption and that has made the Italians "without religion and wicked" (I.12:228)!

So far Machiavelli is entirely within Polybius's tradition, but precisely through these last invectives we begin to see how he goes beyond that influence: because the conception of religion and of life can never be reduced, in Machiavelli, to an element of functionality and of subordination to power. It is also free passionality, it is individual life, enjoyed and hoped, it is rupture of conventions—religion overflows out of the sacred as much as life can and must overflow above conventions:

Anybody who saw our letters, honored friend, would wonder greatly, because he would suppose now that we were grave men, wholly concerned with important matters, and that into our breasts no thought could fall that did not have in itself honor and greatness. But then, turning the page, he would judge that we, the very same persons, were light-minded, inconstant, lascivious, concerned with empty things. And this way of proceeding, if to some it may appear censurable, to me seems praiseworthy, because we are imitating Nature, who is variable.[60]

This "matter that dances" is well beyond Polybius and his tradition.

If now we want to evaluate on the whole the degree of influence of book I of Polybius on Machiavelli's work, the answer is not very difficult: it is an important influence, on the first seventeen to eighteen chapters of the *Discourses*, but it is an influence that is more erudite and taxonomic than philosophical. Indeed, insofar as we consider the insistent and continual return of the Polybian model in the mixed government, we sense Machiavelli's deep unease to let himself be closed in and restrained into the *anakyclosis* and in the profoundly pessimist temperament of the Polybian doctrine.[61] On the other hand, the idea of the mixed constitution is in the ideology of Florentine humanism: Machiavelli may have got acquainted with it through the work of Leonardo Bruni, who constructed the model of the mixed government on Aristotelian sources rather than on Polybius.[62]

Whatever the channels that allowed Machiavelli to get to know Polybius may be, it is certain that the same channels opened other paths to the solutions of the problems confronted.[63] Here we reach the crucial point—that is, the point when Machiavelli, after having for some time rested his theoretical impatience on Polybius's text, comes to pose some fundamental questions: "A corrupt people, if it attains freedom, has the greatest difficulty in keeping itself free" (I.17:238); "How free government can be maintained in corrupt cities, if it is already there; and if it is not there, how it can be set up" (I.18:240). Here we are at the interruption of the

Discourses (or at the putting off of the project of the "book of the Republics"). It is clear that it was impossible to answer in Polybian terms the questions that Machiavelli now posed. *The Prince* becomes the new answer: constituent power. It is an *experientia crucis,* a moment of absolute theoretical innovation. Beyond and against Polybius's method, Machiavelli constructs a method that goes from the structure to the subject, from descriptive phenomenology to natural anthropology, from mixed government to democratic creativity. This new conceptual movement redefines the *Discourses* and completely and definitely tears apart the Polybian pattern. The formal institution of power now needs its absolute content. From now on, the *Discourses* will be nothing but the demonstration that the only content of the constituent form is the people, that the only constitution of the Prince is democracy. A research toward the "institutio populi."[64]

To give immediately the sense of what we are saying, allow us to look ahead briefly at book III of the *Discourses,* at its beginning and conclusion as the moments in which the constructive movement of Machiavelli's thought is crowned. Indeed, by connecting the opening statement of book III, that "If a religion or a republic is to live long, it must often be brought back toward its beginnings" (III.1:419) to the statement with which the book closes, "A republic, if she is to be kept free, required new acts of foresight everyday; and for what good qualities Quintus Fabius was called Maximus" (III.49:527)—well, here reappears, with extreme evidence, all the difference that *The Prince* has inserted into the *Discourses,* by refounding them. Here the conception of history has nothing to do with the Polybian or cyclical dimensions, since here the relation between principle and reform is all-encompassing, and disunion does not require rebalancing techniques of the powers, but on the contrary it embodies a motor of the continual reopening of history.

The constitutional process has become a play of productive subjects. The mixed constitution fades and disappears in front of this productive strength of the princes and of the subjects. The government by now is almost exclusively that which the new Prince had made of it—fury and order, impetus of virtue, creative capacity. The government is a fighting body. Thus in the *Discourses* the relation of Polybius to Machiavelli is a process that, moving in a confused and tight initial confrontation centered on the cycle of the mixed constitution, exhausts itself in the course of the work—as soon as the influence of *The Prince* intervenes in the *Discourses.* Abandoning the theory of the cycle implies abandoning the mixed constitution. Against this, fundamentally emerges the affirmation of constituent power—it is what the Prince invents ("The Duke Valentino, whose work I would always imitate, were I the new prince").[65] Then history is not suffered, the times of history are not those of a sentence, of an empty, suicidal repetition. On the contrary, they are the times of construction, of creation.

Now let's go back to chapters XVI–XX of book I of the *Discourses* around which moves the mutation of the Machiavellian project. It takes such effort to resume the discussion, once it has gone past the theoretical crisis. In fact, the transformation of the point of view is accomplished through a description of a crisis of the State that has become endemic, inert. This inertia of the crisis is assumed into the theory through a consideration of historical time that has become material, solid, enwrapping: in this time the corruption of the customs and the degradation of the laws become irresistible. And yet it is precisely against the background of this historical and institutional framework, inherited from the Polybian conception, that the rupture of time, the overdetermination of the Prince, become now possible, because necessary.

In the following chapters (XXI–XXXII), the tension between historical inertia and institutional crisis on one side, and the prince's initiative on the other, is pushed to the extreme; any mediation must be refused, "the middle ways are very dangerous" (I.27), only radical means will work: "These methods are very cruel, and enemy to all government not merely Christian but human, and any man ought to avoid them and prefer to live a private life rather than to be a king who brings such ruin on men. Notwithstanding, a ruler who does not wish to take that first good way of lawful government, if he wishes to maintain himself, must enter upon this evil once" (I.26:254). Thus we come in an entirely natural manner to those chapters on the Roman dictatorship that constitute, so to speak, the central pivot of book I of the *Discourses* (XXXIII–XXXVIII).

More than as institution, classical dictatorship is in fact studied as the historical outcome of the disunion; and its analysis begins to show how the urgency of the event, the prince's decision, the necessities and wills of the multitude can find an adequate synthesis. The formal principle of command, of power, must be embodied. The Polybian principle of equilibrium and of mixed government cannot but lead us—and indeed it has led us—to an entirely static theoretical and historical condition: in this principle everything withers, consciences as well as the laws, and institutional reality is degraded, while the natural one is "unfortunate." Only the opposite principle, the principle of the prince, spares us this condition. It reopens the genesis of the constitutions; it is the strength that makes them come to life again. The Roman dictatorship is the sign of this creative passage. The disunion cannot therefore be restrained and blocked in the equilibrium of the mixed constitution, but, rather, it must be continually interpreted and renewed, by a powerful and dynamic principle.

Roman history, and in particular the history of the century-long struggle for agrarian law (I.37), is the formidable example of the historical-political rule that Machiavelli is elaborating. The aristocrats sustain, says Machiavelli, that the struggle around agrarian law, from the Gracchi to Marius and Silla, to Pompeus and Caesar, has led to the end of Roman freedom. But if it is true that the conclusion of this fierce class struggle, through which the Roman institutions assumed their character, led to the end of freedom, it is false to affirm that without the class struggle freedom would have been maintained: "So if the quarrels over the Agrarian Law took three hundred years to make Rome a slave, she would perhaps have been brought much sooner to slavery if the people [la plebe], with this law and with its other cravings, had not continually checked the ambition of the nobles" (I.37:274). The plebs are the guarantor of freedom.

From now on the *Discourses* become an apology of the people, of the constitution of freedom, and finally an explicit declaration of the absoluteness of democracy as government.

We can, therefore, sum up the development of the discourse of this Machiavelli, prophet of democracy, around a few key points. First, the analysis of the republic turns against tyranny—to show that, in order to resist, democracy must be strong and armed and that the dictatorship for freedom is not to be feared (I.39). As prophecy, as hope, as resurgence, democracy must be armed. But the first and fundamental arms of the republic is its people: the people must in any case always be kept alive, in the republic, and the constitution must be respected, because it promotes the activity of the people and its own continual renewal (I.45): "If cities of free origin, such as Rome, with difficulty find laws that will preserve them, cities of origin immediately servile have slight possibility for doing so" (I.49:295).

> *This is evidently true of the city of Florence. Since at the origin she was subject to Roman authority and had always lived under the control of others, she remained for a time humble, without planning for herself. Then, when there came a chance for taking breath, she undertook to make her own laws; these, being mingled with old ones that were bad, could not be good. And so she has gone on governing herself for two hundred years for which there are trustworthy records. (I.49:296)*

This movement of thought, exalting the freedom of the foundation and the absoluteness of the republican government, deepens even more: "Public affairs are easily managed in a city where the populace is not corrupt. Where there is equality a princedom cannot be established; where there is none, a republic cannot be established" (I.55:306).

It means that, in these last chapters that outline a real republican synthesis, an open constitution that deeply treasures the conversion of all the parts of society toward the State as aim is set at the center of the discussion, but it is with the ultimate and fundamental condition, that the republican machinery is set on equality: "The would-be founder, then, will establish a republic where there is, or has been brought about, great equality; on the other hand, he will organize a princedom where there is great inequality. Otherwise he will produce a state out of proportion and not durable" (I.55:310). Here, therefore, equality is the condition of freedom. Could we be surprised if the multitude, which each time has been until now considered the guardian or the guarantor of truth, finally here is once again called "capable of truth" (I.4)? The multitude is wiser and more constant than a prince (I.59:319). This must be said and repeated, even if it were against the "common opinion": "I believe . . . that a people commits smaller sins than a prince; therefore one can rely on a people more than on a prince."

Machiavelli the democrat is here fully developed—how much hatred, how many falsifications, how many negations of luster and memory would these pages deserve, then! How much fear has produced in the powerful ones this very radical image of a people capable of truth, equality, organized in its rallies, ethically sustained by civil religion, capable of arms and victory. This people is powerful.

The chapter that closes book I of the *Discourses*—and that anticipates book II—behind the unsuspicious title "The consulate and every other magistracy in Rome were given without regard to age" is in fact the exaltation of youth and its virtue, of its capability to drag the plebs into the adventure of freedom, of being the force of the multitude, in the construction of glory (I.60:320). The virtue of the Roman consul and his youth are called to exalt the force of the plebs in the construction of the republican synthesis. And thus ends book I of the *Discourses*, in the strong, explicit, insisted on vindication of the legitimacy of the government of the multitude—thus of democracy, as the best form of government. The discourse of *The Prince* has been definitively absorbed in that of democracy; the Polybian beginning and the philosophy of history that was implicit in it are reversed: the best government is democracy, and its effectiveness is guaranteed by the determination of the subjects.[66] The effectiveness is the history of a subject.

If in book I of the *Discourses* we have witnessed the definition of the subject as collective entity—plebs, multitude, people—now in book II, in order to reach a high degree of actuality, the subject will have to show himself as dynamic basis of historical production, as strength. While the previous book was concerned, says Machiavelli, with "the decisions made by the Romans with respect to affairs within the city, in this one I shall speak of what the Roman people did pertaining to the expansion of the empire" (II:324). If we were following a triadic schema of exposition, here we could say that we are in the place of the affirmative: indeed, as in book I the dialectic between virtue and fortune, and in general the principle of disunion, had been considered central, so in this book virtue takes the center stage: it becomes the fundamental critical principle, and it is on it that the theoretical plot unravels. "Whether the Romans conquered their empire more through ability or through Fortune," and the answer is a program—it was virtue, the prudence of virtue (II.1:324). Virtue promoted in time by a collective subject. What allowed the Roman power, the construction of the great fortune of that people, was virtue—the virtue that comes from living for the common good: "Because not the particular good, but the common good is what makes the cities great. And doubtlessly this common good is not valued but in the republics" (II.1:134).

Against it there's tyranny.[67] Tyranny, which is a global form of domination, fierce and intrusive, pervasive, as a spiritual fact. Religious? What has the Christian religion to do with tyranny? The association of ideas is not casual; this chapter makes the analysis of religion a central moment in the description of the collective subject. The Christian religion, then: it is not tyranny, but it allows tyranny; it is not against tyranny and suffocates virtue. How much, instead, could the collective character of the virtuous subject be constructed and exalted in civil religion! In ancient times the sense of freedom found its source and fused with the public religion. The ancient one was a religion aimed at the celebration of the collective.

Neither pomp nor magnificence was lacking in the ceremonies and in addition there was the deed of sacrifice, full of blood and ferocity in the slaughter of a multitude of animals; this terrible sight made the men resemble it. . . . Our religion has glorified humble and contemplative men rather than active ones. It has, then, set up as the greatest good humility, abjectness and contempt for human things. . . . Though our religion asks that you have fortitude within you, it prefers that you be adapted to suffering rather than to doing something vigorous. This way of living, then, has made the world weak, and turned it over as prey to wicked men, who can in security control it, since the generality of men, in order to go to Heaven, think more about enduring their injuries than about avenging them. . . . The world has grown effeminate, and Heaven has laid aside her arms. (II.2:331)

Perhaps there would be the possibility of interpreting our religion according to virtue rather than according to inactivity: but this does not happen, so that in our era there are very few republics and none of those "well armed and very stubborn in the defence of their freedom" (II.2:332). Formidable chapter! Common good and public religion constitute the subject, as virtue, as collective and powerful activity.

Nonetheless, the necessities of the exposition claim space: while building the republic, the *Discourses* must show how obstacles are overcome, and how the harsh actuality can be reformed. Thus after chapters I and II, which, as we have seen, are dedicated to the method of virtue and to reproposing the collective definition of the subject, book II proposes a method of exposition by alternatives, counterposing chapters that decidedly show the ontological preeminence of virtue to chapters that instead take us to the political conditions of fortune: the first are "republican," the second argumentative, instrumental; the first "ideological" and the second "effectual." In concrete terms, chapters I and II—which we have already considered—are opposed to chapters III and IV, to define the fabric of actuality; and then, on the one hand, chapters X, XVI, XVII, XVIII, XX, and some others insist on the method of virtue; on the other hand, chapters IX, XI, XII, XIX, XXI, and some others show how actuality constitutes a solid cage. Only from chapter XXII until the end of the book, the unity of the two directions is realized, and the collective subject becomes the motor and the cipher of objectivity, the virtue of the actual.

In this list chapter V—"Change in religious sects and languages, along with the coming of floods and of plague, wipes our records"—is missing, and with good reason. In this chapter Machiavelli makes a digression away from the line of his argument and tries to define the Heraclitean flux of becoming as an experience of freedom. It is an absolute experience of freedom that permeates the constitution of subjects. We always find ourselves on the virgin terrain of history in the attempt to reconstruct virtue "in this mixed body of human generation," but we can still win back memory and construct it in virtue only if we risk this extreme limit of destruction. To save the memory of humanity is to reinvent it—a constituent power. In chapter V of book II blows a great wind of being and of destruction, that poses against a completely negative background the possibility of freedom and of constitution. If there were not this margin of destruction, there would not exist the possibility to speak of freedom as absoluteness. Isolated, but not less relevant, this metaphysical chapter poses what is at stake.

Back to our discussion. Thus the arguments of virtue against actuality unravel following the order of the chapters we have mentioned—that is, the strength of the subjects is constructed in book II of the *Discourses.* The more we advance the more we have the impression that actuality and fortune, against which virtue struggles, are neither irresistible nor invincible. Sometimes, from chapter X to chapter XX, we live the experience of being in the static center of a fading hurricane: that is, if fortune is felt in all its terrible force and in the series of elements of inertia and of deceit that it implies (or imposes on those who want to win it), in the same moment we see that this urgency and this massive objective impact are containable. It is a war that we live; virtue, to show itself as powerful, must structure the obstacles that oppose it.

Virtue is living labor, that little by little can destroy the traditions and the power that have consolidated against life. It is not by chance that here, in the midst of it all, is for the first time argued in a theoretical manner what until now has been either the theme of practical exercises,[68] or rhetorical and inciting discourse:[69] here instead it is demonstrated that virtue can be powerful in arms, or better, that only in arms virtue can be powerful:

> *Riches are not the sinews of war, though common opinion holds them so; but good soldiers are. . . . Money is indeed necessary in the second place, but it is a necessity that good soldiers gain for themselves, because it is quite as impossible for good soldiers to lack money as it is for money of itself to find good soldiers. (II.10:351)*

This inclination, at times naive, other times fanatic, often genial, always impassioned, that pushes Machiavelli toward the arms and the discourse of military orders, is the transcription of the necessity to give strength to the collective subject. "How far the soldiers of our time have turned away from those of ancient times." "How armies at the present time, should esteem artillery and if the opinion universally held of it is true." "On the authority of the Romans and by the example of the ancient soldiery, infantry ought to be valued higher than cavalry." "The sort of danger risked by a prince or a republic making use of auxiliary or mercenary soldiers" (II.16:363; 17:367; 18:373; 20:381). Well, this is how the radicalness of the refounding of history comes to light.

It is from chapter XXII of Book II, and to the end, that the discourse tightens in a synthetic manner, recuperating the destructurated elements, and in general the objective conditions, in order to make them internal to the tension of the project. The relation between virtue and the elements of actuality is completely reversed in terms of productive synthesis. No unbalanced move, in this picture, neither in the sense of a neutral objectivism (that could hide the yielding to a brute actuality), nor in the sense of a blissful subjectivism and of the idealism of virtue. Not at all: here the elements of actuality, previously taken apart and analyzed, are reconstructed and led to be part of a new actuality—of which virtue is itself an actor, because it is virtue of a collective subject, it is strength:

I assert, indeed, once more that it is very true, according to what we see in the histories, that men are able to assist Fortune but not to thwart her. They can weave her designs but cannot destroy them. They ought, then, never to give up as beaten, because, since they do not know her purposes and she goes through crooked and unknown roads, they can always hope, and hoping they are not to give up, in whatever fortune and whatever affliction they may be. (II.29:408)

Here is thus how the project works: there is no dialectic, there is no idealism in it.

However, there are always situations in which virtue cannot constitute itself as new actuality: in chapters XXXI and XXXII Machiavelli lists examples of how virtue crashes against frauds, plots, the problems of the exiles. But generally this terrain of the struggle is what can be negotiated—project of strength, constituent power. If the text of book II seems to have taken as its point of departure too advanced a hypothesis—so that, in the movement of the demonstration, it accumulates and discards hypotheses and demonstrations, often in a prolix manner, sometimes confusedly—however in this way it manages to approach a conclusion, by groping a little, but not less effectively. Thus the new actuality of virtue is constructed, and the difficulties of the argument show the difficulty of the real constitutive process.

Antiquity always remains there to show us the exemplary way, to construct the paradigm that we can reconstruct through all the difficulties of history:

We see, therefore, both from this discussion and from what we have many times said elsewhere, how much in their way of proceeding present republics differ from ancient ones. We also see, for this reason, every day miraculous losses and miraculous gains. Because where men have little ability, Fortune shows its power much, and because she is variable, republics and states often vary, and vary they always will until someone arises who is so great a lover of antiquity that he will rule Fortune in such a way that she will not have cause to show in every revolution of the sun how much she can do. (II.30:411–12)

Thus fortune can be shaped by virtue, but only to the point where the struggle has developed and virtue has triumphed. "Good fortune" exists—it is that which we have constructed, it is that which virtue has imposed as new actuality. The discourse on the "disunion" of book I has become the discourse on the "struggle" of book II, that is, it has become subjectivized. Indeed, we have so far witnessed a theoretical movement that has proceeded toward the identification of the structural dimensions of the collective subject—first in terms of constitution proper, of centripetal direction of the movement; then in terms of expression of strength. First, the possibility of strength, then its actuality. And this process is very impetuous. However, we can never forget the sense of crisis that the entire discourse subtends.

In *The Prince* the discovery of the constituent principle, the application of this theoretical instrument to the question of time and democracy, to the Italian crisis, and to the movement of virtue, propose a solution, but do not do away with the problem. In Machiavelli, no illusion is ever given about the dialectic or metaphysical unity of fortune and virtue; in no case is the ancient paradigm nostalgia for an undifferentiated golden age, ideology, or myth. Rome is not a myth: it is a slice of the human, a space and a time that man has subtracted from the disaster of any history that is not virtuous. In any case, virtue and fortune are, per se, elements of an unsurpassable and profound crisis that pertains to the ontological constitution of the human. Not ironically we can concede that "to such an extent does Fortune blind men's intellects when she does not wish them to check her gathering might" (II.29:407). However, we can always heroically be soothsayers.

Thus we are now at book III of the *Discourses.* We have mentioned above how the discourse of the democratic republic here comes to define itself in terms of absolute government. Now we must carefully study these pages. In order to do so, we must always remember that the passage from the definition of the dualistic constitution of the subject to that of the strength of subjectivity—which we have until now followed—can also lead us into error, if we do not continually insist on the quality leap that has occurred in the meantime, and that from *The Prince* has spread to the *Discourses.* The model of democracy built here, I mean, is a modern and powerful model.

To fully clarify the context, before beginning the reading of book III, let's confront another, more ancient Machiavellian description of democracy—that is, that which he gives around 1508 of the cities of Germany: "Nobody must doubt the might of Germany, because it abounds in men, riches, and arms."[70] Now, this wealth comes from the fact that the public and private expenditure is extremely low, and that the Germans have smaller necessities than the Florentines and the Italians. There is, further, a situation of complete autarchy of their production and their consumption: produced at a low cost, their manufactured goods are competitive abroad. "And thus they enjoy this unrefined life of theirs and their freedom." They do not want war, unless they are "overpaid"; they live in free communities. These cities are inimical not only to the princes, but also to the "gentlemen"—because they demand, within themselves, a certain equality—"so that in their country there's nobody either of one species or of another, and they all enjoy, without any distinction among men, except those who are in office as magistrates, a free freedom." Upon this basis a unified Empire is unthinkable, and only a certain contractual order is possible.

But what is the use of a "free freedom" if it only produces an uncivilized life? Here we are at the point at which, in the *Discourses*, a new conception of democracy appears: there is democracy only where there is constituent power. The German community, on its side, is not State, is not power, is not prince, therefore, in this light, those orders are not even virtuous. Those orders exist at the margins of modernity, there where theological or contractual foundations of right are given—irrelevant for science.[71] Science instead can only study virtue, the genealogical process of the constitution of power: the constituent power of *The Prince* becomes, in the *Discourses*, the content of democracy. There can be other models of democracy, other contracts of citizenship, but they are characterized by a degraded intensity with respect to the constituent characteristics of modern democracy. Democracy is not a half-State: it is a real Princedom. The singularity of this defining approach by Machiavelli cannot ever be forgotten.

And now let's go back to the *Discourses*, book III.[72] If we want a religion or a republic to live long, "I say that those changes are to their advantage that take them back toward their beginnings" (III.1:419). It is in its principle, in its constituting act, there where virtue has become actuality, that the strength of the republic lies. "This regress toward the beginning—as observed in republics—results from either external accident or internal prudence"; thus, either through the structures provided for it (the institutional structures of change), or through the deeds of men and the renovation in the play of virtue-fortune, "in religious bodies—continues Machiavelli—these renewals are also necessary, as we see through the example of our religion, which, if Saint Francis and Saint Dominic had not brought it back towards its beginnings, would have entirely disappeared.... This renewal, then, has maintained and still maintains our religion" (III.1:419, 418, 422).

The reference of the concept of constituent power to that of religious reform is not by chance; we will return to the connection with the religious discourse and with Savonarola's activity later (III.30). It is not by chance, because the intensity of the foundation is the same, both for the republic and for religion: it touches the multitude and constitutes it as creative possibility, both in the case of the republic and in that of the religious community. The secularization of religion and the sacralization of civil life proceed step by step.[73] Here we see that Machiavelli is playing on a terrain difficult to define. After making itself collective subject and having shown its strength, virtue refines itself "with intrinsic prudence"—it moves from the experience of objectivity to the experience of passions, rearticulates virtue and actuality from inside, and from below apparatuses that generate the constituent principle. It is not the modern absolute[74] State that is built, here—this degeneration must be left to the anti-Machiavellians. Here it is the democratic republic that gets founded, the constitutional form of the multitude. The reference to reform is not ambiguous, therefore. Even less ambiguous will be, in the next section, the connection between virtue and poverty (III.16). In fact, here it is the Renaissance that gets reformed, and nobody more than that offspring of hers—Machiavelli—has her passion and enthusiasm.

We have thus entered the terrain of the constitutional dynamic of strength. To begin with, we talk of the return to the beginning, the principle, the foundation. It is obvious, however, that in the discourse is inscribed the opening of a new historical terrain, a new ontological production, and a new texture of freedom. Freedom can live only insofar as it renews itself—freedom is the first product of strength.

What is the Renaissance? It was the rediscovery of freedom and, with it, of the virtue of constructing, of inventing: at the same time it was the discovery of the possibility and the capacity of accumulating. Yet through accumulation fortune was built, and fortune so established opposed virtue—the dialectic revealed itself through this negativity of the result. The only possibility of resisting this perversion of the development of virtue and its dialectic is the foundation of a collective subject that opposes this process, who tries to fix the accumulation not of fortune but of virtue. Who will be able to do it? Only in the forms of democracy and of the government of the multitude will this project be conceivable.

The reform of the Renaissance is the refusal to accept its perverse dialectic, thus the refusal to accept its dialectic as a form of thought and as a conciliation of antagonisms. It is not true that between man and the world there is a relation of conciliation—we do not know this benevolence of reality; on the contrary, everytime we act we risk the reversal of virtue into fortune, and the recognition of the actuality of the latter, against us. How does the picture change? How can the Renaissance be reformed—and virtue itself? Answers Machiavelli: there exists no circle that sums up both virtue and fortune, and nothing else. Virtue can win or succumb: this and nothing else is the alternative that constitutes it. But also its dignity. Virtue is freedom. How can we avoid, then, that the expression of virtue is crushed? That it becomes perverted or neutralized?

The chapters that should give an answer to this question are extremely ambiguous. Indeed, the theory of passions is ambiguous—not its genealogical definition, the insistence on its capability to give origin, but its phenomenology, its descriptive. Thus any passion manifests itself as the right side and the obverse, and the exercise of virtue can become inhuman, when patriotic *pietas* becomes cruelty; as for prudence, to give another example, it reveals itself as repression and exemplary punishment, while the conception of the enemy is totalitarian and obsessive (III.2–5).

But this ambiguity does not reveal an incoherence but, rather, the difficulty of making logical what is a play of forces and counterpowers. Let's see, for example, what Machiavelli says about plots (III.6). A plot per se is an evil, an inactuality with respect to the value of peace, but it can also be, and often is, the emergence, in a situation that is otherwise blocked, of the exigence of change and of the need for reform. A plot can be virtue that presents and develops itself as counterpower. A plot must be refused when it is a possibility for tyranny. But when it is virtue, or even only an indication of an eternal "up and down" of the hoped for actuality, when it is in any case a sign of opening and dynamism, then it may be welcome. A plot is virtuous when it is democratic, because democracy is always virtuous.

In fact, the republic deserves plots when it must be instituted. Once instituted, the republic refuses plots. Rightly so, the republic refuses plots, if they are organized in a way that allows the mobility of the subjects and the flexibility of the times of the reform (III.7–9):

> *Thence it comes that a republic, being able to adapt herself, by means of the diversity among her body of citizens, to a diversity of temporal conditions better than a prince can, is of greater duration than a princedom and has good fortune longer. Because a man accustomed to acting in one way never changes, as I have said. So of necessity when the times as they change get out of harmony with that way of his, he falls. (III.9:453)*

With this said, it is clear that even this example of the plot is only, among many, one discourse about that reform of freedom (that makes a collective and powerful virtue of it) with which we are presently concerned. So much so that it is not strange, in regard to the prince's virtue, that the discussion goes back to poverty (III.16). Paradoxical reference, dubious interrogation. Poverty: what can a man of the Renaissance say about it? He can only say that the only means to avoid corruption is the citizens' poverty, that the only tool to defend freedom is an army of free men (again something that cannot be bought and that poverty nonetheless retains). The fact that Machiavelli, a Renaissance man, supports a drastic reduction of needs, Spartan clothing, the struggle against luxury, and so on cannot but surprise us. We will no longer be surprised when poverty will be seen translating, simply, the struggle of virtue against fortune (could we add: the struggle of living labor against dead labor?). On the other hand, without poverty there is no spirit of sacrifice, no autonomous possibility of armament. Poverty—let's not be stunned by this Machiavellian insistence. After being a discourse on strength, the Machiavellian call for a popular army is a discourse on passions (III.10–15). Passions of freedom, experiences of virtue.

Never before as in this case has the discourse on arms, on the organization and management of the army, on the deployment of war strategies been appropriate. This unity of the spirit in civil armament here is logically requested as a moment of demonstration of the absolute character of democracy, but also as a pure moment of direct expression of the passion of the multitude, of the passional unification of the many. Poverty—like disutopia—lies on the absolute limit of freedom that is the void of possessions (logical and practical); but exactly for this reason it is allowed to be a new element of the possibility of a new prince, of a new urgency and opportunity of transforming reality (III.25).

From the dialectic of forces the discussion has moved to the dialectic of passion, to the apparatus that strength reveals by traversing the passions. If we look carefully, here we are in front of the reopening of the constitutive system of perspectives, but on another level. Again it is the principle of freedom that is taken into consideration, but a principle of concrete freedom, thus the freedom that constitutes itself through the passions. A theory of passions as apparatuses of freedom—therefore nothing stoic and nothing, on the other hand, Christian. Passions can neither be dominated nor controlled: we need to let them go toward the construction of reality, of a new reality. Passions can be ordered only by the principle of reform, that is, by an ethical order of the consequences that takes shape in materiality, in the flux of determined consequences. We are completely inside matter, inside passions, but we can stir up all this in a direction of freedom. With effort. Through actuality.

And so? Let's exemplify. In the republics there is always disunion: on the banality and the natural regularity of disunion passions develop; passions generate riots: "And because no certain remedy can be given for such troubles that rise in republics, it follows that an everlasting republic cannot be established, in a thousand unexpected ways her ruin is caused" (III.17:471). With this said, if a perpetual republic is impossible, the perpetual character of its renewal, of its reform is possible. The principle of foundation becomes that of refoundation and of dynamics. Passion is a plot materially and deeply rooted in time, a plot that can shake time and its inertia. This point—of the inertia of time and of its irreducible objectivity—is crucial in Machiavelli's work. As for the other men of his era, and in general for all those who founded modern science, the necessity/possibility of countermanding temporal inertia is as urgent as can be the decision of the search itself. This breaking with the inertia of time—also with that inertia that is formed by virtue—is a fundamental decision of Machiavelli's (III.25).

Virtue cannot be constructive passion if it is not *cupiditas et amor*; natural instinct and very high ethical condition—and, as we will see further on, also rationality: not simply instrumental rationality, but composing and recomposing rationality, rationality that has the passional bearing of the temporal continuum, which is capable of settling within the liquidity of time and present action.

The last part of book III is completely dedicated to show how virtue knows how to and can reconstruct the city (III.24–25). "How to act in uniting a divided city; there is no truth in the opinion that in order to hold cities a ruler must keep them divided" (III.27). This chapter, not by chance, responds to those chapters of book I that had posed the problem of the democratic disunion generated by corruption, and by the impossibility of maintaining the republic in those conditions: it was there, around those chapters (that pose the same questions), that the drafting of *On Princedoms* had been suspended and *The Prince* had begun (I.16–18).

Consequently, here in book III the mechanism of virtue, already transformed by *The Prince* and remodeled in books I and II of the *Discourses*, fixed as constituent principle, becomes perfectly clear. Chapter by chapter the image of the republic, as the synthesis of the multiple and the one, of force armed toward the outside and of civil peace, of rationality as domination of time, and of love and poverty as civil *cupiditas* that destroys corruption—well, this image constructs itself as the schema of the conclusion of the *Discourses*. And if chapter XXVII has definitely posed virtue as the producer of unity, as matrix of recomposing rationality, the other chapters, from here to the end of the *Discourses*, develop thematics, positive or negative, that integrate that thematic nucleus. Here is, then, on the one side, the strong call to beware that the anxiety for the defense of the civil unity of the republic does not become the basis and the alibi for tyranny (III.28–30). Bad faith, hypocrisy, and envy feed tyranny: we must guard ourselves against the passions that produce tyranny. Machiavelli argues on the ground of passions and on their temporal rhythm. Positivity follows negativity: within the perverse temporality and the inertia of power, "Time waits for no one, goodness is not enough, Fortune varies, and malice receives no gift that placates her" (III.30:497). Only constituent power, then, only the prince, can decide for the republic.

The theme is immediately reinforced: it is again the discourse on the armies (III.31). Once again it is a discourse that shows the apparatus of virtue in the moment when the multitude becomes unity through the militia, and democracy is born armed. Constituent power founds the city and it always represents itself in the militia as activity, so that inertia and fatigue may not take away freedom. Only constituent power—open, repeated, lasting, armed—constitutes the republic. Virtue as theme-apparatus of the unity of the city and of the multitude is once again developed—after being deployed as antityranny motif and as *refrain* of the arming of the people—to define absolute government. In chapters XXXII–XXXVI, the order of the magistratures is discussed, as well as the relations that they entertain among themselves, and the relations between magistratures and people: the scheme that here supports the discussion is that of the play of actual counterpowers. Only in such a way—that is, only when disunion has become the key of institutional relations—absolute government can be formed: as democratic government that does not hide differences, but that asks the citizens to always reconstruct unity out of differences. The principle of the absoluteness of power is that of the multitude in action. A relation between "fury and order," between *cupiditas* and rationality, between innovation and consent, that represents the matter of which the Prince's action is made—even more so that of the republic. "Yet when efficiency is disciplined, it uses its ardor in the right way and at the right time, and no emergency daunts it or takes away its courage, because good discipline fed with the expectations of victory preserves courage and ardor." And all this, as it is by now evident, does not only concern the armies but, above all, the democratic order (III.36). Thus, encountering some other not secondary problem of constitutional architecture, of the art of war and of the theory of virtue (III.37–48), we come to the conclusive chapter: "A republic, if she is to be kept free, requires new acts of foresight everyday; and for what good qualities Quintus Fabius was called Maximus" (III.49:527).

Each day new ordinances.... Even if they were, in the rationality of the aim that justifies them, the destruction of the defeated troops, or the exemplary repression of the multitude (the repressions of "bacchanals and poisoners").... The violence of the example, in this commentary, does not produce fear—on the contrary, it leads itself back to the beginning. And this is constituent power, its continual opening, its renewing itself, the possibility of maintaining the multitude and the army in action. Here the secret of *The Prince* is revealed, here an answer is offered to the questions of the *Book of the Republics*; here we see the principle of reform of the Renaissance: freedom can remain open and constructive, oppose tyrannical dominion and corruption, the church and fortune, only if it is the prince, only if it is constituent power in action. The prince is democracy—precisely the reform of the Renaissance. Machiavelli's problem will never be that of closing down the revolution: the constitution for him is always the opening of the revolutionary process of the multitude.[75]

Critical Ontology of the Constituent Principle

Machiavelli detests Girolamo Savonarola; willingly, throughout his work, he ironically conflicts with the "unarmed prophet." Already in 1497 he describes with diffidence and antipathy the friar's movements: they are those of a politician, who, afraid of being attacked by the new Signoria, threatens it, then soothes it, and tries to unite it to his action against the papacy.[76] Now and later, the difference between Machiavelli and Savonarola goes beyond their disagreement on the ends: it touches the political logic of the former, an old political logic, sustained by an instrumental rationality—Machiavelli sees no possibility to attribute to Savonarola the essential quality of the new politician, constitutive capacity, the dimension of praxis.

Machiavelli recognizes in Savonarola the Christian, the humanist, but the ideal of prudence and virtue that Savonarola develops remains part of a tradition of finalism and transcendentalism that Machiavelli does not accept anymore: now political prudence must move among events, not in order to discriminate among them according to external finalities but, rather, to rationalize them according to the principle that runs through them.[77] Paradoxically, Savonarola's transcendentalism can have perverse outcomes: isn't Machiavelli perchance recognizing in Savonarola the first of the authors of "Machiavellianism," of the transcendence of the "reason of State"? Even when this reason considers itself democratic?

Savonarola is burned on the pyre and Machiavelli obtains the Florentine Secretaryship. He moves here and there as ambassador and inspector. For example, he is in Pistoia in 1500; he tells how, intervening in order to appease intestine struggles, the Florentines found themselves prisoners of their own intervention, to the point of building an actual force of occupation of the city.[78] What could they have done otherwise? The only rationality of the Pistoiese situation, vis-à-vis the confused, medieval intestine struggle, uninterrupted and implacable, is the force of the republic. In 1500 Machiavelli also goes to France for the first time.[79] Once again a reference to prudence: it is not the wisdom of known things, or simply of those practicable; it is not a North star that allows one to pass through the tempests of reality: on the contrary, prudence is the will to knowledge and the will to power; it is (specifically) the capacity to adapt with initiative and dynamism to the rules of life at court. The adherence to reality, which is made into an apparatus, is the first characteristic of Machiavelli's logic. Virtue waits for real apparatuses that are revealed and constructed by the will to knowledge.[80]

The dimensions and the depth of this approach doubtlessly make it an ontological operation. In Machiavelli the will to knowledge presents itself as a productive movement that penetrates being, a knowledge that tends toward the construction of a new being. In 1503, when Machiavelli writes *On the Method of Dealing with the Rebellious Peoples of the Valdichiana*, the relation that logic poses between knowing and acting, and that reveals itself as ontological, constitutive, is by now completely self-conscious: the call to action of the Romans becomes political paradigm; exemplarism is considered as ontological apparatus,[81] which means that the commentary of ancient works is the reading of regional ontologies in which knowing and acting are equally inscribed. In Machiavelli the humanistic tradition has extraordinarily matured, and the scientific positions are already dislocated, from morality to politics, from politics to historiography, and finally to ontology. Rhetoric and exemplarism are torn away from the Ficinian tradition—the new, the event, the prince are by now the mark of originality.[82]

When in 1512 Machiavelli goes back to *On Princedoms* and then to *The Prince*, this methodological horizon has definitely taken shape. Until the *Discourses* this direction becomes more and more definite, and characterized by more and more methodological dexterity, in the sense of a constitutive historical ontology. In the letters of 1514 to Vettori we can see foregrounded the conclusive phase of this process.[83] The discussion tries now to go through the "order of things" that constitutes itself through alternatives and juxtapositions of fields of force, but the rationality of the picture and therefore the sense of the order of things are given only from the point of view from which we are situated—a point of view that is also a point of force. The papacy in particular, writes Machiavelli to Vettori, the Florentine ambassador to Rome, can determine disruptions of the situation through its intervention, but this possibility opens clusters of different variables and of unexpected alternatives.

The linguistic movement in these letters seems to organize itself on the historical being: we go to the event, to the construction of the conclusion through an uninterrupted series of alternative options, followed by the exclusion of a term. A geometrical method, sustained by an extremely dry language. The order of things reveals itself as the product of a historical acting and as determination of the event. It is to say that in the method of analysis reappears constituent power, to give unity to the historical field, to impose the sense of the order of things, as it had done in front of social struggles and in the analysis of the genesis of the new princedom.

Thus we come to the *Preface* of the *History of Florence*, certainly one of the highest points of the Machiavellian definition of method.[84] I convinced myself to write a history of Florence from its origins, he tells us (while in a first moment he had thought of dealing only with the period between the Medici hegemony of 1434 to the present), because the existing histories do not take enough into account, and in any case do not describe well enough, "civil conflict, the internal friendships, and the effects born from them." Rome had the aristocracts against the plebs, and so did Athens, but in Florence the conflict is universal—in any direction and in all senses. And here is the paradox—or, better, what seems to be a paradox but is instead the core itself of Machiavelli's discourse: nothing else can demonstrate the excellence and power of Florence as the fact of not having collapsed under the weight of dissents but, rather, having transformed them into the mechanism of its progress: "I cannot, therefore, see any reason why these divisons do not deserve to be fully described."[85]

The historical constitutive ontology reveals itself, therefore, as historical materialism. The order of things has found action, and dissent, at its basis—as motor and sense of the historical process. Being is constituted by human praxis that organizes itself in universal disunion, and it is through disunion that constituent power is discovered and organized. After having seen, in the first section of this chapter, how constituent power is formed in the midst of mutation as discovery of the possibility of overdetermining time; and after having described, in the second section, how the absoluteness of constituent power can find an adequate subject only in the multitude and a substance only in an always open form of democratic government—now we foreground the materialism of this foundation: that aspect, that is, that makes Machiavelli's thought the chief antidote of any thought of the pacification of history, of social antagonism, of any negation of the constitutive work of ontology.

But the thing is not so simple, and the passage not so direct. It is worth, then, studying in depth how Machiavelli develops these materialist conclusions, and what path he takes, not for a philological curiosity but because it is in this passage that depth, density, and extension of the methodological premises are revealed. The way to materialism is as fatiguing as it is fruitful. Here we are interested in analyzing the *History of Florence*, precisely in order to grasp this conclusive transformation—and also perhaps the definitive internal clarification of the discourse of Machiavelli. To this aim, and in this context itself, we are obliged to make a digression.

As we have seen, in the *Preface* and the *History*, Machiavelli tells us that he first thought of writing the history of Florence starting from 1434, the date of the triumphal return of Cosimo from his Paduan exile, and to have only later decided to narrate Florentine history from its beginning—as history of universal disunion—and to show this disunion as the key of the constitutive and constituent processes. The first question that spontaneously therefore arises is: wouldn't this confession of uncertainty about the project correspond to an actual difference in the drafting times, so that the writing of the last four books (that include the narration of the events from Cosimo's return to the death of the Magnifico) would precede the first four? To answer this question, we have few data.

A first element is entirely generic; it is the type of request that had been made to Machiavelli: "To write the annals or history of the things done by the state and the city of Florence, beginning with the date that seems to him suitable, and in that language, whether Latin or Tuscan, that seems to him best."[86] Nothing, therefore, opposes the fact that Machiavelli is going to start his history from here or there. However, for the period preceding 1434, we already have the histories of Bruni and Bracciolini; to go back to write about this period one needs to have something new to say. If we look only at the *Preface* of the *History*, the answer would be easy: neither Bruni nor Bracciolini have cast enough light on dissension as the crucial element of the extraordinary history of Florence, on conflict as motor of the historical process; therefore I, Machiavelli, will concern myself with this question, according to the new method. The first four books, then, would have been written, initially, on the basis of the new original program—except that in the last four books the new method is only partially at work, partially and equivocally. To make things clearer, let's consider paragraph 1 of Book V of the *History*.[87] It has a programmatic and methodological title: "The cycle of human affairs, the weak rulers, soldiers, and peoples of Italy." Here is contained a theoretical essay that could very well function as a philosophical prologue for the four books of the second part of the *History*. A little treatise of anthropology or, better, of a pessimistic anthropology:

In their normal variations, countries generally go from order to disorder and from disorder move back to order, because—since Nature does not allow worldly things to remain fixed—when they come to their utmost perfection and have no further possibility for rising they must go down. Likewise, when they have gone down and through their defects have reached the lower depths, they necessarily rise, since they cannot go lower. So always from good they go down to bad, and from bad rise up to good. Because ability brings forth quiet; quiet, laziness; laziness, disorder; disorder, ruin; and likewise from ruin comes order; from order, ability; from this last, glory and good fortune. (Book V.1:1232)

This beginning, more pre-Socratic than Polybian, is followed by a further evaluation: Florence has come to the point of reproducing, if not the greatness of the Romans' dominion, certainly a strength as great as theirs, but now the city itself is drawn into this vortex of disorder and ruin, as the other Italian princedoms are, because all have forgotten how to use arms and have married civil life to corruption and deceit—"in this corrupted world." Thus the reborn Italy is coming back to servitude.

Now, returning to the problem of the order of composition of the *History*, we can underline that, on the one hand, the theoretical prologue (V.1), has the characteristics of a preface of the *History*, but that, on another, it excludes precisely those novelties of method and of conception that the *Preface* of Book I claims. From these considerations could then follow and the hypothesis could be sustained that, if the Prologue to Book V and what is developed in Books V, VI, VII, and VIII do not correspond either to the method or to the substance of what had been said in the Preface and done in Books I, II, III, and IV and in fact flatten themselves upon tradition; if, against what was written and developed between Books I and IV constitutes the real methodological innovation of the *History*; well, if all this is true, the hypothesis could be thus developed that the first group of books has followed—by breaking its difficult development and by innovating—the drafting of the second group. Let's repeat this: in the first paragraph of Book V is exposed an Epicurean and pessimist philosophical approach, an ambiguous apologia of Florence, an irrational conception of historical development, which dominate the development of the successive narration. In the first four books, instead, even though against the background of a certain pessimistic naturalism, a critical conception of the history of Florence emerges, by now clearly informed by the methodology of historical materialism. The historical rationality that triumphs here is that founded on the constituent power of the multitude. In concluding the digression, it seems to me that we can reasonably hypothesize that Books V, VI, VII, and VIII were written in a different moment, and probably before Books I, II, III, and IV, and all this because, while the method of the first four books is that of a mature and complete historical materialism, in the last four books Machiavelli is still seeking this method.[88]

Long and diffcult is therefore the path of the construction of a materialist method that can confirm, in historiography, the hypotheses of constitutive ontology. If we folllow the *History* according to the reading hypothesis so far formulated—that is, reading the second group of books before the first—we can see how Machiavelli is little by little getting rid of a naturalistic and formulaic style, of a fragmented logic, to proceed toward a new theoretical passage. However, this is not simply a naturalistic and formulaic style: in these same places the naturalistic context covers over an encomiastic intention, as obligatory as unpleasant for Machiavelli. We cannot forget that Machiavelli, the republican, is describing the Medicis' politics at the moment of their triumph, the return of Cosimo, so that this memory has turned into myth also for the majority of the Florentines,[89] and, finally, that past fortune is so present that the Medici reign now over Florence and that a Medici pope (to whom the *History* itself is dedicated) reigns over Rome (see the *Dedication*).

The combination of naturalism and encomiastic attitudes is a typical figure of mannerism: in our case this combination takes place against the background of the author's exhaustion, his need of money, at times his yielding to a dull drifting.[90] Yet we must get rid of all this, but how? It seems that Machiavelli chases and discovers again truths that he had widely discussed in *The Prince* and the *Discourses.* In any case, it is only toward the end of Book VI that he begins, here and there, to overcome the annalistic and naturalistic formulas of the narration: as in chapter 24, when he talks with great fondness of the great betrayor Francesco Sforza; or in number 28, when he mentions the defeats of the King of Aragon in Maremma by the Florentines; and above all in chapter 29, when Machiavelli tells of the "humanistic plot" of Stefano Porcari in Rome, and here realism and the emotion begin to form historical judgment: "Such an end had this project of his. Certainly anyone can praise his intentions, but everybody will always blame his judgement, because such undertakings, though when planned they give some appearance of splendor, in their execution offer almost always inevitable ruin" (1323). Thus the development of the annalistic treatment can be interrupted, and it is interrupted by the compassion for the humanistic insurrection. And even more so, stylistically and theoretically, by the "terrible storm" that crosses Tuscany in 1456: "When men's arms were laid down, so great was a windstorm that then followed, producing in Tuscany effects unheard of in the past, and for those who in the future learn of it, wonderful and noteworthy results.... But God purposed at that time that this slight example should suffice to refresh among men the memory of his power" (VI.34:1329–31). This passage is characterized by an extraordinary literary beauty. The description of the storm, a natural description of such power and breadth, more than Giorgionesque, is, furthermore, unusual in Machiavelli. But this literary streak has also a chief rhetorical effect: in only one stroke here is reactualized the naturalism of Book V, but in order to break it, to show through the example that history cannot be closed in a flat as well as irrational continuity, even that of a natural context. Nature itself rebels against it. Between humanistic insurrection and extraordinary vortex the old style begins then to break down, and the constituent sense of the historical process begins to appear.

Little by little the perspective opens. Books VII and VIII of the *History* are more interesting. The way in which the narration exceeds the naturalist paradigm and the definition of some dynamic paradigms of the historical process is now clear. "Dissensions" appear as causal moments of the historical process—but toward what? The soul of this story is still fractured, and the dissensions are immediately appeased: in fact, historical development is organizing itself toward an ideal end—the style that supports its demonstration is epic and encomiastic—toward a history of the institutions (in the best hypothesis) founded on the Medician political equilibrium (Book VII. particularly 1–3).

The concept of equilibrium is considered as a material structure of the Florentine and Medician constitution, that can be dislocated onto the horizon of Italian independence. The demonstration of the concept of equilibrium both inside Florence and in the passage to the Italian scene stretches throughout Book VII. The central chapters (17–19), which study the consolidation of Lorenzo's power, result in an analysis of the constitutional becoming of these political dynamics. Through these passages the theoretical picture of the *History* reaches its maturity: the historical and institutional development really begins to appear as effect of the dissensions. In order to measure how, at the beginning of Book VIII, is overcome that very narrow threshold beyond which a modern and materialistic historiography is born in Machiavelli, it is enough to consider the difference between the narration of the humanistic plot of Milan in 1476, at the end of Book VII (chap. 34) and the narration of the de' Pazzi's plot that covers the first chapters of Book VIII (chaps. 2–9).

The first, the enterprise of "wretched youth," cannot be but pitied and used for reproaching the tyrant princes who provoked such insurrections: the second, instead, the de'Pazzi plot, is inserted in a profound phenomenon of institutional change, or reorganization of the powers of the princedom. For the first time, not one but two constituent powers are in play, one in front of the armed other. The narration of the plot, internal to the Medici State, is set in relation to the story of the difficult construction of Italian equilibrium (VIII.10–16). The plot is a constituent power that attempts a constitutional restructuring within the city and a general dislocation of powers among the Italian princedoms. Now, in front of the movement of this motor of transformation, which possesses a general frame of reference and the capability of overdetermining the times of development of its own and others' action, another element appears, suddenly created by popular insurrection in favor of the Medici: popular insurrection is counterposed to the plotting of the great. Upon these dissensions, through them, constructing its virtue with these materials, Lorenzo's politics comes to the fore: "In discussing affairs he was eloquent and penetrating, in settling them wise, in carrying them out prompt and courageous"; "Hence, observing both his frivolous and pleasure-seeking conduct and his serious conduct, we see in him two different persons joined in an almost impossible combination" (VIII.36:1434).

Let's go back to the first four books of the *History*; now we can verify with a high degree of probability the hypothesis of their later and more mature drafting. Book I, even though it is the least significant, nonetheless fixes a sort of determined historical horizon, centered on the function of the papacy as the motor of a practico-inert dynamics: here those parameters of institutional history whose formation we had witnessed in Book VIII seem to be pushed to the highest degree of theoretical intensity. The growth of the Pope's power has as its effect the continual exasperation of Italian disorder and thus determines a self-generating matrix of the dissolutive processes. The papacy "keeps Italy disunited and weak" (I.9:1046). An institutional history of division—what a formidable intuition!

If we consider the history of Italy around the middle of the fifteenth century, we see how it reveals the ultimate effects of the dividing power of the papacy and of the subsequent poverty: "idle principles" and "vilest arms." But this practico-inert determination can be theoretically reversed. From the history of the institutions and from the historical precipitate of dissensions we move, with Book II of the *History* (particularly chaps. 9, 11–14, 28), to a dynamic theory of disunion and class struggle. The general schema gets concretized in a materialist perspective in which it is social class struggle that gives tone to the development and shapes institutions; the medieval history of Florence exemplifies this schema. In Book III, around the Ciompi, the materialist analysis of classes is taken and specified further—people and plebs, aristocracy and artisanal classes, specifically in the art of wool (chaps. 10–17). But what is more interesting here, and represents almost the summa of Machiavelli's political discourse, is the discovery of the impossibility that Florence may have a mixed constitution. Different from Rome, in fact, here the class struggle becomes stronger, to the point of determining the victory of the higher people. With this, the higher people lose the possibility of arming the Republic—the lower people, the plebs, the multitude, cannot be armed, because they represent vanquished subversion. A mixed constitution, therefore, is impossible in the modern development of the market (III.1).

On the other hand, a radical democratic constitution is also impossible: the motors of "riot" are not capable of becoming the motors of liberation.

What is to be done? In Book IV Machiavelli will identify a middle way, the way of a reasonable ideology, as the only possibility: the way that leads to a power and to "the virtue of one man" that can take the place of "good laws and good orders" (IV.1). The central chapters of Book IV (26–29, 31, 33) will thus demonstrate how the dominion of the house of the Medici is formed, through the defeat of the aristocracy and the definitive marginalization of the plebs. Through the Medici the higher people, the bourgeoisie, are then reduced to mediation. Their fortune mediates virtue. The "impossible combination of two different persons" that we have seen taking shape in the person of Lorenzo is here shown as an extraordinary and precarious miracle.

With this we have come to a central point of Machiavelli's thought—that is, to the discovery that, even when all the conditions exist for the ideal to become the real, and virtue to become history, even in this case the synthesis does not realize itself. If something ideal becomes real, it becomes such as an "impossible combination," as an extraordinary case that time will soon consume. In fact, rupture is more real than synthesis. Constituent power never materializes except in instances: vortex, insurrection, prince. Machiavelli's historical materialism never becomes, to use modern terms, dialectical materialism. It finds moments of neither synthesis nor subsumption. But it is precisely this rupture that is constitutive.

The ontology of constituent power in Machiavelli presents itself as critical principle, as ever open possibility: the constitutive process finds its perfection in the process itself. The pain and the toil of the constitutive process accumulate. Virtue explodes and reveals as innovation the network of humanity that dramatically constitutes history. What makes Machiavelli's discourse fundamental in the history of modern political thought is not only the fact that strength is for the first time shown as will and determination of the project in the future,[91] but above all the fact of making the relation between will and result, between virtue and fortune as absolutely problematic. Only radical democracy, where absolute power finds an absolute subject, the multitude, to interpret it, could fully unfold virtue. Beyond that point, virtue is as constitutive as it is problematic. It presents itself as strength, but as critical strength. It constitutes being, but a being that does not not close. But isn't this, precisely, the principle itself of democracy? We could answer positively to this question. But in Machiavelli the conditions are different: the nonclosure of constitutive strength does not derive from the force of the multitude, from the measure and the nature of its project, but from the obstacles that are opposed to strength. From the impossibility, here and now, of the *multitudo* to become subject.

But what has happened in order to make that formidable construction that had been articulated between *The Prince* and the *Discourses* now fade? Or, on the contrary, in order for it to mature toward a contradictory outcome? It happened that, with the *History*, the long developed principle of dissent has become the principle of the class struggle. It has inserted into the surface of history the most intense materiality of experience. And here virtue has not found itself any longer on the same level as fortune: fortune has become the barrier to overcome, the accumulation of inimical energy to destroy in its materiality. So far Machiavelli had developed a theory of the constitutive apparatus, while here he finds himself to define a theory of antagonism determined in the dissymmetry of the relation of forces. In this perspective, the apparatus of virtue is losing—or, better, it is impossible to declare its absolute affirmation. Does this mean that virtue can no longer be identified? No—it is still the territory of our freedom. And it will be so until the people become the prince (*Prince*, XXXIV ff) and the absolute of constituent power will be interrogated by the multitude (*Discourses*, II).

A parenthesis—on fortune, on its consistency, on its force, but also on the horizon of instability that its irresistible advancing imposes on politics and communal life, by intervening not only on the summit, but also on their interstices. In the course of his work Machiavelli often pauses on fortune, both as force and precariousness, above all when he perceives that the alternative virtue/fortune often plays in favor of the latter. But how can fortune—that is, a product—become cause? How can this drift become a source? It happens. This excess, this inversion, and, why not, this perversion are actual. There is no explanation: only tragedy is the fabric of the experience proposed by fortune.

If it is not possible to explain it, what other attitude will be possible? This world is often senseless. But if it is impossible to understand it, it will be in any case possible to laugh about it. The parenthesis on fortune becomes a parenthesis on the comical in Machiavelli. This fact does not surprise us: this inversion is typical of the Renaissance, this reflection is typical, as we will see, of the vitality of youth. The comical, then, in general is the violent juxtaposition of the sublime of power (in all its aspects—religious, state, patriarchal...) and of its precariousness; it is the unforeseen comparison of absolute wealth and absolute poverty.[92] In Machiavelli all this emerges in the forms of popular art, and as in popular art, in Machiavelli the comical is together the product of the crisis and its control, a way of understanding the mutation when we are dominated by it. As in popular art, the prince who does not succeed becomes an expression of the comical. The extreme intensity of the relation between virtue and fortune, between constituent power and constituted power, if it does not become drama, in Machiavelli it becomes comedy. It could become popular or chivalric epic, as in Boiardo or in Ariosto:[93] "I have just been reading *Orlando Furioso* by Ariosto, and truly the poem is fine throughout, and in many places is wonderful."[94]

This is not the path taken by Machiavelli: what interests him is no longer the discourse of virtue, not even in a utopian and poetic form; on the contrary, it is the discourse on drifting, on precariousness, on fortune and its folly. Let's laugh, then, let's laugh—about our virtue and, above all, about their fortune. The sense of the comical debunks (the sublime, the emphatic definitions of power, and even power as such). A popular and tough world emerges from all of Machiavelli's works, but it is here, where constituent power proved itself and has been defeated, it is here that bitterness turns into comedy—a sense of the ridiculous, vernacular, picaresque story.

While writing the *History*, in the new Florentine political climate, Machiavelli is reinserted into some small role of active life. Here he is, in the "republic of the clogs,"[95] but above all, here he is taking up once again his formidable epistolary activity, this time with Francesco Guicciardini.[96] We were saying: blocked *virtus* is comic *virtus*, unfortunate *virtus* makes people laugh. The interstices of political discourse, when it is interrupted by the enemy's antagonism, and the constitutive force are pushed toward crisis—well, these interstices can be covered, in their toughness and unhappiness, by a blanket of laughter. One does not laugh about fortune, properly, but about a virtue maimed by misfortune.

But even the fortune of others is precarious: revolutionary discourse exposes in its specific rhetoric the resistibility of the enemy, and this happens in Machiavelli. Now, in full defeat, discourse assumes, in the form of comedy, its strongest elements, from low pleasure to the grotesque. When the mutation is fixed in a catastrophic dimension, the catastrophe must be turned into laughter. Let's organize, therefore, a "pleasure company": civil wit and vulgar pleasure can now constitute the outlet of the disarmed intellectual.[97] *Belfagor* or *The Golden Ass* in the same period: they represent with extreme refinement a complex of vernacular or imaginative elements, in which the grotesque replaces reality.[98]

In fact, the grotesque is not only a way of seeing the world; it is also a way of defending it or of reconstructing it in defeat, a way so powerful the more it is rooted in the popular style of pleasure![99] If democracy and *virtus* are blocked on the terrain of actuality, we reinvent them on the terrain of enjoyment. The grotesque is a kingdom wrenched away from fortune. Other civilizations have given us stories of defeat at the hand of virtue; only the Renaissance has transformed or, better, has elevated defeat to the level of comedy. In this lies, besides any critique of the modern, the power of the Renaissance—it lives and shifts upon the terrain of vitality the tempo of its critique and is even nourished by it. Through the grotesque the constituent principle is saved even in crisis. But it knows, by now, the difficulty of its clandestine existence. Fortune is master: fury, anger, cowardice define it now.[100] It is no longer the result of virtue, but the static element of the bourgeois order and the basis of its reproduction—labor, dead labor.

This image of a blind and vulgar fortune is even clearer in the coldness of the comedy *Clizia*, all the more as the descriptions of fortune and virtue are didactically connected to the age of the protagonists—father and son, old and young, Nicomacus and Cleandrus, divided by love. So fortune is on the side of old age, and virtue on that of youth. Dead labor against living labor, death against life.[101]

Machiavelli, who rarely makes extreme the tone of either characterization or contrast in *The Prince* and *Discourses*, becomes an extremist in these comedies, where he measures vital vicissitude on the level of passion and desire. Desire is the chief element, the force, the positive impulse: it is virtue. The universal that defines the human does not traverse it horizontally, in an equal manner, but it insists and deepens on the ages of man, on youth and desire. Fortune is the damned background of drifting and idleness. Constituent power is young power, strength, and even if at this moment it is impeded by it, it is predisposed to oppose old power, that is, power *tout court*. *Clizia*, a very elegant comedy, fully develops the concept of a low and full passion, beautiful and powerful as life.

Machiavelli has long recognized himself in this nature. He tells Luigi Guicciardini, already before falling into disgrace: "In order to seem alive I keep imagining endless letters to write to the Ten . . . and I am having a good time."[102] After his fall his desire expresses itself all the more, by standing as the only terrain on which strength sets its feet and finds a force, if not of construction, certainly of resistance. It is in this spiritual climate that the confidences to Vettori are born, throughout all their correspondence: confessions of love for beautiful and young women[103] and continual calls in search of love: "I have abandoned, then, the thoughts of affairs that are great and serious; I do not anymore take delight in reading ancient things or in discussing modern ones: they all are turned into soft conversations, for which I thank Venus and all Cyprus."[104] Here desire appears to constitute the ground of life and to support that comic *virtus* that attaches itself to fortune. Fortune has broken the creative tension of constituent power, and this rupture is registered in the movement of man's passions and can bring death to it. One must break these mechanisms of death and rediscover the creative, vital ontological foundation of an otherwise distorted process. Desire, and only desire, is at the base of the possibility of virtue. And thus it is at the base of the comic, if it is true that each time fortune prevails over virtue, virtue cannot but laugh at its own defeat.

Two more comedies, written around 1518: *Andria* and that absolute stroke of genius that is *La Mandragola*.[105] In the first comedy the plot is banal: it is the story of an impeded marriage, and it is even poorly narrated. The classical references and sources are rigidly and heavily superimposed on the dramatic development, so much so that we lose the sense of its autonomy and originality. Notwithstanding this, we can find positive accents, as in *Clizia*, around the theme of passion and desire, of that human radicalness that can constitute reality. But the fact that it can does not mean that it does, that it is capable of doing so: we find these alternatives of being able and not being able at the basis of *Mandragola*, this metaphysical play of strength.

The characters of the comedy are well drawn: after having read it, nobody will forget Messer Nicia and Frate Timoteo. Against the chiaroscuro of these very strong characters the comedy produces an apology of desire. In this the comedy distinguishes itself from the classics because here passion is not represented as much as subjectively constructed, developed with great psychological intensity. The theatrical machine is organized by passion. I mean to say that we are not, as in the classical model, in front of a preconcocted tangle (a story of an impeded youthful love), managed according to custom: here the freedom of invention and the intensity of passions crisscross, and the tangle, the paradoxes, and the farce become more and more credible and effective in the theatrical representation the thicker the passions become, and the more desperate the clashes. The pervasive strength of desire that Machiavelli makes flow in the text of *Mandragola* represents its absolutely original element. Here the machine is produced by passion. Virtue is open again, even though on the limit of the comic description of the crisis. The tone of life is again discovered in its founding power.

How convoluted and yet, at the end, how linear is Machiavelli's story. Fallen in disgrace, he has reconstructed the theoretical path that he had conceived in his active life—from the definition of *virtus* as pure ontological strength, to the recognition of its crisis, from the institution of an absolute constitutional process to the identification of the conditions of its failure in the social struggle of the classes. Finally, Machiavelli manages to look at this development with irony. And this look is not useless. If, in fact, on the terrain of the project and of its impact on reality, an absolute limit has been touched—and here we can bitterly laugh about it—yet through this experience itself the discourse is shifted from the terrain of the crisis to that of ethical testimonial, once again, in sum, toward that definition of the true that understands it in the perspective of genealogy, in the construction of a subjective point of view.

Then it is not by chance that at the basis of the last period of Machiavelli's theoretical political work, around 1520, stands that jewel that is *The Art of War*.[106] It is a dialogue around one of the themes that is dearest to him and that, precisely because of its continuity in his work, can give us a sense of the intensity of the critical curve of the ontology of our author. Now, how many times we have reproposed here the theme of arms, of armed democracy, in Machiavelli's work? From *Words to be Spoken on the Law for Appropriating Money* of 1502 until the construction of "The New Officers of the Ordinance," of which Machiavelli becomes chancellor in 1506, and to whom he dedicates three important writings, when he was still actively working, with humanistic enthusiasm, on the construction of the republican militiae;[107] from the letters to Ridolfi of 1504 and 1506, in which clearly the division between virtue and fortune is situated in the possession of, or lack of, arms,[108] until the letters to Vettori of 1513, in which the nexus of arms-virtue is again exalted, but only with the purpose of unmasking the Italian princes, and of declaring desperation about the fact that they can never produce their own arms;[109] and then, passing through the humanistic exaltation of *The Prince* and of *Discourses*, up to the by now technical writings of 1526 (the style has become clear and secular, as desire has faded)[110] and to the reflections addressed to Francesco Guicciardini on the military dynamics of the League of Cognac[111]—well, throughout all his life Machiavelli has tied the concept of political constitution to that of military constitution. Such remains, again, the basis of *The Art of War*.

In the dialogue, then, we find all the elements that are part of Machiavelli's technical memory, exactly as those that are linked to his vocation of reorganizing a patriotic army according to the teachings of the ancients—in sum, the same elements that had been developed in the republican Ordinances. And here we find again his sociological knowledge of the city and the countryside, and the urgency of building the defense of the city on the military participation of all the citizens. The precepts given are elaborated in the sense of the imitation of the ancients: to imitate the Roman orders means to see the militia not as an art or a trade but, rather, as a form of civic existence: "Against the great corruption of the century." It means, in a correspondent manner, to consider the exercise of arms as an exercise that accompanies life. Now, the young are invited to realize the teachings of the ancients, also in matters military: "Therefore I have been liberal of it with you, who, being young and gifted, can at the right time, if the things I have said please you, and advise your princes to their advantage. But Italy's condition I do not wish you to be dismayed or terrified, because this land seems born to raise up dead things, as she has in poetry, in painting, and in sculpture."[112] The long chapters on ordering the army day by day, on marching, on lodging, on how to conquer fortresses, are in fact marked by an indefatigable tension—that of making Italy rise once again through arms, the Italy that now is, with its princes and because of them, "the scorn of the world"; "Yet the people are not to be blamed for it, but certainly the princes are to blame."[113]

What is to be done? And said? How can we judge this text? Why have we determined it as critical? On the one hand, *The Art of War* lends itself to very few speculations. In fact, the dialogue is a further confirmation of the Machiavellian discourse on constituent power. It means that through the request of universal and continual participation of the citizens in the arming of the republic, Machiavelli does nothing more than reinstate his theoretical position on the problem of legitimacy: it is not the title of sovereignty that is essential, but its exercise, not sovereignty but constitutive democracy, armed constituent power. Thus here in *The Art of War*, the ontology of the constituent principle is radically reexposed. In the medieval tradition the titularity of power is so important that anytime it overflows into exercise, it is considered tyranny;[114] the same is valid, and will be valid, for all the constitutional theories of the division and of the balance of powers: even in this case the exercise of power can be conceived only in a formal context of titularity.[115] In Machiavelli the inversion of the relationship is total. But be careful: this does not lower and cheapen the exercise to a simple management of power: the title here is born from the exercise of power because only constituent power can build the universal. It is democracy that constitutes the title of the government, its absoluteness: it is the democratic exercise of the government that constitutes its legitimacy. And this exercise cannot be but that of an armed power.[116]

Second, however, this reasoning does not exhaust *The Art of War*, and above all it does not sum up its spirit except partially. In fact, the dialogue is not only the confirmation of the constitutive ontology; it also signals its crisis. To demonstrate this, it is sufficient to notice that the weight of the denunciation of corruption (of the princes, of customs, of arms) in *The Art of War* finds neither consolations nor counterweights other than literary ones. The imitation of the ancients here is proposed in terms that are mythical rather than capable of turning into a paradigm of action—and even when it turned into this, it could produce nothing but a further desperate humanistic plot![117]

As for the preceptist movement of the work, it is often boring, notwithstanding the formidable writing of our author! Indeed, *The Art of War* anticipates the *History*, atoning for its outcome. This is a final attempt to avoid that frontal clash in the fracture of the constitutive ontology registered by the *History*, on a more sensitive and fine terrain: that of class struggle. In *The Art of War* Machiavelli sets in a literary activity and in a mythic aura the last calm before the storm. The disenchantment has not yet turned into scientific function; the crisis tries to rest on utopia.

It is not by chance that immediately after *The Art of War* Machiavelli produces that historical and poetical jewel, *The Life of Castruccio Castracani.*[118] A virtuous man, a new prince by definition, a great Ghibellin leader in Lucca and in Tuscany, the friend of emperors, the Roman senator of the democracy of Cola di Rienzo... But this story is above all a military story. It resounds with the noise of battles and of great armed horses. We are inside Paolo Uccello's paintings, inside the same sequences. The description of the last two victories of Castruccio, at Serravalle and at San Miniato, is wonderful. Machiavelli's spiritual assonance to military virtue, and the enthusiasm for that continual, lasting presence of the people in the enterprises of the prince, show themselves in a very high poetical form. The narration has definitely flowed into myth.

This appearance of myth is not a solution but the declaration of a problem—better, of the problem, of the only problem, that of reuniting virtue and fortune, and of making available to the multitude the extreme radicalness of constituent power. If we can unify art and nature on the outer limit of existence, into a strength that reaches the intensity of the origin and on the point itself from which, in the void, expression emanates;[119] if from this point we can virtually let rise a genealogical and constructive strength—this process is nonetheless arrested. And thus, among the shadows of the myth, the crisis spells itself out in all its substance and range and connects itself to the radicalness of the principle, anytime that this principle tries to situate itself in the absoluteness of the subject.

The constituent principle becomes constituent power only in its relationship with an adequate subject: we have often acknowledged this and in this consists the hoped-for revolution. But this revolution is not yet possible. In the *History* Machiavelli, posing the problem to himself once again, will answer that the class struggle does not yet include universality, that the victory of the bourgeoisie destroys democracy, that fortune chases away and crushes virtue. Then, if you are democratic, if you are in the multitude, what do you do? Little can be added to what has been said so far. Beyond myth, in order to maintain a possibility of knowledge, we must make that crisis participate in our science. The future of the constitutive principle is guaranteed by the fact that it has known the crisis. Only when, beyond the crisis, constituent power will find the absoluteness of the subject, only then the desire for democracy will be answered. Which is the moment in which the democratic project of constituent power becomes utopia? Which is the moment when science yields to myth? The *History of Florence* has shown it: it is when the class struggle of the Florentine proletarians must yield to reasonable ideology and to the Medici pacification. Which one will be the moment when the crisis and the utopia will reopen to constituent power?

Even darker and fiercer horizons are those that the international situation produces in the meantime. By now we are in 1527, and the imperial troops are descending on Italy.[120] The Italian princes are definitely lost, the Renaissance is over, and its reform has not intervened. "Everything will come to ruin," exclaims Machiavelli, and we understand the horror of his statement because he adds: "I love my native city more than my soul."[121] What is to be done? Wait once again:

> *Since the young mule has gone mad, it must be treated just the reverse of the way crazy people are, for they are tied up, and I want you to let it loose. Give it to Vangelo and tell him to take it to Montepugliano and then take off its bridle and halter and let it go wherever it likes to regain its own way of life and work off its craziness. The village is big and the beast small; it can do no one any harm.*[122]

Perhaps never, as in this moment, we can understand what another author of modernity, Althusser, says about him: that he is not the thinker of the modern absolutist State, not the theoretician of a constituent power that wants constitution—he is the theoretician of the absence of all the conditions of a principle and a democracy; and it is from this absence, from this void, that Machiavelli, literally, wrenches away the desire for a subject and constitutes it into a program.[123] Constituent power in Machiavelli is this: and we know it so well that any attempt to deny it (and there were many) and any effort to hide it (and they were very effective) do not touch him.

Althusser also says: "We are taken by Machiavelli as by our oblivion. Because of that strange familiarity, as Freud says, that is that of a *refoulé*." Constituent power had thus found in Machiavelli its first absolute and inevitable definition.

T H R E E

The Atlantic Model and the Theory of Counterpower

Mutatio and *Anakyclosis*

CONSTITUENT ONTOLOGY is part of an absolute mutation. When Machiavelli formulates the concept of constituent power, he moves in a scene of mutation: in 1494, when Charles VIII descends on Italy and the independence, the political autonomy, and the internal equilibrium of a country that represents the world economy are put into question, a sudden and global mutation takes place. Here are born, together with the complex of Niccolò Machiavelli's problematic, the themes of a mature and critical Renaissance thought. The Machiavellian utopia goes hand in hand with a deepening consciousness of the crisis. "The heroic disillusion with which Machiavelli considers the clash between man and fate" resolves itself into myth, a constituent myth that presupposes and wants to resolve an ontology of the crisis.[1] We know all this, but especially now, when we begin to consider the fortune of Machiavelli in Europe, we cannot forget it. This is because constituent power and critical ontology are beginning to branch out onto the thoroughfares of the European Renaissance (and revolution), and they will do so more and more.

Yet this entirely secular vicissitude of a philosophical and political concept (constituent power) implies a complex history, and it is enmeshed in a fabric of different, and often contradictory, determinations, within which it is hard to get oriented. Some great critics of the Renaissance interpret *mutatio* and *renovatio* as the trace that allows us to grasp and go through this richness of determinations.[2] What is, then, *mutatio* and what is *renovatio*? Both terms cover, in different degrees, all the way to their superimposition, the perception of the radical transformation of time. Both terms derive their initial meaning from the humanistic tradition. But when the humanistic revolution reaches its climax, the meaning of those terms goes radically beyond their initial determination and presents itself as the metaphor of a social mutation and of a cultural renewal of ontological dimensions, and thus as the metaphor of the passage through the highest point of crisis. A dramatic crisis: *mutatio* and *renovatio* are crushed together to the point of indistinction, because, indeed, they cannot but interweave semantically there where the mutation is catastrophic, and the catastrophe, alone, is innovative. The nexus between *mutatio* and *renovatio* becomes thus, little by little, charged with more and more critically significant resonances; and those who live this nexus are implied in a practical totality of which unease is a symptom, and myth a production; and of which the crisis constitutes its historical condition, the symbol its linguistic revelation, and prophecy its ethical function. From Charles VIII's descent to Italy in 1494, until the Sack of Rome in 1527, each event is read in the context of this pervasive and dramatic, symbolic and prophetic sensibility.[3]

Many have strongly insisted on the fact that this critical passage of the Renaissance is determined by the hegemonic transformations of the religious, mystical, and reformatory movements of sectarian origin—an anticipation, in Southern European countries, of the ferments of the renewal that in Northen Europe will soon become explicit in the Reformation. Savonarola's vicissitudes in Florence have allowed us to gather and exemplify this great narrative.[4] Some critics see the continuity of the tradition of Joachim da Fiore as passing through these vicissitudes—or at least the influence of that version of prophetic millenarianism and of democratic political thought, of which the Joachiminite currents of the fifteenth century had become the carriers.[5]

Mutatio/renovatio, then, in the Joachiminite tradition? I do not know how much of the first Joachiminite inspiration remains in the continual reappearance of this blurry connection throughout the century; neither do I know whether and how much Savonarola's prophetism was important in rooting this ideological formula at the center of the culture of that world economy that is Florence at the time of the Magnifico;[6] rather, with Machiavelli, I am ill disposed toward those friars who are prophets by profession, "in this city of ours, which is a magnet for all the imposters of the world."[7] With this said, it is certain, however, that only within the sphere of a tragic notion of present history and of a heroic disposition toward the future, of pessimism in considering the *historia rerum gestarum* and of the morality of the intervention in the *res gestae*, or a cold awareness of the destruction of the old world and of the prophetic will of constructing a new one—only by taking into account these ambivalences can we follow the movement of the constituent principle from Florence to Europe. Because in Europe, in the course of the Protestant revolution, historical conditions and innovative situations analogous to those that Florence and Italy had lived are little by little developing.

It should not seem odd that a secular concept, fundamentally materialist and humanistic, spread in cultural terms that are related to religion. Until now we have seen how secular concepts represent themselves in a religious form:[8] from now on we can see how concepts that belong to the religious tradition change into entirely secular concepts. Thus, if in that Florence shaken by mystical ferments, the malaise of the century is figured in prophetic forms, religion on the other hand abandons itself to ethics, to secular behaviors, and becomes religion of the collective *res publica*, civic religion, patriotism.[9]

Exactly when the crisis becomes deeper, the image of the city will become more and more consecrated to the myth. A recent past becomes "the golden age": "the age of Lorenzo" is proposed as mythical image of the ancient times and as model for the future.[10] Upon this myth civic religion produces itself and gets new vigor: the religious imaginary becomes more and more secular, in an irresistible and irreversible manner, while the contents of civic religion are confirmed as absolute. All this would be of secondary importance if this mythology and practice of "civic religion" would not spread all over Europe, between the sixteenth and seventeenth centuries, both as the structure of the definition of a secular ethics, and as the content of a bourgeois and progressive project of politics and of the State.[11] The fortune of the Florentine model lies in its identification with the bourgeois revolution. The Florentine model is the prototype of its designs, of its crises, of its capability of getting through. Since the beginning this schema is experienced in this way, and in this way it is reproposed.[12]

Back to our discussion: it is in this perspective that Machiavelli is interpreted. There where he is read, that is, where the political conditions allow for his reception, where the authority of the State is not strong enough to prevent, or mystify, the interpretation of his works. *The Prince*, *Discourses*, *History of Florence*, *The Art of War* come to sustain the new progressive myth: they become manuals of renewal all over Europe, or at least there where the revolution is open. The history of the diffusion of Machiavelli is that of the diffusion of any revolutionary text or thought: either it is accepted as such, in the strength that it expresses, or it is plundered for the innovative epistemological and practical elements that it contains, while being, at the same time, refused, mystified, hidden. This division takes place around the acknowledgment or the critique of the founding myth, that of the absolute character of the democratic foundation of the State, of the absolute force of the principle of "disunion," of "riot," of struggle.

Thus in France, the country of either anti-Machiavellianism, or of Machiavellianism *tout court*, the choice takes place very explicitly: what is refused of Machiavelli are freedom, democracy, the critique of the Church. Without these elements, Machiavelli can perversely be transformed into an author of the absolutist modernization of the State. Against what the historians generally affirm—that is, that Machiavelli's thought was only partially known in France[13]—it is certain instead that it was fully known and studied. *Discourses* had already been translated between 1544 and 1548, and *The Prince* appears in a translation of 1553. But, above all (notwithstanding the fact that Machiavelli's work had entered the Index of Prohibited Books in 1559), we know a series of commentaries (by Gentilet in 1576, Bodin in the same year, Naude in 1639, and Machon in 1634)[14] that show, through the distance they assume from it, an extraordinary knowledge of Machiavelli's thought.

The problem, therefore, is not to know but to choose: to side with the science of the republics, invented by Machiavelli to explain social conflictuality and to found political democracy, and to wonder, thus, if this democracy can be accepted and developed, or if it must be adapted, distorted, perverted in order to draw from it the knowledge that can be funneled into the absolutist power of the absolutist modern State.[15] In France they opt for this second alternative. Here Machiavelli becomes a taboo author. The same with the Medici, struck by the ostracism that hits the makers of massacre of Saint Bartholomew. And so the Florentine myth, vis-à-vis the refounded Kingdom of France through the wars of religion, the following repressions, and the successive compromises, loses its meaning. Machiavelli, civil religion, *mutatio*, *renovatio*, democratic government all disappear in this difficult situation: these elements are, rather, deployed as the presuppositions of a theory of violence, as apology of a constituent power without subject. "The end justifies the means" is a phrase born in France, and it represents the actual logical condensation of the "Machiavellian" reversal of Machiavelli's teaching. In fact, this is a total refusal of Machiavelli, and even when absolutism will have to give space to mixed forms of government (in its mediations between aristocracy, *noblesse de robe*, and rising bourgeoisie), this will not happen upon the acknowledgment of social conflict, but as expression of a reasonable ideology of power.[16]

Completely different is the reception of Machiavelli's thought in England.[17] The relative delay of the translations, which become frequent only at the beginning of the seventeenth century, is compensated for by the frequency of the publication in Italian of Machiavelli's work in England, where the knowledge of the Italian language is particularly widespread among the cultivated classes.[18] Now, this reception is immediately republican and progressive. Machiavelli is read as the author who introduces the critique of constituted power, the analysis of social classes, the concept and the practice of the popular *militia* as constituent power. In the Puritan experience these elements are not only absorbed into the contents of the political program of reform, but they invest also the genres of propaganda and of apology.[19] Contrary to what happens in France, the Machiavellian myth of democracy and revolutionary realism is not reduced to a neutral knowledge of the political and to the "libertine" and conservative reasons for the construction of and apology for absolutism:[20] rather, myth is pushed into a crisis also in this case, but within the opposite schema, practical rather than epistemological, revolutionary and not conservative. The crisis takes place in myth, in that myth of which we have already begun to taste the practical reality, the religious intensity, and the ethical materiality. Puritanism exalts the possibility of translating the Florentine civic religion into the practice of political vocation. Before becoming capitalist ascesis, radical Protestantism knows how to be political ascesis, foundation of the civil principle, and revelation of the collective *Beruf* of the political.[21]

In England Machiavelli is the prophet of a relation between virtue and fortune that will be never concluded but in myth; yet this relation is nonetheless human, irrepressible, radical: it is a practice. A practice that, like the one that religiously stretches between freedom and grace, must be operated, actualized, and followed even if we ignore what will come at the end of the path. What in Florence had become the medium of an unresolvable crisis, that is, the impossibility to make "fortune and virtue work within the same linguistic sphere,"[22] becomes now a practical hypothesis of unexpected force and scope. Unexpectedly, Machiavelli finds himself mixed up in the discussion of "free will," in an original and powerful manner, because he is the author of a faith that can comprehend predestination, of a freedom that can turn into necessity, on the terrain of political practice.[23] Florentine civic religion is a religion of the world, of its political constitution through the movement of the people in institutions and in the armies: it is religion because it implies the totality of man, it is civic because it assumes the community as its subject, it is civic-religious because it represents a dislocation of knowledge on the level of will and freedom.[24] The most profound and original elements of Florentine humanism[25] are thus renewed within a completely changed historical scenario, rougher in its constitutive elements, but powerful and rich in its expression, revolutionary in its vocation, worldwide in its destiny. What Florence had known—the consolidation of *fortuna* and the ruinous shipwreck of *virtus*[26]—England has not: virtue, freedom, *Beruf* establish themselves, and the horizon of fortune and grace remains fully open. What in France was by now a given—the irreversibility of *fortuna* and only the possibility of constructing *virtus* in symbiosis with absolutism—here in England is refused: a king will be sentenced to death, fortune dissipated, and a thousand virtues let flourish.

In France virtue is already conquered, dejected, made marginal, while in England it is strengthened by the Reformation, by the revolution, and by the practice of freedom. Virtue is represented by a people in arms. The story of the expropriation of virtue by consolidated fortune, or, better, by the contradictory transformation of the same virtue into accumulated virtue, which represents the destiny and at the same time the tragedy of rising capitalism, its immediate and fierce ethical parable—well, this story in England is still completely open. If corruption is capitalism and the genealogy of the State of primitive accumulation, this reality in England is still problematic. Therefore, if the theme of the corruption of virtue, that is, the theme of the transformation of fortune into an independent reality antagonistic to virtue, will become central, it achieves this centrality not by performing an analysis of a matter of fact, but as a critique of a path followed elsewhere, here understood as drift. Again the idea of mutation and renewal opposes itself, with strength and hope, to corruption, to its idea, and to its becoming. This struggle has the strong taste of the Machiavellian discovery of constituent strength and of democratic virtue.

James Harrington was born in this England of virtue. "Harrington was a classical republican, and England's premier civic humanist and Machiavellian."[27] He was formed in the tradition of Bacon and Raleigh, who had moved upon his same terrain: England here is seen as a classical republic, and the English citizen is a *civis republicanus*.[28] Republic-commonwealth: what does it mean to proclaim virtue in this context? It means to affirm that the republic is the place where the "disunion" becomes the State, that the legitimacy of the State is formed through the recognition and the organization of the emergencies that traverse it, that the force of the State is born out of the republican synthesis of the virtue of its citizens, taken individually and in groups.

The republic, in the tradition of Machiavellian humanism, which is deeply related to Protestant ethic, can be nothing but "the mixture or balance of three independently existing powers or virtues, those of the One, the Few and the many."[29] The traditional model of the English monarchy, which precisely in those years had been put again into discussion,[30] here is entirely subjected to the critique of virtue. If the secret of the republic is the maintenance of these powers, this can be so because these powers are virtuous, or, better, they are virtue itself. "Every Commonwealth is a circle," proclaims Harrington, but only if the circle is the circle of virtue—that is, only if the republic receives from its internal dynamic a farther and farther reaching expansive force. Thus, here constituent power reappears: as a power permanent in space, continuous in time.

The Commonwealth of Oceana, Harrington's major work, was published in 1656.[31] In this text the complex of these problems is posed clearly, during a phase of reflection following the king's execution. Here determination becomes abstraction: indeed, it is at this moment that the revolutionary debate reaches a first synthesis, thus going beyond the extreme fury that had animated Putney's debates, and the opposition between chiliastic communism and a traditional notion of property. Here the constitutional principle is affirmed for the first time: "Power follows property,"[32] that is, the principle that virtue at the same time produces and guarantees property, and the republic is a system of materially founded freedoms.

The "disunion" of property structures and of the citizens' social rights must establish in the republican constitution the base and the form of their political rights. The constitution must determine a situation in which virtue will be allowed to express itself freely and continually, without becoming prey to fortune. In 1648 and in the following years we witness war, anarchy, and regicide. Constituent power is now entrusted to the biblical hero, the *innovator*, the "armed prophet" who came forward in this conjuncture—precisely *Oceana*, the product, place, and utopia born out of this constituent phase.

It is not my task here to reconstruct the general terms of the debate that went on during those years, since others have done so eminently.[33] Instead, what is necessary to stress here is the intensity of the constituent climate. All the elements that contribute to the new quality of Protestant Machiavellianism are present and operating in it: Machiavellianism has already turned into the civic religion of a people in arms, that reclaim virtue as the guarantor of the republic and property as its material base. The "army of Saints" no longer looks like a lugubrious representation of Christian ayatollism in the period of primitive accumulation, but as a clear image of the youngest and most glorious force of *renovatio*, of the most vigorous disposition on the *mutatio*, that wants to penetrate the real in order to squeeze new guarantees of freedom out of it.[34]

This remains the fundamental question: how can virtue resist fortune and not be absorbed in the destructive mechanism of corruption? It can do so only by becoming republican: by predisposing, that is, social and political conditions that allow British freedom to organize itself in a real manner. The balance of powers, which stands as a guarantee of freedom, must therefore be filled with social contents—it must be founded on property. Machiavellianism shows its most realist face here. Freedom can be effective only if it confronts the material conditions of the republic and civil life. The Machiavellian utopia must therefore pass through the regimes of property.

What had been impossible to propose in Italy, except in the emblematic form it assumes in *The Art of War*, or in the critical tone of the *Histories*, is accomplished in England: freedom must consciously measure itself with its material conditions; the disunion of the forces and the subjects, established upon the difference of the dimensions of property, must be regulated according to a "material constitution," capable of making these subjects, no matter how difficult it may be, converge toward a single civic aim, an agreement on properties. If the "army of Saints" pushes to the extreme the representation and the practice of the secular religion of Florentine humanism, and if the republican conception takes up once again and absorbs the ancient tradition of the "mixed government" of the different orders, Machiavellianism brings these elements back to the order of property and gives a material quality to the evolution of the forms of the State. The medieval idea of the State is over, and even though the notion of mixed constitution remains, it is so modified that it relates to its medieval image as a real, living bear relates to the constellation of the Ursa Major. The concept of the mixed constitution is radically changed: here it has become a new constituent machine.[35]

We must step back for a moment. Until now we have considered the republican and constituent principle as a form of articulation of virtue, but in the political reality of the period in question, it represents itself above all as a principle of resistance and opposition. I mean to say that in the English Revolution the critical point of the thought is not utopian, formative, or simply a project, but first of all revolutionary. Before proposing it opposes, before constructing it destroys. That is, the paradoxical vicissitudes of virtue, according to which virtue is the true motor of any wealth and progress and simultaneously the cause of the consumption of wealth and of the arrest of progress, must be explained through the logic of contradiction. Contradiction becomes therefore problematic. Now, from the perspective of the history of political ideas (not in general but on the terrain of the debate of the time in England), contradiction is understood as it is theorized in Polybius's history, of which the theory of the constitutional government is only a special case.

We do not need to insist here on the crucial position of Polybius's theory in the period we are studying. We have already seen how it reaches Machiavelli; now we can understand how its absorption into Machiavellianism allows the Polybian system an even more profound, vast, and rapid diffusion.[36] We need instead to remember the specificity of the Polybian cyclical schema, that is, how in *anakyclosis* the theory of the forms of the State—those of the one, of the few, and of the many; the good and the bad; those of Plato and those of Aristotle—is dominated by an inevitable law of progress and decadence that explains the tendency of all forms of government to degenerate into corruption.[37]

Monarchy and tyranny, aristocracy and oligarchy, democracy and ochlocracy [mob rule]: "This is the regular cycle of constitutional revolutions [*politeion anakyclosis*], and the natural order [*fuseos oikonomia*] in which constitutions change, are transformed and return again to their original stage."[38] Against this logic, here is the Roman regime: it is born according to nature but then it develops "backwards"; that is, once it reaches the "zenith" of its development, in conformity with nature, it takes a shape opposite to that which the same conformity would have wanted.[39] Perhaps preceded by the great Lycurgus, prompted only by adversities, the Roman equally produced a just constitution—"the best of any existing in my time."[40] And here therefore is the *Descriptio Reipublica Romanae*,[41] that is, the description of the Roman mixed constitution, a balanced and moderate constitution, the constitution of the reciprocal control of forces and powers.

Polybius transforms the theory of the forces of the State into a theory of the structures of the State, more precisely of the Roman State. The republic, even in its imperial form, is founded on the play of checks and balances (*Histories*, VI.15:1), and if it is true that anything decays, if it is true that "there is in every body, or polity, or business a natural stage of growth, a development according to nature" (that is, a period of maturity [*acme*], then a decline [*ftisis*]), and "everything in them is at its best at the zenith [*acme*], we may thereby judge of the difference between these two constitutions as they existed at that period" (VI.51–56:501). Yet the Roman republic, when it is at its climax, resists decay. Why? Ruin can derive from external and internal causes. We have no power over the external ones, and it is possible that, in the long run, they might have prevailed also in Rome. But regarding the internal causes of decay of regimes, we can certainly say that Rome avoided it because its constitution, what depends on us, is close to perfection (VI.57–58).

Back to England. Also in London, as in Rome, the crisis of the ancient constitution took place, as well as the decay of the mixed regime, which for some time protected the citizens against the unhappiness and the irrationality of the political cycle. A new constituent power emerged to destroy, together with the corruption of the State, the cyclical character of its destiny—the evil of fortune, the brutality of *Thyche*. The critical aim of any political reasoning is to understand how the rupture of *anakyclosis* may provoke a real *renovatio*, itself an experience capable of setting up a constitutional system that the cycle of corruption cannot sweep away. What Polybius really said and whether his theory actually corresponded to the ancient constitutional phenomenology, and to the constitution of Rome in particular, are not very important. It is more essential that the problem of constituent power is, through Polybius, reproposed as the problem of virtue and freedom versus corruption and fortune.[42] Through Polybius, but above all through Machiavelli. If Polybius had indeed forced once again political philosophy to confront the real history of the constitutions, thus drawing philosophy nearer the movement of passions, to the concreteness of needs, of individuals and groups, in poverty and in wealth, Machiavelli showed us all this as a struggle, as an uproar and a mechanism of disunion, as the material and necessary key to the rupture and recomposition of any political constitution, even of the most perfect one.

Polybius brings the constitutional movement into historical objectivity, while Machiavelli recuperates it into subjectivity. The debate is thus dislocated, and even Polybius is interpreted in a different manner; while a strictly Polybian perspective ultimately cannot but crash against the biological model, so that corruption and decay become fate (only an absolute chance event could empty this destiny of its metaphysical characteristics à la Thucydides),[43] on the contrary, Polybius can be interpreted in a very different manner, as we have seen, through Machiavelli. In this perspective the mixed constitution itself is a terrain of ruptures, and as a whole it is the outcome of a multiple and dynamic constituent power. The mixed constitution neither develops naturally nor is it is subjected to the cycle: among all the possible constitutions it is the only one that is the result of acting subjects, and its structure is identifiable only in the forms of its genealogy.[44] The Roman constitution possesses the truth of *verum ipsum factum*, that is, of a nexus subjectively realized between history and institution: it reveals the space of the political.

Harrington understood all this since the beginning of his activity as a theorist and a revolutionary. This is the element that makes his work important for us: the nexus between the objective and the subjective, but most important the connection between formal mixed constitution and the material constitution of property. In this perspective it is therefore true that Harrington is less distant from Hobbes than they claim:[45] both understand the spatial and the temporal component (respectively, property, and the juridical and constitutional emergency) as instrumental in producing political synthesis. It is also true that both Harrington and Hobbes have the same reservations with regard to Polybius: both consider a notion of the constitution of the checks-and-balances type as static and conservative. In chapter 19 of *Leviathan* Hobbes strongly attacks the Polybian typology of the Roman republic, substantially in the same way as Harrington would have done.[46] This said, the directions of their critiques are openly in opposition.

Indeed, Hobbes's refusal of constitutionalism leads to and poses the transcendence of power and crushes the social in the grip of its command. Harrington's interpretation of constitutionalism instead shakes the social from the inside and subtracts it from the substantial *inertia* that the mechanism of checks and balances imposes on it: constituent power is an open tension; it constitutes a permanently open system. It jeopardizes any balance by confronting it with subjectivity, and with the subjective impulses that traverse the materiality of the proprietary constitution. English Machiavellianism (perhaps as much as Machiavelli himself) passes through Polybius's teaching for neither philosophical nor political reasons (in fact, it refuses both the biological foundation and the remote conservatism of Polybius), but simply in order to exalt the materialistic dimension and intonation of classical political science. Those dimensions and that intonation had now to confront, and possibly be counterposed, to the ideology of the "army of Saints"; as such they had to allow the recuperation of that exhausted movement, of that full hope, in order to make it a progressively stabilizing element in the reform, or, better, in the refounding of the State. All this takes place through an analysis of the material conditions of the revolution, and of the subjects involved in it.

The problem of the republican constitution therefore tends to intersect more and more clearly with that of its material conditions. This depended on the fact that if the "appropriative age," at its beginning, imposed on all the actors of the age itself its own ethics,[47] this could only happen insofar as the hidden unconscious of that genesis would also be put on the table. Why does virtue, in its development, bypass freedom and congeal into fortune as wealth, power, destiny? Why is democracy always open to corruption? The analysis of power cannot, at this point, become what it should become: the anatomy of the political economy of rising capitalism. Indeed, only at that level could it have been understood why virtue let itself be crushed by fortune, and why *mutatio* was swept away into *anakyclosis*. Even though the economic critique is missing, we witness nonetheless the founding of a new political science, which also penetrates, and not by mere chance, into a reserved terrain, until now untouchable, such as that of property, into the analysis of appropriation, and into the critique of appropriative classes—in the fact that for Machiavelli the definition of the materialistic context is critical.[48] While in Polybius *anakyclosis* is an instrument of interpretation and a means for constructing models, for Machiavelli the analysis claims to destroy continuity and found freedom: to the biological model is always opposed that of disunion and rupture, and to the naturalistic dialectic of the forms of the State the very concrete terms of the struggle among classes. In Harrington this Machiavellian formulation acquired even more strength and relevance. The conditions of the republican constitutions are all material.

In the next section of this chapter we will analyze these terms in their specificity. Here it suffices to underline the fundamental, qualitative transformation that took place through the translation of Polybius from France to the Atlantic: this is not only a rupture with the biological model, as had already happened in Machiavelli. Nor, more subtly, is it merely a rupture with the Neoplatonic model, which had recently restored with this particular cement the very ancient building of the "mixed constitution" typical of English culture—a rupture that Harrington widely practiced.[49] What happens is the actual reversal of this point of view because it becomes the point of departure, the interpretive key of the process. The rupture concerns the complex of the material determinations of society. Civic humanism becomes a point of view and a generally applied methodology, functioning as a critique that wants and knows how to be transformative.

Going back to the great metaphysical and theological horizons that support the notion of political regimes, we will have certainly to admit that the Polybian perspective is that (easily reducible to the mythical level) of a limited world, contemplated *sub specie aeternitatis.* On the contrary, Harrington's and Machiavelli's world is contemplated from the abysmal perspective of an infinite space and time, from the horizon of a totality without end. It is on this totality, no longer *anakyclosis* but *renovatio,* that modern thought is constituted, thus identifying in the absence of conditions the foundation of constituent power. The order of this development, which in classical antiquity and in particular in Polybius's *anakyclosis* appeared objectivist and immanent, and which in the patristic renovation of *anakyclosis* appears as subjectivist and transcendent, here is summed up in a constitutive schema that is subjectivist and immanent. Rupture is the law of development, and it is virtue, immersed in the world's materiality, that always provokes it and determines its outcome.

Only at this point does the question of how to save virtue from being neutralized, from the heteronomy of ends, from the cumbersome closure that its development determines, make sense. The dialectic of capitalist development with its immediately negative results—that nonetheless affirm themselves within a first formidable effect of productive socialization—is interpreted in its external manifestations, identified with that concept of corruption that is the sign of the alienation of value, with the negation of socializing processes, of the expropriation of the product of virtue, therefore of a construction of an unmovable and mortifying fortune. There's no possibility of "mixed constitution" on this terrain; there's no chance of calling "free" a regime that makes accumulation (and therefore consumption) the turning point of the distribution of power. In Atlantic history, therefore, constituent power was born as a power antagonistic to the Gothic constitution of rising capitalism, as a counterpower. In the passage from Florence to England we are not facing a different problematic, but certainly a substantial modification, which implies specific spatial and temporal determinations. In the Atlantic experience constituent power intervenes upon a critical ontology of continental dimensions and is actualized through a fully displayed range of social classes. It is on these dimensions that, as we will see, its nature as counterpower is affirmed. It is here that the absolute mutation experienced by the Florentine democrats turns into the paradigm of world history. Here the humanistic ideological elegance merges with the Puritan religious furor, and from this monstrous contamination the most beautiful flowers are born.[50] The cycle of the utopian proposal is closed, and the *renovatio* affirms itself as concrete constituent power.

Harrington: Constituent Power as Counterpower

The Commonwealth of Oceana was published in 1656, in the midst of the revolution. James Harrington took part in the war and between 1647 and 1649 was part of the group of aristocrats to whom the imprisoned King Charles had been entrusted. Harrington is a man of the English Renaissance and a man of the civil war. *Civis Republicanus*. We have already seen, in this perspective, what his position on the real would have inevitably been: a fundamental intellectual attention to how the corruption of the government always recurs, and an absolute, practical dedication to the *renovatio* of the republic.

Like other men of his epoch, but with extraordinary lucidity, Harrington lives the intertwining of the spiritual and natural motivations of the revolution and grasps the intimate contradictions of both: the contradictions born from the coexistence of the constitutive process of a liberal constitution, and of the inexhaustible tension, sometimes subterranean, often visible, of a radical social revolution.[51] He tries to resolve this contradiction by proposing a utopia, the constitution of Oceana. This is a utopia that is not very utopian, because it is not a project outside of time, but a realistic analysis of the political and social trends ongoing in England at his time, and of their consequences.[52] Furthermore, the analysis immediately becomes praxis, a means of shaping the real; the prophetic component of Harrington's work is this manipulation of the real.[53]

How can one get rid of this corruption? In Harrington the notion of corruption has reached an entirely explicit logic. This is no longer the corruption theorized by ancient physics, and its successive historico-naturalistic translations; nor is it merely the ethico-political corruption discussed by Machiavelli. In Harrington this concept becomes economic-political. This conclusion is founded on the Machiavellian theme that arms are the foundation of the city, in the sense that "corruption" derives negatively from this foundation and its democratic characteristics: corruption is found where there are no popular arms making virtue the bastion of freedom against fortune, against the wealth of the powerful. But what is the foundation of the arms? It is the land, it is its property. From this perspective we understand how Harrington moves toward the radical positions of the revolution, those positions that, supported by the free-holders-in-arms, anticipate the desire for a socialist redistribution of land property.

On the other hand, *The Art of War* is the foundation of *The Commonwealth of Oceana*. Furthermore, the latter is dominated by a materialist notion of the juridical and political relations that characterize the propositions of the appropriative classes before and during the revolution. According to various critics,[54] the sources of Harrington's position lie, other than in Machiavelli, in Francis Bacon's *The History of King Henry the Seventh* and Walter Raleigh's *The Prerogatives of Parliaments*.[55] From these sources Harrington would derive the awareness of the end of the medieval regime of land property, and of the changes already occurring before the revolution.

Since the War of the Roses, and even more so between the times of Henry VII and Elizabeth, the property structure of the feudal world is shaken by a massive shift toward medium and small property. The medieval world and its juridical relations, the Gothic balance, enter a crisis. In fact, this is nothing to complain about. The Gothic balance represented the corruption of the Roman republican world: it is the development and consolidation of that corruption. But the times have changed, and, in step with the historical tendency that the revolution had extraordinarily accentuated, it is now time to leave the Gothic world in a constituent manner, through the imposition, that is, of a new agrarian law. With this law, property, and therefore power, can be moved toward plebeian subjects. The agrarian law can construct democracy because it constitutes its basis. It is a form of counter-power enacted against the Gothic balance, against the old constitution.[56]

What a formidable anticipation of the political science of modern materialism! What a striking foregrounding of the revolutionary subject matter! If it is true that Harrington had received his awareness of this historical transformation from Bacon and Raleigh, it is certain that the same awareness drew its nourishment from the drive of the revolutionary movement, impetuously living in English society. It is very strange that these affirmations, so openly materialist, so clearly revolutionary, have become a kind of red herring in the interpretation of Harrington's thought.

One wonders whether Harrington's insistence on property as the basis of freedom, and the democratic perspective deriving from it, can be connected to the antifeudal revolt and to the construction of a capitalist model.[57] The answer is no. Harrington would not argue against the Gothic order from a bourgeois point of view; rather, he would be tied to a naturalistic, precapitalist, Aristotelian notion of freedom and property. "Harrington's economics, more than capitalist, would be an 'economics' in the Greek sense, an ethos of home management to which *crematistics,* that is, the art of acquisition, had to be subordinated." I am not at all convinced by these interpretations that sound like logomachies, meant to dislocate Harrington's argument on an abstract categorical terrain, and on dubious templates. Whatever Harrington's notion of economic science was, in fact, it is certain that he thinks that constituent power depends on property, and that the form in which this dependency organized the notion had to be revised. This position was simply revolutionary, certainly very close to the chief claims of the Levellers: as such, it pictured ancient prudence[58] as made of radical democracy. Was this position anticipating the capitalist revolution? I am doubtful, even though it is difficult to think that the capitalist revolution could be independent from this type of men and freedom.[59] On the other hand, the concept of property that Harrington invokes here is not very ancient: it goes back to the previous century, when it was understood that virtue, arms, and the progressive transferral of property were connected phenomena, participating in the new process of redistribution of power. With this, *anakyclosis* is interrupted because here property is defined as spirit of appropriation, and thus becomes the foundation of the republic and of its expansion.[60]

In fact, Harrington is a revolutionary, but he is not a forerunner of capitalism. He is a modern man who conceives the revolution as an alternative to rising capitalism. We will never understand Harrington if we refuse to adjectivize the noun *property.* For him the concept of property is never generic but, rather, is the concept of a property that organizes itself in a collective regime, of a property fundamentally egalitarian and socialistic. Indeed, agrarian law is not only a norm of redistribution of individual private property: from this founding element it derives a constitutional direction, an ordering principle. The *Commonwealth* is a constitutional system in which the relations of property are socialized, and whose legitimization takes place according to the rhythm of that socialization. To take agrarian law as a self-standing phenomenon, to isolate it within the institutional mechanism that organizes it, to recognize that—in isolation—this conception of property is "precapitalist" is foolish. That is, it would be an apology for ideological points of view external to our work.[61]

Indeed, Harrington's conception of property is a fundamentally socialist notion, situated at the limit of the appropriative impulse, and explainable only through this limit. He, who in the midst of a historical crisis of enormous dimensions sides with those who want to destroy the feudal order, is not a "precapitalist." From this point of view Harrington is on the side of the capitalists. But in no way is it possible to confuse him with them, because he is on the side of virtue versus fortune, because he, like Machiavelli, wants to break the perverse dialectic that, in the common battle against the Gothic order, intertwines virtue and fortune. Harrington's notion of property is fundamentally socialist. It is already a modern notion that refuses to be imprisoned in the cage of capitalist development, and claims to go well beyond this limit.

Against *Oceana*, in 1657 Matthew Wren publishes his *Considerations upon Oceana*, to the aim of guaranteeing, with social peace, the force of the contracts.[62] This polemic was aimed above all against the rigorously secular positions that Harrington expressed in his works. But underneath this surface, the aim of Wren's work is well visible: to guarantee the contract. To this end, he demands of absolute monarchy and of theological power (the Church) a coercive overdetermination. Harrington's democracy would be deemed dangerous because it does not allow for the certainty of contracts and thus threatens economic development. On Wren's polemic is founded the accusation that Harrington takes up reactionary positions. But we must say once again that Wren's argument (and similarly the argument of those who side with him) is not probatory: could Wren, and, as we will soon see, Hobbes, lay claim to the monopoly of the economic and political *renovatio* of the century?

Their positions, aimed at maximizing profit, and theorizing the political conditions of this passage, represent one of the genealogies of the rise of English capitalism during the seventeenth century. Harrington opposes this outcome.

Is this an opposition against modernity, or is it, rather, an alternative to this concept of the modern?[63] Here we need to be extremely careful from a methodological point of view, in order to eliminate from the historical picture any apologetic notion, whatever the price, of capitalist development. With this caveat in mind it will be then possible to identify the differences, the anomalies, the positions of struggle that crisscross the century.[64] Harrington is one of these differences: the singularity of his approach to the social and the political is irreducible. His can easily become a philosophy of defeat; however, it is certain that it is not a political philosophy domesticated by power. Here a constituent paradigm of absolute originality is constructed, *within* modernity and *against* the affirmation of capitalism. The Machiavellian principle of the political is further clarified: it is the great appropriative stirrings of the struggle among classes that make the law and the State: the constituent principle is born from these struggles, seeking in them the highest expression of virtue.

Legislation is thus to give form to the Commonwealth. In *The Art of Lawgiving*, a book published in 1659, after Cromwell's death, Harrington believes that the time is ripe for introducing the agrarian law into the political system.[65] Constituent power is here defined as an exceptional power that radically renovates the law in force through the radical modification of its social conditions: "Legislation remains a quasi-divine art of infusing form into matter." The various aspects of constituent power are here defined little by little, and together fused into a creative vision: "Formation of government is the creation of a political image after the image of a philosophical creature, or it is an infusion of the soul or faculties of a man into the body of a multitude."[66] This means that, if needed, agrarian law can be subjectivated, become the soul and praxis of a multitude, and therefore express itself as constituent power. This is a moment of great creative power that invests political physics.

We are still bathed in that Renaissance culture that Harrington's work shows us every time: a creative materialism, a powerful and radical humanistic tension.[67] Finally, the identification of *mutatio* and *renovatio*. Here constituent power does not reveal itself, as it does in Machiavelli, in the *historia rerum gestarum*; rather, it wants to be *res gesta*. Furthermore, it presents itself as a general expression of political creativity. It does not apply only to the societies where the problem of land ownership is fundamental: "In such cities as subsist most by trade and have little or no land, as Holland and Genoa, the balance of treasure may be equal unto that of land in the cases mentioned."[68] In sum, constituent power is founded on a law of equality, which brings back any form of fortune to the balance of virtues and dissolves any bloc to the free expression of productive freedom.

From this point of absolute rupture rises the capability to give shape to the Commonwealth, to give spirit to its fabric. From this radical point of self-consciousness rises the principle of freedom (organized by agrarian law), against any form of command that opposes agrarian law. The principle of freedom becomes constituent principle by manifesting itself first of all as counterpower, and then as a formative power. Harrington's constituent power is a revolutionary power that seeks to express its strength. And this is not only a radical principle, but also a constitutive machine. Now we need to examine the complexity of the interconnection of these dynamic elements.

Harrington immediately immerses us in antiquity: there is an ancient prudence that is proper to the Romans until the fall of the republic. It consists of "the empire of the laws and not of men"; it has been destroyed by the barbarization of the customs, of the reigns in the age of decadence, and of the barbaric invasions. The last condition produces a hybrid consequence, modern prudence.[69] Is there some trace of ancient prudence in modern times? Is there some truth that we can renew on the political terrain? Machiavelli has already sought this: he is indeed "the only politician of later ages" (*Oceana*, 162). In his wake and on the basis of the teaching of the ancients in general, we can further investigate the Polybian analysis of regimes and come to the same conclusion as Polybius and Machiavelli: "the doctrine of the ancients" says that the mixed government is the best among the forms of power. According to ancient prudence, thus, power is not founded on simple force, but on authority, on force transfigured by authority. But how did force and authority combine into power? By means of agrarian law. "If the whole people be landlords . . . [in such a way] that no one man, or number of men"—that is, the aristocracy ("within the compass of the Few or Aristocracy")—can surpass it ("can overbalance it"), the government is then a republic ("a Commonwealth") (164). Therefore, the only possible legality is that founded on the multitude's counterpower—on a counterpower founded, in turn, on the property of more than half of the available land. The Machiavellian riot has become a guarantee of legality.

Ancient prudence, mixed government, agrarian law: in Harrington's discourse, to establish this relationship is like pitting Machiavelli against Hobbes. Machiavelli is the republican, he who imposes, through the ancient prudence, "the rule of law" against that modern prudence and "the rule of men" that Hobbes theorizes. Machiavelli is the law, Hobbes is force. Certainly, the law must be sustained by the sword, and Hobbes is right in this respect. On the contrary, the sword, as Machiavelli claims, can be carried only by the entire nation, that is, by its army

(*Oceana*, 165). It is always the people that must carry the sword because power resides in the people. The people are the force that authorizes the law.

The principle of authority comes from the life, in its entirety and complexity, of a people: the life of the republic is like the life of the human organism—soul and body, reasons and passions that rule and balance each other. The soul is virtue: the republic must help virtue prevail as the soul prevails on the body. But the principle of virtue is reason, it is the collective sovereignty of reason over the body; and it is thus, as the outcome of this process, that the law is born. The soul of a nation or of a city is its virtue, and therefore the law. Freedom is freedom within the law, under the law (*Oceana*, 169 ff). The way this celebration of freedom and its autonomous expression seems to anticipate Kant's theory must not deceive us: here we have a Renaissance culture of a strong and frank materialist tone. It is not by chance that the attack against Hobbes and his claim that freedom can be founded (and limited) only through a transcendental source (170, 173) is continually repeated in these pages. No: law and freedom are materially founded on agrarian law.

Now, from agrarian law we must go back to the constitution of the State: from the fact to the law, from the material constitution of the relations of property and class to the formal, from the structure to the superstructure. The structure, or *balance*, is the material relation of the classes; the superstructure, or *agrarian law*, is the constitutive dynamism of the constitution and the positing of its rules (*Oceana*, 180; see also 164, 181, 204).[70] Agrarian law is an actual constitutional law; it constitutes a juridical order that not only guarantees but also reinforces and reproduces the order of the material constitution. And this is the first aspect. But there is another one: not only does agrarian law reproduce the material basis of freedom, but it reproduces it in an expansive, participatory manner. We remember that corruption wins over virtue, not only because the modern relations of property break the equality of natural relations, but also and above all because the relations of authority, on that base, perversely consolidate, become fixed, and make themselves eternal, against the participation and the movement of the multitude.

To avoid these effects, in the superstructure agrarian law will therefore have to be combined with a law of rotation in the exercise of power, with a Machiavellian law of the reappropriation of time (*Oceana*, 180). Hence the final definitions of agrarian law: "An equal Commonwealth is such a one as is equal both in the balance or foundation and in the superstructures, that is to say in her agrarian law and in her rotation" (180); "an equal agrarian is a perpetual law establishing and preserving the balance of dominion by such a distribution that no one man or number of men within the compass of the few or aristocracy can come to overpower the whole people by their possessions in lands" (181); "as the agrarian answereth unto the foundation, so doth rotation unto the superstructures" (181).

The principle of rotation is therefore extremely important because it allows the republic to continue, and participative democracy to enjoy an expansive form. The periods of rotation must be brief, convenient: they must prevent the Bench from holding office for too long a period, which can lead to the rupture of "the life and the natural movement of the republic." Furthermore, the principle of rotation makes the vote free, in the sense that it ties the elected to the elector with no other obligations but those of the mutual defense of freedom, and of the respect of the rules. Election and rotation, ballot and rotation are concepts that Harrington reduces to a unity: "An equal Commonwealth . . . is a government established upon an equal agrarian, arising into the superstructures or three orders, the senate debating and proposing, the people resolving, and the magistracy executing by an equal rotation through the suffrage of the people given by the ballot" (181).

It can be noted, with full evidence, that here the social balance has already unswervingly turned into the idea of the three powers: the senate, the people (that is, *auctoritas patrum*, *iussum populi*), and executive magistrature. That is, the mixed monarchy has generated a republic where the division of the three powers rules. This happened on the basis of the consolidation of the people as actual constituent power, or, that is, as counterpower, the fundamental limit to an aristocratic or absolutist functioning of the mixed constitution.

The three orders (senate, people, and magistrature) derive from the traditional order but are modified in the expression of popular power. The superstructure does not simply depend on the structure: it *must* depend on it. The descriptive order has become prescriptive, and the structure conditions the superstructure qualitatively. Harrington newly and vigorously affirms his position while answering the objections of those who, even though they accept the republican government, do not believe that the people can constitute its basis and, rather, denounce the fragility of this theoretical assumption. Thus, they conclude, it is in any case necessary to overdetermine and defend the fragile popular power by the means of the dictatorship of one man, as a guarantee of the rule of the laws, as on the other hand happened in the case of the Roman dictatorship (182–85). Even when, as in Rome and London, there is a man who is founder or refounder of the constitution and the republic, this republic must nonetheless maintain its nature: it must consist of the three orders of the mixed regime, and it must be subordinated to the constitutional material rule of the equal division of property. Thus agrarian law is entirely and fully a constitutional law: it poses the material basis of the republic and predisposes the instruments for consolidating and reproducing it.

But agrarian law would not be effective (that is, the relation between structure and superstructure would have no value) if the people would not act from within this passage as a real and actual constituent power, "power of legitimization" enacted, in movement. As far as agrarian law is actualized by the people (owners of at least half of the national territory and, consequently, by the people in arms), it constitutes a semidirect democracy, entirely original in the connection it establishes between the principle of approval and the division of powers, as well as among election, rotation, and the functioning of State powers: in this whole, the concepts of representation and of responsibility are defined and come to intersect (185–87). In this mechanism, therefore, we recognize a reinforcement of the concept of constituent power: the constitution is, in fact, materially established by a counterpower, a counterpower that breaks with the traditional determinations of property, and upon this break it organizes its constituent capacity. With this, the republican and Machiavellian "reduction to principles" is accomplished, as a way of taking the city back to the virtue that destroys fortune.

Now we can understand how *Oceana*, far from being merely a work of constitutional law, is above all a text of political intervention and polemics. We'd better follow this interweaving of the political and the constitutional because it takes us to the foundation of the genealogical apparatuses of modern public law. There is also a second part of *The Commonwealth of Oceana*: in it "I shall endeavour to show the rise, progress and declination of modern prudence" (188).[71]

We have already mentioned how Harrington defined *modern prudence*—as the corruption of the ancient one—by turning to the historical analysis of the development of the English monarchy by Lord Bacon and Raleigh;[72] now the analysis is brought to perfection. Ancient prudence has been ruined by the succession of different conquerors on Oceana's territory, by the imposition of the feudal system, through which the order of the conqueror becomes the order of property (191–96). Consequently, Harrington describes the process that leads toward the dissolution of the modern order: this process is only beginning under the reign of King John, but it takes full shape in the period between Henry VII and Henry VIII: because of the necessity of subjecting the feudal nobility, monarchic power begins to exalt small property holders and urban bourgeoisie (196–201). All this starts a process that goes well beyond all the criteria of modern prudence. The monarchic attempt to weaken the nobility does not manage to build royal absolutism; on the contrary, it prepares the conditions for the republic: "Oceana, or any other nation of no greater extent, must have a competent nobility, or is altogether incapable of monarchy. For where there is equality of estates, there must be equality of power; and where there is equality of power, there can be no monarchy" (201).

Here we have a sharp analysis of Henry VIII's and Elizabeth's contributions to the destruction of the modern order, from the plunder of Catholic abbeys, to the sale of the abbeys' lands. As for Elizabeth ("who convert[ed] her reign through the perpetual love tricks that passed between her and her people into a kind of romance"), she started a real struggle against the aristocracy, so that the crisis of medieval agrarian law reaches its most intense point (198).[73] It is necessary to stress that the crisis of the Gothic model does not concern only the regime of appropriation, but, against the will of the monarch, it also concerns the regime and the mode of government themselves.

Here we have reached one first fundamental point. With the aim of grasping its formal implications, let's compare once again ancient to modern prudence. Both, as we have seen, rely on a specific form of the agrarian law; consequently, both represent the superstructure of a specific social condition. Both, finally, are moved by the same immanent mechanism. The reasons for the dissolution of ancient prudence as well as of the modern one are tied to the dynamics of the regimes of appropriation. That is, in the case of ancient prudence, they are tied to the transformation of common property into feudal conquest, and thus to the imbalance of the regime of appropriation, while in the case of modern prudence, to the redistribution of land ownership and to the consequent weakening of the aristocracy and the monarchy. However, here lies the difference: the crisis of modern prudence takes us back to the principle—that is, to the republic, to democracy, and to constituent power. Harrington's historical materialism is a science of the constitution accompanied by a political choice. Democratic passion and imagination are foregrounded. In *Oceana* Harrington proposes "to follow fancy in the fabric of a Commonwealth" through the revitalization and the mobilization of ancient prudence (208–9).

Now we know what this fancy that intervenes in the making of the republic is: it is counterpower, it is social subjectivity, it is democratic imagination. Pocock, the most recent editor of *Oceana,* justly stresses how there is no modern equivalent to the richness of the Renaissance concept of fancy (208n). However, we can easily recognize some strong and expressive equivalents in seventeenth-century thought, for instance, as we will soon see, the Spinozian *imaginatio.* But it is possible to recognize these equivalents only if one is able to grasp the constitutive function of fancy, of the imagination, that is, of their ontological significance; and for this reason, on the terrain we are studying, the republican-democratic definition of fancy, its capability of being the *multitudo*'s constituent power. Fancy and imagination do not simply mediate between the concrete and the abstract—they are not epistemological functions; on the contrary, they are ontological and constitutive functions. Moving from thought to being, from philosophy to politics, from individual to collective functions, fancy and imagination are nothing but constituent power.[74]

From here and upon this method takes shape the description of the *Model of the Commonwealth of Oceana* (210–340), followed in turn by *The Corollary* (341–59). To comment on these pages could be useless and inconsequential. The constitutional machinery described resembles in fact a great baroque construction in which the polemical and the constructive elements are mixed together in a rhetorical soup. The analyses are prolix, the mode of exposition extremely abstract, and the attention to the details of the constitutional construction quite maniacal, in a way that often produces only contradictions, while leaving us quite empty-handed. With this said, we must nonetheless add that this work is in any case a revolutionary foundation, and that this argumentative tangle, so exposed to daily polemics and to their futile necessities, is still organized around a few key points, or fundamental directions. Let's examine them.

The first one concerns method: "In the institution or building of a Commonwealth, the first work... can be no other than fitting and distributing materials." But the material is the people and its divisions: on this axis everything is articulated, founded, and configured (212–14). The method is and remains materialist, and fully radical. At the end of that same year, 1656, by defending his work against his theological detractors in *Pian Piano*, and yet developing (in chaps. V, VI, and VII, above all) a wide-ranging phenomenology of the useful effects of religious teaching among the people, Harrington nonetheless refuses to consider religion as *fundamentum imperii*.[75] On the contrary, he insists on the fact that authority and the constitutional and juridical orders are created only by the "balance of property," and that, on the whole, the people's constituent power is based on this balance. We can, and perhaps we must, formulate an apology of the republic from the perspective of biblical teaching, but only if we understand how this teaching is not in contradiction with the actual political recomposition, that recomposition accomplished by the people by reappropriating property and reclaiming it as the material basis of the republic. "Balance of property," and not "constitutional balance": the second follows the first, while the second logically and ontologically succeeds the first.[76]

Second, the constitutional construction develops. This is a process that, on the superstructural terrain, goes from the constitution of social groups to the constitution of the three orders, and from the orders to the civil and military magistratures. All this takes place in indissoluble connection with what takes place on the structural terrain, which is organized into parishes, centuries, and tribes (214–28). This is an order à la Cleisthenes, according to what the ancients tell us, but renewed through the schemata of mixed government. The detailed description of the forms in which the government of the commune must be organized adequately expresses the spirit of Harrington's project. Its political sense is made clear and continually stressed by the relation between rootedness in the social and the democratic-republican expression of all constitutional forms. Constituent power is always actuality.

Thus we reach the moment when the organization of the people in a territory, according to the three hierarchical divisions that we know, gives rise to the organization of sovereign power, that is, to the proclamation of the fundamental laws concerning property and the ordering of the State: these are agrarian law, which rules power, and electoral law, which rules representation and rotation. It is the establishment of "the fundamental laws of Oceana, or the centre of this Commonwealth" (230). This is the third moment of the exposition. Here the reciprocal integration, or, better, the incorporation of one into the other, is total (241).[77] Communism and freedom, property and right, multitude and sovereignty are thus systematically connected, and it is no longer possible to keep them apart. That motor of freedom that produces Harrington's entire system consists in this nonseparation.

On this base, after having so clearly affirmed the internal unity of agrarian and electoral law, and having situated this synthesis at the core of his project, Harrington can once again concern himself with the entirety of this project itself and write point by point about the parishes, centuries, and tribes. Thus here is how the sovereign organs of Oceana are formed, its Parliament, for example (245 ff). This is constituted by a Senate and a "people." From this moment on the discussion becomes internal to the constitution of sovereign bodies, and of the magistrates in general. The pedantry of the description of the institutional and regulatory mechanisms does not stop us from seeing, at any moment, Harrington's intention of reestablishing the balance, and of preventing that it might be broken, for any reason, at all levels of the order. The juridical formulation of the institutional machine never conceals the political-constitutional frame, and the importance of the continual expression of constituent power (245–66).

After talking about the Senate, Harrington focuses on the sovereign assembly par excellence, the "people" (266–81). These pages are nothing but an apology for the people and the multitude. The sovereign assembly and the arming of the people appear as the central element of Harrington's entire research: "The multitude is wiser and more constant than a prince." Harrington repeats this Machiavellian principle, thus insisting on the constituent function that he has so prominently derived from Machiavelli.[78] That which emerges here is an entirely positive and constructive Machiavelli, without any shadow, so that his theoretical force is intact. It's the people who govern: "The unity of government consists in such a form which no man can have the will, or having the will can have the power, to disturb" (*Pian Piano*, 378–79). Nobody, either king or dictator or aristocract, can take the place of the democratic organ of power. The people are the foundation of power and constitute sovereignty: they interrupt *anakyclosis* and overdetermine the mixed government. An absolute democracy and a radical republic are described here, on the basis of only one principle: that of popular power, therefore of the impossibility of transferring the basis of sovereignty to any other place but the people.[79]

At the end of this description Harrington proposes some transitory constitutional dispositions. Between *The Epitome of the Whole Commonwealth* (333–38) and *The Corollary* (341–59), he talks of the modalities according to which the archon Olphalus Megaletor should leave the power to allow the new order of Oceana to take the stage. The argument is thus taken back to the political actuality of Harrington's times. *Oceana* is a project developed along the revolutionary cycle, and now, after Cromwell's reign, it looks for its Machiavellian "occasion." What is at stake is to push the ideal project into the political fray, to realize it. And the political fray is ready at hand. During the two years following the publication of *Oceana*, extremely vivacious polemics flared up. We have already mentioned those of Wren and the theologians, where the new capitalist spirit and the old clerical overdetermination of power articulate themselves[80] against the anticapitalist and democratic modernity of Harrington's proposal. For him it's not enough to answer: more and more often he counterattacks. Between the last two works of 1656 (above all *Pian Piano*) and *The Prerogative of Popular Government* of 1658 (389–566), the tone has changed: in 1656, after drafting *Oceana*, he is worried about defending his ideas; in 1658 he is polemical and constructive. It is in this atmosphere that the sense of the propitious moment coming near combines with a stronger and stronger and more and more explicit vindication of popular constituent power. The formalities and rhetorical smudges of the previous texts are here clearly overcome.

"The voice of the people is the voice of God" (*Prerogative*, 390–93). The clerics, à la Wren or Hobbes, will not succeed in taking away from the people the dignity of having founded the law and the constitution of legality. Only in the republic we have "the government of the law" instead of "the government of men," capable only of corruptibility. On this side stands the *multitudo*, the totality of the people (400–404). The law is a normative expression (thus Harrington proceeds in his demonstration), produced by the will of a social agent, by a mover. Now, "the mover of the will is interest," and this needs to be clarified. Because either it is the interest of the few or of the one: and in this case it is a selfish interest incapable of transforming itself into law. Or the interest issues from the will "of the whole people, coming up to the public interest (which is none other than common right and justice, excluding all partiality or private interest)"; in this case it "may be truly called the empire of laws and not of men."

It seems here that democratic deceit turns into utopia. But it is not so. The reaffirmation of public interest and of the general will of the multitude does not imply the demonization of particular interests and their dynamics. Rather, it implies the attempt to describe in an open manner the organization and articulation of the multitude. The concept itself of balance finds here new meanings and a new extension because it presents itself not as the model of an already formed system, but as the regulating key of an always open dynamism. The materialistic relation that constitutes the balance of power is a vital relation: "A political is like a natural body" (485).

This body lives, and its dynamism has nothing to do with natural right theory definitions, nor can it be reduced to static balances, internal to the structure of things.[81] The scientific and the constitutional criteria move side by side. Finally, the balance is, in sum, the form of constituent power, an always open drive within the State, within the republic. The subject that forms legality continues to found it and preserve it. This constituent power never forgets its nature as counterpower. If we don't allow it the possibility of expressing itself, it can resort to sedition. If we give it the possibility of expressing itself, it holds power with its own military strength. On the basis of its own strength it affirms the positive and negative safeguard of the *Commonwealth*.

In *The Prerogative of Popular Government*, in a polemic with Wren the Prevaricator, and answering him on that terrain of biblical exmplification on which the attack had been moved, Harrington explains in more precise detail the themes of *Oceana*. Among these: the problem of the revolution and of appropriation through the revolution (404–12); the theme of the building of public interest in democratic terms (413–19); the reduction of the *ius circa sacra* to political power (423–31); the vindications of the conditions (exceptional but real) of sedition (451–58); the reproposing of the extremely close articulation between agrarian law and electoral law (or rotation) (458–95); and so on. Yet if the aim of the discussion is to demonstrate the coherence of the teaching of *Oceana* and of that of Scripture ("Now, the balance of governments throughout the Scriptures being of three kinds and no other, the balance of Oceana is exactly calculated unto the most approved way, and the clearest footsteps of God in the whole history of the Bible" [463]), certainly this is not the only effect of the work. By now it has defined the terrain of constitutional construction as creative. The Machiavellian concept of constituent power here seems to reemerge from the abyss of a democratic rootedness [*radicamento*] by now ungraspable (and dissolved into myth), all the way up to a level of well-recognizable materiality—a material terrain on which the creativity of constituent power can thus be tested. Democracy, the republic, and the revolution are real possibilities: creativity concerns them not as a utopia but as a determined practice. Creativity is the concept that unifies the multitude by making it a subject.

Nor is this subjectivity merely symbolic. On the contrary, it is very concrete: it is popular representation, participation, democratic expression. In *The Second Book, or a Political Discourse concerning Ordination* of 1658, all this becomes well visible (499–566).[82] Harrington opposes those who consider ecclesiastical ordination a sacred and not a political right. But the theological aspect of the discourse is entirely secondary; here the fundamental aspect is that which reduces ordination to election, grace to representation, the sacred to the civil. This material metamorphosis is strongly subjectivized. In sacred history, ecclesiastical ordination, as Harrington affirms, is always a moment of democracy. The nondemocratic choice of the clergy is, on the contrary, a political weapon of absolutism.

Take notice: if ordination is not democratic, it is lacking that sacred value that only the *ecclesia* attributes to it. The nondemocratic ordination takes place in a reality of servants and slaves, among captive Jews, but cannot take place anywhere else. Only democratic consent can be the basis of representation, in the religious as in the secular sphere. On this foundation lies, furthermore, the election of the magistrates: "Whatever in nature or in grace, in church or in state, is chosen by man according unto the will of God, is chosen by God, of whom is both the will and the deed" (539). Here we are once again within the ideology of the Army of Saints, and we can again feel that formidable drive that is proper to the republican civil religion, not less religious because it is civil and republican.

It is not by chance, then, that in the same year, 1658, in another polemical pamphlet (*The Stumbling Block of Disobedience and Rebellion*) Harrington again takes up the Calvinist claim of the right to resistance, and he does this by extending its legitimate use: no longer attributable only to the lower magistrates, but directly to the popular assembly (567–77). Resistance is part of constituent power, and consequently it is a right/duty attributable to any magistrate as well as to any citizen. In particular, disobedience and rebellion against a monarch are always legitimate when they pass through the multitude. Parliamentary power itself (at this point it is quite evident) was not born simply as the product of agrarian balance, and as its institutional transfiguration; rather, it was born as the product of the subjectification of constituent power, as positive organization of the right to resistance. Here the constituent function of Protestant radical thought, and the formative impulse of antimonarchic action resound once again. Nonetheless, Harrington does not abandon the realism of his analysis: these discussions are polemical moments that remain as positive residual elements in his planning the continuation of the revolution, and in his study of democracy. In the same year Harrington proposes in *Brief Directions* an extremely realist model of popular government, identifying without any great frills the needs of a nation.[83]

The process through which constituent power finds its subject improves also in another sense. In 1658 the Lord Protector dies. This is the time, therefore, to seize the "occasion" and to push constituent power even further toward a full expression of Machiavellian strength. In 1659 Harrington publishes a series of writings, mostly polemical, but also presenting elements greatly constructive in their impact, particularly in *The Art of Lawgiving.*[84] In them the concept of constituent power, developed in the entirety of its determinations, by now was centered in a subjective figure. Thus the process of the definition of constituent power is concluded. The republican canon has been formed. In the materialist spirit of this definition is contained a democratic view of man and the multitude. Freedom is rooted in the material conditions that allow its practice. The concept of constituent power refuses any idealization. It configures itself as a counterpower, as the capability to answer continually a historical occasion; it expresses strength and it is always connected with innovation, and thus it prevents the inversion of the course of history. By expressing itself, constituent power offers some more being to history.

In this way Harrington's political thought comes to be situated in the central current of political philosophy of the modern age. He is not a utopian, he is not a defeated democratic polemicist, he is not the defender of a static society or of a constitutionalism that keeps reinstating the traditional order. On the contrary, Harrington is an author who, even though preceded by Machiavelli, develops a political-theoretical system full of great potential. He welds a theory of the forms of government to a theory of the forms of the State, and then he connects all this to a theory of the appropriative social classes. Monarchy, aristocracy, and democracy are articulated with the executive, jurisdictional, and legislative functions: the whole is subjected to the rules of class struggle. From this point of view Harrington founds a theory of the State and of class struggle that constitutes an unsurpassable grid in modern thought before Marx. But there is more: this fusion of different elements is supported by a constituent power that is active force, basis, and continual reproduction of the system of power. As the heart produces circulation and balance in the human body, so constituent power produces circulation and balance in the political body.

With this schema, Harrington introduces in the political science of his time a constructive element that makes his work superior to that of Hobbes.[85] To the metaphysical atomism of the latter, Harrington opposes all the modern articulations of a dynamic idea of the political: Harrington's analysis is concerned not only with power but with strength, not only with the relations of production but with the productive forces. Over Hobbes, Harrington has the advantage of deploying a dynamic materialist method, capable of identifying not only the determination but also the dynamic of the system. His dynamic attention allows him to express a contradictory idea of the development of the modern State, and to found on this contradiction the possibility of democracy. None of the above is foreshadowed or intimated in Hobbes. Therefore, Hobbes ends up being the apologian of this world ("the best writer at this day in the world," says Harrington ironically), while Harrington's problematic will mark all the crucial moments of modernity, and of the development of the modern State.[86]

By defining constituent power as material counterpower, Harrington further probes Machiavelli's argument. Constituent power as the prince, or the figure of the people that becomes the prince by taking up arms, in Machiavelli is a process passing through struggle and disunion, and at the same time a strength fed by these two elements; it is a structure that builds itself both by the means of compromises and balances of forces, and a passion that pushes movement beyond decadence, tyranny, and the inertia of corruption. However, this is where Machiavelli stops. By decidedly giving constituent power a materialist character, Harrington overcomes this limit. Not that constituent power is desubjectivized, not that its definition loses its intensity with regard to struggle and disunion, or that the sense of history and its occasion are "lost": nothing of all this.

On the contrary, by acquiring its materialist character, constituent power becomes a machine that constructs social and juridical relations, and the balance is not a device for transforming a preconstituted order into a juridical sense of duty but, rather, a motor for stirring both horizons continually. The republic is a "fantasy" of power, "the multitude is wiser and more constant than the prince," and the constitutional structures are a process of continual creation.[87] The radicalism of the Machiavellian notion of the political and of the constituent principle becomes genealogical method in Harrington, and strength constructs an ontological horizon—it accumulates freedom. In the relation of Machiavelli to Harrington we find something like the relation between Machiavelli and Spinoza.

Thus it is not by chance that Spinoza and Harrington find themselves, in not too distant epochs, in polemic with the same scientific tendencies—tendencies that, in political and natural science, had turned atomism into the unsurmountable obstacle of constitutive strength. Harrington's polemic against Wren and the Oxford Good Companies[88] slightly anticipates that of Spinoza against Oldenburg and the rising Royal Society.[89] The strength of the multitude is negated by the former and celebrated by the latter: and here Harrington is entirely on Spinoza's side. Even more, as happens in Machiavelli, this specific political and constitutional possibility pushes him to analyze the immanent and dynamic mechanism through which the democratic republic is constituted in a deeper and more substantial manner than the author of the *Political Treatise*, with whom he remains nonetheless in an ideal relationship. Certainly, Harrington does not even reach the metaphysical intensity of the Spinozian definition of the political. But this is not what matters here. What counts is to notice how constituent power in Harrington is presented as an image and a force that brings it very close to Spinoza's strength, so that this resemblance allows the name of the English author to be put near that of all those authors who, by insisting on materialism and democracy, trace the *maudit* path of modern political metaphysics that goes from Machiavelli to Marx.[90]

The Constituent Motor and the Constitutionalist Obstacle

Much irony has been directed against Harrington's constitutional engineering. George Holland Sabine called "an infantile pleasure" that kind of mania with which he fixes the days, hours, and minutes of any institutional operation, a mania burdened, furthermore, with an incredible obsession with procedural minutiae.[91] Even leaving aside the most evidently useless aspect of this constitutional apparatus, there are more serious elements that make us wonder how appropriate it is to consider Harrington one of the founders of the concept of constituent power. In this context it is enough to think of the extreme formalism of some analyses,[92] and the real fetishism with which he studies and proposes various electoral models, the Venetian one in particular.[93] Again, it is enough to observe how the relationship between constituent power and the development of the constitutional form often rewards the latter rather than the former. This can be felt any time the Venetian model appears to sustain Harrington's engineering.

The myth of Venice, as it has been authoritatively pointed out,[94] acts on Harrington with the same force as the myth of the Platonic city on other utopian thinkers. This is a real motif of political science fiction, the moment when the *Gesellschaft* is experienced as *Gemeinschaft*. Venice is for Harrington an artificial angel, in the same way as Leviathan is an artificial demon for Hobbes. What is the cost of this mythical deployment? Sometimes it is that of fixing the principle of the formal constitution (with the rigid schemata of its electoral mechanisms, of the rotations, and of its aristocratic closures) at the expense of the founding constituent principle.

Other interpreters have defined the ideal context of Harrington's project as Aristotelian, thus insisting on the imbalance between constitutional engineering and constituent principle, a disproportion that benefits the former rather than the latter.[95] This project would take place thanks to the hegemony of the concept of balance over that of movement, of natural law over political law, of the form of the superstructure over that of the founding structure, so that the balance and the laws of representation would form a naturalistic and formal grid of the project. Here Harrington would radically distinguish himself from Ireton's and the Levellers' positions, given the fact that in his thought the constitutional form gets the upper hand over the constituent unity of the armed democratic movement.[96] Finally, other authors, playing on this sort of decompression and formalistic degradation of constituent discourse, have seized the occasion to take Harrington's thought back to the tradition of British constitutionalism. This is a necesssary drift, and, according to these authors, fundamentally positive in its development. Harrington as constitutionalist rather than democratic; Harrington the traditionalist rather than the revolutionary.[97]

I have referred to all this literature out of a sense of duty, but it seems to me that these interpretations are false, and that the limitations of Harrington's discourse cannot, in any way, be taken as the negation of the constituent principle, of its originality, and of its radical expressive capability. If the limitations exist (Venetian formalism, constitutional fetishism, legal mechanicism), they do not suffocate the constituent principle but only make evident the difficulties of its functioning, besides its problems as foundation, and as motor of the constitution. In Harrington the constituent principle is not merely the repetition of the Machiavellian will to power that the multitude expresses; in Harrington (and this is why he goes beyond Machiavelli), the constituent principle also wants to be the medium of this strength.

Here, and only here, on this theoretical progress, do the limitations accumulate. Yet, as a few object,[98] Harrington's system does not destroy but, rather, preserves the classes, within a schema of reciprocal conditioning. The objection is both true and false: it is true because here the political process is realistically founded on the determination of the revolutionary passage, and therefore on the recognition of the existing classes; it is false because those determinations of class are never given as definitive, neither temporally nor in the light of utopia, but, rather, they are given as constitutive elements, or, better, subjects of a play of counterpowers. Notice that this is a dynamic that can be played only if the free-holders-in-arms already own 51 percent of the land. And then? Then Harrington's system is a machine that draws its energy from constituent power, from an affirmed revolutionary principle. Its forming capability is entirely evident. What characterizes and marks as important Harrington's thought is exactly the fact that it has proved itself on this passage from constitutional principle to constitutional structure. With this, we do not deny the limits of the realization of the project, but we do not underestimate Harrington's commitment to measure these limits against historical reality, to verify their impact in the midst of revolutionary struggles and of the development of English democracy.

Harrington, then, wants to fix the constituent principle as a founding form of the constitutional order; he wants to build a machine capable of guaranteeing, at all levels, the reproduction of constituent power. Why doesn't he succeed? At this point the answer cannot but be sketchy, even though it purports to confront different problems. And the first observation is that Harrington's project is situated at the limit of the constructive tension of the revolutionary movement. In 1658, after the death of the Lord Protector, Harrington tries, through the repetition and the more and more politically marked elaboration of his project, to seize again the "occasion," but the revolutionary project is over, and when Charles II came to the throne in 1661, the traditional constitution had been affirmed again. The alliance between gentry and yeomanry is also coming to an end. As for the bourgeoisie, during the interregnum it tries nonetheless to push forward the conditions of a resumption of primitive accumulation.[99]

The second observation is that in these same years a strong infrastructure of the Industrial Revolution begins to take shape, through a more and more rapid transferral of capital from the country to the city. All this will lead to a new alliance between the gentry and the productive bourgeoisie—the alliance on which the Glorious Revolution of 1688 relied, and, from that moment on, the new organization of the English State and economy, in the absolute hegemony of the monetary form.[100] This means that, after the Lord Protector's death, the material constitution, which had presided over the revolutionary development, is subjected to an extremely strong tension, and ultimately to a rupture. And if a new constitution was born here, it registers totally modified class relations. Harrington's constituent principle does not manage to transform itself into the constitution, and it is defeated. The forces and the alliances, the material determinations on whose basis the constituent principle had been conceived are now fading away.

Over this death fly the vultures. Harrington has been defeated because his thought is tied to the past,[101] because he had not understood the dynamics of financial capitalism,[102] and because he has not adhered to modernity.[103] How hard it is to kill off historicism and its silly *vae victis*! It is much more correct to notice that Harrington's defeat, as all the political defeats of a very impetuous class struggle, is nothing predetermined or deserved: it is the defeat of a model of appropriative society vis-à-vis another model, of a tendentially socialist model vis-à-vis a tendentially liberal one.[104]

Certainly, in *Oceana* the concept of money is scanty, to use a euphemism. In responding to Wren, who attacks him on this account, Harrington is incapable of approximating an original and adequate notion of money. He believes that it can have only exceptional functions, and that for the rest it is subordinated to landowning. Usury and bank mediation are similarly underestimated, critiqued, refused, substantially uncomprehended. On the Medici and the King of Spain, extremely established financial powers, Harrington makes ironic remarks (*Prerogative*, 404–12). Should we conclude, looking at this aspect, that Harrington is fully alien to the new concept of time and of the political produced by the "Glorious Revolution"?[105] Certainly not, and this is demonstrated by the fact that Harrington's constituent power is not, however defeated, a dead principle.

Pocock has given us an exhaustive account of the immediate evolution of this principle, when he writes how, in the Glorious Revolution and in the new alliance of power dominated by the hegemony of the bourgeoisie, the "Harringtonian doctrine" is situated on an entirely new terrain, in the sense that it becomes the theory of the gentry tied to landed interest, thus opposing the liberal-bourgeois theory of the gentry tied to monied interest. According to Pocock, within fifty years the progressive theory of property becomes a reactionary ideology, if confronted with the productive order imposed by the new monetary system:

> *What may now be termed neo-Harringtonian doctrine is directed not against a collapsing feudal order, but against a bureaucratic and salary-paying State; not against the past,*

but against modernity. Where Harrington had thought the traditional King and parliament obsolete in face of the revolution of the proprietors, his heirs and successors sought to mobilize parliament against king and ministers, by invoking the independence of property against threats too modern for him to have considered.[106]

But next to the immediate evolution of the Harringtonian legacy—that is, next to the effects of a defeat that takes place, as often happens, through a derisory falsification and through a reversal of the original principles of a revolution—next to these immediate effects there are the longer procedures of the influence of Harrington's thought, exactly as that of the other English revolutionaries of the seventeenth century. The continuity of the concept of constituent power, of that of *militia* and people-in-arms, of permanent counterpower, is attained through an ideal and material reproduction, in theory and in praxis, which we will find again in the history of constituent power that we are narrating.[107]

If the victory of a mode of production crushes the alternative, or transfigures and modifies its theoretical expression, this does not mean that the alternative and the desire that links it to the revolutionary project are themselves crushed. On the contrary, compared with the fixity of the new constitution, the constituent principle renovates itself, too. But history is intact, static, finite. If the title of power is no longer the property titles of the multitude, if the people's arms are expropriated and reorganized under the capitalist order, if executive power dominates and nominates popular power, well, all this defeats that tendentially socialist constituent power that Harrington had theorized. It defeats it in actuality, but it cannot erase it. The old constituent principle becomes clandestine but still lives, accumulates, and renews itself, determines civic unrest and political insubordination, seeks new spaces. The capitalist constitution lives in perennial fear of a constituent principle that little by little becomes alternative. Also from the formal point of view difficulties arise for the capitalist constitution: in order to see to it that its apparatus reproduces itself, the constitution must turn to that defeated and denied principle. As the analysis of juridical thought concerning constituent power has demonstrated, the negation of its strength also blocks the renovation of its apparatus, or, better, questions it and defers its principle of renovation to more and more uncontrollable and unpredictable instances.

Nonetheless, Harrington does not want to hear about all this. Between 1660 and 1661, when the defeat of the revolution begins to become visible, Harrington moves to insurrectional militancy. He changes neither discourse nor tone: he changes his public—a public for the insurrection. Harrington is by now aware that his readers' society is coming to a close, and that militancy is set against a victorious enemy. In this climate he produced the two works of 1660: *The Rota* and *The Ways and Means.*[108] Both repeat the old principle of democratic government, and the model of the free and equal State in its four partitions: civil, religious, military, and provincial. They mark no substantial change in his project. But what strong ethic incitation to resistance, what exaltation of a constituent power that becomes insurrectional! The constituent motor is pushed to the maximum in its weakest moment. But this does not mean that its principle is wrong and its rootedness unreal. On the contrary, defeat emphasizes clearly the enemy, defeat is not irresistible. Arrested in 1661, accused of plotting, heavily interrogated in the Tower of London, overcome by mental crises, Harrington will not say anything else.[109]

It is exactly in the period between the drafting of *Oceana*, and of the polemical works that defend it, to the preparation of the insurrectional phase (before, therefore, this phase gets organized between 1660 and 1661) that the thought carrying Harrington's project beyond the times of his defeat gets explained. Let me clarify: the texts of 1659, those texts, that is, produced between the definition of the project of 1656 and the insurrectional call of 1660–61, program a political perspective that goes beyond the limits of the project itself. Thus, in *The Art of Lawgiving* of 1659, the crux of the argument lies in the distinction between just and unjust government:

> *The art of lawgiving is of two kinds: the one (as I may say) untrue, the other true. The untrue consisteth in the reduction of the balance unto arbitrary superstructures, which requireth violence, as being contrary unto nature. The other in the erecting necessary superstructures, that is such as are conformable unto the balance or foundation; which, being purely natural, requireth that all interposition of force be removed. (603)*

The unjust government is that which deploys violence and arbitrary power to overdetermine the natural balance, that is, to overdetermine an overbalance. Here violence opposes nature. On the contrary, this opposition does not take place, and nature is respected when the material base of the balance (naturally) allows a peaceful and equal development of the superstructure. The material constitution of equality must dominate the formal constitution: in this case violence is eliminated. The materialism of the theoretical formulation in this case is marked by a reflex of justice—that is (and this stands in the way of every natural right theory expanded on in these pages), marked by the desire that the multitude must be productive: positively, that is, as a desire of equality; negatively, as resistance against violence.

Constituent power is therefore the succession of two operations: first of all the fixing of the balance, and then the construction of adequate superstructures:

> *If the balance or state of property in a nation be the efficient cause of government, and, the balance being not fixed, the government... must remain inconstant or floating, then the process in formation of a government must be first by fixation of the balance, and next by erecting such superstructures as to the nature thereof are necessary.* (Lawgiving, *609)*

But this is not enough. The foundation, the erecting of superstructures, thanks to constituent power, is followed by a power of social restructuration. This means that, after shifting from the material to the formal, strength folds on itself, into that common social terrain that is the only referent of the entire process. After having been constructed within the social, the political constructs the social. The political builds the social through the definition of the orders of society (621), and above all through the organization of the *militia* (682–85).[110] Constituent power reaches far, forming subjects and associations, regulatory functions and people-in-arms. What is enacted here is an actual ontological function. *The Art of Lawgiving* does not merely represent, as we have said above, the moment of synthesis between the development of the structural analysis and the emergence of subjects: it also represents a theoretical foray into the ontological terrain and imagines a transformation of the real that cannot be degraded by any defeat.

What has been observed in this context is true: that the insistence on the ontological elements risks dissolving the constitutional horizon of Oceana—the Canon would exhaust the Commonwealth.[111] But this is only true in part, because the Commonwealth goes on, reproduces itself, and relives in the Canon, no matter what the conditions. Harrington's polemical pamphlets issued in 1659 are all touched by the new problematic,[112] that of the latency of constituent power—and we could add, of its capability of reemerging from the ashes of defeat. This latency is a continual and discrete presence, an uninterrupted reproposing of transformation and renovation on the part of the multitude. This point of Harrington's thought really marks a revival of Protestant ascesis in its most radical and even theologically founded dimension: Harrington conceives of constituent power as a sacred background of the movement of *renovatio*, as an ever open possibility of the revolutionary process.

Of a defeated revolution? But up to what point? Until when? We have already seen how the division between strength and violence, where the former establishes the social order of the balance and the latter distorts it, has become key in Harrington's definition of balance, discrimination of its effectiveness, and also affirmation of the necessity of giving it a direction. Now, in the first period of his activity Harrington wrote *A System of Politics*, imperfect but important.[113] It is at this point that the themes of strength and violence are clearly opposite. But violence is no longer something in any case positive, real; rather, it is deprivation. Violence is the loss of being (836). This violence finds no place in Harrington's paradigm: violence is loss of the Commonwealth, it is absolutely the negative form of power. Into this abyss precipitate all the classifications of the forms of government that do not take as their point of departure the opposite pole: that of constituent power. In this chasm are ontologically destroyed the Aristotelian definitions as well as the Polybian periodical schema of *anakyclosis*. On the contrary, the formative processes of the political, and those, equally formative, that the political projects onto the social, determine a surplus of being: they are divine (837). Here is how, therefore, constituent power can live beyond its own temporal defeat. It can live as latency that traverses a world where the violence and the unnaturalness of unjust social relations have triumphed, a world without sacredness and being, thus a world that will be destroyed by the rebirth of the constituent power of the multitude. Here Machiavelli is taken up once again as a fundamental point of reference,[114] but once again our thought cannot, confronted by this ontological emergency, but move toward Spinoza's political thought.

Let's pause a moment and ask: Isn't that concept of "latency," which seems yet to be so significant, actually the representation of a project that is not only defeated, but also definitely consumed? To answer this question it will be necessary to situate ourselves once again in the midst of historical reality: only in this reality can the sense of utopia (both as its consumption and its way of leaving ontological residues) be grasped. If we move to the heirs and successors of Harrington, once again we will nonetheless sense all the ambiguity of their vocation. Pocock has exhaustively shown one side of it;[115] Hill and others with him, have revealed the other side.[116] Pocock has shown how Harrington's republican view became so rhetorical and abstract that it could be deployed in other linguistic contexts; Hill instead has shown us how republicanism, however defeated, however reduced to impotent passion, goes on to live and to reproduce itself, to spread and improve. Thus utopia is on the first side, and passion on the second.

Utopia is ambiguous. It reorganizes itself around the passwords *property*, *militia*, and *ancient constitution*, but it is incapable of posing these terms as the blueprint of a constitutional alternative. When we follow the debate and the political polemics articulated by Harrington's immediate heirs, by Shaftesbury, by Marvell, by Nedham, by Neville, utopia turns into the desperate separation between constitutional demand and new social reality.[117] Utopia reveals itself as the failure to understand the transformation of the real; it is a historical mistake, and no longer an anticipation of the future. The onset of the era of industrial capital, which in England begins in the second half of the eighteenth century, actually destroys all the points of reference of the political-theoretical scenario that Harrington and his contemporaries had foreseen. A gigantic process of abstraction of labor and of its equivalent in new monetary and political terms takes place.[118] In its strict determination Harrington's thought reveals its ambiguity. Property, arms, old constitution mean less and less. Between the individual and the multitude cannot be established any concrete mediations anymore. Harringtonism, as determinate political knowledge, as revolutionary operativity, is cut out of the course of history. The extraordinary inversions of meaning and the way it gets absorbed into a real "heteronomy of ends" become its destiny.

But we cannot neglect the second element that Harrington's constituent thought produces as a residue. In its defeat, this power is also the victim of the particular level of restructuration that social relations have undergone, and it recuperates, from its own tradition, polemical and reconstructive elements—elements that are at work in the entangled debate that marks the reconstruction of the British State, and that are visible, for example, in the kindling of dissent against the reform of the "arms," and their transformation into a "standing army."[119] These elements are part of a long project and a radical battle. Indeed, it is not just a matter of opposing the constitution of the standing army but, rather, of reaffirming that the exercise of arms and the definition of democracy are the same thing: antimilitarism was born here as a polemical instrument, while democracy is defined as an end per se. The problem is to take the arms away from the king and give them to the people, to oppose an organization of the State founded on the expropriation of subjects, on the alienation of arms, and therefore on the transformation of individuals into subjects. Algenor Sidney, Milton, Winstanley and, later, John Toland, Andrew Fletcher, and others take this position.[120] It is true that their resistance is difficult, and that it is often reduced to a heroic residual apology, expressed in deistic and prophetic tones, of the expropriated individual. Nonetheless, in this thought can be recognized another essential force, the constituent strength, which, in latency, fully experiences this resistance and tries once again to become hope, in full autonomy.

Therefore, if there is anything utopian in Harrington's thought and in the thought of his followers, and if this utopia is crushed by an implacable structuration of society, nonetheless, through this structuration a popular drive that moves from the definition of democratic revolution and constitution continues to live and take an ever more definite shape. Here Harringtonism is no longer utopia, but once again constituent spirit emerging from the defeat and passion for renewal and for the founding of democracy. Although here we do not have to follow the history of ideas and the revolutionary thinkers of the end of the seventeenth century in England, we can nonetheless recognize that, beyond the religious and utopian aberrations characterizing some of these writings, lives in each one individually and in them all as a whole a formidable faith in the possibility of rebuilding social and political relations from the depths of a democratic revolution, made by the multitude.[121] Here the constituent principle reveals itself as the motor not of the constitution but of the revolution, as latency of a very strong potential of destruction, and at the same time of transformation of the present state of things. This is constituent power, the Harringtonian legacy, that already in these years will cross the Atlantic, to implant itself in the virgin spaces of colonial America.

These reflections on the fortune and destiny of Harrington's thought allow us to repropose the analysis of its meaning on a terrain that by now has become dislocated with respect to either its literal interpretation, or to the fundamental currents of its interpretation. And it allows us to affirm that the historical determination of the constituent principle in Harrington poses itself directly against the English constitutional tradition. Harrington and his friends, above all Nedham and Neville, between 1656 and 1661 made every attempt to oppose that form of government that had been provided for in *His Majesty's Answer to the Nineteen Propositions of Parliament.*[122] They redefine constitutional power as revolutionary power, as democratic counterpower, which in the mixed monarchy is expressed by the pure and unmixed democracy of the *New Model Army.*[123] If, at the same time, they try to deploy the schema of mixed monarchy as a grid on which to model the relations of counterpower, and as a terrain on which the dialectic between the form of the State, the form of government, and that of social relation could have been made dynamic constitutionally, it is constituent power that, in this perspective, remains central and unique.

It is on this terrain that defeat is determined—when constitutionalism is definitely recognized as the enemy of democracy, when the dialectic becomes antagonism. Only the democratic principle could have been a principle of constitutional construction. When, in the second half of the revolutionary process, during the English Thermidore, between the Interregnum and the Glorius Revolution, the Gothic machine is once again started to serve the new financial power,[124] we should not only, as his critics do, point out the insufficiency of Harrington's thought, the limitations of his concept of power because simply tied to the ancient notions of freedom and virtue,[125] but also we should notice how that process defines traditional constitutionalism through the notion of "corruption."

Harrington's project clashes with the constitution insofar as the latter is a factor of corruption. The mixed constitution is the constitution of corruption. The Machiavellian alternatives of freedom and fortune, virtue and corruption are moved by Harrington to this new level of perspective. In the mixed constitution freedom is always separated from power, and Harrington's story shows how in the end democracy cannot but part from constitutionalism. Harrington's illusory confidence in being able to use the terrain of the mixed constitution as the sphere of expression of counterpower produces not only defeat but also the awareness that democracy can be affirmed beyond this institutional limitation. The constitution is the absolute obstacle to constituent power, to democracy. If Harrington, very sharply and with great tactical acumen, tried to situate constituent power within a constitutional fabric made weak by the revolution, nonetheless, after the defeat, he understands that only a vindication that is absolute, savage, and separated from the revolution can reconstruct virtue and glorious, ancient prudence. And this understanding represents the legacy of Harrington's thought.

The sign of the permanence of this thought, and of its effectiveness, cannot be seen simply in the Atlantic movement of democratic ideology toward the American States. It remains present, as latent and unsuppressible contradiction, in the history of Western constitutional thought, on both sides of the Atlantic. Perhaps we have the most characteristic sign of this threatening presence when we study the passage of political thought from the Polybian tradition to theories of the contract, to those theories, that is, which, through the glorification of "competition," of voluntary consent, of the linear transformation of fact into the law, aim to eliminate any antagonistic element from the notion of the political.[126]

In this scenario, Locke represents the sign of order and the fundamental element of restoration, just as, in the same conjuncture, Spinoza represents the antagonistic element, by refusing the contract, and therefore by reproposing the theme of democracy as multitude in movement.[127] It is here that contractualism invents its proposal of foundation of the modern State; and the contradiction between Locke and Hobbes is minimal if compared to that which pits both against Harrington's and Spinoza's democratic thought. In fact, for these two, democracy is the only absolute government because it gathers into unity the freedom of all and sees all subjects' passion in a light of equality. On the contrary, contractualism is convinced that man's socialization and his transformation into citizen can only be understood through a mechanism of closures and obstacles. The *pactum societatis* is limited or, in any case, reorganized by the *pactum subjectionis*. In Locke constituent power is reduced to a residual power, a power of resistance; consequently, the complex of the constitutional mechanisms becomes a system of divisions and limitations, predisposed to maintain the equality of rights in the inequality of property, to establish therefore the isolation of virtue vis-à-vis the consolidation of fortune.[128]

With the political compromise between gentry and industrial and financial bourgeoisie, from the restoration of 1561 until the Glorious Revolution, the democratic alliance toward which Harrington had worked ceases, and with it the possibility of a constituent discourse. In the old constitution, now renewed, the new dimensions of capitalist appropriation begin to live: the Gothic is remolded on them. On the contrary, the democratic spirit and the absolutism of republican virtue are gone. Harrington had brought to England the republican humanism of the Italian Renaissance. Now also here, as in Italy, the enemy wins: corruption, that is, fortune, that is, capitalist accumulation opposes virtue and chases it away. Virtue, constituent power, and the great appeal of radical democracy had nonetheless existed as principle and hope; they had spread into the spirit of individuals, had invested new civilizations, had experienced the crisis, and taken up new arms. This is what Harrington's Machiavellianism expresses in an irreducible manner, for the first time putting materialism to the service of the freedom of the multitude. And this virtue survives its own political defeat; as constituent power, constituent motor, as hypothesis of a machine for liberation, it lives in modern history, ready to reappear anywhere democratic revolt resurfaces.

F O U R

Political Emancipation in the American Constitution

Constituent Power and the "Frontier" of Freedom

THERE IS an image that dominates Edmund Burke's speech when, on March 22, 1775, he presented his motion of conciliation with the colonies: the image of the Americans pushed beyond the Appalachians by the embezzlements of the British government and by their love for freedom, and here, in the immense plains, become "Tartars": "English Tartars . . . pouring down upon your unfortified frontiers a fierce and irresistible cavalry."[1] Immense spaces and an unrestrainable love for freedom: in this approach we can recognize the man who, in 1756, had published an inquiry on the sublime.[2] But on the other side of this man there is the politician, exhibiting an extreme realism: "We must govern America, according to that nature, and to those circumstances; and not according to our own imaginations; not according to abstract ideas of right; by no means according to mere general theories of the government, the resort to which appears to me, in our present situation, no better than arrant trifling" ("Speech," 111).

Should we continue to close their ports, to impose taxes that they do not want to accept, to prevent their trade, or even to stir up the slaves against Virginia? This means that we have not understood that in America "from these six capital sources: Descent; of Form of Government; of Religion in the Northern Provinces; of Manners in the Southern; of Education; of the Remoteness of Situation from the

First Mover of Government, from these causes a fierce Spirit of Liberty has grown up. It has grown with the growth of the people in your colonies, and encreased with the encrease of their wealth" (125). "In order to prove, that the Americans have no right to their liberties, we are everyday endeavoring to subvert the maxims, which preserve the whole Spirit of our own. . . . [We attack] and ridicule some of those principles, or [deride] some of those feelings [for] which our ancestors have shed their blood" (127). The rebellion is in place, the immense American spaces constitute its background: will the English constitution be able to prove itself in these spaces, to measure up with that nature? Burke understands from the start the expansive character of the American revolt, and he answers positively to the question: "My idea therefore, without considering whether we yield as a matter of right, or grant as a matter of favor, is to admit the people of our Colonies into an interest in the constitution" (136). The English constitution is, then, according to Burke, compatible with American spaces.

It was well known that the government of His British Majesty would not accept this proposition. But the problem posed by Burke was still crucial: how could the constitution and its space, constituent power and its space, develop in the spirit and history of the American Revolution? This is a fundamental rupture of the Polybian schema of the succession of the historical times of the constitutions: it is no longer the control of time but, rather, the expansion of space that becomes the horizon of constituent power and the perspective of the constitution. The battles and the political alternatives taking place here assume the organization of space as their specific object. The "end of classical politics," on which so many contemporary critics have insisted, essentially consists of this passage.[3]

It is the idea of the people that is radically modified by the introduction of the immense space in its concept: if, on the one hand, the people are presented as being of an undifferentiated body, on the other, they are seen as a complex of individual, communitarian, and political activities that expands across an extensive dimension, a territory that can indefinitely be traversed. Insofar as the people were considered an undifferentiated mass, the "classist" assumption of classical politics and of the Polybian tradition, which understood as univocal the relation between class stratification and forms of government, was overcome. Insofar as the people were seen as activity spread across the territory, and thus as an indefinite possibility of differentiation in the expression of power, the residual classical prejudice that, finally, always saw in the people an ultimate and moldable matter, was overcome. The nexus of the polis, the concept of direct and active participation in political life, all this explodes: the political citizen is he who, running through the great territories, appropriates them, organizes them, leads them toward a federal unity, and guarantees through this act of appropriation the general movement toward the constitution of the nation.

Burke was not wrong when, attempting a mediation with the colonies, he insisted on the Tartar sense of freedom that governed here, a freedom to which only that spatial dimension gives sense. While tracing the history of the American refounding of freedom, we need to pay attention to this element. To forget it, to forget this savage dimension of American freedom, its sublime character, results in Tocqueville's formalistic (and potentially pessimistic) closure, or, even worse, in the syrupy expansive utopia theorized by Hannah Arendt, who, in the storm of the Cold War, forgets that once the savage space becomes finite, expansion translates into expansionism and imperialism.[4]

But what, then, is this space, this new reality, this expansive concept, this indomitable will? Burke again helps us to understand this point: "My opinion is much more in favor of prudent management, than of force, considering force not as an odious, but as a feeble instrument, for preserving a people so numerous, so active, so growing, so spirited as this" ("Speech," 118). The fundamental limit to the use of force (besides other obvious ones, listed here) is that "force diminishes the object," leads one to concentrate on an exclusive end inadequate to the strength of the subject that needs to be repressed—and this specific strength consists in the temper and the character of the American colonies, in that Tartar love of freedom that "is the predominating feature, which marks and distinguishes the whole" (119). What Burke says in negative terms, the American rebels say in positive terms. Space is the expression of freedom—but a very concrete freedom, a Harringtonian freedom founded on property, appropriation, and colonizing expansion.

"Power always follows property.... The balance of power in a society always accompanies the balance of the property of land."[5] Space founds power because it is conceived as appropriation, as expansion—in sum, as "frontier" of freedom, the place where the citizens' strength becomes power, synthesis of a positive activity indicated to every citizen as a space of power.[6] Space is the destiny of American freedom, and at the same time its way of finding its origins, the new Canaan—that is, a Wilderness, a "first" nature on which freedom, that is, the American "second" nature, can be shaped.[7]

Space is the place of the American masses, themselves renewed by a freedom that property, appropriation, and the new law will guarantee. There could not be a deeper modification of the concept of power: it becomes completely abstract because it adapts itself to a mass distributed over an enormous space; but at the same time it becomes completely concrete because it leans on the individualized interests of this mass, on their singular insertion into the territory, in terms of appropriation by fact that it must become property by law. Space is the constitutive horizon of American freedom, of the proprietors' freedom.

At the very moment when Harrington's utopia becomes reality, it represents a completely renewed image of power. The subjects of the political are now the masses of free appropriators: the problem will be to organize not the relations with the expropriated but, rather, those among the appropriators. The Machiavellian dimension of the political, on this horizon, affirms itself in a primordial manner because it takes the political back to the spatial ontology of appropriation. But at the same time this dimension is negated because it eliminates all the elements of urgency, of conflictuality, of crisis that the political had assumed in its own genesis. Space is in fact also the place where conflicts are transferred.

The expansive republic, therefore, will be capable of moving the conflicts toward the frontier, a frontier of appropriation, always open. Freedom has at this moment a frontier that is pure and simple opening. The American dream and drama and the story of its constitution will be from now on tied to this perspective: the perspective of the frontier, now understood as frontier *of* freedom, tomorrow as frontier *to* freedom; today as open space, obstacle to overcome, tomorrow as closure, as a limit definitely posed. American political society was born from this alternative, which at the beginning is an open alternative, perhaps not even logically conceivable. But then? How can the Tartar become a citizen? How can the space close while maintaining freedom?

However, these are not the problems to which the American revolutionaries and constituents immediately apply themselves. American constituent power was born on this spatial base, on that new concept, fully complete, as Minerva was from Jupiter's head. What is at stake is not the problematization of the concept, but its interpretation, its orientation, and its reorganization. Even the man most distant from that new intellectual and political sensibility, the John Adams whom Gordon Wood considers, with reason, "ensnared" by the Enlightenment,[8] is profoundly touched by it, at least in the *Thoughts on Government* of 1776, which constitutes his work most deeply immersed in the political struggle.[9] What Adams discusses is not the multitude's strength but its quality, not its virtue but the possibility of its corruption. The basic pessimism that in the *Defence of American Constitution* of 1787 will reveal his class origins and his desperate defense of aristocratic privilege vis-à-vis the rising democracy,[10] and that consequently will make him side with a "mixed" constitutionalism in the Polybian and British tradition,[11] in the *Thoughts* has only the function of warning against a utopian project of parliamentary dictatorship (for instance, monocameralism, then constituted in Pennsylvania), and of giving back to the political the differences of the social.

The assembly "should be in miniature an exact portrait of the people at large. It should think, feel, reason, and act like them" (Adams, *Works*, 195). Representation is a process that, moving from below upward, from the direct to the indirect election, gives shape to an executive branch that in turn is structured by complex functions of control. Only in this way the minorities will be defended, only in this way will it be allowed that they continue to nourish that "virtue" that must be at the basis of the government. And to this aim a series of social measures (such as universal military service, the organization of a general education system in favor of the poor, the adoption of sumptuary laws in favor of the frugality of clothing, and so on) are as important as the constitutional guarantees. In the constitution of Massachusetts, Adams tries to make his political project concrete, once again not by limiting the principle of popular sovereignty but articulating it in a complex system of representation of social interests and of political filtering.[12]

Are Adams's critics right when they attack the *Thoughts* and his *Defence* alike? Are they right when they recognize, in Adams's thought in its whole, even during the revolutionary period, a bitter aristocratic nostalgia, of which the precautions and the bufferings of the *Thoughts* and the explicit adhesion to the model of "mixed constitution" in the *Defence* would be nothing but homologous expressions?[13] This is not what appears in a careful examination.

From the point of view of the search for guarantees against factions and the corruption of the popular will, the political philosophy of the *Thoughts* is closer to the tenth letter of *The Federalist* than to any British tradition: and it's much more Blackstonian than we can imagine in its way of establishing the uniqueness of political society as the source of any sovereignty. Nor, on the other hand, is there minimally present in Adams that principle of "virtual representation," which in the British Parliament wanted to represent the will and the interest of the nation. The Parliament, says Burke, is not a gathering of ambassadors of different antagonistic interests, "but [it] is a deliberative assembly of *one* nation, with *one* interest, that of the whole."[14] Corporations and empire were included in this concept of organic representation, the real black beast of the American insurgents.[15] And yet this concept is deeply, essentially tied to the definition of the modern State, to its genesis and its science. Indeed, from this point of view, there are no real differences and changes in the definition of sovereignty and representation between Rousseau and Burke,[16] nor, as we will soon see, between Hegel and Hamilton.[17] On the other hand,

Adams is part of the new political sensibility, of the sensibility that, through the spatialization of the concept of power, refers him to an unconcluded and progressive dynamic of constitutive experiences. The constitution of the political body of this freedom is the product of a dynamic and limitless constituent power. Adams inserts himself in this tendency as a pessimist: his *Thoughts* are perhaps a preliminary expression in showing the frontier as limit rather than as an obstacle to overcome. But also in the stress given to negativity, Adams is more related to the new American theoreticians (or, if you want, caught in their net) rather than to Burke; he is more tied even to those "extremists" who, like Thomas Young, the representative of Vermont, think that the "constituent people" can well attribute to the legislative assemblies "a supreme delegate power," but only by maintaining to the people themselves the strength to express in any occasion "a supreme constituent power," a real power of control of the government, and power of progressive constitutive dynamics of the people.[18]

Here we are, then, in the midst of the constituent process, of that democratic revolutionary process within which freedom assumes the form of the frontier: "The democratic revolution lived two years . . . not after the Declaration of Independence, but before."[19] Perhaps this rigid temporal delimitation corresponds to the truth—provided that, however, we do not forget that the triumph of nationalist ideology, and the reactivation, on the side of the political elites, of the revolutionary process, does not mean the exhaustion of democratic thought. The practice of a very radical democracy, experienced between 1775 and 1776, cannot be put aside. Even defeated, the democratic movement imposes on the Whig elites a continual and general process of mediation. The relation between spontaneous institutions and the government, between the people in arms and the continental army, has been so widely studied as to give us the sense, in fully adequate terms, of the dynamic ambiguity of the situation.[20] It is a dynamic that is, in extraordinary form, that of constituent power in general. That the phrase "constituent power" has been invented by the American revolutionaries is perhaps possible, as we have mentioned elsewhere:[21] what is certain is that for the first time in modern history we are witnessing such a complex process, so massified, and at the same time so compressed in such a short time, so powerful and rapid, so effective and unconcluded in its action.

The passage from resistance to revolution, from associationism to the constitution of political bodies, from *comitia* to the continental representations, from the *militiae* to the armies—all these elements interweave with one another in a political climate in which the ideological prescriptions and the material pulsions push rapidly toward irreversible results and radically innovative determinations. The constituent spirit is first of all radical. The democratic revolution, whether its origins are religious or social, is the motor of constituent power. In it, political and social, religious, and juridical questions interweave and become cause of total innovation. All relations are put into discussion, everything is shaken from its depths. Here the mobs or the associations have the same revelatory function as the Machiavellian and Harringtonian *comitia*, the same function that will later characterize the French clubs, as well as the masses and the councils of the soviets in the Russian Revolution. Fundamental is the rupture of the hierarchy of the existing power, of the ancient social order, and, at the same time, the formation of the revolutionary process as the process of the constitution of a new subjectivity. These are the youth and the essence of the political.

Let's now explain the armed insurrection. The "people-in-arms" are not only a fact of military organization; they also represent a new constitutional order. The act of recruitment of the *militiae* by the single colonies is considered an act of "constitutent power." Unforeseeable, unexpected, sudden, the process of protest and resistance turns into a moment of innovation. I doubt that in this turn can be simply recognized, à la Bagehot, a set of positive processes leading the "social differential" of the protest to become hegemonic. I have, rather, the impression that the innovation springs out of the radicality of the decision, out of the "arms," or better, out of the fact that the expression of the interests is inclined to the extreme alternative of the war. Only on the radicality of the refusal, on the touching of nothingness is constituent power founded. This is in any case revealed by the radicality of the apparatus that the revolution sets into motion: not only a new form of the State, but the constitution of a nation. A new space is given to the world, and first of all to its citizens. The "return to the principles" (of a just taxation, of a just representation) that animated the protest discovers now the creative nature of a new principle. Something abstract becomes real, a nature is appropriated to the point of transforming it into a second nature.

On this basis, after insisting on democratic radicality and on ontological innovation, there is a third element that characterizes American constituent power: its impact on the imaginary. What finds expression here is a true and profoundly effective cultural apparatus. The organization of the revolutionary struggle is not only radically linked to the interests; it not only expresses and consolidates in new form the abstract idea of the nation. Rather, it sets out to transform man, his interiority, his imaginative capability, his will to power. Virtue can now pose an inexhaustible frontier to itself, a frontier of freedom, as potentiality of a new man. What constituent strength offers to the citizens, to the new citizens, is a progressive power, a formative progressivity. The founding act is extremely radical: it destroys memory, creates new organizations and orders, constructs functional myths: constituent power reveals itself as ontological facticity.

Paine and Jefferson best express, in their time, this concept of constituent power and this image of the frontier of freedom. Thomas Paine's *Common Sense* in 1776 has the effect of a bomb: "The time hath found us"—against the age of corruption, the new American hope: America is the "promised land," and its cause is that of humanity.[22] Society is capable of self-regulation when it is not subjected to rules alien to its principles. It is this state of nature that needs to be reconstructed, constituted into a republic. In it, radical democracy represents the only form in which the contract among citizens is possible. The fact that this book today is basically illegible, in the flat simplicity of its style, in the obviousness of its argumentations as much as in the biblical erudition with which it is filled, does not prevent us from understanding the influence that it exercised on his contemporaries. Liberalism presented itself as radical revolution. And also the reading of the constitution of Pennsylvania (inspired as it is by Paine), which today can appear to us only as a constitution soliciting a wide popular participation, cannot make us forget the revolutionary nature of its genesis and spirit, a genesis directly connected to the class struggle against the local oligarchy and a radical spirit encoded in the declaration of rights and in the definition of the criteria of representation (rotation, year-long mandates, continual control by the people, principle of constitutional control).[23]

What is interesting to underline here are the quality and intensity of the constituent event that Paine expresses, by articulating it in the illustration of the democratic radicality of the process of formation of the new State, and in the attempt to give the innovation social roots. Thomas Jefferson is not less important in this first phase of the constituent process. In his *Summary View of the Rights of British America* of 1774, the target of his polemic is the principle of "virtual representation."[24] If the validity of this institution might ever be imagined, affirms Jefferson in an entirely Blackstonian manner, its sphere of effectiveness could only exist in reference to the king's sovereignty, and not to parliamentary sovereignty: the unity of the empire passes through the crown and not the parliament. The American states have nothing to do with the virtual representation of other English cities, of corporations, and of "putrid villages." American autonomy is irreducible. Now, the originality of this first stand taken by Jefferson lies in the fact that the juridical argument already contains the prefiguration of the constituent event. In the modernity and the elegance of the juridical argument is already running the revolutionary affirmation: the law precedes the constitution, the people's autonomy lives before its formalization. It is the Tartar who founds freedom, in the experience of his own right.

When the drafting of the *Declaration of Independence* is entrusted to Jefferson, we know what he will make of it: he will vigorously and unequivocally reconnect any legitimacy of government to popular sovereignty, to direct democratic consent understood as expression of the rights preceding any constitution.[25] That is, as permanent expression of constituent power.[26] It is the never-interrupted relationship between the text's political aim (that is, the declaration of independence of the American colonies) and its constituent form (the declaration of democratic rights) that makes exceptional the event, and relentless the progress of the writing in the radical synthesis of the protest and of the resistance, of constitutional innovation and political projecting. To a formal analysis the text appears divided into four parts: the first defends fundamental rights, the second is the enunciation of the abuses of power perpetrated by the British crown against the American colonies, the third is a rhetorical discussion with the aim to demonstrate the good faith of the American peoples, and the fourth contains the formal declaration of independence. Yet this formal distinction does not hold when we actually read the text, because each of these parts takes up once again and reproposes as motivations the themes that in the other parts are assumed as the object of the discussion, so that we are confronted by a circular argument, whose first and last support is the constituent will.

The declaration of rights is brief:

We hold these truths to be self-evident, that all men are created equal; that they are endowed by their Creator with unalienable rights; that among these are life, liberty, and the pursuit of happiness: that to secure these rights, governments are instituted among men, deriving their just powers from the consent of the governed; that whenever any form of government becomes destructive of these ends, it is the right of the people to alter or to abolish it, and to institute new government, laying its foundation upon such principles, and organizing its powers in such form, as to them shall seem most likely to effect their safety and happiness.

Here these rights are listed: (a) the right to life; (b) the right to freedom; (c) the right to the pursuit of happiness; (d) the right to a democratic government by consent; (e) the right to resistance and revolution; (f) the right to the expression of constituent power.[27]

In the second part of the *Declaration of Independence* are listed twenty-seven abuses of power perpetrated by the king against the American people. Each of these reported abuses reveals, in its formulation, an aspect of the fundamental rights that have been enunciated: the juridical motivation of the abuse historicizes and makes concrete the abstract definition of the fundamental right. Thus the right to life is determined by the fact that it cannot be left "exposed to all the danger of invasion from without, and convulsions within" (2); rather, that it must be guaranteed by laws of population, of naturalization, of encouragement to colonize, by new ordered distribution of land; that it cannot be jeopardized by the presence of permanent armies and war fleets stationed on the American territory and defended by an emergency legislation; and even less so can it be actually destroyed by piracies, devastations, fires, killings, and finally by ruthlesss Indian wars promoted by the king.

As for the right to freedom, it is made concrete by the people's capability of instituting a judicial power, independent from the king's exclusive will, exercised through free juries and on national territory; it is made concrete through the capability of the people to control their own public administration, so that it will not become too bureaucratic and squander public money; it is made concrete by maintaining military power on an inferior terrain, subordinated to civil power. The king has forgotten to do all this: even more, he has acted against the fundamental rights. The same for the right to the pursuit of freedom. This right positively lies in the exercise of commerce, in the population of the country, in the authorities' inclination to support these and other social politics, necessary and favorable to the public good, often of immediate importance. On this terrain the king has oscillated between a permanent sabotage and a ruthless repression.

The right to a democratic government by consent has been in turn trampled on in all its determinations: that of exercising "the right of representation in the legislature; a right inestimable to them, and formidable to tyrants only" (1–2). A natural right this is, which, in the absence of the institutions, the people can, must, and have exercised directly: that of obeying exclusively to a jurisdiction internal to the constitutions and the law that the citizens have given themselves; that of legislating in an independent manner. The right to resistance and revolution is actualized as duty and necessity where abuse and violence deny the expression of the other rights here listed, and above all where it is the right to life that is put in doubt.

The right to revolution is a negative right, aimed at the destruction of the adversary and the maintenance of the natural basis of survival, but it is also a positive right, in the sense that it opens the constituent will:

Prudence indeed will dictate that governments long established should not be changed for light and transient causes; and, accordingly all experience hath shown that mankind are more disposed to suffer while evils are sufferable, than to right themselves by abolishing the forms [of government] to which they are accustomed. But when a long train of abuses and usurpations, pursuing invariably the same object, evinces a design to reduce them under absolute despotism, it is their right, it is their duty, to throw off such government, and to provide new guards for their future security. (1)

The third part of the *Declaration of Independence* shows the American good faith—a good faith made concrete by the exercise of justice, by a tradition of connection and friendship with the English homeland, by a repeated and humble attempt to make the British king and the Parliament recede from the position they have taken. All this has been followed only by a series of continual and serious provocations: "We must therefore acquiesce in the necessity which denounces our separation, and hold them as we hold the rest of mankind, enemies in war, in peace friends" (3). Here the concept of constituent power becomes the concept of a necessity; in this necessity are summed up, as motivations, the discussions of the fundamental rights and the exposition of a new constructive imaginary. Constituent power is a road to travel. In the last part of the *Declaration of Independence* this road has begun. The fundamental rights begin to be realized in an autonomous form, in a contractual commitment that the states, which have declared themselves independent, establish among themselves, in war as well as in peace. The *Declaration of Independence* reveals itself an act of constituent power.

Let's then go back to the definition of constituent power. In the *Declaration of Independence* it is defined as limitation of the space of British legitimacy, and it is specified as new frontier of American freedom. It is a space already widely filled by the radical democratic activity that is behind and inspires these pages, and by the imagining, on this basis, of a movement of constituent power that comes before any constitution. It is a dense movement of rupture and innovation, not a different function in the continuity of the juridical, political, and ideological history of the United States. "The eternal separation" defines a completely new space, a space that the people's democratic activity has already begun to fill with a new life, with freedom and happiness. In this *Declaration* Jefferson foregrounds a fundamental element in the history of the concept of constituent power: it presents itself as capability of constructing a completely new space, a space redefined by the political, conquered through an operation of founding political emancipation—in universal terms. Jefferson seizes in its immediacy the process that had started between the First (1774) and Second Continental Congress (1775)—through the Associations for boycotting English products and laws; the diffuse experiences of self-government; popular arming; the new experimentations from below of administrative, juridical, and economic management of the States; the reappropriation of power by the armed people.

Let's leave to the apologists of "eternal liberalism" to conjecture what this has to do with the pale Lockean ideologies of freedom, and also with the more astute, but less abstract, Scottish concepts of common sense.[28] Here witness the simultaneous formation of a nation and a State, of a political space and a society:[29] an unforeseeable and unforeseen theoretical situation. If Machiavelli had dug the political until he reached, on the verge of nothingness, the principle of its constituent reality; if Harrington had materialized this creative reality in the relation of counterpower; here Jefferson instead invents the spatial dimension of the constitutive act, showing that the political holds a creative radicality in all its dimensions.

American constituent power throws into an indefinite space that absolute radicality of power that Machiavelli had understood as rupture of cyclical time. Thus are constituted together the concepts of political emancipation and political society. Political society emancipated the individuals, making them citizens and appropriators of an indefinite space. The Harringtonian thematics of liberation can thus be integrated in positive terms: once freed from the British crown, once the American space has been constituted, the liberation no longer has reason to be a moment of separation: it is fully brought to conclusion into political emancipation, in the promotion of citizens, in the freedom to pursue the end of happiness in the spaces of the nation. The democratic experience of the revolution finds therefore in the *Declaration of Independence* the expansive qualification of constituent power. Toward the frontier, always beyond the frontier, democracy consolidates its program.

Contemporary authors have called all this "the Jeffersonian accommodation."[30] But it is not a compromise: rather, here we are dealing with the designing of the "new American relations," as Marx will define them. It is an operative hypothesis: on the Tartar frontier of American freedom a new and rich sociality can be built.[31] It is a real hypothesis, it is the new American constituent power—something running through the political revolution, showing, on the threshold of the national space, the possibility of widening power and social freedoms, a substitute (but how effective!) of the traditional concept of social revolution. And also an illusion? An illusion charged with destructive effects? We will come back to this point, and later in this chapter we will try to answer this question. For the time being it is enough to say that the potential contradictions of the Jeffersonian project are far from finding a moment of rupture, not only at the end of the eighteenth century but also for a long period of the nineteenth. The long polemic that until the 1960s has divided the historiography of the revolution between "the progressive school" and "the school of American exceptionalism" has no reason to be: both schools were decidedly apologetic, and each projected on the American past its judgment on the present revolution, or better, their wish for or refusal of a new revolution.[32] And although our favor goes entirely to those progressive authors who felt the need to recognize once again in the revolution of 1770–1780 the impulse to further probe the democratic debate of the first two decades of the twentieth century, it is very difficult to adhere to those who consider, in the course of the American Revolution, the conflict more important than the consent, the spreading and accumulating of class struggles more important than the event of independence.

On the other hand, if we study the conservatives of the Cold War, who, by using as their motto Tocqueville's statement "the United States were born free," think that "the political revolution" was enough to satisfy strong men, ready to take, with freedom, also property, to fill their stomachs, and to take care of their interests—also in this case it is clear that we are touching levels of pure ideology. In fact, the social revolution is within the American Revolution insofar as it constitutes its edge: it is included in the concept of political revolution because the concepts of sovereign people and constituent power are drawn on the continental space. Also because, furthermore, the concept of property here has deeply changed and, far from representing itself according to the English legal tradition, is defined in terms of appropriation and exalted as a direct product of labor. It is thus not by chance, as Elise Marienstras has demonstrated, and as we have already pointed out, that in the years 1770–1780, both Adams and Jefferson, in one voice, had widely developed these arguments: this shows how much the American space modifies any concept, until the point when "property" presents itself exactly as an inalienable activity for the "pursuit of happiness."[33] This American specificity must also push us to recognize that the idea, so widely spread in Europe toward the end of the eighteenth century, and above all insisted on by Turgot, that the American Revolution is the product of the Enlightenment and of the European revolution (in the founding and innovative globality of all its social and political dimensions)[34] is a myth rather than a reality: the American Revolution could not demonstrate anything, it could not conclude anything, because it was something utterly different. Karl Marx, in his characteristically powerful writing, notices this utter difference. While studying an American economist, a certain Carey, Marx tells us that he

> *is the only original economist among the North Americans. [He] belongs to a country where bourgeois society did not develop on the foundation of the feudal system, but developed rather from itself; where this society appears not as the surviving result of a centuries-old*

movement, but rather as the starting-point of a new movement; where the state, in contrast to all earlier national formations, was from the beginning subordinate to bourgeois society, to its production, and never could make the pretence of being an end-in-itself; where, finally, bourgeois society itself, linking up the productive forces of an old world with the enormous natural terrain of a new one, has developed hitherto with unheard-of dimensions and unheard-of freedom of movement, has far outstripped all previous work in the conquest of the forces of nature, and where, finally, even the antitheses of bourgeois society itself appear only as vanishing moments.[35]

Carey is aware of all this: therefore he counterposes the American relations of production, which from his point of view he sees as "normal and eternal," to the English relations of production, limited, distorted, altered by the past:

American relations against English ones: to this [Carey's] critique of the English theory of landed property, wages, population, class antitheses etc. may be reduced. In England, bourgeois society does not exist in pure form, not corresponding to its concept, not adequate to itself. How then could the English economists' concepts of bourgeois society be the true, undimmed expression of a reality, since that reality was unknown to them?

Space, the great American space, is at the basis of everything: "Carey's generality is Yankee universality. France and China are equally close to him. Always the man who lives on the Pacific and the Atlantic."[36] The American relations consist of this, and of this consists the very strong innovation that they impress on the history of man. Political emancipation includes social relations and develops the theme of liberation within these relations: that is, there where freedom has always a frontier to overcome, a space to run through.

Edmund Burke was right when he warned his colleagues in the Parliament. As for Jefferson, better than any other he gives us an extremely strong image of constituent power's capability to expand. Thus the founding dimension of constituent power that Machiavelli had situated in the radical grip of will over time, and that Harrington had fixed in the materiality of counterpower (each posing, in this way, constituent power as an ontologically constitutive act), in America widens to fill space, to travel it, to reinvent it. Constituent power at this point is destined to constitute a "second nature" proper—in the American case, a nation that spreads between two oceans, an immense territory to construct. American constituent power poses freedom as frontier, as its frontier—and the historical frontier of the American states as an obstacle to continually overcome, to give more and more freedom to its citizens.

American constituent power founds a right that is the first in any constitution: it is the forming form of dynamic social relations that recognize themselves as such and do not even ask, as Paine and Jefferson at times suggest, to become constitution. They want to be effective, but effective in a universal manner, over a space in which the self-government will not create conflictuality but, rather, will express consent, as well as new and dynamic rules. Is this religious utopia, the prophetism of a church of saints, or the anxiety of appropriation and the violence of men seeking liberation from persecution and misery? All the above and none of the above. All of the above if we consider the motivations of the process, in which religious and ideological elements, as well as impulses from the class struggle and impulses of interest combine. None of the above if we consider the dynamic of the process that sees this contradictory synthesis of motivations become the hard kernel of a struggle for independence, that contains within itself the highest expression known so far of constituent power. Constituent of a new society of free men.

Homo Politicus and the Republican Machine

The *homo politicus* that the American Revolution has formed is evidently at the root of the American constitution, but within a deeply modified relation of force and institutional location. If the *homo politicus* of the revolution includes the social within the political as open space and freedom of the frontier, the *homo politicus* of the constitution is by now subjected to an institutional machine that poses precise limits to freedom: it guards its expansion but guarantees it within a juridical apparatus that is an unsurmountable limit. How do we move from the democratic revolution and from the *Declaration of Independence* to a withdrawal of thought and of political practice in the constitution? How do we reach the relative inflection of originality and strength of American constituent power? Why and how is the space of freedom restructured and its apparatus formed?

It is well known what polemics, in the brief period of a decade, led to the victory of the federalists, through the overcoming of the fights of the confederate states, and through the first elaboration of a constitutional project outside of the Confederation itself (substantially in terms of politics of territory and of citizenship).[37] In the period immediately preceding the constitution, it is once again the rivalries among the states, the difficulty to coordinate the commercial politics, and above all the social revolts that impose the necessity to go beyond the "articles" of the Confederation. Without exaggerating the importance of Shays rebellion in Massachussetts, on which, however, Madison reflects dramaticallly and for a long time in the tenth letter of *The Federalist*,[38] it is evident that too many moments of crisis have accumulated by now: so that the conviction about "the incapacity of the present Confederation to maintain the Union" widely spreads among the ruling class.

But there is, above all, a new and unforeseeable element that emerges here: it is the deep pessimism born from observing the internal disunion that can result from the new sense of freedom the revolution had affirmed. This element is confirmed in the fear that, *rebus sic stantibus*, this disunion will produce tyrannical responses. Number 6 of *The Federalist* is, to this effect, exemplary when it insists that dissents among the States are inevitable if a superior authority, outside of local ambition, is not working to resolve them. Equally examplary is number 21, dominated by the urgency to pose the principle on the basis of which, if confronted by the attempts of turbulent and usurping majorities, a confederation may intervene. There must exist constitutional instruments capable of preventing damage making:

any successful faction may erect a tyranny on the ruins of order and law.... The tempestuous situation from which Massachusetts has scarcely emerged evinces that dangers of this kind are not merely speculative. Who can determine what might have been the issue of her late convulsions if the malcontents had been headed by a Caesar or by a Cromwell? Who can predict what effect a despotism, established in Massachusetts, would have on the liberties of New Hampshire or Rhode Island, of Connecticut or New York? (no. 21:139–40)

Pessimism is intrinsic to the constitutional spirit and finds its root in the contradiction between "the requisite stability and energy in government" and "the inviolable attention due to liberty and to the republican form." How can we reach a reconciliation of these two elements? (37:226). The contradiction lies in "the genius of republican liberty," which

demand[s] on one side not only that all power should be derived from the people, but that those intrusted with it should be kept in dependence on the people by a short duration of their appointments; and that even during this short period the trust should be placed not in a few, but a number of hands. Stability, on the contrary, requires that the hands in which power is lodged should continue for a length of time the same.... Not less arduous must have been the task of marking the proper line of partition between the authority of the general and that of the State governments. (37:227)

How can these contradictions be reconciled? *The Federalist* has doubts about the fact that the contradictions can be resolved: rather, they can be made to function. There is no preconstituted form of solution for these problems. In this regard our law is as insufficient as our sociology. But it is true that the wisdom and genius of freedom lie exactly in taking these unsolvable contradictions as a terrain of constitutional exercise:

Would it be wonderful if, under the pressure of all these difficulties, the convention should have been forced into some deviations from that artificial structure and regular symmetry which an abstract view of the subject might lead an ingenious theorist to bestow on a Constitution planned in his closet or in his imagination? The real wonder is that so many difficulties should have been surmounted, and surmounted with a unanimity almost as unprecedented as it must have been unexpected. It is impossible for any man of candour to reflect on this circumstance without partaking of the astonishment. It is impossible for the man of pious reflection not to perceive in it a finger of the Almighty hand which has been so frequently and signally extended to our relief in the critical stages of the revolution. (37:230–31)

The pessimist has become an optimist once again, but only by modifying his point of view, and exalting the possibility of regulating constituent power. The *homo politicus* of the revolution must submit to the political machine of the constitution; rather than in the free space of the frontier, the individual is constrained to that of the constitution.

James Madison's *The Vices of American Political System* is, from this point of view, an extremely important text; even more so because, differently from Alexander Hamilton, the other great author of *The Federalist Papers*, Madison is not a monarchist: he is a real republican, completely tied to Jeffersonianism.[39] Now, in that book Madison attacks localism and above all corporative constitutionalism. To a sociology of the plurality and of the relevance of interests he counterposes a political science irreducible to the former one; political science cannot simply stand above the mediation of social interests: it is autonomous because political action is autonomous. The constitution must therefore be a central axis of political mediation, of filtering, balance, control, and compromise of social interests. All can be accepted by a republic except the absolutization of a particular interest. It is evident how, on these grounds, the "mixed monarchy" is totally out of question. There are no preconstituted interests to the constitution, or social strata concretely and specifically tied to figures of representation. Compromise and mediation are not taking place among preexisting subjects, but among subjects that the constitution creates along its course.[40]

The paradigms of classical political science are here completely modified. In particular, we are faced by a spectacular reform of the concept of constituent power: it is absorbed, appropriated by the constitution, transformed into an element of the constitutional machine. It becomes constitutional machinery. What constituent power undergoes here is an actual change of paradigm. Nonetheless, it is useless to try to determine this change in the "long term" of Atlantic ideology: we have already seen how, on this dimension, the concepts of democracy and freedom present themselves in a new way with respect to the English tradition and the Florentine sources, and how constituent power, in the democratic period of the American Revolution, is given a singular definition.[41]

What becomes essential at this point is to determine the change in the "short term," to grasp, that is, the reasons why American constituent power, which in the democratic period had adjusted its Machiavellian and Harringtonian strength to the new American relations, here changes nature and transforms freedom, shifting it away from its meaning as active participation in the government to a negative meaning—that of an action, or the fruition of its own good, under the aegis of the law.[42] Let's clarify one point: never, either in the democratic period, or in the constitutional one, in America has the concept of people assumed the denotations of "general will."[43] But the fundamental discovery that had constituted the cognitive and practical essence of American constituent power and of its concept of people had been instead "the will of all": the idea of a manifold representation and of a diffused network of particular wills that in their expansion found a limit only in the frontier. In this perspective federalism is a dynamic element of very strong intensity, and its spatial figure mirrors itself in, and overflows with respect to, a functional figure, to a hypothesis verified for the first time, of a grid of horizontal and dynamic powers, through whose exercise constituent power remains continually open. Now, in the short term, in the ten years of the confederate union, this idea of constituent power undergoes a revision. And the constitution was born out of its rocking. "The passage from republicanism to liberalism" does not take place by crossing the Atlantic,[44] but by crossing the short period of the Confederation.[45] Certainly, the idea that the soul of the republic is not the constitution but the frontier will stay alive: the Jeffersonian spirit will live for a long time in its purity and in its might. But, when measuring itself with the constitution and with the opposite series of the constitutional principles, it will be pushed to reveal itself as contradictory (we will see this later in the next section).

Let's return, therefore, to the analysis of the modification of the constituent principle. This will become evident if we follow the discussion of *The Federalist*.[46] There is no need to insist on the practical importance of *The Federalist*: to this aim it is enough to remember a 1790 annotation by Jefferson:

As for political economy, I believe The Wealth of Nations *by Adam Smith is the best work; for the constitutional science Montesquieu's volume* The Spirit of the Laws *is generally credited. Indeed it contains a great number of political truths, but also an equal number of heresies, so that the reader must continually keep a good guard. . . . Locke's little volume on the government is perfect for what it sets as its aim. When we move from theory to practice there's no better volume than* The Federalist.[47]

Now, the first revolution within the revolution is contained in numbers 9 (by Hamilton) and 10 (by Madison) and lies in the explicit redefinition of the political. The union is shown as "internal safeguard with respect to factions and insurrection." But what is the union, and what is the political that cements it? The answer to these questions comes from an observation: "The *causes* of faction cannot be removed. . . . relief is only to be sought in the means of controlling its *effects*" (10:80). "To secure the public good and private rights against the danger of such a faction, and at the same time to preserve the spirit and the form of popular government, is then the great object to which our inquiries are directed" (10:80).

The political, and political society, are therefore the condition sine qua non for overcoming the effects of the factions; they are the constitution of a place within which the causes of the factions, that is, the interests and the ideologies, become elements not of rupture but of participation: "The regulation of these various and interfering interests forms the principal task of modern legislation and involves the spirit of party and faction in the necessary and ordinary operations of the government" (10:79). All is political, because otherwise there would be no society. And the political, and political society, are therefore the machine that orders and reorders the interests: it intervenes on conflicts, it represents, judges, orients.

Democracy then is not enough. It legitimizes the origin of power, but it must, in turn, be organized within power. Representation is therefore necessary, but as necessary is its mobilization within the machine of power. Here American democracy is distinct from "vulgar" democracy, dominated by the illusion that the principles of direct representation, of rotation, of popular control, of an always active constituent principle do not lead to catastrophe, offering thus the best ground to factions. Here therefore American democracy becomes republican democracy:

A republic, by which I mean a government in which the scheme of representation takes place, opens a different prospect and promises the cure for which we are seeking. Let us examine the points in which it varies from pure democracy, and we shall comprehend both the nature of the cure and the efficacy which it must derive from the Union. The two great points of differentiation between a democracy and a republic are: first, the delegation of the government, in the latter, to a small number of citizens elected by the rest; second, the greater number of citizens and greater sphere of country over which the latter may be extended. (10:81–82)

But in order for a republic to exist, and for the dangers of a dictatorship—even of a democratic one, or a dictatorship of the majority—to be avoided, we need guarantees.

The democratic game of power must therefore be dispersed through a multiplicity of offices of government, and the constitutional machine of political society must guarantee its functioning through the divisions of powers:

The science of politics, however, like most other sciences, has received great improvement. The efficacy of various principles is now well understood, which were either not known at all, or imperfectly known to the ancients. The regular distribution of power into distinct departments; the introduction of legislative balances and checks; the institution of courts composed of judges holding their offices during good behavior; the representation of the people in the legislature by deputies of their own election: these are wholly new discoveries, or have made their principal progress towards perfection in modern times. They are means, and powerful means, by which the excellencies of republican government may be retained and its imperfections lessened or avoided. (9:72–73)

What is striking, in this first approach to the American constitution, is the actual *translatio* of constituent power that has taken place here. For the first time it is not conceived as something that founds the constitution, but as the fuel of its engine. Constituent power is no longer an attribute of the people, of those people free and capable of reinventing the great American spaces, and by the means of appropriation, their own freedom, an attribute of that people that Burke had described. Constituent power has become a model of political society: it is this society that forms the people through representation, through the division of powers, through all the cogs of the constitutional machine. The *homo politicus* is redefined by the constitution: without constitution there is no constituent power.[48]

But there is more. After functioning as filter and selection of popular interests, the machine folds on itself and reveals itself as organism. It is sufficient to go back to the passages of *The Federalist* already cited to see how the division of powers and the system of controls do not represent only a panoply of guarantees but constitute also a dynamic of concurring powers that organizes itself through and in the name of the complex whole of the constitutional operations. This is an organism that has its own life: it sanctions the capability, for the government, "to enlarge . . . the orbit" of its own actions according to the necessities that it encounters (9:73). To the linear process of the concurrence of powers is added here the rhyzomatic phenomenon of the affirmation and development of the "implicit powers," determined and constructed by the activity of the government itself.

Later, in the course of the discussion of *The Federalist*, in number 31, Hamilton will affirm: "A government ought to contain in itself every power requisite to the full accomplishment of the objects committed to its care, and to the complete execution of the trusts for which it is responsible, free from every other control but a regard to the public good and to the sense of the people" (194). At this point constituent power becomes a modality of organized power: it is defined as formativity of the government of political society.

Therefore, not only is constituent power defined by the constitution, but it is reduced to a formal element of the government. The original constituent fact is confined within the *Declaration of Independence*, assumed as a patrimony, and now its might is interpretable only as power of government. Without the constitution, outside of the constitution, outside of the constitutional machine and of the organism of government, there's no constituent power.

But what is left outside of the constitution? Are there only factions and irrationality? The rhetoric of *The Federalist* would become obtuse and counterproductive if it would linger only on these first arguments. Simultaneously to the operation of *translatio* of constituent power to the constitutional machine, we witness an attempt to recuperate and reform what constitutional theory and practice have until now excluded or been silent about: American space, the expansion of freedom and democracy. The federalist thematic constitutes the terrain for the antagonism between the principle of republican government and the constituent power that continues to live outside of the constitution. Madison senses this clearly. He enumerates reasons opposed to the conflict:

> *The greater number of citizens and extent of territory . . . may be brought within the compass of republican [rather] than . . . democratic government; and it is this circumstance principally which renders factious combinations less to be dreaded in the former than in the latter. . . . In the extent and proper structure of the Union, therefore, we behold a republican remedy for the diseases most incident to republican government. And according to the degree of pleasure and pride we feel in being republicans ought to be our zeal in cherishing the spirit and supporting the character of federalists. (10:83–84)*

But he knows well, however, that the problem thrown out of the window of the republican building comes back in through the door of federalism, and through the freedom and the political action of those who, in the States, on the frontier, consider American constituent power as the atmosphere of their own freedom.

A mediation is thus necessary. Madison in number 39 of *The Federalist* throws much water on the fire of the definition of republican government:

> *What, then, are the distinctive characters of the republican form?... If we resort for a criterion to the different principles on which the different forms of government are established, we may define a republic to be, or at least may bestow that name on, a government which derives all its powers directly or indirectly from the great body of the people, and is administered by persons holding their offices during pleasure for a limited period, or during good behavior. It is* essential *to such a government that it be derived from the great body of the society, not from an inconsiderable proportion or a favoured class of it. (240–41)*

Good, and now, in front of a constitution that puts itself up to be approved, how can these democratic qualities of the republican government be guaranteed? How can they be guaranteed after having been subordinated to the constitutive machine of political society, when constituent power has been expropriated in this direction, when the government has presented itself as an organism?

The democratic counterweight lies in federalism. The republican constitution will have to submit to federalism, make with it a compromise that invests it in its complexity. The compromise of the national constitution with federalism is the compromise of republicanism with democracy—there where constituent power had presented itself as democracy in the wide spaces of the frontier:

> *The proposed Constitution, therefore... is, in strictness neither a national nor a federal Constitution, but a composition of both. In its foundation it is federal, not national; in the sources from which the ordinary powers of government are drawn, it is partly federal and partly national; in the operation of these powers, it is national, not federal; in the extent of them, again, it is federal, not national, and, finally, in the authoritative mode of introducing amendments, it is neither wholly federal nor wholly national. (39:246)*

In front of these affirmations of Madison's we cannot but admire the strength that, in the ambiguity of the constitutional script, reduced democracy under the wing of a powerful government, whose rule is self-reproduction; yet, from a theoretical point of view, we cannot but denounce the further process of expropriation of the constituent power of the masses that the succession of the constitutional diktat expresses. So people, as mass of individuals, as multitude in the new space, which the democratic and revolutionary power had defined, here are erased, reinvented as political society, as element of a second nature prefigured and produced by the republican government. Madison's and Hamilton's "political science" is a political science of the "second nature," of the deontologization of constituent power and of the popular political.

From all this derive a few fundamental consequences. First of all, let's consider the theme of the organization of force. Numbers 23 to 29 of *The Federalist*, drafted by Hamilton, argue in a fierce manner against those who refuse the right of a regular permanent army for the Federation. Already in the numbers 8, 16, and 22 this theme had been dealt with, but in a rhetorical way, posing the problem of the standing army as a controversy, stressing the resolutive direction that *The Federalist* privileges, as if it were an obvious thing. When the debate reaches its acme, there is no more space for rhetoric. The polemic against the adversaries of a permanent army for the Federation is then developed in functional terms, as necessity of a force for the external defense, and in warrantist terms against the abuse of the federal army by anybody. Marginally, the right to the *militia* is acknowledged, under certain conditions, in number 29. But the hard concept is only one: the decision about the use of force is up to the central power.

Here we have reached a point where the residual ambiguities concerning the relationship of republic to democracy are completely resolved. The United States constituted themselves on the refusal of proxy in regard to the use of weapons: and now this bulwark of constituent power, this fundamental element of American democracy is erased. The refusal of the active participation of the citizens to the arming of the nation, the affirmation of the proxy for the armies is the affirmation of the monopoly of power. The reversal of the democratic position is here fully accomplished. With this we go well beyond the republican-federalist compromise: and we witness the changing of the constituent project of political society by imposing on it a new value. Because the monopoly of physical force defines sovereignty in traditional terms, here even the last democratic illusion is taken away, thus taking republicanism back to an absolute concept of the State. As for the argument that allows the maintenance of the militia, it represents a pure and simple juridical perfidy. The militia, that is, the plan of organizing in arms the nation, they say, is a harmful and unrealistic project: but well-trained contingents of the militia can always be useful, and in any case the militia can constitute an antidote for any standing army claiming to represent a threat to freedom! In *The Federalist* the threat against freedom is always risen to construct, little by little but more and more definitively, a new sovereignty.

Numbers 30 to 36 of *The Federalist* show us how this formidable new deduction, aimed to the reconstruction of the most traditional concept of sovereignty, is developing: these numbers discuss the general power of taxation: "Money is, with propriety, considered as the vital principle of the body politic; as that which sustains its life and motion and enables it to perform its most essential functions" (30:188). The argument is obvious: only the autonomous power to impose taxes allows the central State to exercise its strength and its power with independence.[49] But the rhetoric implies much more. In fact, it proclaims: if there is too much democracy in this independent America; if we do not win over it now, at the moment of the *translatio* of constituent power, we will never win over it:

> *As in republics strength is always on the side of the people, and as there are weighty reasons to induce a belief that the State governments will commonly possess most influence over them, the natural conclusion is that such contests [on taxation] will be most apt to end to the disadvantage of the Union; and that there is greater probability of encroachments by the members upon the federal head than by the federal head upon the members. (31:197)*

And it is not by chance that, in regard to this question, what are above all and widely discussed and organized are those "implicit powers" (whose image we have taken into consideration) that allow a wider and wider definition of central power (as an organism) and of its necessary functions.

To complete the picture, what is taking place here, in numbers 32 on, in a definitive manner, is the transformation of the "mixed constitution" according to the Polybian and Atlantic tradition, into a modern constitution: now the division of sovereignty is no longer tied to the corporative and classist constitution, but to the formal process of its own structure and organization. I do not think I am going beyond the boundaries of my own research if I stress the coincidence between the fiscal and the financial part of the constitution and this moment of modernization: here it is money that assumes that function of giving a direction and a sense of organization that in the democratic constituent power of the first revolutionary stage was performed by the "frontier." In these essays Hamilton certainly does his apprenticeship for the future government of the Bank of America.[50]

But more important is the exactness of the homologies between money and competences, between implicit competences and concurrent competences that take shape here: the constitution is elevated to the kingdom of monetary circulation. The organism by which Hamilton is inspired is that of the "powerful abstraction" of money, of its circulation, and of its pulse. From this point of view he really is a child of Europe, not of Enlightenment thought, however, but, rather, of the England that, at the end of the Glorious Revolution, reorganizes power around financial capital.

The enclosure of the conceptual system of the "mixed constitution" within the abstract artificiality of the new constitutional formalism is further examined in these essays. Three themes (political supremacy [no. 33], the concurrent competences of parallel powers [no. 34], and the relation between taxation and representation [nos. 35–36]) constitute the subject of a real dialectical synthesis, in which affirmation (the centrality of taxation), negation (the pluricentrality of the decisional and executive power), and synthesis (the centralization, with popular legitimization, of the entire mechanism) follow each other: a good Hegelian procedure, therefore, to make constituent power a force of the spirit, a strength completely assimilated to the constitution, a fundamental and independent motor. The perspective of the centralization and the constitutionally self-regulated mechanism are tested also in the numbers (41–46) of *The Federalist* dedicated to commenting juridically on the difference of competences of the States and of the Federation. The theory of the two constitutional orders starts taking shape, while reaffirming, however, the supremacy of the Federation as a force settling any conflict. By now, thus, the constitutional motor is marching, even hastening forward. The masterpiece of transferring the constituent foundation from the people to the constitution is fully realized already at the end of the first part (the first fifty-one numbers) of *The Federalist.*

What's left to the authors is to answer the detractors, while continuing to insist on the force of the constitutional motor. Are there detractors who believe that the constitution of the Union destroys the separation of the three powers, and that in any case it threatens their balance? It is not true, our authors reply. The separation of powers defined by the constitution is purely and simply that of Montesquieu—and this doctrine, far from fixing the separation of powers as absolute, on the contrary, considers them as concurrent (no. 47).[51]

It was shown in the last paper that the political apothegm there examined does not require that the legislative, executive, and judiciary departments should be wholly unconnected with each other. I shall undertake, in the next place, to show that unless these departments be so far connected and blended as to give each a constitutional control over the others, the degree of separation . . . essential to a free government, can never in practice be duly maintained. (48:308)

Therefore, the balance of the three powers passes through their reciprocal control, almost in a conspiracy among powers, toward constitutional ends. Nonetheless, there can be conflicts among powers. How can they be resolved? It is entirely evident that the norms of the written constitution cannot suffice, by themselves, to solve the conflicts. But could a continuous recourse to the people? *The Federalist*, combining, as always in these cases, sociological with juridical considerations, weighs the recourse to the people as a classic "perverse effect" of democracy, as the introduction of a democractic virus in the republican organism. The refusal of democracy is strong, insisted on, repeated, underlined, and on the other hand fully coherent with the logic itself of the constitution:

To what expedient, then, shall we finally resort, for maintaining in practice the necessary partition of power among the several departments as laid down in the Constitution? The only answer that can be given is that as all these exterior provisions are found to be inadequate the defect must be supplied, by so contriving the interior structure of the government as that its several constituent parts may, by their mutual relations, be the means of keeping each other in their proper places. (51:320)

An internal mechanism, a system of checks and balances, a system of reciprocal control of various autonomies. This formal and dynamic criterion relies on the same laws that constitute human nature:

What is government itself but the greatest of all reflections on human nature? If men were angels, no government would be necessary. If angels were to govern men, neither external nor internal controls on the government would be necessary. In framing a government which is to be administered by men over men, the great difficulty lies in this: you must first enable the government to control the governed; and in the next place oblige it to control itself. (51:322)

All the constitution must be read in this key and subjected to this labor. And since in the republican regime the legislative organs are the strongest, they must be divided into two branches, so that they can control each other: "In the compound republic of America, the power surrendered by the people is first divided between two distinct governments, and then the portion allotted to each subdivided among distinct and separate departments. Hence a double security arises to the rights of the people. The different governments will control each other, at the same time that each will be controlled by itself" (51:323). As for the defense of the minorities, how can it be realized? There are two ways: one is that of counterposing society, as such, to the government—that is, to consider society as a counterpower. But this way is very precarious and dangerous. It is conceivable in a constitutional monarchy, not in the American republic. The second way, instead, is that taken by the United States and is the way of pluralism:

Whilst all authority in it will be derived from and dependent upon the society, the society itself will be broken into so many parts, interests and classes of citizens, that the rights of individuals, or of the minority, will be in little danger from interested combinations of the majority.

In a free government the security for civil rights must be the same as that for religious rights. It consists in the one case in the multiplicity of interests, and in the other in the multiplicity of sects. The degree of security in both cases will depend on the number of interests and sects; and this may be presumed to depend on the extent of country and number of people comprehended under the same government. (51:324)

The circle of the constitutional demonstration closes with a paradox, since *homo politicus*, who is constructed by the constitution, has now become the sociological referent of the constitution—a referent so solid from the sociological point of view that he does not admit any other reality outside himself (that is, outside of the figure constructed by the revolution). The constitution has absorbed not only constituent power, but also the subject of constituent power. If in England, around the end of the seventeenth century, the constitution that followed the Glorious Revolution had begun to transform the mixed constitution of the classes into the constitution of the different functions of the government, here, a century later, the republican genius makes another miracle: after erasing in the constitution the subjects that were at its origin, it gives back to society pure and simple constitutional products, juridical individuals. In the course of this process of transformation, one only thing had been forgotten: the creative capability of the subjects, the groups, and the classes. Strength had yielded to power, and nothing was left of it in the constitution.

But constitutions are live things, and even more so is the people's constituent power—and formalism, or, if you want, the republican genius, will never succeed in subduing democracy! Thus the contradictions of the "political science" at work on the constitution, and those of the constitution itself, will appear also in the following part of *The Federalist.* These are not static but dynamic contradictions that put into discussion the exasperated positivism of the constitutionalists and reopen spaces for the work of democracy.

But before returning to these contradictions, let's try to understand why this American constitution, this "machine that can go by itself," exactly in the image of its complete and formal genealogy, fascinates contemporary thought so much. Because they say it is here that the "political space" of democracy is built.[52] It is here that the political, and specifically the democratic political, finds the noble title that prevents it from becoming flattened in the social. The American constitutional machine is appreciated as a machine that produces (and stretches further and further) political space as the constitutive dimension of the *homo politicus.* The constitutional political then becomes a sort of transcendentalism of reason, a free place on which collective freedom can be constituted. It frees us from any subjection to the social, and from all the passions that prevent us from dominating the social.

The political and its space are realistically the only possibility allowed to the social for expressing itself: "The central idea of revolution... is the foundation of freedom, that is, the foundation of a body politic which guarantees the space where freedom can appear."[53] Outside this political space, the social has a voice only as violence or anarchy: the consequences are known. The great difference of the American Revolution and the specificity of its constitution consist exactly in this self-aware transcending of the social; this awareness is so strong to form a constitutive capability, more real than the social, a machine formative of the society enclosed in the political. Through the political, society is returned to freedom, to an organized freedom. The force of Hannah Arendt's image lies in its underlining the difference between the American Revolution (and constitution) and the other revolutions. In the first one are at work freedom as foundation, reason and patience as constitutive virtues, desire as its horizon; in the second triumph the indefinite processes of compassion, of resentment, of freedom and terror; in the American Revolution the crystalline space of truth, in the other revolutions the scripturing of practice. On the whole, to conclude and to go beyond poetry, what Arendt tells us is that the fundamental element of the American constitution is the conjunction of constituent power with constituted power in the emancipation of the political.

As Habermas has noticed, this thesis refers entirely to the Marxian thesis of bourgeois "political emancipation," as it has been elaborated in Marx's writings from "On the Jewish Question" until *The German Ideology*, but it reverses the sign of value.[54] This means that here, in Hannah Arendt, the perfect coincidence of the political and the bourgeois, the linearity of the overcoming of the social conflict, and of its overcoming in terms of freedom, constitute an ontologically unsurpassable dimension and an epistemologically necessary horizon. The Marxian demystification of the passage from the social to the political is understood, but at the same time reversed, shown as affirmation of freedom. Where Marx demystifies in order to build a revolutionary praxis, Arendt constructs a praxis without a subject, and the ideal of this praxis. In this metaphysical apology for the American constitution we can recognize the confluence of the Kantian tradition of the rights State, and of the Nietzschean polemics against democracy. Here we can recognize above all a formidable effort to fix the illusion that liberalism may constitute the sense and the totality, the foundation and the limit of the human community. What an immense price this illusion implies! There is another realism in the Western tradition of political thought: that which links democracy to the constituent spirit and freedom to its social conditions. This realism does not allow one to reduce its constitutions to machines producing political reality; but it wants to maintain the exchange between social subjects and constitutional institutions, between political history and juridical machinations.

On the other hand, if we do not accept this open terrain and this irreducibility of constituent power to constituted power, it is impossible to explain the great juridical constructions of the modern and contemporary age. Isn't Arendt's point of view entirely fallacious when she tries to overcome this real determination? This is what Habermas thinks too, whose insistence on the difference and singularity of the American constitution does not lead him to negate its fundamentally ideological character.[55] Also, the American Revolution consists of a process of philosophical understanding of the bourgeois revolution, in which a spontaneous and optimistic natural right seeks its translation into positive right. This marks its specificity and its limits, this prepares the crisis of the event which already with the "revolution of 1800" affirms itself—in Jefferson's social democratism—a reopened revolution that already begins to exalt the dialectic between the democratic spirit of the masses and the active role of the State, even with the aim of determining the free constitution of the market.

These ambiguities and these possibilities of different outcomes are present in the second part of *The Federalist.* This means that the more we leave ideology behind, the more the self-sufficiency and the autocentrality of the constitution become unstable. In numbers 52 to 61, it is evident that the major difficulties had to present themselves on the theme of representation (and on the House of Representatives). It is here in fact that the constitutional machine, in order to continue to function according to the rules, must present itself as a sociological machine of selection of a representation adequate to the constitution. Hence a series of preoccupations aroused by the outburst of a democratic dynamics insensitive to the general design of the constitutional bloc. How can one resist the representatives' power? How can one resist an organization of public opinion that will become more and more demanding and complex? How can one make compatible the (factual) exigencies of the electorate, exigencies that oppose those of the Union, in the matter of taxation as well as in many other fields? Surely, here are assessed electoral rules that withhold the vote from nonproperty holders, that link the contributive capabilities to the electoral ones; here, in the theory of representation, is inserted some concrete limitation regarding the slaves, to full advantage of their owners; here is reaffirmed the generality of the representative function, and a number of representatives is fixed that must not be subordinated to the demographic growth of the nation. But these, no matter how important, are empirical elements: the guarantee must be higher up, in a safer place.

And it is once again the primacy of the constitution on the political capacity of the representatives' power itself that is strongly reaffirmed: "The important distinction so well understood in America between a Constitution established by the people and unalterable by the government, and a law established by the government and alterable by the government, seems to have been little understood and less observed in any other country" (53:331). "Where no Constitution, paramount to the government, either existed or could be obtained, no constitutional security, similar to that established in the United States was to be attempted" (332).

But this continual rise of the level of the guarantee resolves nothing; the contradiction remains, empirically given, empirically unresolved. How can it be overcome? Once again one turns to rhetoric: "If it be asked, what is to restrain the House of Representatives from making legal discriminations in favor of themselves and a particular class of the society? I answer: the genius of the whole system; the nature of just and constitutional laws; and above all, the vigilant, and manly spirit which actuates the people of America—a spirit which nourishes freedom, and in return, is nourished by it" (57:353). Once again the "genius of the system," Hamilton's romanticism! In fact, nothing is so hard and impenetrable by the genius of the system as free representation. In the American situation one can always work and put into action the conditions of a renovation without ruptures in the republican political class: but when the problem was born at this level, the illusion that the constitutional machine can also function directly as a machine of sociological selection is already destroyed. The sociological process of politics marches in rhythms different from those of the constitutional machine. The constituent spirit, the desire for democracy are always in wait. The American political spirit takes its revenge on the constitutional space.

This becomes particularly evident in the issues of *The Federalist* concerned with the Senate, that is, with the representation of the States (nos. 62–67). These issues represent a formidable apology for the centralization of the functions of the federal State, there where this organ should be representative of the widest decentralization of the Union—to this end is defined a specific constitutional space that is made for the Senate, as much as a specific function of constitutional guarantee that it must exercise belongs to the Senate. The government of the federation of the States, the control of foreign politics, the impeachment of the president and of the other organs, the control of bureaucracy—this is the eminent place assigned to the Senate. With all this the contradiction between constitutional apparatus and representative functions is pushed to the limit.

The American Senate, representing the States, is invested with the highest functions of the Union, almost executive functions, exalted by its pluristate representation. What is realized here is a gigantic transformist operation: the "spatial" determination of sovereignty is concluded in an eminent function of representation of a "firm national consciousness." The debates regarding this point follow the by now well-known safety arguments, against factions and insurrections—the arguments to protect contracts and entrepreneurship. The Senate is the receptacle of a republican order that, by reuniting the aristocracies of the single States, would like to decree the definitive overcoming of the contradictions between functional representation and the democratic force of the masses. Perhaps here the republican solution has demanded too much: within half a century, the crisis and the Civil War will show how unsustainable this process of centralization is, in the exasperated form that it has assumed here. The issues of *The Federalist* on the power of the Senate are soaked in resentment and fear: the constituent spirit, the free and democratic masses that experience the new American space, are their enemy. The American Senate wants to be the machine of the deepest stability of the system, the constitutional Thermidore of the American Revolution. Constituent power stands in opposition to it as a permanent threat, as a ghost to annihilate. In the Senate the frontier of American freedom is definitely erased: with a sublime irony, it is the constitutional "spatial" organ that defines this closure.

But it is exactly in the extremity of their relation that all the elements of contradiction and rupture become more evident. When the "conventionals" and *The Federalist* face the theme of executive power, and then that of judiciary power, it is as if by now they were obliged to a referral in the process of legitimization of a constitutional construction that was alive in their hands, richer in incongruences and contradictions, in mystifications and removals than in a coherent application of "scientific spirit"—as they claimed at the beginning. Within this referral, the push to centralization becomes stronger and stronger.

On the theme of "executive power" (nos. 57–67): What are, in this case, the political values to protect and promote? The same refrain once again: stability, effectiveness, timeliness, independence from factions, the capability to produce a program... We must stop with the revolution, a king is necessary, we seem to hear. But there are innumerable objections: "There is an idea which is not without its advocates, that a vigorous executive is inconsistent with the genius of republican government. The enlightened well-wishers to this species of government must at least hope that the supposition is destitute of foundation, since they can never admit its truth without at the same time admitting the condemnation of their own principles" (70:423). And yet

> *energy in the Executive is a leading character... of good government. It is essential to the protection of the community against foreign attacks; it is not less essential to the steady administration of the laws; to the protection of property against those irregular and high-handed combinations which sometimes interrupt the ordinary course of justice; to the security of liberty against the enterprises and assaults of ambition, of faction, and of anarchy. (70:423)*

All the dangers that have been enunciated with respect to the formation and the constitution of the organs of representation return *a fortiori* when we talk of the figure of the king-president. But if, according to the principles that inform a democratic government, in constituting the legislative organs we must overcome many disadvantages, why reintroduce such considerations in the formation of the executive? It would be superfluous and harmful. The executive cannot be but one. Any alternative would result in ineffectiveness, and it would destroy the spirit itself of the constitution, which, in the complex play of the republican powers, demands an absolute point of centralization and guarantee, an absolute point of decision and effectiveness. Finally, the king is naked, it would be appropriate to affirm. The work of centralization that runs through, from beneath to above the constitution, becomes completed. A pressing logic closes, in the times of the executive synthesis, the residual intervals left to democracy. A pure and tight determination of power blocks any fissure into the democratic process and into popular strengths. A sort of Jacobin spirit here puts itself at the service of a kind of institutional Thermidore. All this is expressed and validated by *The Federalist* in an Enlightenment language, where the examples drawn from ancient history, and the attempts in defining virtue and corruption, alternate as nauseatingly rhetorical motifs, to the ends of instrumental reason.

Here Hamilton, the Hamilton who in the years immediately following will shoot on sight against the French Revolution,[56] gives his best. The powers of the executive are widely analyzed and reinforced in any sense with regard to possible objections: the power of veto, the command of the military and naval forces, the power of grace, the power to stipulate a treaty, the power of appointing, competition with the Senate, and the power of intervention on the Congress, and so forth. The regality of the presidential function is not, at this point, a simple image, but a precise qualification. And all this is drowned in a sea of words of democracy and of republican invocations! To the citizens who ask why the Convention did not vote a *Declaration of Rights*, Hamilton answers that such declarations, born as contracts between the king and the people, "have no application to constitutions, professedly founded upon the power of the people, and executed by their immediate representatives and servants" (84:513). And with pedantic hypocrisy he adds:

I go further and affirm that bills of rights . . . are not only unnecessary in the proposed Constitution but would even be dangerous. They would contain various exceptions to powers which are not granted; and, on this very account, would afford a colourable pretext to claim more than were granted. For why declare that things shall not be done which there is no power to do? Why, for instance, should it be said that the liberty of the press shall not be restrained, when no power is given by which restrictions may be imposed? I will not contend that such a provision would confer a regulating power; but it is evident that it would furnish, to men disposed to usurp, a plausible pretence for claiming that power. They might urge with a semblance of reason that the Constitution ought not to be charged with the absurdity of providing itself against the abuse of an authority which was not given, and that the provision against restraining the liberty of the press afforded a clear implication that a power to prescribe proper regulations concerning it was intended to be vested in the national government. This may serve as a specimen of the numerous handles which would be given to the doctrine of constructive powers by the indulgence of an injudicious zeal for bills of rights. (84:513–14)

With the same spirit we could thus say, reversing the argument, that it is better not to talk of implicit powers, because the constitutional machine, and in particular the competences attributed to the executive, practically already comprehend the possibility of such an expression: the nonsaid is implicit. Thus, between rhetoric and things implicit, the republican mill will grind the American *homo politicus.*

But there is still something of which the *homo politicus* has not yet been dispossessed: his constituent capability, no longer as result but, rather, as activity, as always reproposed strength, no longer as past struggle for independence, in the revolution, but as ever present possibility. This is the last contradiction that *The Federalist* must solve, this is the last energy that it must absorb. The war that *The Federalist* wages against constituent power and against the democratic revolution is always a war of annexation; also for this last *Anschluss* are proposed suitable institutional instruments. The issues on judiciary power (78–83) are, in this respect, exemplary.

What is judiciary power? First of all, it is the great mobile hinge of institutional becoming. It connects and makes possible the competition of powers, by intervening in possible conflicts if necessary, by systematically rebalancing the powers according to the fundamental rules of the constitution. The autonomy of judiciary power and the independence of the judges must, to such end, deeply and very strongly be guaranteed. "The complete independence of the courts of justice is peculiarly essential in a limited Constitution" (78:466) because judiciary power is per se the weakest of powers and because, at the same time, it is the index of the constitutional process. Second, judiciary power is the custodian of the constitution: "No legislative act . . . contrary to the Constitution, can be valid" (78:467).

The interpretation of the laws is the proper and peculiar province of the courts. A constitution is, in fact, and must be regarded by the judges as, a fundamental law. It therefore belongs to them to ascertain its meaning as well as the meaning of any particular act proceeding from the legislative body. If there should have to be an irreconcilable variance between the two, that which has the superior obligation and validity ought, of course, to be preferred; or, in other words, the Constitution ought to be preferred to the statute, the intention of the people to the intention of their agents. Nor does this conclusion by any means suppose a superiority of the judicial to the legislative power. It only supposes that the power of the people is superior to both; and that where the will of the legislature, declared in its statutes, stands in opposition to that of the people, declared in the Constitution, the judges ought to be governed by the latter rather than the former. They ought to regulate their decisions by the fundamental laws rather than by those which are not fundamental. (78:467–68)

Third, judiciary power is endowed with potential political prerogatives: these derive from the fact that its intervention to guarantee individual rights against possible seditious attitudes of the citizens will "have more influence upon the character of our governments than but few may be aware of" (78:470). These political prerogatives, furthermore, derive from the continuity of the jurisprudential production of the courts, from the necessary laboriousness in the building and accumulation of this knowledge. But this political capability is above all exalted by the competences of the judiciary power in reference to the jurisdictional exercise concerning the putting into effect of constitutional norms, or in the case of conflicts between two states, in those conflicts that concern the relations between individuals and the State (no. 80). This is the point, therefore: in the American constitution, judiciary power resolves dynamically the ambiguities that the constitutional machine, in the rigidity that constitutes its guarantee, makes evident. In moving as the dynamic element of the constitutional realization, judiciary power founds and renews. It attributes to itself a sort of constituent power that shows the comprehensive "political force" of the constitution. In this sense judiciary power resolves by itself that problem of "implied powers" of the federal government,[57] that in the constitution had been considered, on the one hand, as a dangerous drifting and overflowing that juridical positivism must stop up; and on the other as the necessary key of institutional development, the adjustment of the means to the ends, and of the system of norms to the exigencies of historical becoming. Judiciary power assumes and exalts for itself the becoming explicit of constituent power, uncontainable in the net of a rigid constitution.

This is a deceit and a fiction. In fact, here the machine appropriates the last terrain on which the *homo politicus* could produce a direct innovation. The political innovation gives its ripe fruits: nothing is left of the sociality and the universality of the political expressed by the revolutionary movement. The strenuous centralization of the constitution takes up an exclusive and total place, from which constituent power is excluded.

Crisis of the Event and Inversion of the Tendency

The final number of *The Federalist* (no. 85) contains an important reference to Hume by Hamilton, a reference that is a tribute to the freedom born of experience. But we can certainly add, of experience insofar as it contains faith in the correspondence between the rational and the real. Scottish philosophy here is presented as Romanticism, as presupposition of the idealistic revolution that organizes experience in the transcendental function of reason. It is useful to underline the density of the Hamiltonian reference because here it indicates the reasons of his distance from Madison's position. For the latter, in fact, the reference to Scottish philosophy is made in natural right theory more than Humean terms, ethical more than idealistic, and the option, common to both authors, for a strong constitutive imagination, in Madison maintains a reference to the problematic character of the ethical subject.[58] The distinction is not irrelevant: it shows how the encapsulation of constituent power into the constituent event reveals, since the beginning, an important ambiguity, capable of producing a crisis. If we suppose that to govern constitutionally means to structure the subjects' field of action, and if we concede that the subject, in such case, is no longer an element counterposed to power but, rather, one of its first effects, the question concerning the consistency of the two poles, constitutional and subjective, remains still open. Now, since the beginning, the glass is cracked.

Nonetheless, what we are interested in here are not the vicissitudes of the progressive ideal and political distance between the two authors of *The Federalist*.[59] Rather, it is the contradiction of the paradigms, the dynamics of their separation, and the contrast that here begins to emerge. In general, we could say that the *Declaration of the Rights of Man* is immediately opposed to the constitution. Indeed, the problem is soon pushed to the extreme: we must decide whether the soul of the republic is the constitution or the frontier. The alternative is more material than philosophical. The last ten years of the century are characterized by the progressive acknowledgment of the alternative. The debate about the French Revolution is called to clarify and explain the two positions.[60]

The problem is to decide whether democracy is sustained by a constitutive subject that tries to organize its own freedom in movement, in the social, toward the limit of the possible, or whether the virtue of this subject ends in the play of interests, in symbolic legitimization, in the circle of commerce. *Homo politicus* or *homo mercator*.[61] It is known how the progressive impulse affirms itself since Jefferson's presidency in 1800, how the thematic of the frontier becomes more and more important during the next thirty years, until Jackson's presidency, where the triumph of the expansive paradigm opens new thematics and imposes new problems.[62] But this is not the place to follow the historical development of this question; what we must take up once again and situate at the center of our analysis is the concept of constituent power, in order to understand its extraordinary force, and at the same time the deepest mystifications that it undergoes in the American constitutional experience.

The extraordinary force of the American constitutional principle is its immersion in space and in the masses; it is the limitlessness and the irresistibility of its proceeding. The old constitutionalism of medieval origin, whatever the way in which reactionary thought theorizes its continuity,[63] is swept away. If in that tradition constitutionalism is the theory of limited government, here the constituent principle is limitless; if in the former the concept of legality dissipates any original normative fact that qualifies the system, here constituted power is materialized by the expansive capability to determine new systems; if, finally, in that tradition and in its apologists constitutionalism means political State opposing social State, here constituent power makes expansive sociality the only place of foundation of the political.

American constituent power constructs an ontology of the constitutive strength of the masses, in space. It does not found modernity but, rather, the actuality of constituent power. But on the other hand, constituent power in America is subjected to an extraordinary effort of containment and mystification. *The Federalist* is the chief document of this tendency. But it does not close the problem; rather, it exasperates it, it pushes it to the extreme. It is on the basis of this exasperation of constituent power that the American "exception" becomes typical. Notice: the three models that mark the genesis of the constitution (Hamilton's, Jefferson's, and Madison's mediation of the two) even in their difference constitute a fabric in which constituent power always presents itself with the newest capability of not being entrapped. The limitation of political participation prescribed by Hamilton, the republican multiplier imagined by Jefferson, and Madison's pluralism interact critically and in any case determine open situations of constitutional compromise.[64] In other words, we can say that for a long period the "material constitution" exceeds the formal constitution, that the constituent principle and its determination of freedom and originality manage each time to materialize and break through the constitutional wrapping. Paine's and Jefferson's natural right theory cannot enclose the positivity of its concept into the narrow dimension—pessimistic and positivistic—of the constitutional system. The juridical guarantees and the economic limits of freedom are, so to speak, always put under pressure, and this dynamism becomes the motor of formation, not of a self-centered and political constitution, but of an expansive and reformist society.[65] This is the theoretical legacy of the American vicissitudes. The unrecoverability of the strength of the constitutive event determines, since the beginning, synchronically, the crisis of the constitutional event, and it is this crisis that becomes the real American political paradigm. "The most perfect example of the modern State is North America," says Marx in "On the Jewish Question." We can add, because the extreme effort to produce the political emancipation of bourgeois society exasperates its contradiction: the event is returned to us as crisis.

In the history of constitutionalism and of the political theories of democracy, this crisis has always been felt, by the great and not by the apologists, as the fundamental element of the American constitutional event. And before Marx, by Tocqueville: "This whole book that is here offered to the public has been written under the influence of a kind of religious awe produced in the author's mind by the view of that irresistible revolution which has advanced for centuries in spite of every obstacle and which is still advancing in the midst of the ruins it has created": the revolution of equality, that is, the revolution of democracy. The last seven hundred years of European history are dominated by it, by this irreversible process.[66] The irreversibility is also irresistibility, the ontological deposit of a history traversed by struggles often qualified by contingency, but determining the destiny of societies. Thus, it is inside the material constitution that the analysis of formal constitutions must venture: "The democratic revolution has taken place in the body of society without that concomitant change in the laws, ideas, customs, and morals which was necessary to render such a revolution beneficial. Thus we have a democracy without anything to lessen its vices and bring out its natural advantages; and although we already perceive the evils it brings, we are ignorant of the benefits it may confer" (Tocqueville, 8).

Soon Tocqueville returns to this remark in the introduction to *Democracy in America*:

> *The social condition is commonly the result of circumstances, sometimes of laws, oftener still of these two causes united; but when once established, it may justly be considered as itself the source of almost all the laws, the usages, and the ideas which regulate the conduct of nations; whatever it does not produce it modifies. If we would become acquainted with the legislation and the manners of a nation, therefore, we must begin by the study of its social condition* [état social]. *(Book I, chap. 3: p. 46)*

What does this study of the *état social* in the epoch of democracy suggest to us? That any limit to freedom, any traditional counterpower against the movement of the masses is taken away. The tendency toward equality destroys the old freedoms; will it also destroy freedom *tout court*? Will it introduce tyranny? Hence America as a problem: "There is one country in the world in which this great social revolution seems almost to have reached its natural limits; it took place in a simple, easy fashion, or rather one might say that this country sees the results of the democratic revolution taking place among us, without experiencing revolution itself" (intro., 18). Hence American as tendency: "I confess that in America I saw more than America; I sought there the image of democracy, with its inclinations, its character, its prejudices, and its passions, in order to learn what we have to fear or to hope from its progress" (intro., 14).

By taking as his point of departure this very strong sense of the American democratic anticipation, Tocqueville expresses the most original and characteristic element of his analysis of the development of democracy: the American constitution is the constitution of a crisis that sees freedom turn into equality, and equality interrupt and reverse the tendency toward freedom. Tocqueville's genius lies in his going to the root of the problem, that is, in his concentrating on the fact of considering American freedom in Jeffersonian terms, and in understanding the inversion of tendency of this freedom in the crisis of the event. In Tocqueville there is no constitutional bigotry but, rather, the sensing of a tragedy that the democratic event carries within itself, as equally irresistible adventure and destiny. Tocqueville is certainly closer to Nietzsche or Burckhardt than to the religion of constitutionalism; his contemporary interpreters pretend not to see, or in any case they do not want to know! The study of a democratic nonrevolutionary society does not accentuate his liberal optimism but, rather, makes his historical and sociological pessimism stronger. In Tocqueville the revolution is not the notion of the democratic principle, but an acceleration of its destiny; democratic society is not only fragile, inert, and conformist, but it is for this very reason provided with an extraordinary potential toward despotism.[67]

To this effect it is enough to turn to those *Souvenirs* where, after analyzing the "society without fanatics," that boring and empty world that is Louis Philippe's France, Tocqueville reacts as if facing a necessary consequence when the Parisian workers take up arms in June 1848, and, astonished, considers the material consequences of what he had, nonetheless, painfully foreseen: the expansion and pervasiveness of revolutionary action, of its democratic, fierce impulse toward equality.[68] Thus the crisis of the event is implicit in its principle, so that the American nonrevolutionary democracy faces the crisis of the event not less but, rather, more typically than revolutionary democratic societies.

Let us see the way in which this reasoning unravels. Thus begins Tocqueville: "The great advantage of the Americans is that they have arrived at a state of democracy without having to endure a democratic revolution, and that they are born equal instead of becoming so" (*Democracy*, II.3:101). This originary dimension undoubtedly implies some consequences: "In democratic society the sensuality of the public has taken a moderate and tranquil course, to which all are bound to conform.... By these means a kind of virtuous materialism may ultimately be established in the world, which would not corrupt, but enervate, the soul and noiselessly unbend its springs of action" (II.11:132–33). But this situation, this well-being is "restless." A restfulness is maintained by the constitution, but those same means that the constitution deploys for the common good impress on society an egalitarian mobilization that leads toward opposite results.

At this point comes the analysis of the American constitution and its functioning. The approach has a freshness worthy of the "founding fathers." The genetic force of the constitution is recognized in the "new American relations," in the democracy stretched across the frontier, spontaneous and expansive. The bursting popular sovereignty, the guarantist machine of counterpowers—implanted in the judiciary as well as in the federal system—is powerful. Another effective counterpower is the press, a new and essential phenomenon, a sphere of freedom guaranteed by the immediacy of the information and of the possible protest. But this is not enough: the administrative decentralization, the spreading of the popular courts, the force of religions, widespread education and popular common sense, the Protestant ethic—all these constitute a strong and real support to democracy. Tocqueville's analysis, above all in Book I of *Democracy in America*, ranges across all social relations and illustrates with exceptional accents, worth of an extremely modern *Wissensoziologie*, the cultural determinations of democracy. The idea of progress; the American, more technical than learned; the spirit, and the moral foundations of industrial production; language and speech [*langue* and *parole*] in democratic regimes, and so on. Where the omnipotence of the democratic majority and the dominion of public opinion could have overflown and determined collective tyranny, here a system of socially founded and socially consolidated counterpowers traces a strong circle of guarantees, an unsurpassable limit (I:2–9).

Nonetheless, this formidable exercise in democracy secretes poisons. The more equality is affirmed, the more political indifference is generalized. The more the mobility of fortunes is exalted, the more virtues are banalized. The more money becomes the fundamental element in the qualification of the individual and in the stratification of society, the more democracy cracks. It is in this situation that the unresolved crisis of the founding act of American democracy (as of any other modern democracy) is revealed. In democracy, in front of the new powers that are born in society, it is always more difficult to identify new political counterpowers. The "simple" idea of one only central power becomes therefore an irresistible tendency:

> *Among [nations] all the idea of* intermediate powers *[between social bodies, between the law and the citizens] is weakened and obliterated; the idea of rights inherent in certain individuals is rapidly disappearing from the minds of men; the idea of the* omnipotence *and* sole authority *of society at large rises to fill its place. These ideas take root and spread in proportion as social conditions become more equal and men more alike. They are produced by equality, and in turn they hasten the progress of equality. (IV.2–5)*

The ideas of "the unity, the ubiquity, the omnipotence of the supreme [social] power" triumph anywhere, and "the notion . . . of government [as] a sole, simple, providential and creative power" arises. "The intermediate powers disappear." Here is the decadence of the spirit: "The love of public tranquillity is frequently the only [political] passion. . . . it becomes more active and powerful among them in proportion as all other passions drop and die." Not anarchy but democratic absolutism, not the unrestrainable development of the passions but a passive homogeneity of all—these are Tocqueville's Nietzschean forecasts (2:291, 293–94). An immense, protective, and paternal power stretches out "absolute, minute, regular, provident, and mild," over equal, similar, and powerless men. "A servitude of the regular, quiet and gentle kind," "a compromise between administrative despotism and the sovereignty of the people": horrible image of horrible slavery. Subjection, enervation of the passions. The freedom introduced in the political sphere is destroyed in the administrative sphere (4:318–19). The crisis of the democratic event implies therefore the inversion of the tendency.

Is it possible to stop this process? Is it possible to keep leading "an active political life within a well-balanced social body?" How can one reach an institutional compromise between freedom and equality, between constituent power and constituted power, a compromise that, if left open, necessarily leads to catastrophe? Tocqueville's paradox is that, while taking as his point of departure Jeffersonian premises, he seeks a Hamiltonian solution to the problem of democracy—a solution that goes toward the definition of a "new aristocracy" capable of blocking the ruinous development of individualism, of freedom, and of equality. It is a new aristocracy that, grafting itself in the midst of the social and institutional dynamics, manages to exercise a function of assemblage and mediation. Social associationism and its great American popularity can allow this solution, but will the extraordinary social development, the birth of new inequalities and new classes, allow its permanence and political effectivness? Very likely not. Then a new aristocracy must be sought and fixed on the political level. Here is its formula: we should "lay down extensive but distinct and settled limits to the action of the government;... confer certain rights on private persons, and... secure the undisputed enjoyment of those rights... enable individual man to maintain whatever independence, strength, and original power he still possesses" (IV.7:329). That which dominates the finale of *Democracy in America* is a desperate liberalism, as ineffective and slightly caricatural. In fact it is the sense of defeat and of the crisis of the event. This critical awareness, implanted in an optimistic and open phenomenology of democracy in America—this gives a sense to Tocqueville's discourse: not the mellifluous apologies of his sense of freedom or an illusory definition of his work as the masterpiece of a triumphant constitutionalism.

In our terminology we could then conclude, with regard to Tocqueville, that he makes the American constituent spirit and the American constitution incommensurable and irreconcilable. He colors the crisis in pessimistic terms and generalizes it as the background to the life of contemporary political institutions. At the same time, Tocqueville grasps the epochal importance of the new concept of constituent power that the American Revolution has expressed, and the crisis of the constitution of the Union, as machine that attempts to compose democracy within liberalism and its State. A fact remains to be taken into consideration: that that irresistible constituent power is an irresistible provocation to imbalance, restlessness, and historical ruptures. As for the solution, certainly it cannot be the one that Tocqueville sadly foresaw. If Americans are born free, if constituent power here operated in a pure form, it will not be a successor of the ancien regime, that more or less balanced aristocratic ideal, that can give meaning and measure to the succession of future institutional forms. Here, in the historical reality and in the succession of events, another pernicious and frightening annotation of Tocqueville's will be verified: "There is a secret connection between the military character and the character of democracies, which war brings to light" (III:278). Indeed, it is in war that the crisis of American constitutionalism first of all makes itself manifest. And we do not need to wait many years for this crisis to open in these forms: it happens during the first fifty years of existence of the constitution.

An extraordinary figure theorizes this crisis: John Caldwell Calhoun.[69] It is doubtful whether his thought is "a sort of intellectual Black Mass" as the democratic Richard Hofstadter claims, or whether Calhoun is "the Marx of the Master Class," as that fine analyst of the American South, Eugene Genovese, affirms.[70] For sure, Calhoun, operating from within the constitution, elaborates an economical and juridical interpretation of it, which brings him to affirm "the constitutional right of the States to interfere, in order to protect their reserved interests." The relationship between the Union and the States is radically questioned, as is questioned the relationship between constituent and constituted power. Calhoun is pushed to assume this position by the accumulation of unresolved questions that agitate the life of the United States, and, at the same time, he interprets the interest of the States of the South. First, he intervenes on the debate about the customs tariffs that favor the industrial States of the North and their protectionist politics, then on the problems of slavery and the frontier.

His ethical principle says that what is unjust for some is unjust for all. A system of tariffs favoring the protectionism of the North is therefore unjust for all, hence the development of his constitutional interpretation. As he tells us, the constitution does not represent the hypostatization of a general interest (or of a will), but the outcome of a complex of antagonistic interests: "In concrete . . . it composes the States in a community only in the measure of their common interests, and leaves to them their character as distinct and independent communities as far as the other interests are concerned, tracing with consumed skill the line of separation."[71]

A measure becomes unconstitutional when it violates the constitutive path originally agreed on by antagonistic interests. Consequently, a system of self-protection of autonomous interests is mobilized. The right of interpretation by the single States thus immediately configures itself as "right to resistance," a right to resistance that must in any case be interpreted as constitutional remedy to the violation of the originally constituted right, with a restorative function internal and not alternative to the system. The economic antagonism must be transferred into the constitutional controversy (how can we not remember Harrington?). Each State has the right to exercise the power of "nullification" (a power of annulment of federal acts that Jefferson had approved in the assemblies of Virginia and Kentucky before 1800), and this exercise cannot be confused with secession. Self-protection cannot put the State that exercises it in the situation of a State external to the Federation.

Even though only in the last instance, secession represents nonetheless an extension of the constitutional right to self-protection. Yet, on the other hand, the right of the majority to govern is not uniformly compatible with the maintenance of constitutional balances. We can in fact distinguish two types of majorities: the first is the absolute, or numerical majority; the second is the concurrent or constitutional majority: "Here the majority is not calculated with respect to the whole, but with respect to each class and to each community of which this is made, thus obtaining the autonomous consent of each interest, so that it is constituted with everybody's concourse."[72]

The difference between constituent and legislative powers lies in the fact that the former demands concurrent majorities, and the latter absolute majorities. The federal system therefore relies essentially on "the maintenance of the supremacy of the constitution over the legislative majority," on the prevalence, that is, of the original constitutional pact about the block of majority interests. Now, when for a series of reasons (the tariff-related politics, the politics of the frontier, the polemics against slavery) the relation of force at the basis of the constitutional pact changes, what happens? The destruction of the original constitutional balance legitimates secession as an extreme form of self-protection. In order to avoid this last consequence, the only chance is to make a compromise. If indeed the constitution is nothing but a set of compromises (even though hierarchically organized), the solution for a situation of radical unbalance cannot take place but through a comprehensive renegotiation of the entire structure of the agreement. Otherwise, there is the conflict, or at least, the emergence of a dilatory formula of the conflict itself.

No doubt the figure of constituent power emerging here takes up some fundamental and radical elements of the American revolutionary experience of the new democratic order. On the other hand, it presents itself as the resolute negation of the contractual element: consent is not a contract but a radical foundation. On our side, repeating Marx's adage, we cannot but add: sometimes it is useful to learn from the reactionaries!

However, thus object the federalists: "What is 'rigorous' about grounding the state in force and Providence after the fashion of Maistre, and then creating a set of constitutional gadgets that would have staggered even Sieyès? What is so 'consistent' about destroying Locke's state of nature and then evolving a theory of minority rights that actually brings one back there for good?"[73] The historical references here are dubious. In any case, things are more complicated. The interweaving (taking place in Calhoun) of a constitutionalism supported by an iron rationalism, and, on the other hand, the abandonment of the contractualist natural right theory of which the fathers of the constitution were drenched (a real parricide, what Calhoun perpetrates!)—this crossing, finally, is not only capable of contradiction: it can also produce a specific constitutional mechanism, in particular, a constitutional mechanism hinging on the prevalence of the constituent powers (the constitutive act) on the legislative powers, and at the same time the hierarchical distinction between the concurrent majority and the absolute majority.

When, through constitutent power, we organize a situation of sovereignty, says Calhoun the "reactionary," we are not renouncing constituent power. Constituent power is not alienable from constituted power. The constitution is a pact: but a pact among constituent interests is always a compromise of position that can become hostile once again. It is in the nature of the constituent compromise to unite opposites, not to annihilate them. Consequently, to give an example that can be easily shared by everybody, it is evident that the constitution cannot be modified through recourse to the simple arithmetic majority; to modify it, we need a majority capable of reconstituting the relationship with the fullness of constituent power, therefore an extremely qualified majority, or, better, unanimity. In any case, when there is not a majority of this type, the power of receding from the pact becomes, with this same condition, reactualized—because constituent power, inalienable as it is, appears to be at this point a negative power, the power of delimitation of agreement, the power of resistance.

Paradoxically, the fullness of constituent power (as well as the complex of its genetic determinations, from the right to resistance through the exercise of counterpower, up to the expression of fundamental rights) is defined in the dissolution of the pact: a negative power shows here its strength:

The normal function of constituent power remains however the preservation of the agreed upon pact by the means of the power of veto, which represents in turn the constitutional extreme of the continuum *of interposition-recession. Thus it is explained the apparent antinomy of a negative power that has an essentially conservative role: the constitutional role of sovereignty is not that of promoting unity, but that of keeping into balance diversity.*

The reference to the conservative function of constituent power also allows us to unmake the knot of the "internal" configuration of sovereignty. (Sundi, 33)

If things are such, how is an agreement possible? Why doesn't it crumble at any obstacle? Simply because, instead of deploying some automatisms, the interests find it reasonable to constitute themselves into majority on the ground of an economic calculation of affinity, composing a system of weights and counter-weights founded on more or less stable aggregations.

A strange reactionary, this Calhoun! In fact, against the entire reactionary tradition, he denies that agreements can take place on the basis of reference to an originary organic solidarity. There is nothing Romantic, nothing Burkean in him. On the contrary, it is always in the contradiction, always reopened between constituent interests and the necessity of self-preservation of the social body, that the constitution is formed and actualized. Is this constitutional conceptualization very different from that progressive one provided for the Charter of Pennsylvania, which claimed the permanent institutionalization of constituent power? Certainly not. Nor is it different from that of the *philosophes* who thought that a generation must not respect the constitutional decisions of the previous generation.

But this is not enough. Calhoun the reactionary opposes contractualism also on that central focal point that erases any revolutionary potentiality of the theories of the contract, and that consists of posing, in absolute terms, subjection as transcendence, that is, as a necessary result of the association. He breaks the teleological unity of the progression of contracts and thus liquidates, in the manner of radical rationalism, contractualism. He restores a radically appropriative point of view (in a Harringtonian sense), whereas the constitution, instead, had qualified in legal and, therefore, in bourgeois terms the *homo politicus* by reducing him to a *homo mercator*.

On this ground,

interest, in order to have a constitutional relevance, must possess the typical negative right, the right of veto, which represents the chief instrument of a preservation of the pact. As far as the system is concerned, it is the negative power therefore, that legitimates interest, and not vice versa, exactly as the constitution identifies the parts of the pact by measuring their contrast. Consequently there are no "sociological" determinations of interests and of their aggregates, whether classes or states: their identity is inferred from their conflictual interaction, from the entitlement of constituent power, "the power of preventing or arresting the action of the government . . . be it called by what term it may, —veto, interposition, nullification, check, or balance of power, —which, in fact, forms the constitution." (Surdi, 34)

The "political space," Hamiltonian or Madisonian, is put out of the game, but on the basis of the constitutive elements of the American constitutive process, on the hypothesis of the permanence of a founding political capability, which continually renews itself through conflictual integration: "The process of rationalizaton (of power) consists of the mechanism of the institutional compromise" (37). And this affirmation is taken to the extreme, in the sense that "the anticipation of the Civil War constitutes the only rational criterion not only of construction, but also of preservation of the constitutional order, since the same order finds its universal law and its close cause in conflict" (40). Only on conflict, on the continual competition of opposite interests, can order and right be founded. They are continually constructed in a process that is allowed by the entitlement of negative power from the side of the competing subjects: thus, once any possibility of reciprocal overpowering, of blocking the process, has been eliminated, order affirms itself, pushed toward ever new balances. There is no pact without sword. Negative power allows positive power to realize itself. Negative power is the condition of possibility of the constitution, understood as constituent procedure.

Truce, compromise, competition allow in this way the constitutional process. If there must be blueprints of the agreements, these will never be formal. If they present themselves as formal, linear, and self-generating, they are hypocritical and ineffectual. Disunion is at the basis of order. Any schema of agreement is material: constituent power is coextensive with the constitution because the latter is nothing but the sum of the effective acts expressed by the constituent powers and gathered in an attempt to compromise. The balance of the forces is not a form imprinted by power on social conflict, but the result of social conflicts. The truce of conflict is nothing but a moment of constitutional physiology. On the contrary, the continual expression of constituent strengths is organic (Surdi, 35). Anarchy and civil war can be avoided in this manner, and only in this configuration democracy is its antidote.

Constituent power has reappeared here in its originary form, but, it is objected, in the service of a slave order. Ridiculous and hypocritical objection. Wasn't the whole American constitution founded on the slave order? Wasn't it meant to hide and make disappear the problem itself?[74] And it will be exactly only a new constituent experience, in terms of counterpower, an experience, and a struggle paradoxically Calhounian, that will allow the African American people to conquer not their formal freedom, but the economic and political capability to sit among the peoples of the Federation. Constituent power appears again in its originary form, but at the cost of the breaking of the Union. The risk and the cost do not make the problem disappear: this is the problem of constituent power and its rising, as positive determination, from a negative essence, an essence of liberation—from that constituent power that cannot disavow its roots in the right of resistance and revolution.

From this point of view constituent power takes once again the shape of permanent revolution. It does not exclude the process of institutionalization; rather, it excludes its rigidity, and, on the contrary, it assumes as its enemy the impossibility to make institutional totality the objects of its critique. If constituent power wants to be grasped as concept, it must be grasped on this point: its irresistibility, the impossibility to restrain it. Liberalism plays with fire when it assumes the legitimacy of the constituent process; and yet it wants to enclose it, in more or less dynamic form, into the system of legality. By doing so, the constitution excluded constituent power, but only to repropose it properly and internally transfigured in the practice of the "implicit powers," and in its jurisdictional activity. But this meaningless and disempowered repetition does not avoid that: in front of the constitution constituent power reappears, as rampant and hostile strength.

How can we answer this challenge? Once again we have the three answers: Hamilton's, Jefferson's, and Madison's. We have already seen them in the functional positivity that, notwithstanding everything, they determine by interweaving with one another. That is, we said that, by intercrossing, Hamilton's sense of the state, the Jeffersonian multiplier, and Madison's pluralism make the critical distance between constituent power and the constitutional system a contradictory "open work," in which the crisis of the event can show itself as functional dynamics of the whole.[75] But here we want to see also how these positions may, each alone and all together, determine negative results, real inversions of the tendency. If Tocqueville sees the catastrophic destiny of democracy traverse also the American sociopolitical system, and if Calhoun sees in the war the only chance of revival of constituent power, no less negative are the consequences that, in the crisis of constituent power and its perverted political configuration, we can see by analyzing the thought of the founding fathers. In its various directions this thought pushes toward extreme absolutizations, which each time emerge as moments of perverted resistance against any emergence of constituent power.

That Hamiltonianism is part of the dialectical family of the theory of the State has been suspected for a long time, but only recently has it been perceived, through an intensive reading of Hegel and an extensive reading of Hamilton, how much Hamilton's conviction that the State is a machine for building civil society—a place of ordered transcendences of political empiricism, a work that reveals civil society as a complex of contracts, morality, family, religion, and ethics within the predominance of the law—is a Hegelian assumption.[76] This State form represents the perfection of civil society and historical development. The dialectic appears here as the key to the most adequate interpretation of liberal constitutionalism, which, not by chance, boils down to an apology for the State. The idea of freedom is embodied in the State and excludes any liberation. The fact that the key moment of identification between the State and civil society lies not in the mechanism of ordered reproduction of the two moments does not destroy Hegelianism but returns it to us in its most mature and refined figuration.[77] While the rights of freedom are integrated by the State, liberation and constituent power are for this very reason excluded from political life. From this follows a self-centered form of the State, an autonomous and independent configuration. How European this American State has become, even though it had been born from the *Declaration of Rights* of the *homo politicus* in the great spaces of the new continent!

A no less perverse destiny is that of Jeffersonian democraticism. Completely projected on the frontier and on the expansive concept of freedom, at the beginning it resounds with the great echoes of a continent to conquer. The initial history of Jeffersonianism is the history of the liberation of an enormous multitude of men and women, a hitherto unknown vicissitude of heroic appropriation of spaces. However, here the contradiction is also evident: it lies in the discovery of the finitude of that space that was thought to be infinite. Again, it lies in the fact that the appropriation takes place in terms of freedom and not of liberation. The contradiction reveals itself in the fact that here the constituent principle in its movement has become exhausted, changing from appropriation of property to spirit of conquest and imperialism. Let's not cry over the Indians, whose civilization and savage independence are sacrificed to freedom. In this we see only the symptom of a more universal heteronomy of effects, the symptom of a revolution blocked in its concept, of a process of liberation that becomes process of destruction, of a principle of freedom that becomes principle of oppression.

Max Weber has well described the processes of "heterogenesis of ends," posing them, in his explicative sociology of political history, as one of the strongest critical points against any philosophy of history.[78] Here we are in front of one of the clearest demonstrations of the reversed teleology of historical concepts. In fact, here constituent power is not denied but degraded in a development that denies its genesis. The imperial configuration of the American constitution is born from a radical reversal of paradigms, which, unknowingly, develops within the abstract redundance of the principle of freedom and of possessive individualism—a reversal of paradigms that totally invests the meaning of the American constitution, definitely detaching it from its universal and revolutionary origins, that is, from the constituent power that had created it.

Nor is the outcome of the third constitutional variant, Madison's pluralistic one, more felicitous. In it constituent power is reduced to a simple figure of society: it has political value only insofar as it is identified with the problems of national integration, and, simultaneously, with those of social exchange/renewal. This pluralism runs as a line through the history of the constitution of American space into the continental State and characterizes many of its most specific and curious figures.[79] But with what effects? It is fenced in, in the social—certainly a social interpreted as different and consistent, as plural and active, but not less discriminated and separated from the political. The beautiful unity of the constitution is thus as if divided into two: on the one hand social pluralism, on the other unity and autonomy of the political, its independent continuity and autocentrality, its discriminatory inertia and integrationist repetition. American society can thus reproduce itself through integration and social exchange/renewal only insofar as it will continually determine new discriminations and social hierarchies—and temporal exclusions, effective and painful, up to the limit of simple and mere racial exclusion.

The three variants of the crisis of the constituent event, therefore, represent per se three negative results, and in any case three figures of only one inversion of tendency, opened by the American Revolution, and implicit in the originary meaning of the constituent power here expressed. Yet the latter was essentially a concept imitating, in a spatially expansive dimension, the Machiavellian concept of constituent power. Besides the Machiavellian radicalness, it contained equality as its founding principle. In the process of constitutionalization, the American constituent principle is defeated, it is condemned to regression. Its space is broken; universality is taken away from it; in the multitude a bitter destiny of loneliness and strict individuality is assigned to the subject. Constitutional America is no longer an ideal: it is the symbol of a circumscribed project, failed, impossible to realize. The constitution is a machine that, to avoid intestine war, each time chooses the cult of the State, imperialism, social division, or exploitation as alternatives of reproduction, all equally fierce and interchangeable.

Yet the constituent power that the revolution and the *Declaration of the Rights of Man* had lived is the most radical thing that popular modern history has experienced. We can never forget that. This idea of constituent power had reached an intensity that only a little Dutch Jew had imagined, in the greatest political metaphysics of modernity. A freedom born from appropriation, a freedom that spread throughout the multitude, that potentially spread into equality.[80]

Individuals maintained their individual singularity, and, further, the more they entered into the community the more this increased. The more society became political society, the more ethical optimism was the correlative of the positivity of the social. The common destiny was built on the joy of the expression of freedom, and appropriation was the form of the expansion of society. The Spinozian character of American freedom is a universal constituent principle; it is the preventive philosophical declaration of an irresistible constituent freedom. Neither Locke nor Hume, who perhaps are behind the variants of the constitution and of its more or less repressive interpretation, are at the basis of the American constituent principle. The secret thread that constitutes it is that which shapes Spinoza's political metaphysics, a thread that constitutes itself in the Protestant sectarian movement, as reform of the Renaissance, running through the glorious adventure of all the libertarian minorities, emerging from the dramatic crisis of the Renaissance.

The frontier of freedom, the collective possibility of strength, the sense of appropriation as the expression of singularity, and the figure of living labor—these are the irresistible contents of American constituent power. Its perversions, the betrayals suffered, the constitutional bloc, the deviant interpretations do not suppress it but launch it once again. Now, in the United States the radical rupture (which successively became inert) of the constituent spirit with the constitution is marked by an originary fact: the preservation of slavery and the question of African Americans in general.[81] This colored rupture is also a conceptual rupture of the universality of the concept of freedom and equality. It is not by chance that any great American constitutional crisis is therefore marked by a revival of the constituent spirit of the African American people, from the Civil War all the way to the sixties. Thus, by traversing and violating constitutions and political apparatuses, the constituent principle always continues to live. It presents itself as the scandal of freedom, and, at the same time, as the only solution to its crisis. On these bases, having gone through such a long history and such enormous perversions, having maintained the capability of newly nourishing its desire, American constituent power is still alive. Probably the next American revolution will not stop halfway through.

FIVE

The Revolution and the Constitution of Labor

Rousseau's Enigma and the Time of the Sansculottes

THERE IS something that not even the most reactionary, the most regressive and continuistic interpretations can erase in the French Revolution understood as event: its temporality. I mean its temporal progress, its temporal rhythm, the dimension of the "mutation" that—either real or imaginary—remains nonetheless the most essential determination of its movement. The French Revolution has an unerasable temporality; all its course is a succession of events; its quality—both for its supporters and its enemies—is temporal. The term *temporal* is a concern for its protagonists as much as for its adversaries: it is a concern with constituent time, against the ancien regime or against the "new order"; it is a concern with "beginning" or "ending" the revolution, or about both things, one within the other, both in any case within time. Twenty years of research, in social and cultural history, centered on the "long duration" of the eighteenth century (or on the immemorable continuity of the French national institution), have not succeeded in erasing the "short duration" of the revolutionary episodes, their radically innovative intensity in their interweaving and in their dramatic concatenation.[1]

The Machiavellian notion of constituent power reappears, in its essential temporality, precisely in the country where Machiavelli had always been a stranger, an enemy, or a doctrinal pretext:[2] on the contrary, here he reproposes a notion of the absolute foundation, that is, a radical transformation of the time of the constitution. After the revolution, writes Tocqueville, "the past has ceased to throw its light upon the future, and the mind of man wanders in obscurity."[3] A true and desperate exclamation, but the revolutionary would have seen, in this darkness, the light of reason and the creativity of action. The revolutionary would have praised this absence of memory. "Our legacy is not preceded by any testament,"[4] but the challenge of the new temporality was born exactly from this negation of the past. This Machiavellian time of mutation, of the event and the foundation, can be qualified in the most different ways, but it remains there, to mark the beginning of the contemporary form of constituent power.

So much so that this reapparition of Machiavellian time is modified by a fundamental element: the revolution is the time of the masses. It is the time of the multitudes, of the Parisian revolutionary crowds, of mass mobilization, of the sansculottes.[5] It is neither the collective mentality nor the naturalistic determinations of gregarious behavior that explain the revolutionary crowds: it is the time of the revolutionary process, woven through by needs and utopias, by interests and discourses, by the will to power, and by a political dynamic.[6] The time of the revolution is the time of the Parisian people, of its poverty and its imagination, the time of the sansculottes.[7] On this temporal reality history ends and begins once again, the obsession of time penetrates passions and reasonings, occupies spaces, and provokes dynamics. The time of the revolution is an absolute, the Machiavellian absolute of a will to power that builds itself up in the origin.

After Machiavelli the concept of constituent power developed in terms of space, as counterpower in Harrington's theory and in the practice of the English revolutionaries, and as frontier of freedom in the new American world. In the French Revolution it reconquers the terrain of temporality, a terrain already reconstructed as public space, therefore a temporal territory of the masses. Constituent power spells its absoluteness as a principle by developing temporally, by expressing a strength that crumbles and spills into temporality. But this temporality is already spatial: in its assault on constituted power is expressed the revolt against production, against the spatial determinations of the slavery of labor. The masses cannot but express this unity of project. Today it has become banal to denounce the Marxist assimilation of the times of the French Revolution in a general model of the revolution:[8] this just criticism, however, does not make less true the density of the specific temporality of the revolution, of the movement of the masses, of their reaction in the political and in the social. It is an implacable temporality that, even though there is nothing teleological about it, yet proceeds in an unarrestable concatenation of resistance and attack, on the political and the social, toward the target of a deeper and deeper democratization. These are a time and a space that manifest themselves as the abyss of democracy. But the abyss of democracy is the very definition of constituent power. And it is so because constituent power is a material essence that implants and renews itself in the totality of the political and of the social equally—at least here, where it begins to be expressed in its mature form.

First, the counterrevolutionaries, then the moderates, finally the extremist and utopian minorities all sense this. From the conquest of the Bastille to the days of Germinal, in the entire revolutionary trajectory of the masses, temporality has as its target the entire, absolute realization, in the political as in the social, of the democratic process. The masses consider democracy as an absolute, political and social, and constituent power as an absolute procedure, in the political and in the social. The qualitative leap from the political to the social, of the social into the political, is a change to which the masses, necessarily, operating in time, subject the constituent principle through a radical practice. In exercising constituent power and in constructing democracy, the masses begin to express the entirety of their experience of criticism of society. In this political production they situate their political and social program of liberation. When constituent power is reborn in France, it carries with and impregnates with its specific temporality, the entirety of the social dimensions of the principle, by now constituted in its modern form.

In the eyes of the bourgeoisie the principle has thus degenerated. Here are the new barbarians at work! When Mallet du Pan, "alone," as Bronislaw Baczko tells us,[9] senses this unknown character, this unheard-of novelty of the revolution gathers all the Estates, and, above all, the politicians, to stop this attack on civilization, this movement that, by proceeding, reveals itself as "other."[10] In 1790 Mallet du Pan is the only one to feel this challenge; after some years, at the beginning of the Thermidore, in the days of the 12 Germinal and of the First Prairial of the Year III, it is the entire Convention that sees this challenge in terroristic and destructive terms.[11] "Bread and the constitution of 1793," ask the insurgents: social criticism and democratic constitution have definitively joined. The Barbarians are back, the Thermidore reacts.

"The people," writes Quinet, "appeared more frightening than at any other period of the Revolution. They frightened their own friends. This moment was the worst." Michelet talks of "a terrible drunkenness, a strange thirst for blood" and cites, approvingly, Carnot's words: "It is the only day that the people appeared to me to be ferocious."[12] Here the always ambiguous judgment on the Parisian crowds changes itself remarkably: the bourgeois observers and the historians begin to express their class hatred.

The French Revolution, which had been a radical expression of democratic constituent power, at this point has become a different revolution. As its temporality will be enclosed in the new Thermidorian order, so will it try to break through the cage and turn into a movement of proletarian, social liberation. It is difficult to interpret the French Revolution from the point of view of the struggle among classes, but it is certain that the French Revolution, while taking place, gives shape to the new political subjects of class struggle: the bourgeoisie and the proletariat.[13] Not its origin, but its result is the class struggle.

Where was this potentiality hidden? Is it perhaps from the development of constituent power that it emerges and affirms itself? Everything seems to demonstrate this hypothesis. The French revolution is a path within which, through a specific temporality, the revolt against the ancien regime begins to indicate, little by little, and then fully reveal, the proletarian struggle against labor. The temporality of mass behaviors, their progression, leads toward and insists on the aggressive quality of a new founding content, and on a new alternative—labor or its critique, the bourgeois organization of its emancipation, or the proletarian liberation of labor. The universality of the constituent principle becomes critical materiality, concrete universality of labor or against labor. Time is a fabric on which this concretization runs.

It is not difficult to see this transformation, or, better, this translation, of the radicality of the constituent principle into the social, following the order of ideological representations: it is enough to look at the way the masses use political Rousseauism. The diffusion of Rousseau's thought, the fate of his works, the far-reaching and subtle forms of this diffusion have been widely studied.[14] But what is important to underline here is how, in the time of the revolution, the "vague Rousseauism" of the beginnings becomes sharper, how the ideology of constituent power and of the popular sovereignty contained in the concept of "general will" becomes a subversive practice and leads the vindication of a democratic society to implant itself within the critique of society.[15] Now, it is the concept itself of "general will"—that is, the foundation of constituent power as democratic principle—that is assumed by the popular masses and brought to a crisis at the same time.

While for the bourgeoisie "general will" is the abstract foundation of sovereignty, generically indicating the people as the subject of power, for the sansculottes sovereignty, in its historical concreteness, resides directly in the people, not as a principle but as a practice. In the Year II of the revolution, the transformation of the principle from abstract to concrete is practically brought to completion: popular sovereignty assumes an "unprescribable, inalienable, undelegable" character.

The *Declaration of the Rights of Man of 1793* acknowledges the right to insurrection as extreme application of the inalienability of popular sovereignty—a subjective public right—and the people take this right literally, as individuals and as mass. The interpretive clash takes place within the political debate and in the life of the movement. The whole political class (in this case the Girondins and Montagnards can be put one next to the other) affirms that sovereignty, if it belongs to the people, belongs to it insofar as the people is one and indivisible, "a purely metaphysical being, that is the expression of the general will." On the contrary, "for the Sansculottes the sovereign has nothing metaphysical, it was made of flesh and blood, it was the people that itself exercised its own rights in the assemblies of its sections."[16] Title and exercise of sovereignty: the old scholastic separation was taken up once again by the politicians, and negated by the populists. But what was the meaning of this separation and this claim to the direct exercise of sovereignty if not the expression of the absolute character of constituent power? What else but the wish that constituent power was temporarily connected to the existence and the continuity of popular movements and to their capability of political expression? Rousseau's ambiguity is demystified, popular sovereignty is constrained in the thematic and in the practice of the exercise of power, not only in counterpower, but in the universality of its radiating. The rupture could not be, as the bourgeois and the politicians say, "more furious."[17]

But this rupture does not imply yet the preeminence of the thematic of labor, neither in the sense that its bourgeois oganization must be conceived as the key of political society, nor in the opposite sense, that is, that political society must intervene to modify the antagonism of the social organization of work. What does this deepening of the critique produce? The answer is: this rupture on the terrain of labor is operated by the same development of the constituent power of the masses, as far as it refuses to be transformed into constituted power; on the contrary, it wants to continue to exist as constituent power, as the exercise of this power. Here the temporality of constituent power reveals itself as fundamental. As exercise of power, little by little it uncovers and measures itself with the project of the adversary: that of codifying in abstract form the overcoming of a constitutional order inadequate to support the development of the bourgeoisie, that of destroying the ancien regime, and of fixing constitutionally the social organization of labor.

Here the constituent power of the masses encounters the time of the bourgeoisie—that is, the organization of the time of the working day—as its obstacle. It is on this point, that the productivity of power, its economic organization, and its social power manifest themselves, for one and the other, for the bourgeoisie and the proletariat—because both rely on this awareness of temporality (during the revolution and the further the conflict goes) to build up antagonistic class consciousness.[18] Thus time confronts the Parisian masses as limit. Time is finite. Time must be that of the repetition of the working day. It is this obstacle of time that, on the contrary, increases the consciousness of the masses: it leads them from politics to society, from the critique of power to the critique of labor. The masses respond to the obstacle of time with sudden and formidable accelerations, accelerations that each time reach beyond the obstacle and push the limit forward. The rupture of time touches and covers more and more the social space: it breaks it and tries to invert it. Situated in temporality these accelerations of the revolutionary movement of the masses reveal the will to rupture of social time, of working time.

The sociality of the constituent power of the masses in the French Revolution and the critique of labor that through this process presents itself as a central element in contemporary history descend from lived temporality, from *Erlebnis* and the taste for the direct exercise of constituent power. It is not in the contents of the bourgeois revolution, nor through their radicalization, that the self-making of the proletariat reveals and realizes itself: rather, it is through the concrete, practical, and continual exercise of constituent power. Hunger, pain, desire, movement, struggles all organize the discovery of the critique of labor.[19] Through the acceleration of revolutionary time is formulated the idea of time as strength—of a time that is "other." Of a time as strength, that is, the discovery of a political space defined by the entitlement to and by the exercise of sovereign power. Of an "other" time, that is, the discovery of a social space traversed by strength, and by this ordered and configured according to the instances of liberation. The time of the sansculottes subverts the concept of political space because it defines it not as space of representation, but as the place of the mass exercise of power; not as constituted and fixed space, but as continuous space of constituent power. In the continuity of constituent power, and in its name, social space superimposes political space. The novelty that the French Revolution introduces in the theory of constituent power consists in the practical reappropriation of its temporality, a temporality that breaks any intermittence and/or separation of the political, and therefore that introduces constituent power into the terrain of society and its organization: it poses constituent power as principle of the critique of labor.[20]

Once again here we are face to face with Rousseau. Indeed, the critique of labor initially presents itself in the form of the vindication of equality.

But what is Rousseauean equality? It is first of all a declaration of political equality that hints at the desirability of social equality, presupposing it in some way, and therefore disembodying social equality, and turning it into an ideal question, in any case detemporalized. Faithfully, on this basis, the bourgeoisie seeks and finds in Rousseau the foundations of its juridical construction. By what strange paradox, on the contrary, can Rousseau's notion of equality, at the same time, become element of a mass movement whose fundamental characteristic is that of transforming the claim to formal equality into a question of social equality? How can the temporality of constituent power include this substantial modification of the revolutionary objectives in its movement?

If we consider Rousseau's thought itself, the paradox of the interpretations threatens to produce a theoretical enigma. But we should not be afraid. In fact, the mass revolutionary movement patiently digs into the Rousseauean concepts, transforming their reception into hermeneutical innovation, and their use into new projects. This effort turns around three concepts: that of constituent power, that of representation, and that, rather ambiguous, of the division of powers on the side of Rousseau. Let's introduce ourselves to the mass reading of Rousseau through the last of these concepts.

When in Book III of *The Social Contract* Rousseau distinguished the legislative from the executive power, he makes a purely terminological distinction, which derives from Montesquieu and Locke.[21] Rousseau says that the first is will and the second is force. In fact, for Rousseau nothing exists but sovereignty and government.[22] Sovereign power is something absolutely superior to the distinction between the two powers. Sovereignty is certainly the exercise of legislative power, but only because the latter is comprehended in the totality of sovereignty, in the dimension of general will. If we immediately want to talk of sovereign power in general, in Rousseau it is defined as "exercise of the force to impose a will, an executive constitution of the legislation"; as for constituent power, in a first approximation, it is nothing but an exclusive sovereign power, in the shape of a continuous temporality. With this said, we can move further into the analysis of the unity of the two powers: it can be positive or negative. It is positive when the legislative dominates the executive, negative when the legislative becomes subjected to the executive. The negativity of this second situation is so heavy that it can lead to the breaking of the social pact itself (*Social Contract*, III.10:137–39). Thus we must avoid the supremacy of the executive over the legislative. The weakness of the latter with respect to the first depends on the fact that the executive has the force and possesses permanence in the continuity of the exercise of power. Instead, legislative power does not possess directly force and has only intermittently the capability of expressing itself. We must therefore impose the supremacy of the legislative through adequate constitutional instruments—which is to say, through a permanent exercise of it, or, better, through a permanent exercise of constituent power. Rousseau affirms the people's right to change its legislation and also its constitution because there is "no obligatory fundamental law for the body of the people, even if it were the social contract."[23] "Whatever the circumstances," he adds, "a people is always free to change its laws, even the best ones" (II.7:109; II.12.:117). The two powers are reunited in the legislative; the legislative is always constituent power. Finally, the continuity of constituent power passes through the reappropriation of representation: "The moment the people is legitimately assembled as a sovereign body, all jurisdiction of the government ceases, the executive power is suspended, and the person of the humblest citizen is as sacred and inviolable as that of the foremost magistrate, because wherever a represented person is found, there is no longer any representative" (III.14:142).

We can well understand how this ideological body could be deployed by the masses, in a strong and active manner, in the development of the revolutionary process. But this does not solve all the enigmas. Indeed, everything stands, notwithstanding Rousseau's contradictions, on the "general will." This last concept, in the same measure as it allowed that construction of constituent power that we have seen, denied it. General will was in fact an ancient concept, shaped outside of temporality, even defined in opposition to temporality. Its abstract nature was ineluctable. As long as constituent power was put under the tutelage of the general will, it remained prisoner of an atemporal essence. Again Rousseau's paradox: the paradox of a thought that nourishes an immediate and radical notion of constituent power, only insofar as it simultaneously affirms the omnipotence of an abstract sovereign power. This paradox becomes unsustainable above all when the temporality of constituent power becomes key in transferring the concepts of freedom and equality from the political to the social. How can, let's ask this again, an abstract and generalizing thought, a metaphysical hypostasis (such as the general will) be made actual and be so radically transformed by a mass political practice that wants to establish real equality socially as well as politically?

On the other hand, this paradox does not concern only Rousseau. It characterizes the entire relation of the progressive philosophy of the Enlightenment with the revolution, with the temporality of constituent power that the latter practices. Diderot, under the heading "Droit naturel" of the *Encyclopedie*, had amply demonstrated this: "The particular wills are suspicious, they can be either good or bad, but the general will is always good: it has never deceived, it will never deceive."

The general will is "a pure act of the intellect that reasons, in the silence of the passions, upon what man can demand of his fellow man, and upon what this fellow man has the right of demanding from him."[24] Pure act of the intellect: here is that general will that constitutes, within an uninterrupted continuity, the content of modern sovereignty, that is, the concept of an indirect and transcendental mediation that subtracts itself to the singular determinations of existence. From the Renaissance natural right theorists to the philosophers of the Counter-Reformation, and then from the Jacobins to the Girondin Kant, and to the foundation of contemporary constitutional public law, this metaphysical transformation of the constitutive action of the masses constitutes an indestructible paradigm.[25]

This is the other aspect of the solution of Rousseau's enigma, and it represents its bourgeois side. An often despotic solution, as the morbid and astute intelligence of Benjamin Constant could quickly underline: "The advocates of despotism can draw an immense advantage from Rousseau's principles. I know one who, like Rousseau, having supposed that an unlimited authority resides in the society in its entirety, supposes then that this authority is conferred upon a representative of this society, upon a man that he defines as the species personified, the whole individualized."[26]

But let's go back to our question, to Rousseau's paradoxical relation to the masses. The enigma becomes bigger if we touch on another aspect of Rousseau's thought and influence, his proto-Romantic insistence on the spontaneity of consciousness. Of this spontaneity of consciousness we find examples in the *Nouvelle Heloise*, anytime the characters manage to avoid prejudices and errors; obviously in *Emile*; in that apology of conscience that constitutes the end (and the aim) of *La Profession de foi du Vicaire savoyard*; but we find its application also in *The Social Contract*, not only in the doctrine of the sovereign which "by virtue of its special nature, . . . is always everything that it should be" (I.7:94), but also in the theory of the general will, which is "always in the right" and which always "remains as the sum of the differences" (II.3:100–101). And Julie sums up its spirit by describing its real virtue thus: "Be what you are" (*Nouvelle*, IV.12, in *Rousseau's Political Writings*).[27]

What happens at this point? It happens that the already complex dialectic of general will and direct representation is connected to, and fuses with, a phenomenology of spontaneity that is entirely individualistic. It is thus that the transcendental solution of the general will finds a way to triumph in the struggle over the interpretation of Rousseau: so that the individual logical statute is affirmed as the premise of the constitution of the "formal" general will, and thus it can present itself as its basis in terms of juridical normativity.

The spontaneity of consciousness is the pre-Romantic sensibility of individual consciousness: its substance is contained in individuality. The individual cannot express himself beyond the individual, except by jumping (and it would be a fatal somersault) toward the general will and its absolute abstraction. Another paradox. Exactly this proto-Romantic infusion of sensibility and passion into the theoretical whole seemed to demonstrate Rousseau's capacity to apprehend the thick temporality of the rhythm of historicity and of politics. Well, this new passionality is secured away inside the individual, is crushed within him. The general will will become a transcendental dislocation of the will of more and more divided singularities. The temporality of individual consciousnesses—and their spontaneity—moves now in the opposite direction from the constitutive temporality of the revolutionary masses. In Rousseau the political is structured as alienation. Not differently from what happened in Hobbes. But all this happens ambiguously, and within an unresolvable play of contradictory elements. In any case, the social equality that the political equality in the constitution of the general will seemed to presuppose is here destroyed: the ultimate actors remain the individuals.

Is, therefore, the mass attempt to use Rousseau in the course of the revolution a muddle, a colossal quid pro quo? Perhaps. In any case, a theoretical enigma. And an enigma that can only have a practical solution. That is what happens.

Rousseau is assumed by the masses because his concept of constituent power, if isolated from his theory, practically allowed (in fact, demanded) to take a stance against any constitutional line that made of social inequality an essential element in the organization of the State. And since social inequality is represented, in the Gothic tradition, by the principle of the separation of powers, here Rousseau is assumed as the constitutional inspirator of the opposition to Montesquieu, in whose thought could justly be recognized "a feudal enemy of despotism."[28] The separation of powers is social inequality; it is the society of the ancien regime that opposes the social and political unity of the revolutionary constituent power.[29] Through a practical decision that derives from the polemic and the struggle, Rousseau becomes thus, without actually being it, the constitutional theoretical means of passage from social inequality to political inequality, the continental fixer of the Gothic theory of the division of the classes in the separation of powers.[30] "It is necessary from the very nature of things," Montesquieu wrote, "that power should be a check to power."

But what power? What "nature of things"? Montesquieu's historical positivism was so deep to allow him to see as natural social divisions, and as organically sympathetic, à la Menenio Agrippa, the powers that they expressed. If the constitutional thought of the bourgeoisie will adapt to this (*Declaration* of 1789, sect. XVI: "Any society in which the guarantee of Rights is not assured, nor the separation of Powers determined, has no constitution"), democratic constituent thought radically excludes it.[31] Here is thus a motif of Rousseau's apology in the course of the revolution. A fundamental motif in which the translation from political to social equality is entirely implicit. Therefore, Rousseauism is a lexical form and a perspectival image in which the mass movement finds an opportunity to advance its project. To be faithful to the theory does not matter much; what matters is to find in it the polemical stimuli that allow the fundamental moves forward.

Will we now wonder at Benjamin Constant's judgment on Rousseau and on the despotic potentialities of his thought? Certainly not, insofar as, well knowing Constant's liberalism,[32] we will recognize that even his decision is practical, and that his judgment of Rousseau is modeled on that which he gives of the free movement of the revolutionary masses. Constant understands, and opposes, the fact that Rousseau's thought is traversed by the peremptory temporality of the masses, by their capability to destroy not only political but also social despotism; by the necessity, running through and ripening in this movement, to shift from the critique of politics to that of society, from the critique of labor to the perspective of liberation. The temporality of the revolutionary movement is posed between these terms: political equality versus social inequality, social equality versus political inequality. Rousseau becomes the practical means of this dynamic, from the critique of the political to the critique of society, and from this to the critique of labor.

With equal and contrary strength, the bourgeoisie will see, in this passage of the revolution, the necessity to concentrate on the codification of labor, on the terroristic isolation of its critique, and on the dislocation of the theme of the organization of labor outside any democratic implication. In this passage, and from this opposed and extreme point of view, Rousseau becomes the exclusive supporter of general will. An abstraction of society that becomes sovereign body, the reduction of the multitude to the one: to the one of power against and above the multitudes of strengths. The way that German Idealism, from Kant to Hegel, will refer to and take up again this Rousseau[33] represents the consciousness developed by the necessity to take away from the masses the use of his thought, and, on the contrary, to foreground the ideological content of general will, its abstraction and the capacity of manipulation to which the content was open. Is this a contrivance, an abominable falsification? We cannot tell: rather, we are once again confronted by Rousseau's ambiguity, by the impossibility of solving theoretically the enigma, and therefore by the practical decision to decide, in an interested and unilateral manner, the meaning of his thought. General will becomes thus the will of the nation, not democracy, but the nation or the republic becomes the paradigm of the new order. And constituent power, as well as its incompressible temporality, its impetuous sliding toward the totality of freedom, social and political, will become removed—that is, a product of constituted power.

As in the American Revolution, also in the French the *Declaration of the Rights of Man* is fundamental. But in the French Revolution we have the advantage of having not one but several declarations, and possessing a series of projects that, far from being concluded in the declaration of 1789, prolong themselves and make felt the presence of a very hard struggle going on until the declarations of 1793 and 1795, of that of the Jacobins and that of the Thermidore: a subterranean spring that feeds different sources.[34] The analogies, the identities, and the diversities of the declarations will be extremely important for understanding how, in time, the democratic radicalism of constituent power manages to become stronger, and to measure up more and more intensely to the opposite power, that of the bourgeoisie, expressed in more or less liberal forms; and it will be important for understanding how for both the theme of equality—of its affirmation or its critique—becomes more and more central.

Now, if we begin to analyze the three declarations, it seems important, first of all, to clarify the similarities in their organization. The first similarity is formal, in the sense that the representatives in the declaration of 1789, or the people in the other two, proclaim in the charter of rights a set of general rules that determine social life and its constitutionalization. What is the value of these rules, from the formal point of view? The discussions about this point, both from the logical point of view,[35] and on the historical[36] and constitutional terrains,[37] are still open. We are not interested in going through them once again. It is enough to notice the essentiality of the constituent reference. In all three the declarations, the formulated propositions, more than representing the schema of a constitutional schema, constitute the skeleton of constituent power. This is true both in the declaration of 1789, where the constituent subject unravels the plot of his design with "a beautiful soul," and in that of 1793, where the constituent subject is defined in an antagonistic relation with the enemy, and in that of 1795, where the stress is posed on the intrinsic relation between the law and the duty of the citizens.

In each declaration the fundamental problem is thus that of the production of the constituent subject. The "formal" constituent is subjected to an operation of singularization, of political concretization. It is here that, as we were stressing before, the enigma, or, if you want, the muddle of Rousseauism, is first tested. The constituent subject, within the process itself of its production, finds, opposed to his own formativity, the stability of a natural right code, overdetermined by the presumption of general will. It is easy to notice that here, in this way, a bourgeois content superimposes itself on the constituent form. In each of the declarations the principles of freedom, security, and property are affirmed in a homogeneous manner; and yet in each declaration the general will is the new formal into which constituent power is translated, expropriated of its mass radicality and exposed as mere foundation of individual rights.

1789, sect. II: "The aim of all political associations is the conservation of the natural and imprescriptible rights of man. These rights are liberty, property, security and resistance to oppression." 1793, sect. II: "These rights are equality, liberty, security, property." 1795, sect. I: "The Rights of Man in society are liberty, security, property."

These declarations deal with the formulation of the fundamental rights. Their overdetermination through the general will, however, is another matter and here again we find the deepest resemblance.

1789, sect. VI: "The law is the expression of the general will. All citizens have the right to take part in person or through their representatives in its formulation. It must be the same for all, whether it protects or whether it punishes. All citizens being equal in the eyes of the law are equally eligible to all honors, offices and public employments, according to their abilities and without other distinction than that of their virtues and talents." 1793, sect. IV: "The law is the free and solemn expression of the general will; it can ordain only what is just and useful in society; it can forbid only what is harmful to society." 1795, sect. VI: "The law is the general will, expressed by the majority of the citizens or of their representatives."

But it is not in any case sufficient to stop at the foregrounding of this muddled web of definitions. In fact, starting from these similarities, and perhaps thanks to the muddle that they constitute, the differences among the declarations unravel—differences that take us immediately back to the themes that qualify constituent power in the French Revolution. These differences touch on two problems: that of equality and that of the qualification of the subject, both in reference to the definition of constituent power. The first group of differences concerns therefore the articulation of the right to freedom and that of society, that is, the content itself of the general will. It directly takes us to the theme of equality, that is, to the paradox of political equality, to which social equality can more or less succeed. On this terrain the declarations more or less articulate first of all the definition of equality. In 1789 the concept has not yet become problematic, so that, with Rousseauean naïveté the section proclaims: "Men are born, and remain, free and equal before the law. Social distinctions can be founded only on public utility." In 1793, the generic affirmation "All men are equal by nature and before the law" (sect. III) follows a series of operative norms (sect. V): "All citizens are equally eligible public employments. Free peoples know no other causes for preference in their elections than virtues and talents"; sect. XVIII: "Every man can hire out his services and his time; but he cannot sell himself nor be sold; his person is not an alienable property. The law recognizes no domestic service, but only an agreement of care and recognition between the man who works and the man who employs him"; sect. XXI: "Public assistance is a sacred debt. Society owes subsistence to unfortunate citizens, whether in procuring work for them, or in assuring the means of existing to those beyond the ability to work"; sect. XXIII: "The social guarantee consists in the action of all to assure to each one the enjoyment and conservation of his rights; this guarantee rests on the national sovereignty"; sect. XXIX: "Each citizen has an equal right to take part in the formulation of the law and in the nomination of his proxies or his agents"; sect. XXX: "Public posts are essentially temporary; they can be considered neither as distinctions nor as rewards, but as duties." Thus, a series of operative norms that break with Rousseau's ambiguity and proceed on the path of the concrete determination of social equality.

The political space becomes social space; constituent power identifies social space as the direct terrain of its operativity. The concept of the political is entirely embedded on the social terrain. 1793, sect. XXXIX: "There is oppression of the social body whenever a single one of its members is oppressed. There is oppression of each member whenever the social body is oppressed." Equality is not an abstract concept but a terrain to cross. The transcendental concept of general will is reversed, and constituent power poses itself as social strength. The right of society completes and improves the right to freedom. If a man is oppressed, if he suffers, there is no freedom.

One interpreter, Hannah Arendt, has considered the equality of 1793 as the triumph of compassion; she bears the responsibility of the contempt toward a multitude that does not want to be the populace, of a constituent power that does not want to be the bourgeoisie, of a freedom that doesn't want any limit.[38] Indeed, what divests this concept of any vulgarity is its historical destiny, the impossibility of removing the definition of freedom and equality from the terrain of society in the future centuries. The irreversibility of the definition of constituent power on the social terrain is posed here, once and for all. From now on, we can only resist it.

The declaration of 1795, at first, tries to limit the effects of this project. If equality is affirmed ("Equality consists in the fact that the law is the same for all, whether it protects or whether it punishes. Equality admits no distinction of birth, no heredity of powers," sect. III), if security is reaffirmed as "the result of everybody's concourse to assure the rights of each" (sect. XV), if the inalienability of the person is newly guaranteed (sect. XV), the order of equality and security is then reconducted to the norm of property. Sect. V: "Property is the right to enjoy and dispose of his goods, his revenues, the fruits of his labor and his industry." However, within this reaction something has happened: the dislocation of the point of reference from the abstract terrain of general will to the concrete terrain of the law and the order of property. The advancement of constituent power in society obliges the reaction itself to make manifest the social discrimination on which it is founded.

Here we are, consequentially, facing another series of argumentations relative to sovereignty—arguments that are articulations of the theme of the dissolution of the enigma of the general will. In 1789 the concept of sovereignty is given in its Rousseauean integrity, although hybridized with that of the nation: "The principle of all sovereignty resides in the Nation. No body, no individual can exercise authority which does not emanate directly therefrom" (sect. III).

In 1793 the rupture is limited but significant. The principle is reaffirmed ("Sovereignty resides in the people; is one and indivisible, imprescriptible and inalienable," sect XXV; "No portion of the people can exercise the power of the whole people," sect. XXVI), but, at the same time, the immediacy of the action limits the principle ("But each section of the sovereign assembly must enjoy the right to express its will with complete freedom," sect. XXVI). The reaction of 1795 is radical: "Sovereignty resides essentially in the universality of citizens" (sect. XVII); "No individual, no partial meeting of citizens can attribute sovereignty to itself" (sect. XVIII); "No one can, without legal delegation, exercise any authority or fill any public office" (sect. XIX); "Each citizen has an equal right to take part, immediately or mediately, in the formulation of the law, in the nomination of the people's representatives and public officials" (sect. XX); "Public offices cannot become the property of those who exercise them" (sect. XXI).

But again this reaction is constrained on a different terrain from that of the general will—on the terrain, that is, of a social reconstruction of inequality that again takes up the themes of English constitutionalism and the socially organized, and consequentially defined, counterpowers: "The social guarantee cannot exist if the separation of powers is not established, if their limits are not fixed, and if the responsibility of public officials is not assured" (sect. XXII). To respond to the new, the men of the Thermidore take refuge in the ancient but are nonetheless forced to go through the new. The relation between freedom and equality, between political and social rights, is once again out of balance, in the opposite direction than the constitution of 1793, but with as much backbreaking force.

A new articulation of the relation between equality and freedom presents itself at this point: it concerns the participation and the control of the administration.[39] Here the significance of the differences and of the articulations is less backbreaking and less productive than elements of substantial contrast. In fact, the principle of the control over the administration and of the responsibilities of the administrators impinges only partially on the problem of sovereignty, while it is directly and practically affected by the single notions of sovereignty. But the problem cannot, for this reason, be undervalued: the administrative practices are strongly characterized by the divergent ideas of sovereignty, and the signs of the latter, theoretically fine, become enormous when the administration is executed. We could thus follow this theoretical-practical template and draw useful indications for our own research. But why, when the thematic proposed by the second group of differences among the various declarations of rights expects us, and can allow us, to reach the core of the problems?

The second group of differences among the declarations directly concerns the subjectivity of constituent power, as an activity that develops in time. If equality is the abstract time of general will, brought back to the concreteness of historical subjects, the subjectivity of constituent power is the lived experience of the latter. The lived experience of revolutionary time, the lived experience of the transformation, or of the passage from the idea to the concrete, and—in the concrete—from passion to productive imagination. Here the Rousseauean enigma is deliberately broken: if we cannot solve the puzzle from the theoretical point of view, we might as well destroy it practically. A perverse short circuit? We will see later; we will have to decide whether this is the case or, on the contrary, whether it is a radical ethical decision. Now temporal subjectivity manifests itself: the time of the event is that of its manifestation. The declaration of 1789 does not face the problem: it remains in the enthusiastic indistinctness of the movement, without identifying the problem, and even less the solution. Only the time of the sansculottes, of constituent power in action, poses the problem and its solution. It is what happens in 1793: the theme posed is the most urgent. The right to resistance is constructed as a practical principle deriving from the development of constituent power.

The constitutive logical process has the clarity of the temporal process, and the necessity of its strength. A first observation: "The law must protect public and individual freedom against the oppression of those who govern" (sect. IX). A first consequence: "Every action taken against a man beyond the cases and without the forms determined by law is arbitrary and tyrannical; the one against whom this act is to be carried out by violence has the right to repulse it by force" (sect. XI). However, here we are still on the terrain of constituted right, while constituent power is latent. It is in section XXVI that the tension explodes: constituent power leaves its latency, organizes itself, and is brought to a subjective figuration: "Any individual who would usurp sovereignty will be instantly put to death by free men" (sect. XXVII).

On this basis the revolutionary subjectivity becomes explicit: "The offences of the people's proxies and their agents must never go unpunished. No one has the right to claim himself more inviolable than other citizens" (sect. XXXI), until the definition of the principle: "Resistance to oppression is the consequence of the other rights of man" (sect. XXXIII); "There is oppression of the social body whenever a single one of its members is oppressed. There is oppression of each member whenever the social body is oppressed" (sect. XXXIV); "When the government violates the people's right, insurrection is, for the people and for each portion of the people, the most sacred of rights and the most indispensable of duties" (sect. XXXV).

It is clear that the principle resistance and insurrection is not only negative: here freedom has become a productive substance. It has definitely articulated itself, it has implanted itself into equality. The subject that has constituted itself measures itself with the problems of time: it is a collective subject, capable of moving in time. Its constituent capability is continuous: "The right to present petitions to the guardians of public authority can in no case be forbidden, suspended or limited" (sect. XXXII); and it is absolute: "A people always has the right to revise, reform and change its Constitution. One generation cannot subject future generations to its laws" (sect. XXVIII). Temporality reveals itself as the first foundation of subjectivity. Power must be reconnected to this radical temporality. An open temporality, continually revolutionary. An ontological condition of revolution as condition of the constitution. Here the modern concept of constituent power opens thoroughly, never to yield its concept again.

But, one could object, this claim to renovation of constituent power, from generation to generation, was not so new. It was already present, for example, in the constitution of Pennsylvania (see chap. 4) and in the ideologists of the Enlightenment, particularly in Condorcet.[40] How can we claim that it is so radical and significant? We can for a fundamental reason: because it was felt as such. The constitution of the Year III deploys every means to avoid that even a reminiscence of revolutionary, constituent democracy is possible. It becomes evil. On this contrast, on this refusal of temporality and its constitutive quality is built the modern concept of constitution—that concept predisposed to devour constituent power, and to leave no traces of constituent temporality. The constitutions following that of 1793 are all shaped not on the principle of constitutivity, but on that of counterrevolution.

The Thermidorians react, then, first, fiercely on this terrain. Constituent power, as the right of the permanent exercise of the masses' constitutivity, is their nightmare and their terror. Here we are faced with this affirmation: "Those who solicit, dispatch, sign, carry out or cause to be carried out arbitrary acts are guilty and must be punished" (1795, sect. IX); notwithstanding the lexical identity of this section and of others with the declaration of 1793, we are witnessing a complete inversion of the discourse: because what is struck by the sanction here is, immediately, the constituent movement, the right to resistance. Sect. XVII: "Sovereignty resides essentially in the universality of citizens"; sect. XVIII: "No individual, no partial meeting of citizens can attribute sovereignty to itself"; sect. XIX: "No one can, without legal authorization, exercise any authority nor fill any public office": all these sections pose the negation of the right of resistance and of the dynamic of constituent power, in the most radical and fierce manner. To the point that, in the declaration of 1795 the discourse of constituent power is reversed into a discourse on the "duties" of the citizens—a faded reproposition of the duty of obedience that any contractualist theory proposed to the aim of fixing the political obligation. This reversal is appalling: it reaches paradoxical limits and, without irony, shows political obligation as a convinced and demanded alienation. "The obligations of each member to society consist in defending it, serving it, living in submission to the laws, and respecting those who are its instruments"; "No one is a good citizen if he is not a good son, good father, good brother, good spouse"; "No man is good if he is not a frank and religious observer of the laws"; "Whoever overtly violates the laws declares himself to be at war with society"; "Whoever eludes the laws, without overtly infringing them, by ruse or cleverness, wounds the interests of all: he renders himself unworthy of their benevolence and their esteem" (1795, *Devoirs*, sects. III–VII).

The reversal is complete and total. The good political order stands not on the masses' creativity, but on their obedience. The political space takes the place of social space. Rousseau's puzzle is resolved into a cold image of impotent universality. The conservative social matrix explicitly begins to organize political reaction: "On the upholding of property rests the cultivation of the earth, all production, all forms of labor, and social order" (1795, *Devoirs*, sect, VIII). The reaction asks that the masses' constituent power accepts the time of the counterrevolution. Actively: "Every citizen owes his services to the fatherland and to the upholding of freedom, equality and property, whenever the law calls upon him to defend them" (1795, *Devoirs*, sect. IX).

Thus it is the time of the sansculottes that resolves Rousseau's enigma. It remains, nonetheless, a theoretical enigma, but the sansculottes resolve it practically. For them and for all the others. It means that it is in the time of the sansculottes that constituent power finds its positive maturity, and that it is against the time of the sansculottes that the reaction, in the French Revolution and in future centuries, finds its specific definition. It is the time of the sansculottes that illuminates the alternatives to power, the utopian tensions, and the repressions, pitted against the others, that will live in the coming times. With a fixed point: from now on it is constituent power that defines everything, even for its adversaries. Constituent power comes first. It precedes even the reaction and forces it to model itself on constituent power, on the productivity of the masses. From now on the ancien regime, in all its renovated forms, will always be Gothic, and ancient. The modern perversions of totalitarian power can be explained only on the basis of this definitive loss of autonomy on the part of bourgeois thought vis-à-vis the revolutionary one, of constituted power vis-à-vis constituent power.

A final observation—on the role of the Jacobins in the turning point represented by the appearance of constituent power and its dynamic in the course of the great French Revolution. Now, the problem is not at all felt in its intensity by the Jacobins. They make an already resolved problem out of it: for them equality is given as continuity of freedom, and political rights are the substratum of the social ones. In the Jacobins there is not the sense of the puzzle that keeps these terms really separated: they are, through a somersault of reason, linearly taken into consideration and unified. For Robespierre and Saint-Just constituent power is a direct expression of the social, which, without contradiction, is embodied in the political.[41] It is not strange that Robespierre thinks of himself as "anti-Machiavellian,"[42] by sustaining that morals fully identify with the political, and that one single politics of virtue and the heart exists! This is not odd, because, in moralistic terms, here they say exactly what had been proposed in logical terms: the normal continuity of freedom and equality.

Thus they are right, those scholars who, in analyzing Jacobinism, wonder why "the production of a maximalist language" becomes in them so fundamental, and why constituent power is defined by them in negative terms, as counterposed to the enemy. This happens because constituent time is reduced to a word that presents itself as "the dominant symbolic position, the people's will";[43]

because constituent power cannot be defined by them as production, as struggle to build a new world, but it is simply the revelation of a subjected organic unity that the revolution restores. In fact, the Jacobins are the only ones—against the Girondins and against the movement of the masses, on opposed fronts—that consider the revolutionary temporality as indifferent. They are convinced that the political and social exigencies expressed in the course of the revolution are part of only one design. They take seriously the constitutional formality that is expressed in the words "general will, nation, equality, freedom, brotherhood." They live the constitutional abstraction. Their purity and their probity are moral idealities—as pale as ideas, as desperate as is their detachment from the life of the masses.

The Jacobin tragedy consists in their incapability to see the fabric on which Rousseau's enigma exploded: for the Jacobins there was only the transcendental solution of the enigma, and they considered this solution as a divinity. The production of the maximalist word, in absence of a radical immersion in the struggle, becomes a priestly function. When clashing with the real, they are prisoners of a violence that they do not understand, and that they cannot avoid. For the Jacobins, and in any case for their leaders, the revolution and constituent power are not a constitutive temporality, within which enigmas break apart practically, and thus the levels of solution are dislocated: for them temporality is a horizon celebrating the restoration of ancient virtue.

When Michelet tells us that Robespierre is no longer only a dictator but, rather, he has become a pope, he forgets to add: a pope of ideas, a pope of the general will, something more abstract and fragile than a Roman pope. The temporality of the French Revolution, however enigmatic, will take its revenge on this fact: the fact that the Jacobin priests are outside of the temporality of the revolution and of the constituent power of the multitude.

The Constitution of Labor

To the temporality of the sansculottes is opposed the constitution of labor. Where the first seeks, Emmanuel Sieyès finds.[44] While for the first, constituent power is an opening, a search, a process, for the second it is an accomplished fact, the epiphany of a subject that reduces the political and social world to his own image, that carries out its own norm. What is the Third Estate? asks Sieyès (*Third Estate*, 51 ff). It is everything, it represents nothing, it wants/must become something. This something is a totality. It is such because the Third Estate is a complete nation, because it organizes and supports all the productive activities, it is per se free and flourishing.

But the Third Estate is excluded from the political command, and any function of representation is usurped away from it. Consequently...

Before touching on the consequences, we should underline that, in the debate about constituent power, Sieyès is the first to introduce labor as an exclusive theme. The definition of the Third Estate is an economic definition, and it is on this economic content that other concepts are shaped, from that of nation to that of representation, from that of constituent power to that of constituted power.[45] Sieyès represents society as "a laborious, unified and compact whole," standing on the social work organized by the bourgeoisie, and whose development is "obstructed by the contradiction between labor and public functions, on the whole usurped by the aristocracy."[46] Sieyès considers contemporary society as a modern commercial society, in which complex functions develop, rich in mediations and political interferences: it is this power of mediation that the aristocracy usurps.[47] The indignation against this economic usurpation is thus the fundamental key to the definition, as well as to the proposal, of reform of the Third Estate.[48]

However, it is important to underline that if the description of society is rich in mediations, not as rich is the comprehensive image of the Third Estate; even more, this image is singularly atemporal; it is not so much a matter of transforming, as one of restoring an already existing order of labor, preconstituted, naturally just,[49] which the aristocracy dominates, without being part of it.

The idea of a constitution of labor thus makes its solemn entrance into history, but in static terms, à la Montesquieu, according to a juridical more than a sociological perspective.[50] Even in the most precise interventions on this question, which Sieyès will make in the course of the revolution, this characteristic of his point of view is confirmed. In Sieyès the concept of labor is always a conservative concept; it is sustained by a concept of property that becomes untouchable by revolutionary power. He defends the necessity of tithes and the inalienability of property, supports the liberation of the lands and the expansion of peasant property. Nothing in Sieyès's concept of labor and in the vindication of its foundational value refers to the concept of class and class struggle.[51]

The clarification concerning the notion of labor in Sieyès, if it is useful in preventing undue assimilations of his thought to that of the liberals of the Restoration (Guizot and Mignet, above all), cannot in any case make us forget the impact of the insertion of labor as the key to understanding the political world, and its value as part of the weave of constituent power. What has the Third Estate been, until now? continues Sieyès. Nothing. If what produces a nation is a common law that, starting from the social organization of labor, establishes an adequate representation, nothing like this exists in France. The General Estates are founded on an unjust criterion of representation, that is, one that does not correspond to social order, and that overvalues minorities in a disproportionate manner—scandalously. What does the Third Estate demand, then? To become something. It demands that its representatives are not virtual but real; it wants the number of the representatives of the Third Estate to be equal to that of the other two Estates; it wants the votes of the General Estates to be cast by head and not by order. Here ends the pamphlet-like part of Sieyès's *Third Estate*, on this more than legitimate, and nonetheless moderate, request: that a little power be given to the class that, socially, is everything. That labor be given representation.

What can we say? The force of self-evidence assumes here a Cartesian effectiveness. But extremely evident is also the conservative character of the proposal. The system of representation must be changed in order to maintain intact and to make functional the order and the social-economic fabric of the nation. The theme of labor enters the modern constitutional debate as a conservative theme. Sieyès's problem is to build a modern political society that may represent correctly, without encroaching on the social-economic structures of the country. The radical force of constituent power is *ab imis* taken away from its dimension of social formativity.

Rousseau's enigma is hypostatized, presupposed as such: that is, it is beforehand freed from the temptation to convert political equality into social equality, and celebrated in its theoretical opacity. The temporality of constituent power, which should have first of all put into crisis Rousseau's enigma, is not even glimpsed at: "It's evident that Sieyès' demagogy, put in front of the social situation of France, and having reached the point of rupture, couldn't but feed the extremely strong subversive tensions present, without offering any serious possibility of political mediation."[52]

With this said, how does the concept of constituent power, even in its narrow sense, develop in Sieyès? How does representation organize itself in his thought?

Chapter IV of *The Third Estate* ("What the Government has attempted and what the Privileged Classes propose, on behalf of the Third Estate," 89–118) is made of seven paragraphs: the first five discuss the proposals that the governments have until now made to pacify the protests of the Third Estate. These are unacceptable proposals, often actual booby traps, *pieges*, and deceits. How can we imagine that the Third Estate may fall into these traps? The last two paragraphs (106–

18) debate a much more consistent proposal: "It is proposed to imitate the English constitution." To imitate the English constitution means, in any case, to introduce an Upper House. But to what end? What would its purpose be? To represent the most privileged part of the aristocracy? But aren't the aristocracy and the Church already represented, and without losing their privileges, in the House of Representatives?

The only aim of this proposal is to reaffirm, in any way, a constitution representative of the social orders. This is the only meaning of the reference to the English constitution. In any case, on the contrary, "the Third Estate must never consent to the admission of several orders to a so-called House of the Commons because the idea of a Commons composed of different orders is grotesque" (108). But even more monstrous is the project of a bicameral system, when its idea is that of an overdetermination of the constitution of the orders: "The differences which we have just mentioned [from a truly representative constitution] are real; never will a nation sliced into orders have anything in common with a nation which is a *whole*" (109).

The idea of an Upper House, even though the proposal has more and more supporters, is thus unacceptable. A "constitution of the orders" and a "constitution of representation" can never be mediated. Then let's put aside the spirit of imitation: it will not lead us properly. Even more so since the British constitution is unacceptable and inimitable not only in the case of bicameralism: it is so per se. It is not imitable, because (the entire paragraph 7 of this chapter is dedicated to its critique, 112–18), the Upper House is "a monument of Gothic superstition" (113); because the national representation, divided into the three figures of the king, the House of Lords, and the House of Commons, is bad in all its three elements. To what aim should the legislative capability be divided among three actors? Only a free and general election can found a national legislative power.

The English constitutional complexity (to whose history we can bow, but we do not understand why it must constitute a value), more than expressing the "simplicity of good order," rather, reveals itself as "a framework of precautions against disorder" (114). Finally, the only elements that make the English constitution a good constitution for the English are those that, directly coming from the social, have settled into the constitution, such as the very ancient rule of being judged only by one's own peers, or such as the complex of conventions that forbid the formation of a standing army capable of threatening freedom. The British constitution is an ancient product, going back to the seventeenth century: it does not know the Enlightenment, it does not know science: "The true science of society does not date back very far. Men were building cottages for many a year before they were able to build palaces. Surely it is obvious that the advance of social architecture had to be even slower; for this art, the most important of all, could obviously never expect to receive the slightest encouragement from the hands of despots or aristocrats" (117–18).

Let's then apply this science. "What ought to have been done?" (119–39). If in a free nation there exist differences of judgment with respect to the constitution, it is thanks to the nation itself. Not to the notables, not to the old powers, but to the nation. In what form? Through the expression of a "government by proxy" (122). Notice: although the representatives cannot hold the power of the nation in its entirety, they can nonetheless exercise a part of it. This part, insofar as it is a projection and portion of the great national common will, is full and unlimited in its quality. However, in its partial quantity, the common will is exercised as mandate, although actually containing the power of the nation. Here is a first product of science: the imperative mandate is dissolved, and the distinction between quality and quantity of representation is put into play in order to detach the representative from the represented. Having given this definition of representation, a definition that immediately protects him from any extensive interpretation of constituent power, and from the possibility of prefiguring into it an organization not of labor but of democracy, Sieyès starts working at the problem of the division of norms, which he separates into constitutional—that is, ordering the constitutional—machine, and purely legislative, normative.

Two different powers are at the basis of the two functions: a first one, extraordinary, that is, constituent power; and a second, this time ordinary, that is, constituted power. The difference is a qualitative one: the second power, in fact, works according to the norms of positive law, while the first one, constituent power, according to natural right. Constituent power must produce the political constitution of society and set it in a correct relation with the nation itself. Constituent power is the representative of the nation. It is its immediate expression. Here is a second product of science: the nation comes before anything else, as much as natural right, of which the nation is the interpreter, comes before anything else. Thus constituent power produces the fundamental laws that activate the legislative and executive bodies set by the constitution. The constitution is therefore the means, the machine to produce the laws and the government. Obviously, the precedence of the nation is total, and it would be ridiculous wanting to consider the nation as subjected to the constitution: "The nation owes its existence to *natural* law alone. The government, on the contrary, can only be a product of positive law" (126).

The national will is not legal, but it is at the origin of any legality. Constituent power is thus "a body of extraordinary representatives . . . [that] does not, of course, need to be in charge of the whole of the national will; it needs only special powers, and those only in rare cases; but it is in the same position as the nation itself in respect of independence from any constitutional forms" (130–31). Here is thus the third product of science, the synthesis between the limitation of the principle of representation and the limitlessness of its action, at the service of labor.

"What remains to be done" (140–74). The Third Estate must take the initiative: it is not an order but, rather, the nation itself. It is capable of expressing the "special powers to settle the great problem of the constitution ahead of everything else" (155). It is capable of annulling all the privileges that oppose the order to labor, a liberated society. It wants an Assembly that exercises constituent power on the basis of a general election without privileged parties, on the basis of an assembly of the nation.

It is a formidable war machine, what has been constituted here. Until now, we have seen it function, explicitly, against privilege and usurpation. Now, we must see it function, as explicitly, against all the social forces that oppose themselves, or could oppose themselves, to the order of labor. We must see, in sum, not simply how the revolution of the Third Estate is theorized but how a preventive counterrevolution against any possible attack on the new order is organized.

To this end, let's go back to the concept of political representation. In Sieyès, this is a concept essentially tied to the "division of labor." Indeed, it's a complex and articulated division of labor that distinguishes modern society—a commercial society established on an adequate social structure—from ancient society: in the latter the simplicity and immediacy of social relations allowed democracy. The "mediated competition" is typical, instead, of the "representative government."[53] Mediation is the fundamental element of complex commercial societies, and representative government is in them the only form of legitimate government. "Constituent power" itself is valid only if it is representative power: a "commissioning power" must, therefore, be hypothesized and distinguished from "constituent power" as well as from "constituted power."

Constituent power and constituted power are always representative powers; mandated power, instead, is the people understood as the whole *singulatim* [one by one] of the active citizens. Representation distinguishes the "*re-pubblica*" from the "*re-totale*."[54] It is not by chance that one critic has been able to see emerge here, more than the concept of "general will," a sort of vague expansion of Rousseau's "will of all," almost a demystifying anticipation of it.[55] But the demystification is only defensive. It works to introduce naturalistic elements and arithmetic means in the configuration of sovereignty, and, above all, to introduce rigidly selective criteria in the formation of representation—selections of taxation systems, culture, and so forth. The electoral body is becoming an open corporation of proprietors and starts organizing itself as a complex system that strengthens the criteria of tax distribution. Sieyès comes to the point of reintroducing the *pactum subjetionis*, which Rousseau had excluded from the tradition of contractualism. A tortuous combination of representation and government sanctified thus the power of an assembly of notables and excluded mass popular participation. Is this a realistic development of Sieyès's thought, a conscious self-distancing from Rousseau's utopia of the general will? No: all this represents only an episode of instrumental reason, and a typical moment of its organization into the political ideology of the bourgeoisie. In fact, Sieyès granted the assembly of notables the absolute sovereignty that issued from Rousseau's general will. The game of dice on which the entire modern concept of representation is founded was thus completed: democratic sovereignty, the idea of constituent power become the element of legitimation of limited and divided government.[56]

What does the concept of nation itself become, at this point? If it is true that the nation continues to exist, before other qualifications, as a fundamental reference-idea, yet through the mechanism of representation its concept is definitely duplicated, from the category of social body to that of juridical subject. That is, after having emptied Rousseau's concept of general will of any possibility of democratic grounding, after having operated this reduction through the construction of a representative mechanism completely modeled on the division of labor, Sieyès does his last act of prestidigitation: he transforms this representation into juridical absolute, into the exclusive seat—if it is not yet the exclusive source—of sovereignty. If the absolutism of the constituted powers is excluded, in principle, and now only marginally, by a possible, and in any case problematic, permanence of constituent power, national sovereignty is nonetheless conceived in an entirely reversed manner with respect to any mechanism of foundation: in fact, it is the elective principle (the principle of labor and of its division) that traverses it, constitutes it, and, alone, legitimizes it. The elective principle proposes itself as the only and ultimate foundation of the legitimacy of the exercise of power, and as the only and exclusive juridical practice of interpretation of society.[57] This is an elective principle subordinated to the norms and the urgencies of the social division of labor. Outside of these conditions there exists nothing but a *démocratie brute*.

Constituent power becomes, therefore, not only an extraordinary power, but also a power that does not pose limits—limits that first of all concern constituent power itself. Beyond these limits, it is a power *sans force*. Within this complex game, the contract of association dynamically subordinates itself to a rule of subjection. We perfectly understand why, considering these results of Sieyès's thought, the critics have been able to affirm that his idea of constituent power, from being Rousseauean, little by little becomes Montesquieuean: "Sieyès develops Montesquieu's terminology upon an idea of Rousseau's."[58] We must add that terminology wins over ideology.

One understands how, on this basis, the evolution of Sieyès's thought is entirely meant to establish further limits and obstacles to the expression of constituent power.[59] When in the constitution of the Themidorian Directory the elective principle will be so developed that "the elected ones will choose their electors," we will be finally able to say that the doctrine of the Third Estate has triumphed. With coherence, with rigor. The representation, starting from this moment, cannot but itself "[rest] on the rational principle of division of labour which, applied to politics, demanded the consideration of the latter as a specialised activity, confined to educated and competent persons."[60] At this point the concept of constituent power reenters the game, in Sieyès's project of the Year III, as a caricature of itself: it is delegated to a "constitutional jury," that is, to a representative agency commissioned to watch over the continuity of the institutions, and to reimpose, if necessary, the rule of legality against any attempt to renew the criterion of legitimization and exercise of sovereign power.[61]

What happens at this point, to the polemics and the differences, so strongly insisted on, against the British constitutional mechanism? Sieyès, as other men of the Enlightenment,[62] opposed since 1789 the English constitution, and we have seen with what virulence. In fact, starting from Year III, the discourse is reversed, and the inspiration of Jean Louis de Lolme and of his *Constitution of England* is revived.[63] The political space is once again thought in classical constitutional terms, that is, in terms of separation and balance of powers, of autocentrality of the representative system, and within a formalism that systematically operates the recomposition of the constitutional structure. The selection of the electors on the basis of their tax-paying capability and cultural criteria will not be the last consequence of this huge change of route.

Why does this happen? From the point of view of the immediate cause, undoubtedly it is the movement of the masses and their extremely singular concept of constituent power that determine this passage, and that impose on the dominant class the drifting of the concept. But from the formal point of view, this passage and this drifting would not have been possible if the idea of constitution hitherto elaborated did not stick so closely to that of economic society and of organization of labor.

Sieyès's idea, never discussed, never made critical, but always implicitly developed, is that political space is the organization of a social space, and therefore of a determined temporality and of a specific mode of production. The constitutional imagination registers the social dynamic. Sieyès's thought is always marked by this solid concurrence of the constitution and the image of society, as if the first should only bring to light the implicit norms and the latent tendencies in the second. From this point of view Sieyès's constitution is the direct superstructure of that commercial society of the first capitalistic *essor*, which makes of the order of labor its exclusive assizes. Here we can measure the enormous step forward that the constitutional thought makes with Sieyès because he makes labor the center of the debate and of constitutional construction. Thus it will not be by chance if the clash between the revolution and the constitution of labor will be felt by Sieyès as central. In fact, the revolution also puts labor at the center of its discourse and its movement because here, at this point, the connection between the social and the political imposes it. On everybody: on Sieyès and his adversaries. And since society, as the economy, is separated around the concept of labor and the reality of its organization, and is separated on the rhythm of its division, the clash will be determined on this point: we will have to decide who is hegemonic in the world of labor.

Once labor has been defined as the ordering value of the constitution, the struggle will open in the social. Here the time of labor and the time of the revolution crisscross in an antagonistic manner. When the time of labor is concluded in the constitution, the revolution will try to keep it open. The identification of labor as proper constitutional fabric allows us now to clarify some difficulties that the study of the temporality of the masses and its difficult reference to general will had handed on to us. The centrality of labor in fact unifies that which the constitution and the revolutionary temporality develop on antagonistic sides. But at the same time, the centrality of labor separates different strengths that define themselves around labor.

It is a real dialectical spectacle that Sieyès has introduced to us. Through time, in labor, according to Hegel, "this movement of self-consciousness in relation to another self-consciousness has in this way been represented as the action of one self-consciousness, but this action of the one has itself the double significance of being both its own action and the action of the other as well. For the other is equally independent and self-contained, and there is nothing in it of which it is not itself the origin": thus a great dialectical witness describes the passage.[64] And he continues: "Thus the relation of the two self-conscious individuals is such that they prove themselves and each other through a life-and-death struggle." This is the centrality that Sieyès has proposed for the work that poses the point of the discrimination of the opposites. The constitution of labor opens toward the temporality of the sansculottes as toward an extreme experience of life and death.

If in the first part of this chapter we have seen how the temporality of the sansculottes broke apart Rousseau's enigma, even while remaining a prisoner of it, here we glimpse the formal possibility held by that same temporality to directly oppose the constitution of labor wanted by Sieyès. The temporality of the sansculottes finally presents itself as a project of liberation that evokes Sieyès's constitutionalism while reversing its sense: this is allowed by the centrality of labor and imposed by the antagonism that could not, at this level of the development of constituent power, but open itself between a project of liberation and a project of constitutionalization of labor.

Yet what is this but the reactualization, now rooted in labor, of the opposition that Machiavelli had found in temporality, between constituted time and constituent time? What is this but the reactualization of the Spinozian concept of strength, now rooted in labor, and all absorbed into the process of its liberation? The proletarian history of the French Revolution has no need to return to the rigmarole of the "radiant future," to recognize itself as the history of a liberating strength. For it, it is enough to be founded on itself, on the recuperation of the past of the humanistic revolutions, and on the vicissitudes of constituent power, on the successive enrichments that it synthesizes. To Sieyès goes the merit of taking the contradiction of the general will on the terrain of labor: from this point of view Sieyès is really a "second Rousseau." And if the temporality of the masses had broken Rousseau's enigma, now it takes up the task of filling up this rupture with the contents of the liberation of labor.

On this terrain we must confront the Marxian reading of the French Revolution, a reading that continually relies on the Machiavellian and sansculottic temporality, in order to oppose it to the time of constituted power, of the constitution of labor:

[Marx's] work on the French Revolution can be divided into three great chronological groups, corresponding to three successive modes of treating the same problem and reusing the same materials; but they obey a systematic logic, which varies in accordance with the evolution of his thought and the circumstances of history. First came the Feuerbachian

Marx, who during the apparent stability of the July Monarchy treated the modern bourgeois state according to the model of religious alienation. He is followed, during the years that witnessed a rekindling of the revolutionary phenomenon, by the materialist Marx, who envisioned this state as a mere product of the social domination of bourgeois interests. Finally, there is the Marx of the Capital, who constantly interrupted his meditations on English history and on the secrets of capitalism to interpret and reinterpret the instability of the forms of the state in bourgeois France, from 1789 to 1871.[65]

Furthermore, Furet affirms that Marx never confused 1789 with the successive revolutions of the nineteenth century and considered the first as the event that has in any case "shook the very foundation and structure of the state, whereas the various regimes of the nineteenth century merely altered the organizational forms of power and the political equilibriums."[66]

But what is Marx saying, then, and why does it seem to us that we can assume his reading as the interpretive key of the temporality of the sansculottes? What does radically unify and oppose Sieyès and Marx? Different from what some critics think,[67] the Marxian interpretation of the French revolutionary phenomenon (of the event and the structure) is homogeneous and continuous throughout the different periods in which it unfolds. For Marx the French Revolution is not any revolution: it is not even a revolution that can simply be explained on the basis of historical materialism (as, for instance, the English Revolution).[68] The French revolutionary archetype consists of the fact that it poses the theme of the mediation between the social and the political, it fixes the concept of constituent power, and it introduces us to the problematic of the "party" (that is, of the subject that lives and operates the passage from the social to the political). Marx is not so much interested in the causes of the revolution; rather, he is interested in understanding how these objective causes are configured as subjectivity, how the movements of the masses have become creative. If a little paradox is permissible, we could say that the Marxian point of view is not readable in the terms of Furet the historian, but in those of Foucault, the genealogist of subjectivity.

In "On the Jewish Question" and in *The Holy Family* of 1844, the problem is posed in terms of the identification of the "political space," that is, of the "public situation"—terms created by the French Revolution. Now this political space, which is also the social space of movements and struggles, celebrates in the so-called "political emancipation" the strength of bourgeois hegemony, and it does so in the semblance of "constituent power." Why and how do the *déplacement* and the juridical hypostasis of constituent power in the apology of the social status quo take place? How do we move from insurrection and from the interrogation of all the foundations of the State to the reconstruction of the "present state of things" and of its juridical exaltation? We are not so interested here in underlining the theme of political alienation and the critique of the universal rights of man, as forms of political emancipation counterposed to social liberation, to communism: these are well-known themes, and relatively inessential for our research. Instead, we are interested in grasping the subjective links of these processes, the resolute reduction of the political to the social theme, of the politico-philosophical analysis to historical materialism.

When Marx talks of political emancipation, he talks about it as of a huge progress; what he critiques is the new civil mediation that is determined by this progress, and he critiques it in the specific form assumed by the French Revolution.[69] Here Marx does not construct the solution of the problems relative to the interweaving of constituent and constituted power, between society and State, but he constructs the categories of their singular revolutionary synthesis, and therefore of the possibility of their practical criticism. I mean that here the theme of "equality" is not simply taken as critical subject, but it can become such, if equality is developed outside of ideology, outside of the enigma that constitutes it, as essence made antagonistic between the polarities of work and law. Marx poses the solution of Rousseau's enigma on the terrain of constitutionalist practice.

In *The German Ideology* the critique is once again referred to the subject, therefore the critique of "political emancipation" here becomes real. In "On the Jewish Question" and in *The Holy Family* we were still within structural criticism, before the subjective caesura that makes Marx a thinker of modernity.[70] Now, in *The German Ideology*, the division of labor constitutes the presupposition of the critique: the powerful abstraction of the State and its constitutional figure are explained on the basis of the critique of the social division of labor.[71] What else did Sieyès do? Only the point of view changes. Indeed, Marx immediately assumes the point of view of constituent power, of a temporal universality that becomes power. His concept of constituent power is fixed in that intermediate zone, between society and the State, between movement and institution, which cannot be superseded, because, if this supersession would take place, it would be in the form of the illusion and of the "general" harnessing of the real movement.

Constituent power shows itself thus as communism: "Communism is for us not a state of affairs which is to be established, an ideal to which reality [will] have to adjust itself. We call communism the real movement which abolishes the present state of things. The conditions of this movement result from the premises now in existence." Thus we are touching on a first important element: the French Revolution must not be considered as the revolution of labor, but as the "bourgeois" revolution of labor; it assumes the division of labor to exalt it, as such; this is the movement of its constitutional work: a movement meant to block the liberation of the social forces exploited in the slavery of the division of labor. To this block is opposed the real movement; this resistance is a power that transforms the basis on which the division of labor and its constitution stand. This resistance, this movement, this strength are constituent power. A social power, open, dynamic, implanted in temporality. One subject is recognized as capable of constituent power: the proletariat.

First of all, it presents itself as "universal class"—"a class which forms the majority of all members of society, and from which emanates the consciousness of the necessity of a fundamental revolution, the communist consciousness, which may, of course, arise among the other classes too through the contemplation of the situation of this class" (*German Ideology*, 94). The proletariat presents itself in a struggle against the bourgeoisie: "The conditions under which definite productive forces can be applied are the conditions of the rule of a definite class of society, whose social power, deriving from its property, has its practical-idealistic expression in each case in the form of the State; and therefore, every revolutionary struggle is directed against a class, which till then has been in power" (94). Finally, the proletariat presents itself as radical temporality:

> *In all revolutions up till now the mode of activity always remained unscathed and it was only a question of a different distribution of this activity, a new distribution of labour to other persons, whilst the communist revolution is directed against the preceding mode of activity, does away with labour, and abolishes the rule of all classes with the classes themselves, because it is carried through by the class which no longer counts as a class in society, is not recognized as a class, and is in itself the expression of the dissolution of all classes, nationalities, etc. within present society. (94)*

Therefore as revolutionary subject: "Both for the production on a mass scale of this communist consciousness, and for the success of the cause itself, the alteration of men on a mass scale is necessary, an alteration which can only take place in a practical movement, a revolution; this revolution is necessary, therefore, not only because the ruling class cannot be overthrown in any other way, but also because the class overthrowing it can only in a revolution succeed in ridding itself of all the muck of ages and become fitted to found society anew" (94–95). Never was the founding force of constituent power revealed better than here:

Communism differs from all previous movements in that it overturns the basis of all earlier relations of production and intercourse, and for the first time consciously treats all natural premises as the creatures of hitherto existing men, strips them of their natural character and subjugates them to the power of the united individuals. Its organization is, therefore, essentially economic, the material production of the conditions of this unity; it turns existing conditions into conditions of unity. The reality, which communism is creating, is precisely the true basis for rendering it impossible that anything should exist independently of individuals, insofar as reality is only a product of the preceding intercourse of individuals themselves. (86)

From now on, the definition of historical subjectivity, that is, temporal and evolutionary, of constituent force, as well as the radicality of its work of foundation, are only further probed. In the *Poverty of Philosophy* we read:

Economic conditions had first transformed the mass of the people of the country into workers. The domination of capital has created for this mass a common situation, common interests. This mass is thus already a class as against capital, but not yet for itself. In the struggle, of which we have noted only a few phases, this mass becomes united, and constitutes itself as a class for itself. The interests it defends become class interests. But the struggle of class against class is a political struggle. . . . An oppressed class is the vital condition for every society founded on the antagonism of classes. The emancipation of the oppressed class thus implies necessarily the creation of a new society. For the oppressed class to be able to emancipate itself it is necessary that the productive powers already acquired and the existing social relations should no longer be capable of existing side by side. Of all the instruments of production, the greatest productive power is the revolutionary class itself. The organization of revolutionary elements as a class supposes the existence of all the productive forces which could be engendered in the bosom of the old society. Does this mean that after the fall of the old society there will be a new class domination culminating in a new political power? No. The condition for the emancipation of the working class is the abolition of every class, just as the condition for the liberation of the Third Estate, of the bourgeois order, was the abolition of all estates and all orders. The working class, in the course of its development, will substitute for the old civil society an association which will exclude classes and their antagonism, and there will be no more political power properly so-called, since political power is precisely the official expression of antagonism in civil society. Meanwhile the antagonism between the proletariat and the bourgeoisie is a struggle of class against class, a struggle which carried to its highest expression is a total revolution. Indeed, is it at all surprising that a society founded on the opposition of classes should culminate in contradiction, the shock of body against body, as its final dénouement?

Do not say that social movement excludes political movement. There is never a political movement which is not at the same time social. It is only in an order of things in which there are no more classes and class antagonisms that social evolutions will cease to be political revolutions.[72]

In *Revolution and Counter-Revolution in Germany*, the constitution of subjectivity and the definition of the process of "permanent revolution" as "constituent power" reach a very high expression for the first time. On the one hand the reaffirmation of the universality of the proletariat and on the other the historical perception of the real movement reach a synthesis. The proletarian revolts of the Germinal, Year III, and of the Parisian June 1848 become the symbol of a constitutive permanent revolution, or of a permanent constituent power, that forms the plot of the history of the nineteenth century:

The working-class movement itself never is independent, never is of an exclusively proletarian character until all the different factions of the middle class, and particularly its most progressive faction, the large manufacturers, have conquered political power, and remodeled the State according to their wants. It is then that the inevitable conflict between the employer and the employed becomes imminent, and cannot be adjourned any longer; that the working class can no longer be put off with delusive hopes and promises never to be realized; that the great problem of the nineteenth century, the abolition of the proletariat, is at last brought forward fairly and in its proper light.[73]

But it is the fate of all revolutions that this union of different classes, which in some degree is always the necessary condition of any revolution, cannot subsist long. No sooner is the victory gained against the common enemy than the victors become divided among themselves into different camps, and turn their weapons against each other. It is this rapid and passionate development of class antagonism which, in old and complicated social organisms, makes a revolution such a powerful agent of social and political progress; it is this incessantly quick upshooting of new parties succeeding each other in power, which, during these violent commotions, makes a nation pass in five years over more ground than it would have done in a century under ordinary circumstances.[74]

In Marx, the constitution of labor—which, from the French Revolution on, in the nineteenth century constitutions becomes the central element of the definition of the modern State—opens thus to an immanent and continuous alternative, characterized by the ever new aperture of constituent power. This temporality is solicited in two senses: extensively, that is, in the sense of the permanence of the revolutionary and constituent process; and intensively, in the sense of a process that through accelerations, moments of crisis and offensives makes the contents of constituent power itself develop in theoretical-practical directions, in the direction of the consolidation of collective consciousness and of its conditions of freedom, more and more universal.[75] It is the time of the masses that makes constituent power.

The further development of the Marxian thought on constituent power does nothing more than further probe this passage, while more and more integrating the synthesis of temporality and subjectivity. In *The Eighteenth Brumaire of Louis Bonaparte*, this relationship is stretched to the highest degree:

> *Between 1848 and 1851 French society, using an abbreviated because revolutionary method, caught up on the studies and experiences which would in the normal or so to speak, textbook course of development have had to precede the February revolution if it were to do more than merely shatter the surface. Society now appears to have fallen back behind its starting-point; but in reality it must first create the revolutionary starting-point, i.e., the situation, relations, and conditions necessary for the modern revolution to become serious.*[76]

Temporality and subjectivity shrink so much that, at this point, the principle of constitution, as opposed to constituent strength, seems to consist essentially of a mute and atemporal function; the bourgeoisie senses this impotence and is taken by the terror of this situation, by this estrangement from the life of constituent power: so that, if it is true that "in the bourgeois republic, which bore neither the name 'Bourbon' nor the name 'Orleans,' but the name 'Capital,' they [the executives of capital] had found the form of state in which they could rule jointly" (165). It was also true that

> *they realized instinctively that although the republic made their political rule complete it simultaneously undermined its social foundation, since they had now to confront the subjugated classes and contend with them without mediation, without being concealed by the Crown, without the possibility of diverting the national attention by their secondary conflicts amongst themselves and with the monarchy. . . . It was a feeling of weakness which caused them to recoil when faced with the pure conditions of their own class rule and to yearn for the return of the previous forms of this rule, which were less complete, less developed, and, precisely for that reason, less dangerous. (175)*

Constituent power in its vitality, the progressive content of the so-called bourgeois freedoms and institutions themselves, put under attack the political domination of the bourgeoisie—because, simply, the constituent subject kept open in temporality its action. The parliamentary regime, the regime of "constituted power" becomes thus the "reign of restlessness," pushed to the point of powerlessness and negation:

Thus, by now branding as "socialist" what it had previously celebrated as "liberal," the bourgeoisie confesses that its own interest requires its deliverance from the peril of its own self-government; that to establish peace and quiet in the country its bourgeois parliament must first of all be laid to rest; that its political power must be broken in order to preserve its social power intact; that the individual bourgeois can only continue to exploit the other classes and remain in undisturbed enjoyment of property, family, religion and order on condition that his class is condemned to political insignificance along with the other classes; and that in order to save its purse the crown must be struck off its head and the sword which is to protect it must be hung over it like the sword of Damocles. (237)

The catastrophe of freedom presents itself as destiny where the constitutive nexus of power and might is broken. A catastrophe that is not only the triumph of Bonaparte's dictatorship, but the crisis of the form itself of the constitutional State. In the extreme and continual urgency to oppose the revolutionary constituent strength, and to challenge it constitutionally, "Every common interest was immediately detached from society, opposed to it as a higher general interest, torn away from the self-activity of the individual members of society and made a subject for governmental activity" (348).

If we reflect on the way Marx's constitutional thought proceeds, we must stress that his claim to separate the philosophical and structural considerations of the "Jewish Question" and of the critique of the political emancipation from those that we report here on the subjective, dynamic, and antagonistic of the analysis of the historical procedure is strange: the different "manner" of the Marxian way of proceeding confirms the philosophical assumption, while the historical critique exposes it—that is, demonstrates it.[77]

The passage from here to the writings of *The Paris Commune* is linear and definitive. In these writings constituent power reveals itself in all its fundamental characteristics: as a breaking power, that is, as the power of a radical reformulation of social organization; as expansive power, that is, as the unarrestable movement that, to the synchronic effects of rupture, adds the diachronic effects of continuity, of uninterrupted formativity; as permanent revolution, and therefore as procedure of freedom and equality.

As to the first point: "But the working class cannot simply lay hold of the readymade state machinery, and wield it for its own purposes."[78] Faithfully, Engels can comment: "From the very outset the Commune was compelled to recognise that the working class, once come to power, could not go on managing with the old state machine; that in order not to lose again its only just conquered supremacy, this working class must, on the one hand, do away with all the old repressive machinery previously used against it itself, and, on the other, safeguard itself against its own deputies and officials, by declaring them all, without exception, subject to recall at any moment."[79] As for the second characteristic of constituent power, its expansivity, Marx's insistence is continuous, as he continues in *The Civil War in France*: "The direct antithesis to the Empire was the Commune. The cry of 'social republic,' with which the revolution of February was ushered in by the Paris proletariat, did but express a vague aspiration after a republic that was not only to supercede the monarchical form of class rule, but class rule itself. The Commune was the positive form of that republic."[80]

The Marxian typology of expansive constituent power develops on this basis: "The Paris Commune was, of course, to serve as a model to all the great industrial centres of France. The communal regime once established in Paris and the secondary centres, the old centralized government would in the provinces, too, have to give way to the self-government of the producers" (*Civil War*, 210). The national unity should then have to be recomposed through a system of houses of representatives, but "each delegate [would] be at any time revocable and bound by the mandat impératif (formal instructions) of his constituents."

The unity of the nation was not to be broken, but, on the contrary, to be organized by the Communal constitution and to become a reality by the destruction of the state power which claimed to be the embodiment of that unity independent of, and superior to, the nation itself, from which it was but a parasitic excrescence.

The multiplicity of interpretations to which the Commune has been subjected, and the multiplicity of interests which construed it in their favour, show that it was a thoroughly expansive political form, while all previous forms of government had been emphatically repressive. Its true secret was this. It was essentially a working-class government, the produce of the struggle of the producing against the appropriating class, the political form at last discovered under which to work out the economical emancipation of labour.

Except on this last condition, the Communal constitution would have been an impossibility and a delusion. The political rule of the producer cannot coexist with the perpetuation of his social slavery. The Commune was therefore to serve as a lever for uprooting the economical foundations upon which rests the existence of classes, and therefore of class rule. With labour emancipated, every man becomes a working man and productive labour ceases to be a class attribute. (210, 212)

Finally, the dynamic of the constituent principle cannot be brought to a conclusion: "The working class did not expect miracles from the Commune. They have no ready-made utopias to introduce par décret du peuple.... They have no ideals to realize, but to set free the elements of the new society with which old collapsing bourgeois society itself is pregnant." "The great social measure of the Commune was its own working existence. Its special measures could but betoken the tendency of a government of the people, by the people" (213, 217).

The revolution is permanent, the constitution is a procedure, the liberation of labor a process. This continual process, which so radically distinguishes Marx's positions from those of the anarchists and all the insurrectionists, is the ontological basis of the concept of constituent power in Marx. In his polemic against Bakunin, Marx exclaims: "The ultimate object of the political movement of the working class is, of course, the conquest of political power for this class, and this naturally requires that the organisation of the working class, an organisation which arises from its economic struggles, should previously reach a certain level of development. On the other hand, however, every movement in which the working class as a class confronts the ruling classes and tried to constrain them by pressure from without is a political movement."[81] He could have added: it is a Constituent Movement. The radicality, the expansivity, the continuity and permanence of constituent power are thus the characteristics of a strength that, grafted onto labor, liberates it. Sieyès and Marx are counterposed on the same terrain, that of the constitution of labor. The problem of the constitution of labor is revealed by the clash between these two positions, immersed in the same matter, with opposite points of view. But the enigma of the French Revolution lies here, in this passage of Rousseau's puzzle to a new opposition: between dominated labor and liberated labor, between constituted labor and constituent labor.

To Terminate the Revolution

The time of the French Revolution dominates also its term. The active and passive usages of the verb *to terminate* are at play: *terminate* as bringing to completion, as bringing to a closure. Around these variants "constituent power" becomes a concept: it must be brought to conclusion, or it must stop producing its effects. "To terminate the revolution" is the password of the *Acte d'insurrection* of the *Egaux*: "The revolution is not finished, because the rich appropriate any property, and command in an exclusive manner, while the poor work as slaves, languish in misery and count for nothing in the State": this is the premise.[82] "To terminate the revolution" is, on the other hand, the theme of the Thermidorians ("How could the 'present circumstances bring an end to the Revolution?'" wonders with lucid consciousness Madame de Staël,[83] and Benjamin Constant adds: "Property and talents, these two reasonable reasons for inequality among men, will take back their rights").[84] In both cases "to terminate the revolution" means to act upon time—to dilate it or shrink it, to expand it or close it. And in both cases time is not an abstract element: it is the time of labor that liberates itself; or it is the time of property that is confirmed, open time or consolidated time.

Only the French Revolution funnels the concept of power into the concrete temporality of social life, and only social life makes time a constitutive strength, radicalizing the alternative between the revolutionary dimension of labor and the conservative dimension of property. This alternative persists at the limit of the revolutionary process, completely undecided, open to the extraordinary history of both these positions. Hence the historical exceptionality of the time of the French Revolution: its actors enter it dressed as ancient Romans and exit dressed in bourgeois garb or in blue collar; they penetrate into it thinking as men of the Enlightenment and are expelled from it either as modern revolutionaries, or as new conservatives, ambiguously divided between historicism and reformism. Here constituent power is conjoined to history—*res gestae*, historical becoming, concrete temporality, open or closed—in any case a general transformation had been accomplished, a sort of gigantic sublation of European men into a new and shared destiny, within which new and alternative choices became actual. The *Declaration of the Rights of Man* takes place in temporality and immediately takes shape—where it is claimed as the beginning of the age of individualism—as a paradoxically tight common dimension. Cooperation or privilege assume a new figure; production and measure become the alternative characteristics of historical time.[85] It is in fact true that the discovery of sociality is the fundamental qualification of the French Revolution and its distinctive character, with respect to the revolutions that had preceded it, but this sociality is configured, and, so to speak, constituted, by the collective temporality. Within temporality, subjects are defined: they are born, they live, and they die; they open themselves to the collective and comprehend the future; they comprehend desires and the hopes that they place in the future, in their principle of individuation. Or, on the contrary, they nourish the principle of individuation of the past, of its vicious repetition, of tradition and the will to renew it.

Constituent power moves between these alternatives. Its constitutive temporality is drawn to hope and to the whole range of possibilities that the future opens, toward the production of a new wealth and a new humanity; or otherwise it is brought back to history, as the supreme principle of a becoming that has its roots in the past, in the necessary preconditions of what exists; and in the past it is seen producing the present. Constituent power, after going through the French Revolution, is no longer the same concept as the one on which we had previously meditated; it has become the principle of a constitutive temporality so profound that its formal characteristics (if not the material ones) must be qualifying elements in the sense of historical becoming. I mean that constituent power is revolutionary if it is open, reactionary and conservative if closed. The aperture or closure of time determines the substantial sense of constituent power. At the end of the French Revolution, aperture of time means permanent revolution and communist revolution; closure means liberalism or, worse, reaction. But the historical scene has changed, the insertion of time has multilateral effects: thus also the reactionary will be different; he will be nourished by a new spirituality, the theoretical aura will be in any case different and irreducible. If the revolution must end, constituent power is there, it persists. It is as if history had revealed a new substratum, an ontological level on which productive humanity anticipated the concrete becoming, forcing it or being blocked by it.

Constituent power, with the French Revolution, becomes historical strength—ontologically stable, historically versatile. As such it is recognized by all—even by the reactionaries, and by the revolutionaries a fortiori. Indeed, this fundamental transformation takes place in the obscure awareness that time and productivity are dimensions of only one substance, labor.

The obscurity of the presupposition does not hide the clarity of the conclusions, and it is not by chance that, as we will soon see, the "master and slave dialectic" (and its direct references to labor and its capitalist organization) constitute in Hegel a reflection on the French Revolution.[86] Thus the generic dimension of sociality is specified when we refer it, within the French Revolution, to constituent power as figure of labor. Slave, master. *Egaux,* Thermidorians. Exploitation and domination. Constituent power casts its shadow, in a definitive manner, on the theory of power as the practice of the organization and of the social division of labor.

It is at this conjuncture, on the other hand, that the juridical theory of constituent power is born. Here the awareness of the inherence of its action, and of the relevance of its effects on the totality of the order is, since the beginning, so clear to the point of inducing the exclusion of constituent power from the sphere of the juridical categories. Or, better, to confine it to a neutral terrain, on which actions and effects become aleatory and extraordinary (see chap. 1). The omnipotence of constituent power is declared with the sole aim of opposing it to the omnipotence of the arrangement, so that when there is one there cannot be another. Constituent power is treated in the same way as the labor whose preconditioning of the arrangement we accept, for the sole purpose of being able to order it totally. Within this muddle, "to terminate the revolution" certainly means to choose—with regard to the sense of constituent power—but without forgetting, even when one wants to repress its effectiveness, its extraordinary presence, and its incompressible activity. *Quod factum infectum fieri nequit.* Or, even better, *hic Rodhus, hic salta.*

It is clear, at this point, that all our attention will go to the reactionaries, toward those who want to close with the revolution, because from the point of view of the theory of constituent power, it is they who, paradoxically, better reveal not so much its new figure as the unsuppressable quality of the concept, its having become a fundamental element of the political theory of modernity. It is on the reactionary unraveling of the constituent principle that the constituent power of the French Revolution above all shows the intensity of its revolutionary effectiveness.

Edmund Burke's work, from this point of view, dominates the picture. Its greatness is measured by the fact that he writes in 1790, at the beginning of the revolution, but he talks about it as if he had gone through it, and now it would be time to terminate it.[87] He is still wearing a wig, and yet he is already speaking bourgeois. The politician already famous for his support of the American Revolution moves an attack against the French Revolution (see chap. 4). What is he attacking in it? The metaphysical abstraction of the idea of freedom. It is good that the idea of freedom has finally appeared in France—but careful: the power of freedom is that of a "wild gas . . . broke loose" (90), it must be measured with the real, regulated by nature, and not escape into the abstract.

Freedom is power, it is the constituent principle. But of what, and how? In actuality the French Revolution disdains the real. It formulates a constituent principle that is a democratic foundation of legitimacy, multilateral expansion of the right to resistance, affirmation of democratic self-government, and therefore of the democratic identity of title and exercise of power. This democratic rationalization of constituent power is against history. The English experience demonstrates it. The principle of democratic legitimacy is in fact against the English institutions, real institutions of freedom. On the basis of democracy it is the institution of monarchy itself that is put into discussion, and with it the system of government founded on custom and on the jurisprudential tradition.

The English Revolution of '88 has made this clear, putting an end to that "small and temporary deviation" (101) that is constituted by the revolution of 1648. The Glorious Revolution is the restoration of a constitution founded on tradition, and it is sanctioned by a hereditary monarchy. The historical, and with it natural, foundation of freedom consists of this. As for the right to resistance, it negates the original contract. This contract cannot be broken. The claim that freedom can replace the monarchs, even in the case of their bad behavior, is extremely dangerous. With this, the principle itself of sovereignty is radically threatened, and the certainty of the law is radically put into discussion. Extremely dangerous is also the principle of democratic government—and its affirmation is abstract, where the concrete freedoms are a hereditary privilege, belonging to all citizens, as are the institutions. It is history that creates the institutions of freedom, within a felicitous conformity to nature. "All the reformations we have hitherto made, have proceeded upon the principle of reference to antiquity" (117); on the contrary, "a spirit of innovation is generally the result of a selfish temperament and confined views" (119). "Our political system [inasmuch as it is historically founded and developed] is placed in a just correspondence and symmetry with the order of the world."

What should we conclude? That all the French have made of their revolution is against the spirit of history, and consequently it is "against nature." Only ruins, errors, and crimes can come out of it, with an unarrestable subversion of the structures of the State (96–135). And this is what actually happens. "Plots, massacres, assassinations, seem to some people a trivial price for obtaining a revolution." In France the terror of the bayonets and the lantern triumphs. The Assembly is not free but blackmailed by extremism. "The Assembly, their organ, acts before them the farce of deliberation with as little decency as liberty." The whole of Europe is drawn into this abyss, where violence replaces the law, and the will of the mob substitutes the history of the institutions. The Europe of chivalry and honest customs is attracted into the whirlpool of vulgarity. "All has changed" on the rhythm of the revolution. Statistics substitutes chivalry. "On this scheme of things, a king is but a man . . . [and] a woman is but an animal." "The principles of this mechanic philosophy" triumph. "But power, of some kind or other, will survive the shock in which manners and opinions perish; and it will find other and worse means for its support." Without the old foundations the path is open to despotism and terror (154–74). Let's stop the new barbarians! Let's lift up the flags of nature against philosophy!

What does nature teach us? That the social order must conform to it. First of all with "real rights," those determined by original convention and by custom. These rights, originally attributed, cannot be modified. They are a given, a sacred and inviolable a posteriori: if we substitute them with new abstract rights, it is the structure of society itself that is destroyed. We must clarify a few things regarding some minimal anthropological concerns, if we want to understand the complicated nature of man and the complex structure of society. Now, on this basis, simplicity is defective and murderous. Real rights live in an intermediate zone of the essence and the history of man—as mediations that together traverse human identity and the structure of society (149–54).

It is worthwhile to make a first pause of reflection, and to try to understand Burke's singular approach to the theme of constituent power. It is directly placed within the commingling of nature and history, and this allows Burke's juridical hermeneutics to graft itself onto a natural ontology, and his polemic against abstract rights (and the adequate right that constitutes them) to become violent—without, for this reason, negating the importance of the principle. This means that Burke situates himself on the terrain of constituent power and its temporality and denies it, from the point of view of preservation, exactly what, from the point of view of transformation, the French radical revolutionaries denied it—the claim to constitute a "political space," free and immaculate with respect to the social. Whereas freedom is expansive, Burke tells us, by repeating the adage of his intervention on the American Revolution, political will, force, violence are not.

In this perspective constituent power is not a political principle, but an ontological one. The singularity of the Burkean approach lies in the inversion of the principle of constituent power, that is posed on an ontological terrain.[88] In the way that the French radical revolutionaries wanted. But the ontology is not empty: it registers an arrangement of society that is organization and division of labor. The "real rights" must be called with their name, and the real right that in a fundamental manner guarantees freedom is called right of property—the right of property whose "characteristic essence is to be unequal" (140). In the new French constitution this beacon-value of property is instead tendentially subjected to values of equality: with it can be destroyed the freedom and all the values that are founded on property (140–44).

Here we are touching on the nucleus of the most interesting problems raised by Burke, in his polemic and in his underlying ontological methodology. What are the real rights that rely on property and that realize its synthesis with freedom? First of all, land property. This property is the sacred foundation of juridical order and of the social organization of labor. It is not by chance that the philosophical group, that actual plot of intellectuals and money-makers that constituted the *Great Encyclopedia*, turned against it (211–14). On the contrary, land property is the unsubstitutable basis of the constitution, of any possible constitution (140–46, 170–95, 214–26, 270–74). "We are resolved to keep an established church, an established monarchy, an established aristocracy, and an established democracy, each in the degree it exists, and in no greater." "Society is indeed a contract. . . . It is the first and supreme necessity only, a necessity that is not chosen but chooses, a necessity paramount to deliberation, that admits no discussion, and demands no evidence, which alone can justify a resort to anarchy" (170–95). The principle of property, thus the principle of inequality, constitutes therefore the actual constituent power of the orders. It is a principle of a superior order. Here, thus, against this principle rebels the French Revolution. It demands a break, a constituent power *ex novo*; it preaches the discontinuity of the orders of the State and the end of the contracts of property. "Few barbarous conquerors have ever made so terrible a revolution in property" (214–226). The polemic becomes invective: its object is the confiscation of aristocratic and ecclesiastical possessions. The French Revolution is the organ of a radical and complete destructuration of the law.

The rest of Burke's argument is formidable: here in fact is clarified the polemical concept of abstraction that he deployed at the beginning—then in ideological terms, now in political and economic terms. What do we achieve, in fact, when we destroy the real basis of the law? Its abstract substitution, that is, with abstract means, monetary, made of paper. The real values are substituted by abstract ones; violence takes the place of legitimacy. The confiscation is mediated by money. On the revolutionary principle of confiscation a new sect has formed, more dangerous than the Anabaptists of Munster, a sect that puts everything on the monetary commune in order to cut away for themselves despotic parts without legitimation—or, better, on the basis of the legitimacy of money, of abstraction, of the appropriating violence (145, 261–70).

The consequences will soon be evident. What is the new government of France? "It affects to be a pure democracy, though I think it in a direct train of becoming shortly a mischievous and ignoble oligarchy" (227–38). It multiplies the abstraction of French society: behind the confiscation comes an unjust principle of taxation (289–90, 35–72), and a figure of the representation without responsibility (303–4), perverse multipliers of an oligarchy without morals. Abstract, irresponsible, perverse. Hatred, outrage, irony, and farsightedness succeed each other in this polemic that comes to the point of having a premonition of the bourgeois distortion and then, liberal and Thermidorian, of revolutionary constituent power. The vision is exhausted in the anticipation of a terroristic and dictatorial tendency that the revolution, under these conditions, cannot but produce.

If "the democracy has always the same tendency towards a party tyranny," so much more this tendency will be revealed in the consequences of the French Revolution. All the elements that today form the cohesion of the nation contain in embryo the reasons of its inevitable rotting. The first element is the confiscations, and it relies on the compulsory course of currency: on these conditions a new ruling class is formed, necessarily a "financial oligarchy": "Your legislators, in everything new, are the very first who have founded a commonwealth upon gaming, and infused this spirit into it as its vital breath" (390–10); "few can understand the game"; "industry must wither away" (311).

The second element of cohesion is the superiority of Paris over the nation: but this destroys the different nationalities and superimposes a unifying, abstract force, powerful and terrible, onto the diverse body of France. The third element of constitutional cohesion is represented by the supreme power of the assembly, by its omnipotence. The executive power, the army, and judiciary power depend on it. Thus all independence of the powers is taken away, and any reciprocal control eliminated; justice, first of all, will be fatally damaged by this arrangement, and we can already see the embryo of a "political army," of a military democracy... Who will resist it? (317–50). Abstract are therefore the new bourgeois order, the new measure of wealth and power—worthy of this abstraction and emptiness of any foundation is the ruinous wait.

At this point we must not think we are facing one of Burke's radically antibourgeois polemics: his point of view is not such, except insofar as it is an attack against the evolution of constituent power in the French Revolution. He does not attack the bourgeoisie exactly—even though his point of view is certainly aristocratic—but, rather, the abstract constituent power to which the French bourgeoisie entrusts its success.[89] Here there is reason for a second pause of reflection on the theme of constituent power. Indeed, we must once again recognize that the Burkean polemic, far from positing itself outside the thematic of constituent power, denounces its perverse historical logic when, distancing itself from the historical foundation, constituent power not only produces the separate sphere of the "political," but also the private one of the "economic." And when it substitutes the will of the State for the dimension of the social, and in this establishes particular interests. Also from this point of view Burke grasps the deeply historical nature of the constituent principle, as the radical revolutionaries had interpreted it—thus trying, through an inverted polemic, to reintroduce it into the real dimensions of the historical and social development.

There is, in Burke, a critique of the political and the economic, in their reciprocal interconnections, that, without anticipating Marx's critique, gives credence in any case to Marx's invitation "to learn from the great reactionaries." What is always striking is that, in that "revolutionary work on the revolution" that is the *Reflections*,[90] the discussion never becomes flattened in the apology for the old feudal order, as happens in Mallet du Pan and in Joseph de Maistre: also the Burkean apology of the English constitution, and even the most infamous pages in defense of land property, recuperates in an inverted sense the register of the "revolutionary event" and is subjected to the fascination of constituent power. For Burke the problem is never to negate it but, rather, to "terminate the revolution," to reconduct constituent power to the time of history—to what was "its" historical time.

In this perspective Burke's *Reflections* present a method, the method of "reform." For the first time the discourse of reform is opposed to that of revolution. And this happens in entirely new terms: that is, the power of reform is grafted onto the same dimension of constituent power: "Its operation is slow, and in some cases almost imperceptible," "a slow but well-sustained progress," "a prolific energy" (273–84, specifically 280–82). Let's not be frightened by these words, which in the coming centuries have assumed a banal and mystified meaning. Here Burke thinks of real modifications, obviously in the context of his conception of the world and of the social organization of the division of labor. The process of the reforms must pass through the nature of man, and this nature is complex; it must constitute itself upon the mediation between nature and history; it can realize itself through jurisprudential hermeneutics and the progressive modification of the administrative organization. Nobody can miss how this perspective may be reactionary, and how effectively it is aimed against the revolutionary event: but it is intelligent and inserted in an ontology of history that is the same to which the revolution aspires. Consequently, he forces constituent power toward a historical horizon: it is the invention of Romanticism.[91] Historical innovation is opposed to revolutionary will—but both are born from the revolutionary event and its alternatives. With Burke, constituent power is attributed that historical quality, that constructive temporality that the most advanced fraction of the revolutionary movement had unceasingly sought. The opposites meet in this identification of the event as origin. To terminate the revolution is, from the point of view of constituent power, to discover its new configuration, that of a strength situated in the historical process, the constitutional productivity of social labor. The fact that Burke affirms the strength of social labor in the form of the division of labor, while the most advanced and consistent revolutionaries pose it in the form of the liberation from exploitation, does not change the place of the concept. The place of social labor is constituent power—on this point both sides agree. The ontological nexus between constitution, labor, and temporality is achieved by Burke, as it had been lived in the movement of the popular masses. It is that liminal point of the definition of power, ontologically decisive, that Burke perceives here. It is also for him the solution of Rousseau's enigma:

> *Mr. Hume told me, that he had from Rousseau himself the secret of his principles of composition. That acute, though eccentric, observer had perceived, that to strike and interest the public, the marvellous must be produced; that the marvellous of the heathen mythology had long since lost its effect; that giants, magicians, fairies, and heroes of romance which succeeded, had exhausted the portion of credulity which belonged to their age; that now nothing was left to a writer but that species of the marvellous which might still be produced, and with as great an effect as ever, though in another way; that is, the marvellous in life, in manners, in characters, and in extraordinary situations, giving rise to new and unlooked for strokes in politics and morals. I believe, that were Rousseau alive, and in one of his lucid intervals, he would be shocked at the practical phrenzy of his scholars, who in their paradoxes are servile imitators; and even in their incredulity discover an implicit faith. (283–84)*

This fantastic and marvelous is exactly the constituent principle. From Rousseau, resolved in the practice of his admirers, to Burke, inventor of a new horizon on which that constituent principle terminates the revolution, thus becoming principle of historical becoming itself.

Leo Strauss's affirmation that in Burke that which "could appear as a return to the primeval equation of the good with the ancestral is, in fact, a preparation for Hegel" will not at this point appear untimely but, rather, a propos and, as usual, precise.[92] This is exactly what Thomas Paine does not understand. His *Rights of Man*, which is born in France in the course of 1790, but which only after the publication of Burke's *Reflections* becomes the book dedicated to the contestation of the new reactionary historicism, notwithstanding the incredible success that it obtains, does not absolutely grasp the revolutionary meaning of Burke's work.[93] Pale is the counterpositioning of rights to history, tenuous and ineffectual is the vindication of American democraticism in front of the strength of the French revolutionary process.

The vindication of the revolution, in terms of law, is a pious intention and empty rhetoric vis-à-vis the might of its proceeding. In the face of catastrophes, of war, of the mechanism of confiscation. The vindication itself of constituent power as permanent power, and the example of Pennsylvania for the application of this power, can be easily derived by Burke—different and irrecoverable is by now the thematic of the American Revolution: the political space has become ontological space; the extension of the transformation has been substituted by its intensity. What an incredible difference! It is up to Burke, Paine's old friend and defender of the American Revolution, to acknowledge it, with all the polemical force that he was capable of putting in this acknowledgment.[94] To terminate the revolution is therefore to understand it not only in its institutional vicissitudes, concluded with the Thermidore, but in its historical essence, in its radicalness that touches the organization of labor. Burke understands in advance this new characteristic of constituent power, its temporality, the subversion of time that is engendered here. It will be Tocqueville who, then, will proceed on this terrain of analysis, by making revolutionary time his exclusive and dramatic object.

But before reasoning about and with him, let's try to understand how the thematic of "terminating the revolution" founds a new culture that continues and reverses the constituent principle. It is in Germany, country of conquest, that this reversal is enacted. Already Leo Strauss talks of Hegel as the product of Burke's historicism. But Hegel is a result—the result of a brief but extremely intense work, a work toward the transformation of constituent power into productive historical principle. This is the result of a formidable period of theoretical acceleration, entirely Germanic, anticipating an analogous movement that in the other European countries will take place in the first decades of the nineteenth century and that of these forms the paradigm—the paradigm of sublation of constituent power. Let's consider for example von Gentz, the German translator of Mallet du Pan and Burke.[95] Here as in Novalis, but in a substantially different manner from the pure counterrevolutionary theorists Rheberg or Brabdes, the polemic against the French Revolution is carried on in entirely historicist terms.[96] What the revolution attributes to the movement, von Gentz attributes to the ethical dynamics of the "spirit of the people." The ethics against the revolution—thus a symbiotic and popular operating against voluntary and mass action. The constitutive principle is not put into discussion: on the contrary, it is exalted, promoted, developed. What is put into discussion is the subjectivity of the event, the materialistic dynamic individuated by its mass becoming.

From *Bildung der Geistes*, the constituent principle is reduced to *Bildung des Volks.* The revolutionary theme is reconducted to ontological creativity, and only in this aspect attacked. But the displacement is more important than the critique.[97]

If Burke wrote a revolutionary work against the revolution, the pages of von Gentz's commentary are worthy of the English original:[98] because they similarly transfer the counterrevolutionary polemic onto the principle of constituent power, as ontological machine of historical foundation. Also in von Gentz, as, and even more than in Burke, this profound action of historical foundation crosses the entire society, and, in particular, the organization of labor. The productive sense of labor becomes constituent principle, thus bringing along the totality of social conditions of productive and reproductive strength. The contents of revolutionary constituent power are fought on the terrain and in the extension on which they are applied: the principle of authority as ethical dimension is vindicated against freedom, the necessity of the classist society of labor is posed against equality; the real foundation of society is order, which is also its end—that is, the ordered reproduction of the conditions of order. The reformist impulse is very strong in this perspective because order is not an abstract principle but the form of the historical process, the determination of its dynamic. The Kantian ethical ideal has become historical force.

Hegel takes this new political awareness to the summits of the philosophy of the spirit. Hegel makes the constituent principle an essential modality, if not the unique and exclusive one in the historical process. Hegel takes up Rousseau's enigma by resolving it entirely on the side of general will, of the translation of the people's strength into the sovereign's power. But this process is work. The work of the spirit and the productive labor, the work of the dialectic and the labor of the popular masses historically defined. Through his juvenile writings, the *Phänomenologie* and the *Rechtsphilosophie*, Hegel progressively and impetuously carries on this project.[99] Labor is per se constitutive, but it must be tamed. Its substantiality constitutes the foundation of human society, but "need and labor, raised to this universality, constitute per se . . . an enormous system of communion and reciprocal dependence, a life of that which is dead that moves within itself, that stirs in its own movement blindly and in an elementary fashion in one sense or in another, and that, as a fierce beast, needs to be constantly subjugated and tamed."[100] This subjection and this domination, this recuperating the "absolutely sour" in the movement of the conciliation of the spirit are the forms in which Hegel provides his reading about "terminating the revolution."

Freedom becomes substantial by recognizing the process that makes constituent power the necessary being of the spirit. The State must be restored because it is the immanent of the constitutive movement and of all its figures: of those of the bourgeois society ("In contrast with the spheres of private rights and private welfare [the family and civil society], the state is from one point of view an external necessity and their higher authority; its nature is such that their laws and interests are subordinate to it and dependent on it. On the other hand, however, it is the end immanent within them, and its strength lies in the unity of its own universal end and aim with the particular interest of individuals, in the fact that individuals have duties to the state in proportion as they have rights against it"),[101] but above all of the figures of historical movement, of the constitutive process, which philosophy and political knowledge must assume, in order to live off it:

> *Therefore it is of essential importance to know what the true constitution is.... This insight can be reached through philosophy alone. Revolutions take place in a state without the slightest violence when the insight becomes universal; institutions, somehow or another, crumble and disappear, each man agrees to give up his right. A government must, however, recognize that the time for this has come; should it, on the contrary, knowing not the truth, cling to temporary institutions, taking what—though recognized—is unessential, to be a bulwark guarding it from the essential (and the essential is what is contained in the Idea), that government will fall, along with its institutions, before the force of mind. The breaking up of its government breaks up the nation itself; a new government arises—or it may be that the government and the unessential retain the upper hand.*[102]

History seems thus to come to a conclusion, the constituent principle to come to an end.

But is it really possible to close and determine that temporality? Once it has been brought to such ontological depth, once constituent power has been transformed into historical strength, can they really be considered in an ordered movement? The negative, radically negative answer to these interrogatives comes from Tocqueville. *The Old Regime and the French Revolution* is from this point of view a doubly revolutionary work: first, because Tocqueville, as Burke, gives us an antihistoricist and counterrevolutionary interpretation of constituent power; second, because he radically attacks historicism and attempts the reduction of the constituent principle to a category of negative thought. It is on the perception of temporality that Tocqueville works—but his temporality is definitely tied to the event, and the event is the precipitous embodiment of the negative, senseless abyss of modernity.

Let's examine these two theoretical episodes within Tocqueville's historical analysis. The first episode is historicist: a very modern historicism, embodied in the awareness of the historical effectiveness of great systems, not only constitutional, but administrative. The three books of the *Old Regime* combine in an exceptional manner historical hermeneutics and the sociology of institutions.[103] Tocqueville is the Max Weber of the nineteenth century.[104] From the bottom of French history, from its medievalism, emerges in fact the administrative apparatus of royal centralization that introduces itself with an irresistible force among the old powers, displacing them without destroying them, matching the rules of effectiveness with those of legitimacy. *Machiavelli redivivus.*[105]

Never as in the France of the old regime the administrative tutelage of the interests, the administrative justice, the equality of the juridical treatment of the subjects had been progressively constituted, thus determining an exceptional fullness of social power. But it is exactly from this creativity of the old regime that its death proceeds. Through administrative centralization, it has in fact accentuated the processes of definition and separation of the social classes, the stiffening into caste (in particular of the aristocracy): in sum, it is this evolution itself that blocks the social and political dynamism, the dynamism that constitutes freedom.

In the eighteenth century there emerges, and becomes more and more powerful, the contrast between the entrepreneurial and centralizing capability of the State and the political determinations (exhausted in the evolutionary process) of its command. It is here that the revolutionary process opens, that is, when the great administrative revolution of the old regime and the regime of juridical equality founded on virtue clash with the generalization of the demand of freedom and equality, with the democratic demand. The old, within which the new had manifested itself, must be erased: the new must now be reproduced by erasing its genesis. The feudal privileges and rights become hideous to the people because in France, more than elsewhere, the administrative machine (legitimated by those old powers themselves) had determined a fullness of social powers. Which are now asserted: this product of the ancient is the revolution. A strong historical causality sustains the argument of the *The Old Regime and the French Revolution*, a multilinear causality that does not precipitate the paradox of the heteronomy of historical finalities, but that, rather, analyzes how these unify, articulate, and explode into the revolution.

Against this vast historical web the subjects stand out, and in particular that essential subject that in Tocqueville is the aristocracy. The latter is the guarantee of freedom because the existence of aristocracy is ancient, and it is thanks to the antiquity of its function that it can exercise socially and politically (although its participation in the political has progressively weakened) a real constitutional counterpower, in defense of everybody's freedom. Since the foundation of aristocracy is virtue, and therefore the basis of an order of values for the social—of a real civil religion, that in concrete allows society to become community, homeland, beyond (and before) abstract values that have become predominant in contemporary society. Finally, since the aristocracy is an intermediate body of society, therefore the guarantee of its diversity and its pluralism. So proceeds Tocqueville's historicism—such a sociological historicism and yet entirely capable of grasping in the long run the constructiveness of constituent power. The recuperation of the ontological temporality of the revolutionary principle is operated here, as it is in Burke. Up to this point, we could say, Tocqueville adapts Burke to the specificities of French constitutional development.

But it is on this point that the reasoning gets inverted and the phenomenology of constituent power grows substantially. The aristocracy, median and axiological point of French constitutional development, is beaten by the revolution: democracy affirms itself. The long duration of ontology dramatically and decisively clashes with the short time of the event. "Au milieu des tenebres de l'avenir on peut déjà découvrir trois vérités très claire." The first truth is that all men of our time are driven by an unknown force (which we can hope to rule or slow down, but not to overcome), which, sometimes slowly, sometimes hurriedly, leads them toward the destruction of the aristocracy. The second truth is that, among all the societies of the world, those that struggle the most to avoid an absolute government are those in which the aristocracy is no longer and can no longer exist. Finally, the third truth is that in no other society can despotism produce more damage than in these societies—ploughed by the principle of equality—because it favors every social vice that the societies that have destroyed the aristocracy keep within themselves "as natural inclinations."

When men are no longer tied to one another by ties of caste, class, corporation, and family, they tend toward a "narrow individualism," from which any public virtue is erased:

> *Far from trying to counteract such tendencies despotism encourages them, depriving the governed of any sense of solidarity and interdependence; of good-neighborly feelings and a desire to further the welfare of the community at large. It immures them, so to speak, each in his private life and taking advantage of the tendency they already have to keep apart, it estranges them more. Their feelings toward each other were already growing cold; despotism freezes them.*[106]

The revolution put off balance the process that kept freedom and authority in equilibrium. It frees the destructive strengths of individualism, of money, the subversive strengths linked to equality, by projecting them into a subversion that only despotism can block.

Democracy generates an uncontainable state of precariousness and hazard of values and behavior. The inevitability of the historical process from now on collides with a permanent instability of its results. If the constitutional process of centralization has created the revolutionary conditions, the revolution has torn off the long time of stability and has not reconstructed analogous conditions. It has precipitated history into the short time open to the strength of the multitude. Temporality is generally constitutive of constituent power. Now what changes is not the temporal rooting of constituent power, but the quality of time: short time is opposed to long time, the present is opposed to memory, subversion to tradition. Short time is now the irreplaceable dimension of history.

In the negative quality that temporality assumes in Tocqueville, constituent power finally reveals itself in its modernity. Tocqueville's negative quality cannot answer the question of how "to terminate the revolution": he gives a first definition of constituent power as intensive and shortened temporality, as an assemblage of alternatives, as unarrestable alternative. Consequently, only despotism can resist constituent power and democracy.

Thus with Tocqueville a tragic episode in the definition of constituent power opens—a long and consistent episode in the history of political ideas of the nineteenth century. Here lies the understanding of the irresistible relation of constituent power and of radical democracy, and an anguished retreating in front of this social tendency. It is here that, on the juridical terrain, the theoretical tangle we often brought to the fore was born, according to which the definition of the juridical and constitutional arrangement must exclude or submit, in a prolix, formal, and inconsequential manner, constituent power. It is here that, with the reactionary interpretation of the French Revolution, a catastrophic interpretation of the modern begins to take shape. Tocqueville is certainly closer to Nietzsche than the authors of *The Federalist* are. If in the historiography of the French Revolution, done by French historians, Tocqueville is more and more drawn into writing an apology for liberalism, however tired and disenchanted it may be,[107] much more correctly he could be brought near those philosophical currents that, from Burckhardt to Dilthey to von Sybel, make a tragic element of considerating the modern of the critique of the French Revolution.[108]

But if we probe and develop, interpret and reverse these last readings, there appears a new space of understanding of the concept in Tocqueville: a new, for him irresolvable, but as real as ever, definition of constituent power. A power that, by spreading into the multitude, opens to the task of the unification of the title and the exercise of sovereignty—which, in turn, gives back the concept of sovereignty to the activity of the masses, thus secularizing it, subtracting it from separateness, and constituting it as the government of the systems from below, and their creation, by making power humane, by seeing it as temporal dimension, as the resolute activity of multiple temporalities. What the aristocracy had been able to do—to unify, consolidate, and develop these multiple functions of power—today the multitude must do. Temporality is reversed: the scandal represented by the masses in the course of the revolution, that progressive temporality of the event, must now be recognized as permanent condition. Inevitable, irreplaceable horizon. The constructive capability of history here is elevated to the problem of the specific temporality of the event: this is what returns historical constructivity to the subject. Tocqueville's historicism opens a new front of the interpretation. His pessimism does not replace the aperture and the hope of the previous American experience but merely specifies it in the new situation: here, in fact, time is opposed to space, and if in Jeffersonian democracy all games seemed possible, in the time of European democracy all the problems are reopened. Tocqueville's pessimism is only the pale surface of an intelligence that poses the problems of the future.

There is nothing in the whole of his thought that can hint at an irrationalist, immobilist and reactionary exasperation of the function of aristocracy, nothing that can indicate an eternalization of this function. Nothing that draws him close to, or makes us presume Gobineau's disciple in him.[109] In the latter the exaltation of the aristocracy becomes an absolute principle. Aristocracy is transformed into a natural force, into a race: "The Christian religion ineffective and impotent, Buddhism a moral perversity, patriotism a Canaan monstrosity, law and justice mere abstractions, art a seducer and prostitute, compassion for the oppressed and pity for the poor sentimental illusions: the list is complete. This is the triumph of the new principle."[110] But neither can we notice any proximity to the new theories of the "liberal political space."[111] And this is so for at least two reasons. The first is that in Tocqueville there exists no theory of the political space understood as his contemporaries understand it, that is, as space of representation separated from that of society, or, better, articulated through it according to the exigencies of political mediation. The pale anticipations that *Democracy in America* had produced in this sense are completely inverted (but also, and above all, developed, and thus integrated into the new tendency), where the administrative State is seen as the constitutive machine of a democratic society in the grip of contradiction. In Tocqueville the isolation of the State is not the guarantee of civil society, but the motor of a deeper and deeper contradiction between the necessity of command and the consequences of the egalitarian processes.

The second reason, and a fortiori: in Tocqueville there is no idea of a "liberal" political space, because democracy, far from determining freedom, mixes it with equality, takes away its essential dynamic, and thus makes society enormously fragile. If the concept of democracy is detached from that of the revolution from the point of view of its genesis, it is brought closer to that of despotism through the analysis of its tendency.

Already in *Democracy in America* democracy is described as the limit of the depoliticization of civil society, as the triumph of a generalized conformism: when, then, the organization of the State will have gone through the administrative modifications of the old regime and the revolutionary convulsions, its destiny will be definitely entrusted to an unsolvable tragedy, to the alternative between two equally destructive machines, the revolution and despotism, coexisting, complementary in the concept of democracy itself. "To terminate the revolution" is at this point a tragic nonsense. Tocqueville's journey into temporality ends in catastrophe.

This takes nothing away from Tocqueville's greatness. On the contrary. By proceeding in this way he reopens the problem of constituent power that the historicist interpretative line—from Burke to the Romantics to Hegel—had tried to neutralize in the long term, or to pacify in the dialectic process. Tocqueville ideologically renews the conception of constituent time, bringing it to an antagonist contradiction. He can do this because he perceives, at the same time, the long dimension of the constitution of the social order of labor, and the intensive dimension of the democratic time of the masses, of the time revolution. He renders to us, in its split, that Rousseauean enigma by which the entire history of the French Revolution is dominated, from the beginning to end. He renders it to us after having seen it in the thousand facets of a broken mirror. He renders it to us by maintaining for us the sound of the breaking. In Tocqueville the long development of the constituent principle, from the indistinct temporality of the Machiavellian *virtus* to the counterpower of the English revolutionaries, from the American political space to the ontological rooting in the productivity of social labor typical of French revolutionary thought, is thus conclusively reproposed to us, in the form of synthesis and a new problematic.

The intensity of the analysis is extraordinary. It provokes the definitive displacement of the concept beyond the possibility of synthesis of being and of movement, and it poses the question on this terrain of interruption. Constituent power could at this point present itself as the concept not simply of a historical crisis, but of a metaphysical one. That is, the conceptual crisis does not seem possible anymore if the concept of crisis does not situate itself on the same level as that of constituting, and the dynamic concept of constituting does not adequately modify the essence of power. No longer, therefore, a power and a constitution, but a constitution of power, only one time, one strength—and one strength only.

This is the question that negative thought will pose throughout the nineteenth century. This metaphysical displacement of the concept derives from the insertion of temporality in the definition, as much as, from another perspective, it comes from the fact that only temporality gives the sense of the new productive conditions in which social labor takes place. On the metaphysical terrain temporality means productivity, and productivity means labor. Tocqueville reveals as conceptual crisis this huge metaphysical displacement that the French Revolution, its "constituent men," but above all the movement of the masses, had provoked, historically lived, debated, and suffered. The revolution for a constitution of labor reveals itself as impossible to execute: exactly because, in the attempt to realize itself, constituent power had been transferred to the terrain of temporality, implanted on a new ontological substratum: both reveal a new metaphysical dimension. Here "to terminate the revolution" will be from now on always impossible.

S I X

Communist Desire and the Dialectic Restored

Constituent Power in Revolutionary Materialism

MODERN CAPITALISM brings to maturity the concept of constituent power by constructing it as the pervasive force of the entire society, as the continuity of a social power that absorbs and configures all other power, State power first of all. In modern capitalism all the characteristics of constituent power, which a long historical process had been shaping, are powerfully summed up and reorganized. Its ontological rooting, its function as social counterpower, its spatial dimension, and the continuity of its temporal action—all these become the figure of a constituent power that the modern force of industry distributes among the actors of the market and the social subjects, turning each one into a protagonist and turning collective capital into the Lycurgus of a radical, pressing, and continuous constitutive process of the world. The world, society, and the State are built *ex novo*, reshaped, or radically transformed.

In modern capitalism constituent power immediately reveals itself as social strength. The historical trajectory of capitalist development from primitive accumulation to "postindustrial" society is nothing but a continual process of the subsumption of society under capital, a process in which capital has been insinuated into every relationship and become the connective key of every apparatus, the finality of every initiative. Capitalist development is also the dissemination of powers in productive society, the constitution of a dialectical network that always can or must be brought back to unity and redefinition within command. The modern concept of constituent power can be conceived only on this basis.

On the other hand, only on this capitalist actuality, only on this totality of modernity can it be liberated. It is not by chance, therefore, that the one who reveals this figure, this structure, and this nature of modern capitalism, Karl Marx, is also the one who shows in the most radical manner how constituent power runs through this gigantic machine in a contradictory and yet continuous way. After Marx we can only say that power in capitalist society is held by the one who, day by day, holds constituent power.

This Marxian conception of constituent power in capitalist development cannot be found in his so-called political and historical works. In those writings Marxian subjectivity is most often located in the revolutionary militant, and communist desire becomes tenuous both in utopia and in the immediate political proposition, modeling itself on the movements of the masses (see chap. 5). Marx really deals with modern constituent power in *Capital.* This is where he confronts the riddle of the originary, constitutive violence of the social and political order. This is a double problem that points on the one side to the identification of founding violence and on the other to its ordering function.

Marx makes the crisis that constitutes the concept of constituent power (as a concept perennially open on the social and closed on the political) the keystone of his reading of the historical process, the ontological epistemology of the social systems, and the schema of the alternatives of the forms of the State. Constituent power is in Marx the dynamic relationship of power and cooperation, the progressive line through which successive syntheses are fixed, from subjects to struggles, from cooperation to command, from command to crisis, and from crisis to revolution. All this is grafted on the materiality of history according to a methodology that, more than any other, can illustrate the concept of constituent power. On the whole, constituent power will appear as the synthesis of necessity and freedom, as the practical point on which the traditional concepts of political thought—of force and contract, domination and consent, innovation and revolution—come to confront each other, presenting the entire range of the alternatives of modernity.

When we enter into the heart of Marx's discussion, we can see that he presents the schema of the concept of constituent power along two vectors or logical schemata that go from accumulation to law. The first is mediated by violence and the second by cooperation. Accumulation is the originary state, dynamic and not idyllic, in which modern society is formed. Law and the State are results of the process. In the middle stand the modalities of development, sometimes separated, sometimes interwoven, or, even better, always dialectically connected even in their difference. The crisis lies in the relationship and alternation between violence and cooperation, but the dialectic does not deny difference. It is therefore possible for us to follow the two vectors in their relative separation.

First of all, then, we need to follow the line that leads from accumulation to violence to law. Constituent power is here the originary exercise of violence by the ruling class. We are at the center of the "secret of primitive accumulation," the "original sin" at the heart of political economy. This is where Marx demonstrates how force and violence are typical phenomena of capitalist accumulation: "In actual history, it is a notorious fact that conquest, enslavement, robbery, murder, in short, force, play the greatest part." Only political economy does not acknowledge this violence: "In the tender annals of political economy, the idyllic reigns from time immemorial. Right and 'labour' were from the beginning of time the sole means of enrichment, 'this year' of course always excepted. As a matter of fact, the methods of primitive accumulation are anything but idyllic."[1]

Through violence capital has created the conditions of "capitalist" development, conditions reached through the polarization of the market of commodities. On one side stands the "free" worker and on the other the conditions of the realization of labor. "So-called primitive accumulation, therefore, is nothing else than the historical process of divorcing the producer from the means of production. It appears as 'primitive' because it forms a pre-history of capital, and the mode of production corresponding to capital" (*Capital*, 1:874). Violence is thus the constant element of the process, and it is a violence that is determined in the foundation and the maintenance of the alienation of the worker: "The starting-point of the development that gave rise both to the wage-labourer and to the capitalist was the enslavement of the worker. The advance made consisted in a change in the form of this servitude, in the transformation of feudal exploitation into capitalist exploitation" (1:875). But violence is not only the starting point. Constituent power is a process that founds new social institutions and new conditions of citizenship, and that at the same time transforms and functionalizes all that it touches, old or new:

The spoilation of the Church's property, the fraudulent alienation of the state domains, the theft of the common lands, the usurption of feudal and clan property and its transformation into modern private property under circumstances of ruthless terrorism, all these things were just so many idyllic methods of primitive accumulation. They conquered the field for capitalist agriculture, incorporated the soil into capital, and created for the urban industries the necessary supplies of free and rightless proletarians. (1:895)

Violence is the constituent datum: datum and continuity, fact and organization, effectiveness and validity. It begins to be dressed in juridical forms when it is exercised most intensely. It puts on and off legal garb. Once the expropriation has taken place and accumulation manifests itself in a first capitalist "organization" of the new mode of production, then the law—the direct expression of the revolutionary violence of the bourgeoisie—takes on a prominent form: "The rising bourgeoisie needs the power of the state, and uses it to 'regulate' wages, i.e., to force them into the limits suitable for making a profit, to lengthen the working day, and to keep the worker himself at his normal level of dependence. This is an essential aspect of so-called primitive accumulation" (1:899–900). Violence thus constitutes the vehicle between accumulation and right. It has no problem presenting in legal terms, or better, making law a subsidiary element of accumulation. It insinuates itself as master between the direct alienation of the producer and the organization of the mode of production. It celebrates right and law as shock-producing tools in the genetic phase of capital, and then, once the new conditions have been consolidated, violence grants right and law a crucial place. Violence ceases to be immediate and becomes habit. The silent coercion of economic relations sanctions the domination of capital on the worker:

The different moments of primitive accumulation can be assigned in particular to Spain, Portugal, Holland, France and England, in more or less chronological order. These different moments are systematically combined together at the end of the seventeenth century in England; the combination embraces the colonies, the national debt, the modern tax system, and the system of protection. These methods depend in part on brute force, for instance the colonial system. But they all employ the power of the state, the concentrated and organized force of society, to hasten, as in a hothouse, the process of transformation of the feudal mode of production into the capitalist mode, and to shorten the transition. Force is the midwife of every old society which is pregnant with a new one. It is itself an economic power. (1:915–16)

Constituent power has become a constituted power, a sort of average level of violence that overdetermines every social relationship.[2]

This is the first vector: violence is constituted as the center of every power and every right, a fortiori as expression of constituent power. We might think of this as a Hobbesian Marx, who defines right as immediate superstructure of violence and as process that refines violence, and thus who reveals the secret of right. The reasoning develops from this starting point, but always within this vector that poses violence at the center of the constructive dynamic of right. Violence fabricates right, but this right that is constructed from violence is cast over reality, history, and the space and time of the world. Certainly, "the law [is] a product of the material relations of production" and only from the standpoint of "juridical illusion" can it appear that "the relations of production [are] products of the law." (Marx adds sarcastically: "Linguet overthrew Montesquieu's illusory *esprit des lois* with one word: *L'esprit des lois, c'est la propriété* [The spirit of the laws is property]") (1:766, n. 4).

Certainly, it is absurd to proceed as Proudhon does. He

creates his ideal of justice, of "justice éternelle," *from the juridical relations that correspond to the production of commodities: he thereby proves, to the consolation of all good petty bourgeois, that the production of commodities is a form as eternal as justice. Then he turns round and seeks to reform the actual production of commodities, and the corresponding legal system, in accordance with this ideal. What would one think of a chemist who, instead of studying the actual laws governing molecular interactions, and on that basis solving definite problems, claimed to regulate those interactions by means of the "eternal ideas" of* "naturalité" *and* "affinité"*? Do we really know any more about "usury," when we say it contradicts* "justice éternelle," "mutualité éternelle," *and other* "vérités éternelles" *than the fathers of the church did when they said it was incompatible with* "grâce éternelle," "foi éternelle," *and* "la volonté éternelle de Dieu"*? (1:178–79, n. 2)*

To forget that violence and domination are the constitutive forces of the system is illusory and hypocritical. It is tantamount to entrusting ourselves naively to the "pompous catalogue of the 'inalienable rights of man'" (1:416).

The sphere of circulation or commodity exchange, within whose boundaries the sale and purchase of labour-power goes on, is in fact a very Eden of the innate rights of man. It is the exclusive realm of Freedom, Equality, Property and Bentham. Freedom, because both buyer and seller of a commodity, let us say of labour-power, are determined only by their own free will. They contract as free persons, who are equal before the law. Their contract is the final result in which their joint will finds a common legal expression. Equality, because each enters into relation with the other, as with a simple owner of commodities, and they exchange equivalent for equivalent. Property, because each disposes only of what is his own. And Bentham, because each looks only to his own advantage. The only force bringing them together, and putting them into relation with each other, is the selfishness, the gain and the private interest of each. Each pays heed to himself only, and no one worries about the others. And precisely for that reason, either in accordance with the pre-established harmony of things, or under the auspices of an omniscient providence, they all work together to their mutual advantage, for the common weal, and in the common interest. (1:280)

And we could continue to follow Marx's indignation on this point ad infinitum (see, e.g., 3:459–79).

In capitalist development the process develops, and this right constructed in violence is cast over reality. Violence dominates more and more, even with respect to the transformation of the originary conditions of accumulation. In capitalist development,

the laws of appropriation or of private property, laws based on the production and circulation of commodities, become changed into their direct opposite through their own internal and inexorable dialectic. The exchange of equivalents, the original operation with which we started, is now turned round in such a way that there is only an apparent exchange, since, firstly, the capital which is exchanged for labour-power is itself merely a portion of the product of the labour of others which has been appropriated without an equivalent; and, secondly, this capital must not only be replaced by its producer, the worker, but replaced together with an added surplus. The relation of exchange between capitalist and worker becomes a mere semblance belonging only to the process of circulation, it becomes a mere form, which is alien to the content of the transaction itself, and merely mystifies it. The constant sale and purchase of labour-power is the form; the content is the constant appropriation by the capitalist, without equivalent, of a portion of the labour of the others which has already been objectified, and his repeated exchange of this labour for a greater quantity of the living labour of others.

In short, "Originally the rights of property seemed to us to be grounded in a man's own labour.... Now, however, property turns out to be the right, on the part of the capitalist, to appropriate the unpaid labour of others or its product, and the impossibility, on the part of the worker, of appropriating his own product. The separation of property from labour thus becomes the necessary consequence of a law that apparently originated in their identity" (1:729–30, see also 1:929–30, 3:569).

This violence that creates right and law is thus presented as a real and structural force, that is, a constitutive force. Far from confining itself to the form of the process, it spreads and multiplies in the real relation that humans articulate among themselves in the production. It produces the producers:

Capital developed within the production process until it acquired command over labour, i.e. over self-activating labour-power, in other words the worker himself. The capitalist, who is capital personified, now takes care that the worker does his work regularly and with the proper degree of intensity. Capital also developed into a coercive relation, and this compels the working class to do more work than would be required by the narrow circle of its own needs. As an agent in producing the activity of others, as an extractor of surplus labour and an exploiter of labour-power, it surpasses all earlier systems of production, which were based on directly compulsory labour, in its energy and its quality of unbounded and ruthless activity.

As soon as a certain sum of money is transformed into means of production, i.e. into the objective factors of the production process, the means of production themselves are transformed into a title, both by right and by might, to the labour and surplus labour of others. (1:424–25)

The immediate violence of the exploitation and the juridical superstructure become a mediated violence and a structure internal to the productive process. The law—or really, the form of violence—becomes a machine, or really, a permanent procedure of the system, its constant innovation and its rigid discipline.

From the world of sovereign violence we have entered the pervasive and customary world of discipline. The capital relation constitutes not only the law but also a new world. It changes humans, increases their productivity, and socializes them. It imposes itself as structure of their existence. This transformation of violence into a structure, of the juridical superstructure into a historical and institutional system, becomes more intense the more the capitalist mode of production develops. In this transformation violence does not disappear but is organized, becoming more and more a violence that orders and transforms reality:

Even if that capitals was, on its entry into the process of production, the personal property of the man who employs it, and was originally acquired by his own labour, it sooner or later becomes value appropriated without an equivalent, the unpaid labour of others materialized either in the money-form or in some other way. (1:715)

Therefore the worker himself constantly produces objective wealth, in the form of capital, an alien power that dominates and exploits him; and the capitalist just as constantly produces labour-power, in the form of a subjective source of wealth which is abstract, exists merely in the physical body of the worker, and is separated from its own means of objectification and realization; in short, the capitalist produces the worker as wage-labourer. This incessant reproduction, this perpetuation of the worker, is the absolutely necessary condition for capitalist production. (716)

The capitalist process of production . . . seen as a total, connected process, i.e. a process of reproduction, produces not only commodities, not only surplus-value, but it also produces and reproduces the capital relation itself; on the one hand the capitalist, on the other the wage-labourer. (724)

Accumulation is the conquest of the world of social wealth. It is the extension of the area of exploited human material and, at the same time, the extension of the direct and indirect sway of the capitalist. (739–40)

The capitalist reproduction of society corresponds to increasingly deep and structural forms of violence. The originary expropriating violence of capitalist domination remains a latent potentiality of the system and a constitutive element of its effectiveness:

The antithetical social determination of material wealth—its antithesis to labour as wage-labour—is already expressed in capital ownership as such, quite apart from the production process. This one moment, then, separated from the capitalist production process itself, whose constant result it is, and as whose constant result it is also its constant presupposition, is expressed in this way: that money, and likewise commodities, are in themselves latent, potential capital, i.e. can be sold as capital; in this form they give control of the labour of others, give a claim to the appropriation of others' labour, and are therefore self-valorizing value. It also emerges very clearly here how this relationship is the title to, and the means to the appropriation of, the labour of others, and not any kind of labour that the capitalist is supposed to offer as an equivalent. (3:477)

Originary violence has become entitlement, even though, within this totality, it is no longer originary. In this first constitutive vector Marx unveils the mystery of the relationship between constituted power and constituent power, against which the constitutionalists have long beat their heads.

But Marx also goes further. Time and space, their generality and our perception of them, are comprehended in the totality of the capitalist investment of society and in the omnipotence of its constituent power. Indeed, the valorization of capital always takes place in the temporal dimension of "presence," even though "production time is always greater than working time."[3] This excess is based on the fact that productive capital exists in a "latent state" in the sphere of production, but always in function of its own effectiveness as "presence." This latency or relative inactivity constitutes a condition of the uninterrupted flow of the production process: "During its circulation time, capital does not function as productive capital, and therefore produces neither commodities nor surplus value" (2:203). It remains there, however, latent, anxiously waiting the moment when it will become productive, the moment when the metamorphosis of "latency" into "presence" will take place. The tendency of capitalist production to shorten as much as possible the excess of production time with respect to working time is constant, but what capital cannot stand is the limitation of its process of valorization. This acceleration of time toward presence is something like proof of the totality of the originary constitutive act. It reappears here as the presence of a greedy impatience to reduce all to the foundation:

Industrial capital is the only mode of existence of capital in which not only the appropriation of surplus-value or surplus product, but also its creation, is a function of capital. It thus requires production to be capitalist in character; its existence includes that of the class antagonism between capitalists and wage-labourers. To the degree that it takes hold of production, the technique and social organization of the labour process are revolutionized, and the economic-historical type of society along with this. The other varieties of capital which appeared previously, within past or declining conditions of social production, are not only subordinated to it and correspondingly altered in the mechanism of their functioning, but they now move only on its basis, thus live and die, stand and fall together with this basis. (2:135–36)

The capitalist Moloch thus reorganizes space itself, and it breathes to the rhythm of the conquering will to reappropriate everything. This is the vector that leads from accumulation to violence to right and that defines the first figure of constituent power in its totality and in the force and complexity of its effects.

The process of the constituent power of capital, however, is not only radical but also antagonistic. It also presents an alternative. At the same point where violence rules, in the same space and time another process opens: the process of "cooperation" and of its becoming antagonistic subject. All the passages that the series from accumulation to right has shown us as constructed on violence can be critically reconstructed from the standpoint of cooperation. Cooperation is, in fact, in itself, an essentially productive force. Its position is immediately constitutive:

Apart from the new power that arises from the fusion of many forces into a single force, mere social contact begets in most industries a rivalry and a stimulation of the "animal spirits," which heightens the efficiency of each individual worker. This is why a dozen people working together will produce far more, in their collective working day of 144 hours than twelve isolated men each working for 12 hours, and far more than one man who works 12 days in succession. This originates from the fact that man, if not as Aristotle thought a political animal, is at events a social animal. (1:443–44)

When the worker co-operates in a planned way with others, he strips off the fetters of his individuality, and develops the capabilities of his species. (1:447)

The productive powers of cooperation grow with its complexity. Association and contact become more and more productive the more complex the conditions of production become, with respect to the volume of the means of production, the number of the cooperating subjects, and the general degree of social evolution.

As capital develops, the force of associative productive labor increases at such a rate that it begins to become indistinguishable from social activity itself. We will return to this point later, but we should clarify immediately the form in which the constitutive strength of cooperation unfolds with respect to capital and the vector that constructed right and law. In large part, we need to clarify how cooperation opens constitutive dynamics that oppose the relationship between violence and law. Marx insists on the fact that cooperation is initially constituted by capital: "The collective working organism is a form of existence of capital.... Hence the productive power which results from the combination of various kinds of labour appears as the productive power of capital. Manufacture proper not only subjects the previously independent worker to the discipline and command of capital, but creates in addition a hierarchical structure amongst the workers themselves" (1:481). Marx sees the realization of this tendency especially in the system of the large-scale factory:

The technical subordination of the worker to the uniform motion of the instruments of labour, and the peculiar composition of the working group... gives rise to a barrack-like discipline, which is elaborated into a complete system in the factory, and brings the previously mentioned labour of superintendence to its fullest development, thereby dividing the workers into manual labourers and overseers, into the private soldiers and the N.C.O.s of an industrial army. (1:549)

In the factory code, the capitalist formulates his autocratic power over his workers like a private legislator, and purely as an emanation of his own will, unaccompanied by either that division of responsibility otherwise so much approved of by the bourgeoisie, or the still more approved representative system. This code is merely the capitalist caricature of the social regulation of the labour process which becomes necessary in co-operation on a large scale and in the employment in common of instruments of labour, and especially of machinery. The overseer's book of penalties replaces the slave-driver's lash. All punishments naturally resolve themselves into fines and deductions from wages, and the law-giving talent of the factory Lycurgus so arranges matters that a violation of his laws is, if possible, more profitable to him than the keeping of them. (1:549–50)

Consequently, cooperation itself insofar as it is ruled by capital seems to become something independent and to be concentrated in command against the concrete cooperation of the workers and its productive strength. This dialectic of capital, however, does not come to a happy resolution but becomes more contradictory and untenable the more complex cooperation becomes. In fact, although command has been historically linked to associative labor in such a way that it appears that the *contractum subjectionis* issues directly from the *contractum unionis*, in the capitalist system this relationship is configured in a specific way that reveals its proper antagonistic content. By making the power of command and thus also the juridical sphere increasingly independent as the process of socialization of production proceeds, capitalism destroys the relationship, determines its conditions of rupture, and prepares the liberation of cooperation from its antagonist link to capitalism (3:493–514).

Up to this point, however, we are still on the terrain of possibility—an extremely important but limited terrain and only partially relevant to the thematic of constituent power. Productive force linked to cooperation in fact only seems to be able to break itself away by following the negative path of the capitalist capacity of organization. This is a destructive strength that is more revolutionary than it is constituent. This is not the only terrain of Marx's analysis. In another sense, in the very moment when the antagonism of the relations included in capital builds up to the point of rupture, Marx follows the physiology proper to the subject-worker—or, better, the mechanisms through which productive cooperation becomes a political subject and its productive strength becomes constituent power. Marx develops this theme in the sections of *Capital* in which he studies English factory legislation and the struggles against the excessive length of the working day (vol. 1, chaps. 10, 15). Command and working cooperation, the collective capitalist and the collective worker stand against one another. Each expresses its own right: right against right. We have seen what right and law are for the capitalist. What is the right of the workers? It is an effort of reappropriation against expropriation, and it is the claim that the organization of production can be posed through cooperation, equality, and intelligence. It is the idea that productive strength cannot be alienated but must instead be transformed into a constantly open and developed constituent power:

If we were to consider a communist society in place of a capitalist one, then money capital would immediately be done away with, and so too the disguises that transactions acquire through it. The matter would be simply reduced to the fact that the society must reckon in advance how much labour, means of production and means of subsistence it can spend, without dislocation, on branches of industry which, like, the building of railways, for instance, supply neither means of production nor means of subsistence, nor any kind of useful effect, for a long period, a year or more, though they certainly do withdraw labour, means of production and means of subsistence from the total annual product. In capitalist society, on the other hand, where any kind of social rationality asserts itself only post festum, *major disturbances can and must occur constantly. (2:390)*

But, again, this idea of planning is weak. Constituent power, seen from the standpoint of cooperation, seems to stretch between rebellion and a utopia traced on an extreme planned rationalization of the productive process.

And yet within these limits of the analysis and the project there is more than rebellion and utopia. What we begin to perceive here is the absoluteness of the cooperative moment as the basis of production and constitution, a conjoined and exclusive basis. Constituent power should not be read only in the totality of the spatial and temporal relations of production and thus as synthesis of the rule, nor should it be seen simply as a radical founding moment. These are the philosophy and the practice of capitalism, and it is not enough merely to invert them formally. Here constituent power is conceived as the inversion of the capitalist "sense" of the process. This inversion destroys the capitalist dialectic and frees the strength of cooperation. Constituent power becomes the originary absolute of the expression of a productive community, constituted with difficulty but at this point capable of developing freely. On this new basis, the utopian content frees itself from the analysis of the economic process and becomes, so to speak, a hypothesis of materialist research. And it is successful in this new endeavor! The strong result of Marx's analyses of the struggles around the length of the working day and the Factory Acts consists thus in indicating a new constitutive process, not inside but outside the dialectic of capital and situated in the autonomy of cooperation, that is, in the subjectivity of the working class. Far from presenting itself as indeterminate possibility of a rupture and as vague utopian projection, constituent power founded on cooperation becomes a material force: "As soon as the gradual upsurge of working-class revolt had compelled Parliament compulsorily to shorten the hours of labor" (1:533).

The most strictly economic analyses of *Capital* are the ones that, not paradoxically, sketch the new theory of constituent power and define the formal conditions of the antagonistic process that emanates from cooperation. These antagonisms are far from being resolved by fixing the equilibriums of production—as it has appeared for too long to many of his interpreters.[4] Marx in fact analyzes the relationship between production and reproduction as a process in which the subjects (capital and labor) are not merely dialectically separated (and therefore reunited) but they progressively separate more and more and thus run counter to each other.

The cycle of total social capital in its various transformations "is not the result of a merely formal change of position belonging to the circulation process, but rather the real transformation which the use form and the value of the commodity components of the productive capital have undergone in the production process" (2:175). This means that, in reference to the total social capital and the value of its product, "The transformation of one portion of the product's value back into capital, the entry of another part into the individual consumption of the capitalist and working classes, forms a movement within the value of the product in which the total capital has resulted; and this movement is not only a replacement of values, but a replacement of material, and is therefore conditioned not just by the mutual relations of the value components of the social product but equally by their use-values, their material shape" (2:470). All this means that, far from closing within itself, the dialectical process opens and that its constitutive elements attain full autonomy.

Elsewhere Marx wrote with regard to this same point:

> *In this circulation, capital constantly expels itself as objectified labour, in order to assimilate living labour power, its life's breath. Now, as regards the worker's consumption, this reproduces one thing—namely himself, as living labour capacity.* Because this, his reproduction, is itself a condition for capital, therefore the worker's consumption also appears as the reproduction not of capital directly, but of the relations under which alone it is capital. . . . *But in so far as capital is a relation, and, specifically, a relation to living labour capacity, [to that extent] the worker's consumption reproduces this relation.*[5]

This passage indicates the formal possibility of the autonomy of the cooperation of living labor. Once he defines this formal possibility, Marx can state,

> *The way in which the various components of the total social capital, of which the individual capitals are only independently functioning components, alternatively replace one another in the circulation process—both with respect to capital and to surplus-value—is thus not the result of the simple intertwining of the metamorphoses that occurs in commodity circulation, and which the acts of capital circulation have in common with all other processes of commodity circulation, but rather requires a different mode of investigation.* (Capital, *2:198)*

This "different mode of investigation" has to be able to grasp the separate dynamics of the conflicting subjects, no longer simply revealing the conditions of their separation but their reality. Since we have seen at length what this means on the terrain of command, it is now time to analyze it on the terrain of cooperation. Here constituent power is the power of living labor, which wants to subtract itself from expropriation and seeks its enjoyment—for itself, as cooperation, as social living labor. This process of self-valorization is presented as an unsatisfied tension toward enjoyment, which wants to subtract itself from the block that capitalist objectification tries to impose and in this operation of self-subtracting, in this process, constitute itself. Antagonism is founded but not exhausted (on the contrary, it opens new paths of constitution) within the relationship of exploitation:

> The most extreme form of alienation, *wherein labour appears in the relation of capital and wage labour, and labour, productive activity appears in relation to its own conditions and its own product, is a necessary point of transition—and therefore already contains in* itself, *in a still only inverted form, turned on its head, the dissolution of all* limited presuppositions of production, *and moreover creates and produces the unconditional presuppositions of production, and therewith the full material conditions for the total, universal development of the productive forces of the individual.* (Grundrisse, *515)*

At this point, within the theoretical framework of the critique of political economy, the analysis can come back to the phenomenology of class struggle and see how its constitutive process passes from the formal possibility to the rupture of the process of domination and finally to the open expression of mass constitutive subjectivity. This is where Marx's analysis gives a direct definition of constituent power, where it sees capitalist production arrive at the production of the "social individual which appears as the great foundation-stone of production and of wealth" (*Grundrisse*, 705). As its constitution develops, this subject becomes the explosive element that will "blow this foundation sky-high," that is, destroy capital's ability to rein back and regulate the subject's antagonism in a unitary and repressive relationship: "The more this contradiction develops, the more does it become evident that the growth of the forces of production can no longer be bound up with the appropriation of alien labour, but that the mass of workers must themselves appropriate their own surplus labour" (706). Constituent power is that which, through cooperation, frees social living labor from all domination; it is the constitution of this liberation. It is filled up with content by developing this process of liberation—a productive content, living labor. This process is thus not tautological but always creative.

This process, in the first place, creates crisis as we have already seen. But this crisis that the processes of the socialization and concentration of capital necessarily determine is itself creative.[6] The concept of constituent power is always the concept of a crisis, but in the opening of crisis and in the crisis of the realities that it involves—the becoming-objective of power, exploitation, and expropriation—stands also the creative element of liberation. Living labor is this same concept of crisis and constitution. Living labor is constituent power that opposes constituted power and thus constantly opens new possibilities of freedom. Constituent power determines, according to the rhythm of living labor, a space: the space of social cooperation pushed to the point of a communist redefinition of all activities and all interdependencies. It also determines a time: the open time of the destruction of exploitation and the development of liberation.

Living social labor takes the place of the capitalist *mise en forme* of the social totality. It becomes the absolute protagonist of history. A radical inversion takes place: all that constituted power codifies, constituent power frees. But neither this reversal nor this freedom is defined as a movement between homologous terms. There is no homology, no mechanical inversion, and no negative freedom in this displacement of the sense of history. This inversion is not something that happens between homologous elements, even opposite ones. It is an inversion that liberates creative force and that no longer defines the opposite as negative but only as residue. The dialectic is over. In Marx constituent power is the real movement of communism.

We know how difficult it is to find in Marx a complete definition of communism. In his materialist methodology the only kind of anticipation allowed is the one that moves in the rhythm of the tendency. This is therefore a radical refusal of utopia and a limitation of his research on the contemporary historical limits of capitalist development. This explains the prudence of Marx's definitions of communism, and at the same time it helps us to understand that communism is nothing but an activity—an activity and therefore an opening, a radical practical act that connects freedom to desire, desire to sociality, and sociality to equality. The theory of constituent power here becomes the theory of a practice of liberation, desire, socialization, and equality. A practice as intense as Machiavelli's practice of rupture, as socially rooted as Harrington's counterpower, as extensive as the American practice of space, and as educative as the time of the French revolutionary masses. Finally, it is as powerful as constituted power, that inversion of constituent power into a practice of expropriation and objectification that modern capitalism has shown us.

Marx brings to an end a historical cycle of definition of constituent power, and he does so without any illusion about constituted power: He calls on constituent power to be a strength completely free from power: "All political upheavals perfected this machine [of the State] instead of smashing it."[7] "We call communism the *real* movement that abolishes the present state of things."[8] Between these two propositions stands the new sense of constituent power and its reduction to a conscious, innovative, free, and egalitarian social activity. But is this not the profound tendency that has always run throughout the development of the concept in the various eras and episodes that we have followed? Marx's coherent exposition brings this development to an end. The concept of constituent power is the practice of liberation. Marx eliminates from this concept every disempowered aspect that historical experience has encrusted on it and plants the concept of constituent power firmly in the creative ontology of being. With Marx, constituent power is fixed in the dimension of living labor, as producer of being and freedom.

But we should be clear about this. When we speak of constituent power as liberated labor, we are not flirting with idealist positions that lead the distinction between strength [*potenza*] and power [*potere*] toward the space of pure subjectivity or pure objectivity.[9] Marx's problem is materialist and ontologically grounded so that there is a continuous and uninterrupted relationship between strength and power, constituent power and the mode of production, the process of liberation and the institutional horizon. The Marxian subjectivization of constituent power is objective. The materialist paradox consists in continuously rooting the subject in material activity with no possibility of interruption. This methodological principle is not without fundamental consequences. Being in materialism means conceiving constituent power as determinate practice—both of destruction and of creation. It means confronting the determinate conditions and depths of the historical passages. The adequacy of Marx's definition of constituent power derives from the fact that its subjectivization emerges from the critique of labor, the critique of that collective, everyday activity that constitutes and constructs the worldly reality of existence. Marx's subjectivization of constituent power does not detach it from reality but shows that all reality is production—or, better, it demonstrates the continual bifurcation of strength and power in a sphere that is totally material.

But the decisive argument that guarantees both the irreducible materialism of the Marxian concept of constituent power and its creative strength is the reduction of the social and the political. This is an irresistible and ineluctable reduction. The insufficiency of the definitions of constituent power that have preceded Marx's definition was demonstrated by the fact that the "political" appeared as a space relatively independent from the "social." This is unthinkable in Marx, not only because the concept of "labor" is an inseparable essence but also because only in the interaction of the social and the political does the human world take shape—an interaction that the separation of the political from the social destroys. The separation of the political is an idealist operation, a political rupture, a moment of exploitation and expropriation. To the extent that capital closes the entire society in its economic-political command, this little materialist truth (that constituent power is an inseparable social and political activity) assumes an ever greater importance. Class-based social movements, before and after Marx, have given extraordinary demonstrations of this fundamental truth. Not the "invention of the social" by the State but the "self-making of the working class" has characterized contemporary history.[10]

All of modern history has been characterized by the impossibility of distinguishing the social from the political in the exercise of constituted power by the subordinated classes. Not one episode of the rebellion that for several centuries has counterpoised capital and proletariat has been safe from the common process of the social and the political that the proletarian class has imposed—with a violence adequate to the importance of what was at stake. The abolition of the political as a separate category is nothing but the definitive hegemony of constituent power, of creative free labor. Constituent power does not eliminate the political but makes it live as a category of social interaction, in the entirety of human social relations and in the density of cooperation. Marxian materialism is reaffirmed in today's supposed utopia of the "end of politics," which only means bringing it back to constituent power and bringing constituent power back to living labor, which in turn means denouncing the mystification of any conception that wants to give different images and formally independent categories of the social and the political. The category of the political, as independence or as "relative autonomy," is celebrated only to block, order, and dominate the omnipotence of living labor: the category of the political is part of constituted power.

When we consider its activity in the context of capitalist development, the maturity of the Marxian concept of constituent power as founded on cooperation and on living labor (and always from the standpoint of the inseparability of the social and the political) is revealed even more clearly. In this context, which is our contemporary reality, the capitalist subsumption of social labor and the entire society is by now realized. But this means that social life has become immediately productive, that the sphere of labor corresponds to that of the political, and that economic rights and social rights coincide in any concept of citizenship.

Whereas classical politics configured the political according to social orders and modern politics configured it according to representation, in the postindustrial era politics can only be configured as the universality of the social relations of cooperation. The social that dominated the classical age and the political that dominated modernity have both come to an end and the social-political inseparability of citizenship takes over. This identification of living labor and citizenship completes and extends the Marxian tendency. Constituent power becomes more and more the public subjective right of each person—a constituent power realized on the socioeconomic terrain as much as the political one, without one becoming hegemonic over the other. We will return to this point in the final chapter.

Lenin and the Soviets: The Institutional Compromise

When constituent power meets Lenin's revolutionary practice, we can see a first substantial limitation of the Marxian approach. The relation between the soviet of the 1905 and 1917 Revolutions and the constituent power of the masses is posed problematically—sometimes elaborated in polemical terms and sometimes open in an innovative way, but finally closed in the perspective of the party dictatorship. In all of Lenin's experience (however contradictory it was) the opening of the theme of constituent power nonetheless prevails over the sectarian and bureaucratic closure that will be characteristic of post-Leninism. It is thus important to follow carefully this crucial experience—Lenin and the soviets. It provides us with a series of initial solutions to the problems posed not only by the Russian Revolution but the entire history of the modern industrial system.[11]

In his analysis of the soviet, Lenin assumes first of all a theoretical point of view. The tradition of proletarian struggles offers a great number of council experiences. The councils had marked the highest moment of the proletarian organization in the most acute phases of the revolutionary struggle. They were the direct expression of the exploited class, rooted in that class and organized in radically democratic forms, and fruit of the revolutionary struggle. In particular, the tradition offered at least three typical models of soviet organization: the council as directive organ of the revolutionary struggle (the councils of soldiers in the English Revolution); the council as representative of the interests of the proletariat in the structure of bourgeois republican power (the Luxembourg Commission in 1848); and the Communard council as "class organized in State power." The analysis and the ideological projects of socialist theoreticians had been based on these examples. It was no accident that anarchic populism had exalted these examples of the council-moment of the mass management of the struggles, up to the utopia of a "federalism of the barricades," whereas the Proudhonian tradition rediscovered in the democratic radicalism of the councils the foundation and decorum of the pluralist ideology.

As for Marx, he had only irony for the uselessness of any institutionalization of the councils, and, in general, for a proletarian self-government in the world of capitalist production. The committee of Luxembourg appeared to him as "a socialist synagogue" (which it was), and he thought the project of a democratic organization of labor was simply a support for the capitalist organization of labor and thus nothing but a sign of immaturity and political impotence.[12] But in the same text, *The Class Struggles in France*, he already arrives at the definition of the relation between the struggle of the working class and the political movement of capital. Beyond the mystifying effect of the reformist institution, there is the fact that the proletariat had won it as a concession from the bourgeoisie. The workers "imposed" the bourgeois republic, and the February republic was forced to proclaim itself a republic surrounded by social institutions. The result, in the very moment when the proletariat has imposed, is dissolved and gradually becomes the substance of the reformism of capital.

For the proletariat this is now nothing but the new starting point for a workers' struggle at a higher level:

It is our interest and our task to make the revolution permanent, until all more or less possessing classes have been forced out of their position of dominance, until the proletariat has conquered state power, and the association of proletarians, not only in one country but in all the dominant countries of the world, has advanced so far that competition among the proletarians of these countries has ceased and that at least the decisive productive forces are concentrated in the hands of the proletarians.[13]

Only in this framework, therefore, can a Marxian rediscovery of council power be justified. And the history of the Paris Commune verified this hypothesis: "Its true secret was this. It was essentially a working-class government, the produce of the struggle of the producing against the appropriating class, the political form at last discovered under which to work out the economical emancipation of labor."[14] The revolutionary power of the working class is configured in the continuity of the struggle and only in that continuity, as its product. There should be no indulgence, therefore, with respect to utopian positions but, rather, an affirmation of the councils as organizations of struggle in the permanent process of the workers' revolution and as the initial figure of revolutionary class government.

Lenin's interpretation of the council tradition integrates and validates Marx's discussions. Lenin does not assume the truth of Marx's interpretation from a doctrinaire point of view: its theoretical validity must be analyzed and proved. Lenin's is a singular revolutionary pragmatism that seeks—given the scientific investigation of the specific conditions of the revolutionary movement in Russia—to illustrate the theoretical lessons of the classics through a series of strategic and tactical determinations.

We should first look at Lenin's analysis of the 1905 Revolution:

The peculiar feature of the Russian revolution is that in its social content it was a bourgeois-democratic *revolution, but in its methods of struggle it was a* proletarian *revolution. It was a bourgeois-democratic revolution since the aim toward which it strove directly and which it could reach directly with the aid of its own forces was a democratic republic, an eight-hour day and the confiscation of the immense estates of the nobility—all the measures achieved almost completely in the French bourgeois revolution in 1792 and 1793. At the same time the Russian revolution was also a proletarian revolution, not only in the sense that the proletariat was the leading force, but also in the sense that the specifically proletarian means of struggle—namely, the strike—was the principal instrument employed for rousing the masses and the most characteristic phenomenon in the wave-like rise of decisive events.*[15]

On one side there was an extraordinarily backward economic situation that made a bourgeois revolution inevitable; on the other, there was as extraordinary a degree of political maturity and aggressiveness of the proletariat that made its hegemonic function possible in the revolution. Lenin's position on the revolution in Russia, and consequently on the revolutionary organization of social democracy, is taking shape in the continual confrontation of these two terms. Given the degree of development of Russian capital, the revolutionary objectives of a radically democratic management of capital can be thus assumed by the proletariat and by the industrial working class as its leader—only on the condition, however, that the party is "independent" and its direction "hegemonic." This condition transforms the character of Plekhanov's analytical premise and dissolves its economist residues. The Menshevik affirmation of the necessarily bourgeois character of the ongoing revolutionary phase, the programmatic deductions about the type of political organization of the Russian proletariat, the implications of the democratic function that once a bourgeois republic is achieved would be the role of the proletarian organizations—all these are transformed by Lenin's definition of the relation between democratic revolution and workers' struggle, and by the subsequent definition of the structure and the tasks of the party. The interest of the working class is in fact only occasionally—even though necessarily—tied to the aim of a democratic-bourgeois revolution: therefore it must be guaranteed that the absolved "alternative" function can be soon overcome in the further stages of its progress toward communism. As already seen in Marx, the relation between objective determination of the movement and the general meaning of the revolutionary struggle is all resolved in favor of the second. And Lenin's theoretical and practical struggle to emphasize and impose practically these objectives and the relative organizational conditions on Russian social democracy has this same meaning. This leads back directly to the indications contained in the "Address to the Central Committee of the Communist League."[16]

Such an approach to the strategic and organizational problem of the revolutionary movement in Russia has direct implications when Lenin confronts the problems of the mass organizations, that is, the problems that pertain to the form of organization of alliances that, according to the plan of the democratic revolution, are the necessary premises for the development of the movement, even though we should not jeopardize but, rather, favor the uninterrupted development of the struggle toward more advanced aims. Now, the mass organizations, as well as the entire movement, must be directed by revolutionary social democracy and destroyed by it insofar as, in the course of the movement, the democratic aims of the revolution are in their turn realized and overcome. When this is not possible, social democracy will negate the function exercised by such organisms, even if they are mass and popular organizations. Their inevitable destiny, once they are excluded from the permanent action of the workers' struggle and the direction of its avant-garde, will be that of joining in the development of capital and becoming—in the best hypothesis—useful tools for its reform. Hence, Lenin's suspicious and fiercely polemical attitude from the beginning. Hence his bitter denunciation of all the forms of mass organization that tend to become institutional outside of the revolutionary process and that therefore must subordinate the permanent and real aims of the class movement to the organizational ends assumed by social democracy.

Nor are the soviets an exception. In fact, if Lenin correctly defines them, since their first appearance, as mass organizations—democratic organizations, "a million times more democratic than any bourgeois democracy"—their function will be assessed according to the general strategic and tactical criteria of revolutionary social democracy. This is how Lenin affirms the soviet as an instrument of proletarian struggle, and in it Lenin's discourse will gradually prefigure the organization of the dictatorship of the proletariat, at least insofar as the soviets can be ruled hegemonically by the independent organization of the working class. When these originarily and radically democratic instruments deviate from the project of a "revolution without end" and when the revisionary forces tend to make them function within the political dialectic of capital—at least insofar as such forces succeed in their intent—then Lenin unleashes a polemic against the mystification of these organisms and proposes the sacred sectarian alternative: either the liquidation of the soviet as reformist instrument or its conquest of the movement as moment of revolutionary organization.[17] It is immediately clear that Lenin reads the concept of constituent power in Jacobinist terms and that the legitimacy of its practice is exclusively attributed to the party. The Marxian polemic for the "permanent revolution" has become, without break, apology of the party as the sole bearer of constituent power. But in history things go differently. Let's see how.

The working class in struggle in the course of the 1905 Revolution invented the soviets. In fact, we can recognize many anticipations of their organization in the history of the Russian working class. Given their fragmentary and inorganic character and the strong and continual autocratic repression waged against them, the movements of the Russian working class, from the first wave of industrialization in the 1870s, had in fact been fundamentally spontaneous. They became mass struggles in the course of the second industrial wave since 1895, and that mass character substantially modified the spontaneous characteristics of the movement and restructured it by imposing on it necessary forms of self-organization. Thus in this phase strike councils or workers' strike funds are often born. Already in 1895, a strike-council organized permanently in the Morozov textile factory in Tver. In 1895 there is the first appearance of the Ivanovo-Voznesenk council in the textile area around Moscow. Its new formation in 1905 will be considered as the official date of the birth of the soviets. Thus since the soviets of 1905 have their roots in a long tradition of struggles and experiences of the Russian working class, they are consequently intrinsically characterized by them. If "the history of the Russian revolution is the history of the Russian mass strikes,"[18] then the genesis of the soviets is itself internal to this type of struggle, which discovers once again—beyond the merging of economic and political elements, through the circulation and succession of ever new forms of management, and in a political structure that is defined step by step—the unifying effectiveness of the continual process of the revolutionary working-class struggle. This does not mean that 1905 does not represent the moment of the true birth of Russian sovietism. Only now, in fact, the spreading of the struggle in a brief period, its immediately political character (at least beginning in October), and the insurrectional forms that it assumes free the soviet from the extraordinariness of the previous experiences and attribute to it a definitive figure in a fundamentally expansive dynamism.

We do not need to mention here the various phases of the revolutionary struggles that grow continuously from January until October to December. The insurrectional action, which took place mostly in Moscow and its surroundings where between May and July were born the soviets of Ivanovo-Voznesenk, Kostroma, and the Moscow printers, spreads to the other zones, until, in October, it reaches St. Petersburg, where the local soviet is constituted the thirteenth day of that month: "The Soviet came into being as a response to an objective need—a need born of the course of events. It was an organization which was authoritative and yet had no traditions; which could immediately involve a scattered mass of hundreds of thousands of people while having virtually no organizational machinery; which united the revolutionary currents within the proletariat; which was capable of initiative and spontaneous self-control—and most of all, which could be brought out from underground within twenty-four hours."[19] Recognized by the working class of St. Petersburg, which adheres to the strike, the soviet of St. Petersburg assumes the leadership of the revolutionary movement. In St. Petersburg it spreads to all the representatives of the capitalist factories of the capital, and it is recognized by the nonlabor unions and by the different sections of social democracy. The example of St. Petersburg prompts the organization of soviets in all the major cities and expands and unifies the movement everywhere. In Siberia the first soviets of soldiers are born.[20]

The soviets, mass labor organizations formed by responsible and revocable representatives, thus constitute in the last insurrectional phase the center of revolutionary organization. They appropriate the slogans of social democracy for an eight-hour workday and a constituent assembly and fight their democratic battle with proletarian tools. The ambiguity of the relationship—which the worker's spontaneity always carries with it—between the immediate aims of democratic reform and radical revolutionary refusal is thus represented in the soviets in a typical manner, the direct product of the workers' spontaneity. Nor could it be different, given the democratic, and not always radically democratic, aims imposed by the level of capitalist development. On the other hand, the form of the workers' self-government is necessarily ambiguous, even though insurrectional, due to the persistence of the institutions and the power of the bourgeoisie, since—inevitably, given the backward situation of development of Russian capitalism—there remain wide margins of reformism for the bourgeoisie.

The insurrectional form, in fact, is not sufficient to guarantee the effectiveness of the organizational instrument when the content of the demand is still situated on the margins, not so much of the immediate possibilities of the concession of bourgeois power, as of its necessary development. In an exemplary manner, the authority of the soviets expressed itself in their being at the same time organs of insurrectional struggle and organs of internal self-government of the proletariat: the initiatives and the resolutions of the St. Petersburg soviet are in this regard very significant. But on the other hand the destiny of the soviet rests squarely on the solution of this ambiguity. In fact, two different revolutionary programs result when prominence is given to one moment or the other; the affirmation of one aspect or the other of the structure and function of the soviets follows two different analytical premises.

It is doubtful that the Menshevik slogan of "revolutionary self-management" had an impact, even a minor impact, on the formation of the soviets, even the St. Petersburg soviet. It is certain, instead, that this slogan had been for a long time solidly rooted and now widespread (at the Menshevik Conference of April 1905, for example), since it was adequate to the definition of the strategic and tactical aims of that fraction. The fundamental argument was that the backward character of Russian capitalism would keep the proletariat from the immediate conquest, total or partial, of power. Nothing was left but to exploit the situation to "construct and strengthen the class party," achieve conditions that would allow its free development, and therefore to build—in the articulation of the social and State structures of capital—an analogous articulation of instances of revolutionary struggle.[21]

It is obvious that the idealization of the strategy of German social democracy played a predominant role in this schema and that it exercised an important theoretical influence on Menshevism. Apart from this, however, what was determining in the definition of the Menshevik strategy was the type of relation—fixed in terms of an almost mechanical identification—between the growth of the subjective and objective elements of the revolutionary process, between the (undoubtedly correct) recognition of its material conditions and the awareness of the class movements, which was entirely subordinated to the first recognition and perhaps too disenchanted. From this point of view, the ripening of the economic material conditions for the passage to socialism implied the parallel, mechanical ripening of subjective forces: social democracy had precisely to recognize and follow this process. If we should talk of "proletarian dictatorship," then we should have talked of it as "dictatorship of the majority," of the "enormous majority of the people." Now, this situation had to be attended to: to prepare it was only the guarantee that, after overthrowing czarist autocracy, there would have been created the conditions of the autonomous political growth of the proletariat in its autonomous party and union organizations, a growth meant to determine the passage to socialism. The democratic, majoritarian, yet peaceful passage still remained secondary.

It seems to the Mensheviks that the soviets fit this pattern perfectly. They prefigured a widespread fundamental process of democratic organization and found it in the moment of highest revolutionary tension, in the fight against autocracy, so that beyond this limit they can verify the presumed hypothesis with all the prestige and force that comes to them from having won their first revolutionary victory. The affirmation of the commune as "dictatorship of the majority" and as an instrument of "revolutionary self-management" from which the program of "democratic self-management" is extrapolated is characteristic of the Mensheviks in this year.

Even to the Bolshevik base organizations, the birth and the spreading of the experience of the soviets seem at times to verify the Menshevik program. There is a widespread attitude or suspicion that the soviets reproduce irresponsible, chaotic, and irrecuperable forms of labor organization, or in any case incompatible with the organization of the party. There is an attitude that polemically undermines the soviets, which they want reduced to simple union organizations. In St. Petersburg, where the memory of the workers' organizations of Gapon is still fresh, they even come to the point of proposing the boycotting of the soviet. Only Trotsky's intervention of Krassin succeeds in warding it off. And this attitude spreads from the center to the periphery. The Bolsheviks remain, except in rare cases, foreign to the formation of the soviets.

In fact, the revolutionary councils that Lenin had proposed as instruments to impose insurrection and achieve the aim of the "provisional revolutionary government" shared few traits with the soviets. In the former the ruling function of the party is absolutely clear. Precisely because of the direct action that the party exercises in them, they can simultaneously guarantee the two necessary ends of the insurrection: the development of the permanent revolution and, in it, the development of the movement toward the immediate conquest of power. But in Lenin the rise and spreading of the soviets are not interpreted as in any way contradictory with the Bolshevik line. The soviets are "peculiar mass organizations," spontaneous forms, and organizations of the insurrection.[22] They are eminently the fruit of the workers' spontaneity, and spontaneity is not a problem: it is the normal condition of class existence and expression and must be recognized, followed, affirmed; and overcome. It is contradictory, instead, to consider the soviets as organs of revolutionary self-government in the Menshevik sense. That would make spontaneity, the keystone of the insurrection, fall in the worst kind of democraticist utopianism and eliminate the function of the party.

"While quite correctly condemning a passive boycott, the *Iskra* contraposes to it the idea of the immediate 'organization of revolutionary self-government bodies,' as a 'possible prologue to an uprising.'" With this the neo-Iskrists would like to cover the country with a network of organs of revolutionary self-government:

Such a slogan is absolutely useless. Viewed in the light of the political tasks in general it is a jumble, while in the light of the immediate political situation it brings grist to the mill of the

> Osvobozhdeniye *trend. The organization of revolutionary self-government, the election of their own deputies by the people is not the* prologue *to an uprising but its* epilogue. *To attempt to bring about this organization now, before an uprising and apart from an uprising, means setting oneself absurd aims and causing confusion in the minds of the revolutionary proletariat. It is first of all necessary to win the victory in an uprising (if only in a single city) and to establish a provisional revolutionary government, so that the latter, as the organ of the uprising and the recognized leader of the revolutionary people, should be able to relegate it into the background by proposing a slogan demanding the organization of a revolutionary self-government is something like giving advice that the fly should first be caught and then stuck on the fly-paper.*[23]

Opportunism breaks the continuity of the insurrectional process and blocks it on the absurd project of constructing self-government, which is not possible without first destroying autocracy. The value of the spontaneous experience of sovietism remains outside the utopian and dangerous Menshevik program, against the attempts of absorbing the entire movement of liberation into one single stream of democraticism. Insofar as it is spontaneous, it must be overcome and won by the rules of the political organization of the proletariat. In December 1905, when the Executive Council of the Soviet of the Workers' Deputies refuses to admit the anarchists, Lenin grasps the occasion to stress the position of the Bolsheviks: "If we were to regard the Soviet of Workers' Deputies as a parliament of labor, or as a sort of proletarian organ of self-government, then, of course, it would have been wrong to reject the application of the anarchists." The soviet, however, is not a parliament. It is "a fighting organization for the achievement of definite ends, . . . an undefined, broad, fighting alliance of socialists and revolutionary democrats."[24] As such, it must refer to the criteria of the socialist international organization, insisting in particular on the exclusion of the anarchists. Its end is only insurrection.

Lenin's refusal to accept the either-or alternative between soviet or party, his claim that the soviet is the organism immediately instrumental to the insurrection while to the party are entrusted the permanent and final ends of the revolutionary movement, and his urgency to resolve (and here he is simultaneously engaged in a polemic with and trying to demystify the Menshevik program) the ambiguous nature of the soviet we cited above are further clarified by Lenin's writings during the period of 1906–1907, the year in which the bourgeoisie was making a comeback. Whereas during the most acute period of struggle when the soviets were directly invested and configured by the workers' struggle the danger of their being entrapped in the institutional mechanism of bourgeois democracy could be considered merely theoretical, now in a phase of the ebb of struggle and of a bourgeois comeback the danger became instead immediate. This process of the sterilization of the soviet foreshadowed its elimination, not only as the instrument of struggle but also as an instrument of political representation in democracy. To think that there could have been a different development was to yield to the worst constitutional illusions and to conceive once again, in Proudhonian terms, the soviet as a constitutive moment of pluralist democracy. And this was twice illusory: first of all with respect to Russian capital, which cannot even imagine forms of popular self-management functional to democratic development; and second, in more general terms, because such constitutionalism, if it were possible, far from changing the power of the bourgeoisie, would merely strengthen it. The soviets are, in sum, the products and organs of the workers' struggle and cannot be anything else. Outside this way of understanding them there is only utopianism and the betrayal of the struggle, if not pure and simple opportunism.

The Mensheviks reject the election of deputies to the Duma, but wish to elect delegates and electors. What for? Is it in order to form them into a People's Duma, or a free, illegal, representative assembly, something like an All-Russian Soviet of Workers' (and also Peasants') Deputies?... Why supply the police with the lists of our representatives? And why set up new Soviets of Workers' Deputies, and in a new way, when the old Soviet of Workers' Deputies still exists (e.g., in St. Petersburg)? This would be useless and even harmful, for it might give rise to utopian illusions that the decadent and disintegrating Soviets can be revived by new elections instead of by making new preparations for and extending the uprising.[25]

In November 1905 Lenin had actually hinted at the possibility that the soviets might assume the function of provisional revolutionary government.[26] Insofar as they had widened their representation and had rooted themselves in the struggle, and in the struggle became recognized as leaders of the people's majority, as in fact happened, Lenin suggested the possibility of making largely representative soviets function as the basis of the provisional government in place of the Duma, which was itself in any case the fruit of revolutionary struggle. Considering the soviets as the embryo of the provisional revolutionary government was an integral part of Lenin's schema: the ambivalence of the spontaneous character of the birth of the soviet and of the mass and basis democratic elements of its present form can be in fact resolved by this newly assumed function. Even better: in the very moment when the soviet would assume the functions of a provisional revolutionary government, it would have been dissolved in it.

Anticipating a conclusion about Lenin's consideration of the 1917 Soviet, we can say that here Lenin begins to define the soviets as an instrument of proletarian dictatorship. But we mention Lenin's position on the Soviet of November 1905 because it confirms, in the parallelism and plasticity that it establishes between the soviet and the instruments of democratic representation in general, the concept of the soviet as organ of revolutionary struggle and nothing else. From this point of view, even the Duma, if it is to exist, must paradoxically sovietize itself since it too cannot escape the laws of revolutionary struggle that make it its organ:

The objective cause for the downfall of the Cadet Duma was not that it was unable to express the needs of the people, but that it was unable to cope with the revolutionary *task of fighting for* power. *The Cadet Duma regarded itself as a constitutional organ, but in actual fact it* was *a revolutionary organ (the Cadets abused us for regarding the Duma as a stage and an instrument of the revolution, but life has fully confirmed* our view*). The Cadet Duma considered itself to be an organ of struggle against the* Ministry, *but in actual fact it was an organ of struggle for the complete* overthrow *of the old government.*[27]

Yet the Duma was not an instrument of "workers' power." In fact, all organizations are suitable to carry out the revolutionary task when, formed and sustained by the workers' struggle, they free themselves from the bourgeois democratic content of the revolution. Class struggle and the generality of its revolutionary determination are the fundamental elements of this refusal of the bourgeois democratic content. All the rest is secondary and, in any case, limited. "Workers' power" is the power of struggle; it is a moment and a stage in the conquest of "State power." It cannot be conceived separately from the totality of the movement and, even less, institutionalized outside of it. If then we want to prefer the soviets to other types of instruments of struggle, this must follow a pragmatic assessment of their effectiveness.

The ambiguity of the relation between "soviet as self-government" and "soviet as organ of struggle" of the proletariat that is established within the relation between democratic struggle and socialist struggle is here fully resolved. Concluding his speech on the soviets in the first Russian Revolution, Lenin can thus on the one hand exalt the soviets exactly in their spontaneous capability as organizers of struggle and on the other warn against their fetishization and the danger of overvaluing them:

The role which the Soviets of Workers' Deputies . . . played in the great October and December days surrounded them with something like a halo, so that sometimes they are treated almost as fetishes. People imagine that these organs are "necessary and sufficient" for a mass revolutionary

> *movement at all times and in all circumstances. Hence the uncritical attitude towards the choice of the moment for the creation of such bodies, towards the question of what the real conditions are for the success of their activities. The experience of October–December has provided very instructive guidance on this point. Soviets of Workers' Deputies are organs of* direct mass struggle. *They originated as organs of the* strike *struggle. By force of circumstances they very quickly became the organs of the* general revolutionary *struggle against the government. By the force of events and the transition from strike to uprising, they* irresistibly *became transferred* into organs of insurrection.... *It was not some theory, not somebody's appeals or tactics devised by somebody, it was not party doctrine, but the force of circumstances that caused these non-party mass organs to realize the need for insurrection and then transformed them into organs of the insurrection. To form such organs in the present circumstances means creating organs of insurrection; to call for the creation of such organs means calling for insurrection. To forget this, or to slur over it before the great masses of the population, would be unpardonable shortsightedness and politics of the worst sort. This being the case—and undoubtedly it is the case—the conclusion to be drawn is quite clear,* viz., *that "soviets" and similar mass institutions are not* sufficient *for the purpose of organizing the insurrection. They are necessary for welding the masses together, for creating unity in the struggle, for passing on party slogans (or slogans advanced by agreement between parties) of political leadership, for awakening the interest of, rousing and attracting the masses. But they are not sufficient for the purpose of organizing the fighting forces proper, for organizing the insurrection in the most literal sense of the word.*[28]

If the soviet will be in various occasions preferred to other organs of the revolutionary struggle, it will simply depend—we have already said—on pragmatic considerations. The problem is generally considered closed. In the years following 1905, in the process of general strengthening of the tactics and strategy of the Bolsheviks, the discussion on the soviets therefore seldom reappears: this is confirmation of the believed sufficiency of the pragmatic criterion in a decision about this problem, that is, tied to the tactical contingencies of the insurrection, that—in the midst of the counterrevolutionary phase—cannot obviously be foreseen. Some premises regarding the effectiveness of the soviets that were given on the basis of the most recent experience were nonetheless kept in mind. First of all, the fact that the soviets were mass organizations not yet destroyed by the bourgeois tradition. We could, in fact, very unscrupulously establish an analogy between the functions of the soviet and those of the Duma as basis and organ of the provisional revolutionary government, but we could not misrecognize the fact that beyond this rather theoretical analogy of functions there was in the genesis, the organizational nature, and the reality of the soviets a profound and irrefutable originality, which perhaps could be newly deployable for the resumption of open struggle. This fact does not escape Lenin: sometimes he prefers to be silent about this originality of sovietism, at least insofar as it seems to him invalidated by "anarcho-syndicalism."[29] On the other hand, in the rare and less official occasions in which he confronts the problem during these years, he explicitly wonders, by keeping in mind these facts, if and how soviets could become centers of revolutionary socialist power.[30]

After 1905, however, the problem is not that of further defining the relation between soviet and party. The problem is now that of keeping the struggle open and relaunching it in a permanent manner. Permanent revolution remains in fact the strategic line of the Bolsheviks: "After the democratic revolution we will fight for the passage to the socialist revolution. We are for the permanent revolution. We will not stop half-way." They hoped in 1905 and still hope that "the revolution in Russia would have given the signal to begin the socialist revolution in Europe."[31] But only the party is suited to this end, and Lenin insists over and over again on the necessity of the "autonomy" and "independence" of the party of the proletariat.

Beyond the *practical* problems of the relation with the soviets in the insurrectional phase, however, Lenin's defense of the Bolshevik view of the party reopened the *theoretical* problem of this relationship, implicitly if you want, but continually, as moment of the widest discussion on the relation between political direction and mass organisms, and on the alliances of the proletariat in the process of the democratic revolution and, beyond this, toward socialism. It necessarily reopened, therefore, the problem of constituent power. This reopening was unavoidable because this problem is the central, most decisive, and ambiguous one, which is always imposed on workers' theory by effectual reality at that level of capitalist development. Now, the particular form of the debate is determined by the great amount of writings that the Second International produces on the Russian 1905. The soviets are launched in the international discussion of the workers' movement and thus become, perhaps more than within Russian social democracy, occasion for further thematic investigation and political conflict. Here it is not important to follow the lines of the polemic, particularly its reformist tendencies. It is sufficient to keep in mind two positions, which were similar although somehow antithetical: that of Rosa Luxemburg and that of Leon Trotsky. Lenin's thought can be clarified by comparing it with these two.

To Luxemburg the soviets appear as the living proof of the validity of the theses she proposed earlier around the polemic on the *Massenstreik* in

Belgium. That "the living dialectical process makes the organization rise as product of the struggle" resulted from the soviet experience more than from any other possible example.[32] The Russian proletariat, even though politically immature and of recent formation, had learned in the struggle how to impose its own political experience and move to a very high level of "procedural organization." All the forces of struggle circulated in it and were constantly once again launched in a continual interchange. In such interchange the nexus between union struggle and political struggle finds a way to achieve a full realization. As for the soviets, they are represented as propelling elements of this revolutionary procedurality: their being rooted in the life of the masses carries them completely to movement. Organs of insurrection on one hand and prefigurations of the uninterrupted development of the workers' struggle from democratic radicalism to socialism on the other, the soviets are the real embodiment of Marxism among the masses.

Also in Trotsky the emphasis on the spontaneity of the formation of the soviets and their democratic radicalism in the life of the masses is extremely strong: these characteristics make the soviets the "typical organization of the revolution" because "the organization itself of the proletariat will be its organ of power."[33] This concept of the dictatorship of the proletariat, directly exercised by the soviets without the mediation of the party, is the corollary of the affirmation of spontaneity as much as it is the consequence of Trotsky's experience in the soviet of St. Petersburg, which was executive organ, centralizer of the revolutionary struggle, and, at the same time, instrument of democratic and socialist self-administration of the masses.[34]

Trotsky's and Luxemburg's views have, as we have said, some common elements and some that are contrasting or even antithetical. Among these elements we should emphasize in particular the *expansive* nature of the soviets in Luxemburg's thought, whereas Trotsky gives privileged attention to the centralizing phase of the revolutionary functions of the soviets. In the slogan "all power to the Soviets" in fact he sees prefigured, according to the schema of democratic centralism, both the successive revolutionary movement—also in its tactical phases—and the fundamental structure of the socialist State. Other elements are shared: the affirmation of spontaneity in the genesis and development of the soviets, the affirmation of their radical democratic foundation in the life of the masses, and finally, consequently, the theoretical foregrounding of the continuity between democratic struggle and socialist struggle that would be revealed both by the structure and the functions of the soviets.

Lenin refuses both these positions. He has in mind the conditions of the movement in Russia and all the ambiguity presented by revolutionary struggle in the context of a backward capitalism. He does not rhapsodize over the forms that the struggle can assume but, rather, subordinates this consideration to the concrete determinations that result from it for workers' science. What can the theory of the organization process mean in the Russian situation? Simply the return of the movement to generic popular positions? That would present a danger and an obstacle to the irresistible will to create an autonomous revolutionary class organization that now and here cannot be but *minoritarian.* Only this organization can guarantee, as an institutional end to the organization itself, beyond the conditions determined by the present democratic phase of the movement, the conquest and the destruction of autocratic or democratic bourgeois power. And in the affirmation of the democraticism of the soviet does not the danger of subordinating the hard work of organizing the party to a simple prefiguration of the future, take root, the danger eliding its necessary function as *avant-garde* in the illusion of an entirely utopian revolutionary unanimity? Certainly, neither Luxemburg nor Trotsky would have accepted—and they did not accept—such criticisms. In the writings of both the affirmation of the executive function of social democracy does not seem ever to vanish. On the other hand, they had good reasons, in the midst of the polemic, to accuse Lenin of "ultracentrism" in his concept of the party, maintaining that from such a point of view he was inclined to undervalue programmatically every potential element of democratic life and the basis of revolutionary organizations. And on Luxemburg's side such accusations will assume, after 1917, a strong polemical vigor.

But doubtlessly Lenin's discourse revealed the substance of the description and the consequent theory of the soviets proper to Luxemburg and Trotsky; and Lenin's polemic, which was in this respect extremely pertinent, recognized a theoretical overestimation and a fundamental strategic error both in the expansive model of the former and the intensive model of the latter. The overestimation consisted, according to Lenin, in entrusting to spontaneity functions that did not belong to it. It might well be that spontaneity plays an eminent role (more than once Lenin the "romantic" and "anarchist" had acknowledged and celebrated it) but not always and not automatically. If there is a rationality of the spontaneous history of the struggles, it is either capital or class that determines its most aware or political qualities. And the party is all here: a class-based party that recuperates from the spontaneity of the struggles the workers' nostalgia for an alternative organization and that structures class autonomy and consciously plans its expressions. This is an avant-garde party, *always* avant-garde, because it permanently goes beyond the material limits that the capitalist structure imposes on class movement. "Party as constituent power." And here—after the overestimation, however motivated, of spontaneity—

lies the frank error of Luxemburg and Trotsky: considering the revolutionary process a continuity that does not find any solutions—in particular, solutions between economic demands and political demands. Yes, Luxemburg and Trotsky had beaten, in a classical manner, the reformism of the workers' movement and international social democracy, and they had demystified it in each of its aspects, but now, and even more so, the more the situation and the occasions of struggle were backward, also the reformism of class movements had to be beaten. The party was born and functioned for this reason. Therefore the dyad *class autonomy-class organization* could not in any moment be broken. By autonomy we mean, negatively, to isolate class from the people and the workers' class struggle in its permanent necessity of overcoming the given material limits from the concrete tactical determinations of the movement; positively, to impose the problem of its organization. Without autonomy there is no organization: and this, in Lenin, was posed against any theory of democratic organization. Without organization, though, class autonomy is always episodic and risks being crushed—above all, at a backward level of capitalist development—by the reformism of capital and within the wide margins that are conceded to it. It is therefore defeated as workers' struggle. And this in Lenin was held against any hypothesis of process organization.

And the soviets? Only the party can decide how to use them. It is not a matter of undervaluing the typical instrument that spontaneity has offered to the revolution, but situating and affirming it in the tactics and strategy of the party, of constituent power.

Keeping in mind these premises, we must assess Lenin's theoretical and tactical judgment on the soviets in 1917. This is a central moment because this is precisely the moment of the "Leninist revolutionary compromise." This is a *compromise* in the very concept of *constituent power*, between soviet and party, and in the ambiguous synthesis between the Marxian concept of *living labor* and Lenin's concept of the *party* as supreme mediation of the movement of the masses.

Now, the first aspect of Lenin's judgment on the immediate spreading of the soviets in 1917 is his great emphasis on the spontaneity of this phenomenon: "The Soviets arose without any constitution and existed without one *for more than a year* [from the spring of 1917 to the summer of 1918]."[35] It must immediately be recognized that such affirmation of spontaneity is all but generic and populist: since the beginning Lenin defines the spontaneous development of proletarian organization as a specific and characterizing element of the class situation and uses this affirmation as the occasion to define the nature and dynamic of the revolution: "The Soviets are not important for us as forms. What interests us is of which class they are the expression."[36] Nor is he interested, as Plekhanov was, in seizing the movement of the "'creation of the people' in the revolution" but, rather, in fixing in the soviets the expression and the immediate political form of the class insubordination to the general experience of exploitation.[37] "It was objectively inevitable that the imperialist war should have immensely accelerated and extremely intensified the class struggle of the proletariat against the bourgeoisie; it is objectively inevitable that it shall be transformed into a civil war between hostile classes." The soviet is the spontaneous product of this situation: "The embryo of a workers' government, the representative of the interests of the *poor* masses of the population as a whole, i.e., of nine-tenths of the population, and is striving for *peace, bread* and *freedom.*"[38]

Since the beginning of the war Lenin had foreseen this intensification of class struggle, and his activities within the Second International were the result of this foresight. During the war, on the basis of his forecasts, he had fiercely attacked all the attempts at making the working class in the factory coresponsible for the war production and had refused to accept, in exchange, the "factory constitutionalism" that the opportunists of the Duma promised.[39] This was the moment to verify his analysis: his forecast proved correct at the highest level of revolutionary insubordination. Spontaneous is thus the constitution of the soviets as the center of militant insubordination of the proletariat to the exploitation by capital, which in the imperialist war has reached simultaneously its apotheosis and its limit. The assessment and the consequent affirmation of spontaneity offer thus the basis for the definition of the very high degree of development of the revolutionary consciousness of the Russian working class, and the material conditions of the political planning of the passage from the first to the second phase of the revolution.[40]

This definition of spontaneity is not surprising. It is not really contradictory but, rather, a necessary, if not sufficient, element in the political design of the proletarian revolution. We have seen how such method is typically Leninist. What changes is only the intensity of the definition: spontaneity here has grown to the point of being the *embryo* of the revolutionary government; it is so *self-aware* to allow the passage to the construction of socialist power. Since 1902 Lenin had described the process of worker spontaneity as the growth to a higher and higher level of mass revolutionary consciousness.[41] Here the process reaches its acme; spontaneity defines the situation and materially conditions its extremely advanced developments.

Here also falls away the supposed contradictoriness of the judgment and consequent tasks that Lenin gives to the soviets in 1917 with respect to his previous assessments. Once again the new configuration of the nature and tasks of the soviets derives from the definition of the level reached by spontaneity, which is in turn an expression of the level reached by the class antagonism, and from the connected planning of the *leap* beyond the first phase of the revolution. The "April Theses," developing the indications of the "Letters from Afar," acknowledge in the Soviets of the Workers' Deputies "the *only possible* form of revolutionary government": "Not a parliamentary republic—to return to a parliamentary republic from the Soviets of Workers' Deputies would be a retrograde step—but a republic of Soviets of Workers', Agricultural Laborers' and Peasants' Deputies throughout the country, from top to bottom."[42]

From "organ of the insurrection" to "organ of the insurrection and power of the proletariat": this transformation of the function of the soviet derives therefore from the real, material development of the revolutionary ends. Lenin believed they had to be able to complete and correct the old formulas, the old Bolshevik formulas, because they have proven to be correct in general but their concrete application had given different results.[43] The fact is that the mechanism of the permanent revolution had found a new terrain, a more advanced perspective to follow. To the old Bolsheviks who rely on the formulas of 1906, Lenin responds with the analysis of the new situation of 1917. The party must be able to grasp the new situation pragmatically. There is thus no contradiction in modifying the tactical indications of the party. There is, if anything, a continual verification of the strategic line and in it the necessary adjustment of intervention. The correct relation between spontaneity and consciousness and between class and organized class movement that the party must establish in any new situation is expressed—since February 1917—in the affirmation of the revolutionary function of the soviet and, beyond this, in its theoretical function as foundation of a new type of State.

Lenin's analysis exactly recognized the new reality of the soviets. To the mass success of their birth and their immediate propagation in the first week of the February insurrection and to the proof of their terrific organizational capability, which was expressed in the constitution of an "executive committee" with executive functions for the entire movement, were added specific political conditions that configured the soviets in a way profoundly different from 1905, the memory of which, however, still had enormous effects on the genesis of the movement. These political conditions are essentially the (undoubtedly socialist) political character of the entire movement and the particular definition of its mass character. Different from 1905, the Soviets are really born with the victory of the insurrection. They are not confronting the old autocratic apparatus to be destroyed but, rather, the new government of the bourgeoisie. Therefore, their task becomes immediately socialist.

The soviets define themselves as "organs of radical democracy," mass class organs whose task—whatever may be the strategic end of the forces operating in them—is to express an alternative political potential with respect to the power of the bourgeoisie. And also their mass character is modified with respect to 1905: not only by the enormous quantitative dimension of the phenomenon and not only by the wide spread of soviets in the army—which arms the soviets and unifies the political and military organization of the proletariat—but above all by the political radicalization of the masses. This element in the following months will be clarified by the clash between the St. Petersburg Soviet, conditioned at the formal political level by the function of "controller" of the bourgeois government, and the peripheral soviets, extremely permeable, instead, and more and more swept by the radicalism of the masses to further revolutionary movements. Lenin gave this clash his full attention and took advantage of the situation to push the process to its conclusion.

As result of these conditions, the soviets thus constitute a pole of the so-called "dual power," by which some characterize the first phase of the Russian Revolution. We can consider it either as a system of power distribution in a *democratic* revolutionary phase or as a first result of the development of the permanent revolution toward socialist ends. In the first case the soviet will be defined as "control organ of revolutionary democracy" and therefore simply obliged, negatively, to guarantee against counterrevolutionary resurgences and, positively, to ensure the democratic development of the institutions and the politics of the executive. This is the Menshevik and social-revolutionary position founded on the well-known theses about the nature of the revolution in Russia. But even the old Bolsheviks, albeit with many ambiguities, seemed to accept these formulas about the soviets before Lenin's return.[44]

Only the opening of the April crisis, Lenin's return, and the struggle around the "theses" provoke a first settling in this situation. The personal unity of the heads of the soviets and the ministry reveals in fact the class direction according to which the bourgeoisie intends to resolve the duality of power and therefore its necessarily contingent character. It is clear that "dual power" is not a juridical relation that can be institutionalized but a mere relation of force between opposite classes. It is "not a constitutional fact but a revolutionary fact"—*a constituent fact.* It cannot but be resolved in the victory of one of the two rivals: "Really we cannot transform the civil war into a component of the State regime." Any conciliatory position, at this point, is impossible and, from the class standpoint, merely opportunistic. The ambiguity of dual power therefore must be confronted and resolved from the worker standpoint: first of all the proletarian moment of the antithesis must be emphasized and thus affirmed to the point of founding the dictatorship of the proletariat in its soviet form.[45]

The Bolshevik strategy, which in this first phase implies the dissolution of "dual power," is articulated along three lines: strengthening and extending the power of the soviets, their conquest by the party, and the socialist transformation of the State through the soviets. The Bolsheviks dedicate themselves to the first task with all the strength of their organizational capability. In the cities they reconnect the action of the soviets to the struggle for the eight-hour day, thus accentuating in the slogans the proletarian character of soviet organization. But above all in the countryside, where they carry forward extremely refined slogans, they contribute to the spreading of sovietism and the radicalization of the movement.[46] The results of this action will not be delayed: in May workers and sailors proclaim the proletarian republic in Kronstadt. But simultaneously to these peaks of radicalization, in the same period, the process tends to flow back: "dual power" definitely assumes the features of bourgeois power insofar as the Mensheviks and revolutionary socialists accept government responsibilities. At this point the very slogan "All power to the Soviets" begins to appear outmoded and the "peaceful way," which beginning with the first consolidation of the soviets could be imagined as feasible, becomes entirely illusory:

> *The slogan demanding the transfer of the state power to the Soviets would now sound quixotic, or a sheer mockery. This slogan would virtually be a fraud on the people; it would be fostering in them the delusion that it is enough even* now *for the Soviets merely to want to take power, or to proclaim it, in order to secure power, that there are still parties in the Soviet which have not been tainted by abetting the butchers, and that it is possible to undo the past. . . . And the real political issue consists in the fact that now power can no longer be secured peacefully. It can be obtained only by victory in a decisive struggle against the real holders of power at the present moment. . . . The real issue is that these new holders of state power can be defeated only by the revolutionary masses of the people, whose movement depends not only on their being led by the proletariat, but also on their turning their backs on the Socialist-Revolutionary and Menshevik parties, which have betrayed the cause of the revolution. . . . Soviets may arise in this new revolution, and are indeed bound to arise, but* not *the present Soviets, not organs of compromise with the bourgeoisie, but organs of a revolutionary struggle against the bourgeoisie.*[47]

The June crisis then makes the Bolshevization of the soviets an immediate necessity. Here we are touching on one of the most characteristic aspects of Lenin's method. Not even now, in fact, is the theoretical relation between soviet and party modified. On the contrary, as we see once again, in the moment when the Soviets are no longer in the revolutionary movement and when they abandon their conflictive force and settle into democratic development, the party must intervene and bring them back to the class function. After June, in a phase of resurgence of the bourgeoisie, the soviets are therefore once again reconfigured as "organs of insurrection" and nothing else: this is the task that they must carry out and this is the aim of the moment. The events of 1905 seem to return. The party and the subjective reorganization become at this point the primary element because when the relation between revolutionary class and soviet as its organized expression has ceased, the party intervenes to reestablish a correct relation. The Bolshevization of the soviets is not at this point simply the attempt to conquer through them the majority (and the majority, in any case, between July and October is won). It is above all the demand to relaunch, in the soviets and the masses, the revolutionary struggle and radicalize it through the goal of immediate power. The Bolshevik action in the summer of 1917 succeeds in this. It is the necessary and sufficient premise of October.[48]

Lenin's theoretical contribution to the definition of the soviet is, in these years, no less relevant. The positions assumed in *State and Revolution*, where the soviet is at the same time considered as organ of the dictatorship of the proletariat and instrument of the communist abolition of the State, are well known.[49] There is no need for us to repeat here the fundamental arguments of that book. Rather, it will be useful to consider the relation that brings it close to Lenin's revolutionary practice, in particular that of 1917. Lenin's practice stands in continual counterpoint to the studies on the nature of the bourgeois State and the Commune, and on the communist abolition of the State. And on the other hand, it is perhaps legitimate to hypothesize that, without this preliminary further investigation of the problem, the "Letters from Afar" and, even more so, the "April Theses" would have never been written. But also, if imperialist war had not so sharpened on the one hand the class struggle in the single countries and on the other the process of rationalization and centralization of the executive power of the bourgeoisie, Lenin's intensive study beginning in 1916 of Marx's and Engels's writings (as well as Pannekoek's, Kautsky's, and Bucharin's) on the problem of the State could have not brought him to recognize in such a radical way the teachings of the classics. Lenin now sees the abolition of the State as the task of the proletarian revolution and as a material possibility at a certain stage of development of class struggle.

Apart from these hypotheses, it is nonetheless certain that Lenin's analysis of the complex problem derives, first of all, from his political judgment of the effects, present and future, of the imperialist war. In this phase, in fact, the centralization and rationalization of the powers of the executive, their immediate functionalization, outside any mystification, to "pure" capitalist ends of mercantile domination, motivate and develop most the perfecting of the bourgeois State machine, which in its classist foundation is a mere instrument of accumulation and exploitation. The imperialist war is like the cross section and macroscopic exemplification, in addition to being the motor of an extraordinary acceleration, of capitalist development in its political form. Faced with this material development of the structure of bourgeois power, Lenin's program of the transformation of the imperialist war into a civil war opens to the analysis of the problems of the State and the relationship between the victorious class struggle of the working class and the State.

The analysis of the development of capital that Lenin attempted in *Imperialism* must now find its correlative at the level of class science. Therefore, in *State and Revolution* the central object becomes the commentary on the famous pages where Marx poses the relation between worker revolution and reformism, its internal restructuring of the power of capital, and its political machine. Marx concludes: "All political upheavals perfected this machine instead of smashing it."[50] Now, the internal restructuring of power that the war imposes on the bourgeoisie stretches to the limit its present capabilities of internal reform. In Russia, the last step in the reform in the capitalist order of power is provoked and follows the February revolution:[51] this proposes now to the workers' struggle an adversary that is already in itself reunified. Thus, beyond this limit, the problem of the destruction of the bourgeois State machine is simply reopened; thus, beyond this limit, the ambiguous relation, already discovered and theoretically defined by Lenin, between democratic revolution and socialist revolution, dissolves. The dictatorship of the "proletariat organized as dominant class" does not repeat the reformist development of the modernization of the State functions but, rather, "immediately" opens the process of abolition.

In Lenin the analysis always functions as the direct premise of the revolutionary slogan. The soviets are therefore entirely absorbed in this theoretical scenario: they constitute that "superior form of the State" that repeats the experience of the Paris Commune. Therefore, they are not simply the destruction of the *bourgeois* State machine: rather, they represent the first condition and the first moment in the process of abolition of the State as such. In the "Third Letter from Afar" of March 1917, this evaluation of the soviets and the subsequent program, with an explicit reference to the experience of the Commune, is already hinted at.[52] The "April Theses," the article on dual power, the successive resolutions up until

October continually relaunch this program.[53] And the theory seems to support the Bolshevik praxis in the days of October, in which the party destroys any residual democratic slogan to invest the second congress of the soviets with all the power.

But what is the relation that ties, at this point, the party and the soviets? The correct relation, defined and verified by Lenin in the course of his long political battle, was one of subordination of the soviet to the party, of the mass movement—even though it had come to a high degree of development—to the conscious leadership of its avant-garde. Now, notwithstanding any appearance, this relation is practically maintained and imposed in the most acute period of the revolutionary struggle: between February and October it is the party that little by little conquers the direction of the movement. The same conquest of the struggle is the work of the party and not—or only in form—of the soviets. But then do the great emphasis that Lenin puts on the soviets and the model of the Paris Commune have a purely *ideological* and not scientific meaning? Why then let survive such a utopia at a theoretical level by not recognizing the inadequacy of the soviets to determine—at that level of development—the material basis of the dictatorship of the proletariat itself, as well as of the communist process of abolition of the State?

In fact, we must immediately say that Lenin's theoretical analysis had by far overestimated the actual level of development of capital and the degree of political formation of the Russian working class. It is not by chance, then, that after the July crisis of 1917 the great theoretical emotion that had pushed Lenin to see in the imperialist war the last act of the internal reform of capital and that had pushed him to understand—beyond this limit—as open the process of reunification of the working class and its avant-garde (and therefore to see as dissolved the ambiguous mechanism of the dualistic growth of the working class) is forced to recede when Lenin is faced with such a different experience and when he recognized that capital has still wide margins of resistance and resurgence—for counterattacks against the first worker revolution both within the Russian borders and at an international level. Yet besides this, and in a much more decisive manner, it is the successive development itself of the revolutionary movement in Russia that makes clear the political inadequacy on which Lenin's theoretical hypothesis was based. Even though, in fact, the soviet begins to function as "organ of proletarian dictatorship," nonetheless it is the party that actually exercises power, in the form and only in the form, of the soviet. The soviet tends thus to be reduced to a democratic instrument of the "organization of consent," and as such it is once again interchangeable with other instruments of advanced democracy. Therefore, far from being configured as a moment of the process of the abolition of the State, the soviet ends up being, in the best of instances, "organ of the administration of the State." The fact is that we must reconstruct and again push forward accumulation to the point to make materially possible the existence of a unified working class, one that knows how and is able to manage social production. In this context, Lenin situates the soviets within the process of social production. They must organize production and increase productivity. They are first of all organs of the democratic management of production.[54] One might suspect at this point that the arguments of some of the bourgeois ideologues who simply considered sovietism as a model of enlarged and extremely advanced parliamentarism have a certain validity.[55]

Lenin desires all this to the extent that it is necessary. He does not mystify the reality in front of him. He recognizes the *democratic* character of the soviet form of management of production and power, and he talks of it as "the beginning of the socialist form of democracy."[56] Fully aware of the huge tasks that await the revolution, he attributes to the soviets minimal objectives: the power of the soviets is "an apparatus by the aid of which the masses can begin immediately to learn how to govern and to organize industry on a national scale."[57] But if this is the reality, it must be further pushed forward by the class avant-garde. The identification of the party with class and the reversal of the relationship between party and soviet have to be achieved. Until the party does not succeed in this, it needs the State. State and party are in fact equally children of the capitalist division of labor; only a high level of worker unification and class recomposition can therefore allow the overtaking—both to return the soviet to its function and start the process of the communist abolition of the State. We must get to this level: the revolutionary proletariat has not inherited it from capitalism, to the extent that its recent struggle has not imposed it on capital. Paradoxically, the situation confirms Marx's claim: "All political upheavals perfected this machine instead of smashing it." At this level of development, sovietism perfects it even further. "But the revolution is thorough. It is still on its journey through purgatory. It goes about its business methodically." In order for the revolutionary process not to stop, it must be sustained in a high moral and political atmosphere: after 1918 Lenin's work is fully committed to this.[58]

Lenin's propaganda of the soviet experience in the world is, from this point of view, highly significant. Yes, Lenin perfectly understands that the success itself of the revolution in Russia is conditioned by the international extension of the movement. But we are not simply dealing with the material conditions of resistance of the soviet experiment in Russia; it is not simply the problem of the defense of the October revolution. It is also the relation of the development of the Russian Revolution toward its most advanced aims. In this perspective, Lenin's writings in the Third International are not meant so much to generalize the determinate figure of the soviet as the practical form of the proletarian dictatorship, as much as to unify the various and at times autonomous council experiences in one single political design, in one single revolutionary tendency capable of by far overcoming the limitations of the movement.[59] Only in this way will it be able, on the other hand, to beat the democratic resurgence that threatens the revolutionary institutions of the working class in Russia and elsewhere. For example, as the chief agent of the counterrevolution, European social democracy tries to block the movement on positions of democratic reformism. Therefore, it deprives the council form of its revolutionary content and tries to institutionalize it as the basis of bourgeois power, renovated according to Enlightenment principles. Here Lenin once again unleashes the polemic against any theorization of "dual power," constitutionally mummified (and therefore beaten) outside of the general revolutionary class struggle; against the proposals of the "yellow" International to legalize the soviets, to concede to them State rights, and to introduce systems of direct democracy; against Hilferding's and Kautsky's proposals to give importance and constitutional function to the *Rate* as control organizations of production; and against any proposal, in sum, that wants to consider the soviets as organs of democratic representation and not of class dictatorship, grafted onto the international process of the revolution. The communists must always answer no; the movement must continue and go beyond itself.

What we have said works to clarify definitely Lenin's concept of constituent power. Lenin provokes a short circuit between mass action and the command of the party, in which he sees constituent power organized as dynamic reality, foundation, and project at the same time. The compromise of the soviet and the party is a compromise between living labor and a perspective of new originary accumulation, which should result in the determination of the conditions of communism.

Socialism and Enterprise

Something extraordinary happens in Lenin's thought and practice in reference to the concept of constituent power. Lenin gives a definitive shape to this concept, the highest form in which it had been taking shape in the whole tradition of Western political thought—and makes it extreme as strength of mass liberation, as power implanted in society and in the mode of production, and, above all, as organized political power. The "Western" Lenin encloses the masses' constituent power, the soviets, in full awareness, into the grip of political organization and enterprise organization.

Lenin attempts the solution of all the aporias that constituent power had shown in its long history—the aporia between active constitution and institutional constitution, between the productivity of living labor and enterprise organization—and all this contributes to the form of the party. A compromise? Certainly—a compromise confronted with the vitality and the real strength of the movement of transformation, but an active compromise, founded on a philosophy of nature and history that is itself the fruit of the Western tradition, and on a concept of the political that is an alternative to it. In the problematization of the Western political tradition his effort is decisive. The concept of constituent power is posed as a concept that is the synthesis of mass creativity, political organization, and the reappropriation of the rule of enterprise. Social movement, political party, and rule of enterprise: here is the Leninist dislocation of the concept.

Here it will be useful to insist on the last relation that we have mentioned: constituent power and rule of enterprise. Around this relation, Lenin takes up again the Marxian teaching, that is, the definition of a concept of production that is not only economic but social and political at the same time. He considers constituent power not only as the capability of reappropriation of property but also as *mise-en-forme* of industry. He tries to unify democratic spontaneity and instrumental rationality. This work of foundation cannot happen but in the richness and complexity of the relations that configure the modern concept of production. The Promethean quality of this operation simulates, while reversing it, the capitalist sense of the constitution of the social and imposes the reappropriation of capital not as a thing but as an activity. A new concept of constituent power, and at the same time the highest verification of modernity, consists of this radicalness of the apprehension of the creative unity of the social, the economic, the political. The modern economic and the creativity of the capitalist enterprise are assumed as elements of constituent power, and constituent power is reinterpreted as essential moment of the rule of the enterprise. In Lenin the strength of accumulation can and must become prerogative of the masses. Once again, here is Lenin's "Occidentalism"—the essential, repeated, and convinced definition of his thought. This is a pervasive definition that above all manifests itself in the concept of the party. The party is, in fact, on the one hand, the directive organ of the movement, but on the other it is the organ of mediation of the movement. In Lenin, the revolutionary of 1917–1919, the concept of party irresistibly shifts from its function as avant-garde to that of organizational mediation of constituent power. The problem of giving shape to the spontaneous movements becomes even more central. A specific organizational dynamism, which adjusts itself to the necessities of the spontaneity of the constituent process, is built here. A Western dynamism that affirms the productive function of the masses in the constitutive process of the new State.

Why does this masterpiece break down? Why does this positive and dynamic compromise, the fruit of Western tradition, this tendency to synthesis fail to come to its realization? Why does the compromise become short-circuited? Why does the synthesis shortly reveal itself as impossible, making us inherit, together with an extraordinary theoretical dislocation of the problem, a new historical crisis?

A first answer to this question—how disenchanted, but how far-sighted!—is Max Weber's.[60] Between 1905 and 1917 he commits himself to an indefatigable effort of understanding the Russian Revolution. Weber characterizes the Russian social situation as the terrain of a precocious and very violent capitalist development that cannot find a political form. In this situation the possibility of identifying a bourgeoisie that can turn into the carrier of an effective and democratically valid constituent power is missing. For a long time the battle has been taking place around this end, but for a long time it has been lost. The structure of the ancien regime is out-of-date and unable to recuperate the constituent pressure of the bourgeoisie itself as well as of the people, within a politically adequate mediation and process. Nor can the revolution win—not its battle for the taking over of power but that for the realization of a constituent power that guarantees at the same time democracy and development. The revolution of 1905 has had a pseudoconstitutional outcome; the revolution of 1917 will have a pseudodemocratic outcome. Why? Because the hypothesis of a socialist constituent power, such as it has been theorized by Lenin, cannot be realized? Rather, because, just as Weber sustains, the conditions demanded by that model do not exist. The revolt of the masses exists, the dimension of the capitalist development exists, not the mediation, society, thus the premises of democracy. The Leninist party is a poor substitution for this void: in any case, if it managed to win, it would not be able to govern, because a civil society with which it could intensely interchange does not exist. The only solution is that of "State socialism," of a party and State bureaucracy that interprets—necessarily in a foul manner, Weber anticipates— the constituent potential. The alternative cannot in any case be but a capitalist autocracy, right-winged in its principles, itself bureaucratic as for the administrative functioning. In the Leninist solution, the lack of a civil society worthy of this name will soon transform the democratic dictatorship of the proletariat into the bureaucratic dictatorship of the party. The Leninist synthesis, perfectly understood by Weber, explodes in the void of conditions that the Leninist Prometheanism will not succeed either in regulating or in inventing. Weber has no illusion, therefore, about the Russian future. His understanding of the Leninist concept of constituent power leads him to critique not the strength of the concept but the poverty of the conditions to which it is applied.

It is from these conditions, therefore, that the Leninist compromise is necessarily short-circuited.[61] What Weber expresses negatively, insisting on the negative conditions that necessarily lead to the failure of the Leninist concept of constituent power, Rosa Luxemburg expresses positively, that is, critically, moving from a consideration internal to the Leninist practice of constituent power.[62] If Lenin's party has the enormous merit of having led—the only one among the Marxist parties—the masses to power, by sustaining with the highest commitment, coherence, and radicality their revolutionary spirit and their aspiration to democracy, later it has yielded to passivity and compromise, considering the international isolation of the revolution and the immediate solution of some problems (the question of peace, the recognition of nationalism, the agrarian question) not as obstacles to be overcome but as absolute limits of the constituent process. But on these compromises a just tactic does not win: rather, a change of the nature of the constituent subject comes into play.

In the difficult play between the masses' movement and party initiative, the party takes over. This predominance of the party over the masses means the defeat of democracy and the affirmation of dictatorial and bureaucratic management. Yet, sustains Luxemburg, all the conditions for an authentic development of constituent power in a Marxist and revolutionary sense were present. Constituent power is formed by four elements: first, the masses' initiative, their democratic organization, and sovietism; second, the temporal progression of this initiative, its capacity to articulate time according to the phases of transformative strength, and the limitlessness of this project; third, the economic foundation of constituent power, its capacity to impose innovation not only on the political terrain but also and above all on the industrial one—economic democracy and advanced collectivization; and fourth, the spatial dimension, that is, the dialectic between national centralization and self-determination, such as in it the strength of the international workers' union can victoriously confront the political space of the disaggregation and separation prompted by the enemy (Luxemburg, 567–85). Here we identify, as in an academic catalog, the historical characteristics of constituent power—its radical democratic nature, such as it is described by Machiavelli; the temporality of the Parisian revolutionary masses; the counterpower and the appropriation theorized by Harrington; the centrality of the new political space constructed in the American Revolution and by democratic constitutionalism: Luxemburg unifies and affirms these characteristics, rereading their synthesis and crisis, the project and the limit in the Russian revolutionary experience. Here it is thus, by consequence, where constituent power can touch its crisis, as concept and practice: there where this formidable initiative does not become direct exercise of a mass democracy. Because it is only mass democracy that can organize functionally all the revolutionary components of constituent power and transform the new power into democratic dictatorship of the proletariat. Luxemburg has no doubt about the compatibility of proletarian dictatorship and universal suffrage.

"Dictatorship consists of the system of application of democracy, not in its abolition. . . . class dictatorship activates the participation of the masses" (601). "The idealism and social activism of the masses" are in fact prompted by "unlimited political freedom" (598). Thus it is not the sociological and historical condition of the realization of the constituent principle that blocks and puts into crisis its effectiveness, as Weber claimed, but the Bolshevik limitation of the expansion of the principle, as Luxemburg claimed.

Luxemburg's critique of 1917–1919 must be brought back to the critique of Russia in 1905. In this situation, Luxemburg had insisted on the constituent power of the masses as element of organization. Spontaneity is not a negative fact; on the contrary, it is the result of past experiences and struggles, intelligence that has become body and will, and that therefore becomes insurrectional activation. "The struggle is not only the product of the organization at a certain level of force. On the contrary, the living dialectical process makes the organization rise as product of the struggle" (283). The party, social democracy, it is the direction of the mass movement only at the condition of being completely internal to the movement itself: there is no distinction between dictatorship and democracy—better, the distinction concerns only the degree of the movement and its revolutionary maturity (288). It means that, according to Luxemburg, there are no objective conditions that can block the realization of the constituent principle. Also in this case the mature definition of Lenin's concept is not put into discussion; nor is put into discussion Lenin's political practice or, even less so, Trotsky's. Rather, it is the prudence and the tactics of the Bolsheviks and their resistance to push democratic radicalism all the way that are criticized in this moment of the highest expansion of constituent power. Even in the highest moment of the polemic, Luxemburg asks the Bolsheviks to recuperate the fullness of democratic substance of the constituent project (569 ff). But this does not happen. The short circuit of the Leninist compromise appears here to be on the side of the subjective conditions of the process: it does not come into being, insists Luxemburg, because the democratic participation is not synchronically present with the other elements. It is only in the radicality of the democratic project that communism can conjoin proletarian liberation and the project of the productive reconstruction of social wealth.

Let's take a leap of many years, and come to the threshold of contemporary experience. In the second volume of *Critique of Dialectical Reason*, Sartre poses the problem of the intelligibility of history as the problem of the understanding of the failure of the Leninist experience.[63] Now, in Sartre we find, so to speak, the synthesis of the critical positions of Weber and Luxemburg. In Sartre, as in his forerunners, the concept of Leninist constituent power remains intact, even more valorized by the theory of *praxis* as foundation; but it can hold only when, adds Sartre, it is conceived as disutopia, and only, anymore, as *assemblage [agencement]* of subjectivity. The conditions of Leninist constituent power, Sartre explains to us, in historical reality have necessarily become prey to the "practico-inert"—the groups in fusion, that is, constituent power in a subjective sense, have been in fact attracted to the conditions of the "rarity" (more specifically, the isolation and the solitude of the soviet experience) and thus have become prey to institutional objectification.

The crisis of Leninism consists in its inability to make an open project of the project itself—better, in its not assuming the crisis of the project as its uninterrupted foundation. The problem, then, is not that of the Leninist compromise, its conditions of subjective actualization, and its objective realization: the problem comes after that. We are not dealing with preconditions but with consequences. The problem lies therefore in the fact that the Russian Revolution cannot prevent the fact that its constructive work is blocked and that the richness of the *ruptures* [*déchirures*] is extinguished. The problem comes from the fact that Leninism is transformed from a theory of ruptures into a practice of dialectical restoration. We must instead give space not to the work of the dialectic but to the "antiwork" of continual *rupture*. "This antiwork," that is, the negative and contradictory conditions of constituent power, "is productive." "Within this relation constitution is given," since every struggle "is objectified and alienated in the product" and this product is at the same time a new "practice of duality." Consequently: "Anti-work, a synthesis that is passive and reanimated by action, is the overcome inertia that itself constitutes the fundamental support and the crucial secret of its intelligibility."

The political sense of antiwork and its inexhaustible practice consist in keeping the dialectic always open. Weber's negative conditions and the tensions of Luxemburg's critique must not be given as the negative moment that closes the dialectic in a defeat, but must always also critically reopen the dialectic—reopen the dialectic as the inexhaustibility of the revolutionary event. "The totalization of the contradictions in the communist praxis" is "the revolutionary incarnation," it is the specific rationality of its moving. Leninist thought owes its greatness to the proposition of a constituent power that is a product of the antiwork, of the rupture of the dialectic; antiwork is negativity, it is contradiction, but now it is given in the form of going beyond negativity: "The result of the common union and of the totalization of the encircling—implication of all the conditions of the process of transformation." Sartre's question of whether "our aim is that of establishing whether in a practical whole, divided and torn by antagonisms, the same *déchirures* are not totalizing and do not entail and imply a totalizing movement of the whole" finds here, therefore, a positive answer. But why, then, has the Russian Revolution become "a monster"?[64] Because, Sartre concludes without coming to a conclusion, the urgency of the synthesis has become stronger and stronger and because the dialectic has wanted to be restored at all cost. Because constituent power has been crushed on the rule of enterprise, in the fetishization of labor, in rigid constitutional institutionalization. Because the democracy of the groups in fusion and the totalizing dynamic have been eliminated.

The crisis of Leninist constituent power is not determined by its conditions but made real by its result. Having reached the level of comprehensive synthesis to which the historical dynamic of the principle has brought it, Leninist constituent power is broken and suffers the erratic dispersal of its constitutive elements, each in its absoluteness, in the years that immediately follow its institution. The Machiavellian element becomes dictatorship, the temporal element becomes theory of the "phases of development," the spatial element becomes imperialist practice, and the element of counterpower becomes bureaucracy and corporatist defense. This happens because the unity of the Leninist proposal is broken, because the unity-from-below of constituent strength is dissipated in unilateral moments that are only forcedly reunified, in a by-now reestablished dialectic of differences. To reaffirm the freedom of society here, the maximum of State power is realized. Each moment of the synthesis is exasperated in a unilateral manner and subjected to the mediation of State power: dictatorship instead of democratic foundation, bureaucratic management instead of counterpower, the "theory of the phases of development" instead of a conception of the time of the masses and its progression, and imperialism as a practice of space. The singularity of constituent strength is broken and recomposed in the dialectic of absolute differences. Stalinism is the representation of all this: restored dialectic, in rough and centralized forms, against the original impulse, negative and progressive, of the Leninist dialectic. Restored dialectic against negative dialectic. Any singularity of the Marxist and Leninist constituent potential is subjected to an administrative decomposition and to an executive recomposition, whose definitive sign is the absoluteness of constituted power.[65]

Was all this necessary, and inevitable? This question is answered positively by all those who, on the side of Stalinism but also the theories of capitalist development, maintain that only "a revolution from above" could have determined the solution of underdevelopment, or, better, the formation of the modern mode of production in Russia; that the real alternative was not between a liberated constituent power, including (according to Marxist teaching) the rule of enterprise within itself and defeat, but between defeat and the construction of a State capitalism that would mobilize the masses, forcedly, toward accumulation and production. But to that same question must answer negatively all those who, in a constituent power summing up the rule of the enterprise, do not see a closure but, rather, a higher opening of strength. On the terrain of the rule of enterprise, on which Marx had forced constituent power, on that same terrain on which the Leninist compromise had developed, what mattered was the contradiction, its continual reopening, and the vitality of the negative and progressive function of constituent power. The rule of the enterprise was not a fetish, but a new terrain on which constitutive praxis could and should continually reopen.[66]

And this finds definitive evidence in the fact that, however things went in Russia, this necessary and contradictory relation between constituent power and rule of enterprise cannot be removed anymore. Today any exercise of constituent power that frees itself from the necessity of the relation of enterprise is not imaginable. This terrain discovered by Marx is the terrain of communism. Here it is affirmed the irreversibility of the contemporary political imaginary, of social constitutive strength. It cannot be taken away from the unity of the social, the economic, and the political. It can no longer be, and freedom and democracy must be measured (and cannot but be so) in no other place but this terrain. That bleak economism that blocks the constituent process in the Soviet Union is paradoxically also such a new terrain of expression of constituent power that the problem of the latter cannot be reconsidered and historically reopened but on this level.

This is so true that the soviet constituent experience, immediately after 1917, far from being limited to the socialist State, becomes the problem of the capitalist State. In fact, it is from the block of the revolutionary experience of the soviets in Russia and from its recuperation within the structures of a rigid planning—it is from this awareness that the reformist practice of capital comes up against the soviet. Notice: it is not from the knowledge of the *mere institutionalization* of the soviet that capitalist practice seeks the possibility of a new control (the attack on institutionalization as such is the prerogative of the anarchist positions and has little to do with the analysis of the dialectical complexity of the revolutionary power's self-affirmation); instead, it is from the *form of institutionalization* that capital draws precious teachings.

The Soviet is institutionalized as participation in the organization of the production, as support of the ideology of labor, as instrument of planning. From this point of view it offers, for the first time in the history of capital, an example, at mass levels—that of large-scale industrial production (therefore well beyond any cooperative experience, the tradesmen's or the peasants'), of how, then, the worker variable can be democratically imprisoned in its vicious figure as commodity, and here socialized and dominated as commodity. In sum, what capital is little by little recuperating it is the dynamic and participatory form of the institutionalization of the worker variable within the necessity of the organization of labor and of the capitalist finalities of production. We get the first hints and indications, at a still fragmentary level, in the theories of enterprise, in the socializing and strongly ideological form that Weimar constitutionalism, first and not last, in particular offered.[67]

A second phase, much less ideological, can be identified with the triumph, after the great crisis of 1929, of the politics of planning inspired by Keynesianism. Here the participation comes direct, in terms of great proportions, toward the distribution of income. The planned capitalist State thus bows down in front of the necessity to reconfront in itself, in any case, the dimensions assumed by the relations of force among classes—but always in order to immobilize these relations, in order to congeal them within its structure and its finalities. It is not by chance that the monetary and fiscal instruments are the punctual correlative, in Keynes as in the other economists and political planners, of the maneuver on the worker forces, and constitute determinate levels of mediation and participation.[68] Today, from within the history of the reformist modification of praxis, in the postindustrial epoch, we are witnessing a third phase of adjustment and redimensioning of worker participation. The fact is that constituent power has destroyed the possibility of an understanding of the instance of power or communism within the strictures of capitalist planning. Only a relation that pushed itself deeper into the life of the masses, only a profound interpretation of the relation of capital, which defines it, in the dialectic itself of the capitalist perspective, exactly as *relation*—well, only this intentionality can be victorious. In this perspective the council movement has reached a new, unhoped-for actuality: the capitalist necessity of an effective internalization of the relation of control, the bourgeois ideological urgency of pluralism and participation, the reformist smudges of social democracy, and the residual cynicism of the Third International have gone to town around this possibility to found a balanced State of labor.

But let's go back to our point, that is, to the Leninist concept of constituent power, to its greatness and its crisis. As we have seen, it concludes the Western history of the definitions of constituent power, by inserting the rule of enterprise and its critique in the complex of the constitutive elements of the concept, by posing the synthesis of the productive rule and the rules of democracy, and with adequate projects of temporality and space. On the other hand, the crisis of the Leninist concept of constituent power is given and shown by history. No matter how heavy and painful, it is nonetheless endowed with expansiveness. Notwithstanding the crisis, in fact, the constituent character of living labor must be recognized as the foundation of the rule of enterprise, both in socialism and in capitalism. Hence the series of apparent paradoxes that we have considered, so that the abolition of constituent power in the State of the soviets has seen that same constituent power prompted and reaped, even though in a mutilated and mystified manner, in the recent evolutions of the capitalist, Weimar, Keynesian, and postindustrial State.

At this point we should also emphasize the irreversibility of the Leninist synthesis. In simple terms, it consists in the fact that there can be no political democracy that is not an economic democracy and that is not a reappropriation on the side of the masses of constituent power, in time and space, in the mechanisms of social production and reproduction. Constituent power becomes with Lenin an extremely radical terrain and founding activity. Time and space can be produced—even better, must be produced—so that the liberation of the masses becomes possible, so that democracy may be thinkable, and so that freedom is configured as universal activity. From this point of view the relation between Marx and Lenin represents a continuity. After Marx and Lenin it is not possible to talk of political freedom without talking of economic freedom, free production, and living labor as the political foundation. Freedom has become liberation and liberation is constituent power. The irreversibility of the paradigm of constituent power, at this level of the definition of the category, empties of meaning any other understanding or vulgarization of the concept and imposes this determined intensity—of foundation and original constitutive activity—on the term and the problem. Constituent power is affirmed as the exclusive foundation of the political. And history. And the world. Whereas socialism stoops to the rule of enterprise, on the contrary, constituent power by touching enterprise crushes its concept. From its collusion with socialism, constituent power springs forth again by incorporating enterprise and the modern concept of productivity within the project of the radical constitution of a new world.

S E V E N

The Constitution of Strength

"Multitudo et Potentia": The Problem

THE HISTORY of constituent power, considered in its development, reveals at least two continuities. One is demonstrated in a linear manner in the expansion and deepening of the Renaissance revolutionary principle of the *ex novo* constitution of the political arrangements of the new society. The great revolutions that followed expressed the continuity of a constituent principle that responds to the necessity to rationalize power. The rise and the development of capitalism and its form of organization of society revealed the constituent principle as crisis: crisis of the relation between the productive strength of society and the legitimation of the State.

The successive conceptions of republican, democratic, and then socialist constitutions are continually reproposed as attempts to found a "political" capable of stabilizing its legitimacy on the constituent power of the "social," and on the antagonisms that are present in it. But this continuity is also negative. In fact, this project fails in each instance. Machiavelli brilliantly poses it as a problem and gives it only a utopian solution. Harrington and the English republicans try a solution in terms of the political counterpower of the producers—an ineffectual solution that will be neutralized by a simple leap forward of the productive system. The American constitutionalists, through a wily effort, enclose the contradictions of political space within a juridical machine so sophisticated that it is manipulable and soon distorted. Jefferson and the "freedom of the frontier" are eventually reversed into political mystifications and imperialist projects. The French revolutionaries' rapid temporal acceleration that had brought them from the terrain of the emancipation of the citizen to that of the liberation of labor collapsed into terrorism. Finally, the Bolsheviks take the mortal leap by raising up the power of the State in order to affirm the freedom of society. And yet, even among these failures, the pattern of rationality that the Renaissance revolution had proposed as plot of the political is affirmed. And, as if within a process of ontological accumulation that lies behind and extends through each of these experiences and each of these failures, the concept and the practices of constituent power widen and impart a sort of irreversible tendency to the development of the concept.

In proposing constituent power as *virtus* of the multitude, Machiavelli prepares the terrain for Harrington and for his constitutional conception of armed counterpowers. And whereas the American Revolution, by introducing an undefined constitutional dialectic of the singular and concrete rights of freedom, spreads the process of political emancipation, the French Revolution works this space in terms of equality and from the standpoint of the liberation of labor—thus posing the foundations of the Bolshevik effort to constitute the political arrangement of living labor. Therefore, this process has an initial continuity, that of an increasingly complex, complementary, and progressive plot: the rational expression of a dense project of the emancipation of social freedom and its realization in the political.

Within this first trajectory a second historical continuity of the concept of constituent power is revealed. This time it is not a continuity of accumulation, but a process not of objective configuration but subjective action. Inside all the episodes of this story another uninterrupted thread in fact manifests itself: the continuity of what Spinoza called the constituent passion of the *multitudo*. This passion is the keystone of all attempts of constitutionalization, as much as it is the pole that reveals their successive insufficiency. In sum, it is the logic of both their development and their crisis. Each practice of constituent power reveals, at its beginning and its end, a tension of the multitude to become the absolute subject of the processes of strength. Around and against this claim we read the discontinuities and the inversions of the constituent process of Western rationality, as much as in the continuity and in the steady sense of the action of the multitude we can read the indefinite tendency and constant resurgence of the process.

In Machiavelli, Spinoza, and Marx we grasp the conceptual development of this second continuity in the fullest manner—but it is better to say metaphysical development, because the real political science of modernity lies in metaphysics. Machiavelli, in his phenomenology of constituent power, casts the foundation for this perspective. If the Prince is constituent power, and the people are the prince when he takes up the arms, then the historical definition of constituent power, that is, its practice and its tendency, are realized in a process that passes through social disunion and whose strength is fed by the struggle. Constituent power is therefore the passion of the multitude, a passion that organizes force by soliciting its social expression and that moves there where the historical course tends to extinguish power in decadence or to trivialize it in the inertia of *anakyclosis.* Constituent power is the capacity to return to reality, organize a dynamic structure, and construct a forming form that, through compromises, balances of force, different orders and equilibria, always recuperates the rationality of the principles, that is, the material adequacy of the political with respect to the social and its indefinite movement.

The movement of constituent power is indefatigable—again, "virtue" will always be faced with "fortune" and the labor of society will clash with the dead labor accumulated by power. But constituent power lives in this continual crisis, pushing forward its own becoming. Spinoza recuperates and elaborates Machiavelli's definition by transferring its figuration onto the horizon of high metaphysics. The plot of the constitution of the political here is sustained by the unstoppable and progressive expansion of *cupiditas* [desire], which is the determinant force of the constitution of the social, determinate in the formation of the political institutions resulting from the interweaving of the multitude of singularities, and surpassed and exalted by the absoluteness of democratic synthesis. It is the moment of full interpenetration of the will of all and sovereignty. This process is always constituent, but also always conflictual. Strength is both unstoppable and aleatory. The process is always recomposed and always broken down further by a *cupiditas* that becomes the passion of society and sovereignty—and that then becomes redundant, as love that constitutes in the multiplicity the image itself of the living god. *A democratic living god.* The strength of the multitude, the different degrees of a constitutive *cupiditas,* and the transformation of this density and complexity of processes in union and love are thus the determinations that constitute an always new social being. As Machiavelli's phenomenology shifts imperceptibly into Spinoza's metaphysical project, constituent power is configured—without losing its material characteristics—as a creative project, in a way that fully expands strength. Precisely by considering the contradictions and conflicts of the passions as background of the process, constituent power is realized as a tendency. It is continually reopened and defined as absolute in its reopening. It exists in reality, it exists in war and crisis, but this is the divinity of the world.

Marx enters this theoretical process of Western metaphysics, reestablishing its principles in material possibility. The theme of constituent power maintains its creative characteristics but makes them newly explicit, so to speak, as in a new book of Genesis. Creative force becomes here as concrete as the force that in the contemporary world constructs the force of producing and with it a second figure of the world, an enormous and entirely artificial "second nature." Marx expresses the creative tension that Machiavelli felt as a quality of the new man and that Spinoza had metaphysically described as the omnipotence of *cupiditas*. He expresses it as the actuality of objectification and the possibility of a new world.

The strength of constituent power shifts from the sphere of possibility to that of the concretization of the will, from the world of politics to that of the natural prosthesis. The world is seen as the realization of associated living labor, and constituent power assumes alternative meanings and directions through the modalities of association. In Marx the tension of constituent power toward democracy is not only a fundamental perspectival act, an act that in its radicality expresses a superhuman intensity of the project, as it is in Machiavelli. It is not only the absoluteness of the relation between the will of all and sovereignty, between the contingency of the multitude and the totality, as it is in Spinoza. It is a creation that simultaneously follows the Machiavellian rules of strength and the Spinozian rules of the *multitudo* and that embodies the conditions of the absolute. This absolute is not—for the same reasons as in the other authors—an absolute in the proper sense: it is, rather, the product of open and negative dialectical conditions and the result of a historical process. It is the determination of concrete subjectivities. The absolute comes to be the prosthesis of the world and a second nature that men want to govern—precisely because it is a second nature, not an object that conditions us but a collective subject that we have built together. The constituent principle thus represents and concludes the principle of modernity because it leads the structure of modern producing to the subject of production, and to this it ascribes its production and the responsibility and meanings of this producing. In this absoluteness of the relation between subject and world, the alternatives of constituent power are posed by bending its force and truth toward the multitude.

Only in the multitude, insofar as it is capable of expressing living labor, lies the truth of the constitution. Democracy, a real democracy of right and appropriation, equal distribution of wealth, and equal participation in production, becomes the living god. In it subject and structure, strength and the multitude become identical. According to Marx the history of constituent power is the progressive experience of the rationalization of the collective subject. What Machiavelli and

Spinoza had perceived at different levels of metaphysical intensity and in different historical conditions leads here to an absolute hypothesis. The constituent project is explicitly a creative project. Democracy as the "absolute form" of government, as both Machiavelli and Spinoza define it, becomes an effectual possibility—that is, it transforms theoretical potentiality into a political project. The project is no longer that of making the political coincide with the social, but that of inserting the production of the political into the creation of the social. Democracy is the project of the multitude, a creative force, a living god. This is the second terrain of the historical continuity of the concept of constituent power.

Having said that and having identified the two historical continuities, the problem nonetheless remains. We must admit that the problem of constituent power is open even after tracing this development and recognizing the alternatives of its historical course. Why? Because this course is never overcome but, rather, keeps taking place: it gives a sense and a critical fullness to Western rationality and develops it in a critical and radical manner. It treats Western rationality's immanent opposition by pushing it toward explosion and anticipating the results of this outcome. In order to explain this critical course and establish its crucial point it is necessary to emphasize and study the relation that ties the development of constituent thought to three ideological dimensions of Western thought: the Judeo-Christian tradition of creativity, the theory of natural right concerning the social foundation, and the transcendental theory of the foundation. Now, the development of the concept of constituent power, even in its radically critical figures, is somewhat limited by these three ideal conditions—and no matter how much it works to unhinge them, it remains partially tied to them. By following, above all, the second continuity of constituent power, represented by the continual rupture of the historical development and the permanent reproposition of the constitutive strength of collective *cupiditas* and the expression of the *multitudo*, it will become evident how certain limits always prevail and how the problem of constituent power will always be reopened.

The first limitation is thus that deriving from the Judeo-Christian tradition of creativity. It is clear that Machiavelli's, Spinoza's, and Marx's constituent theories are all radically atheistic. The concept of creativity is tied essentially to man. In Machiavelli this radical humanism is tinged with skeptical colors and with a cynical consideration of positive religion. In Spinoza the world is an absolute horizon where the divinity's action becomes a necessity, and for this very reason it is complementary to existence: if the modes are in substance, it is because substance is in the modes; if God is in things, it is because the thing is God. In Marx atheism is expressed and declared as a vindication of being against its own alienation. But there is more in each of these authors: atheism becomes a constructive moment. In Machiavelli atheism provokes the critical reaction of the existent against the ideal—that is, the affirmation of realism, method, and its constructive strength. In Spinoza atheism shifts the ascetic process from the transcendent realm to the world and therefore to the dynamism of the modal being, of the existent itself according to its own strength. In Marx atheism is a fighting weapon against the always theological abstractions of capital's economy.

In each of these authors and in the converging totality of their arguments, atheism is an affirmation—of strength, the revolution, the concrete against the abstract, what is living against what is cold, alienated, inert, and fixed. Moreover, in each of these authors atheism becomes a creative moment. In Machiavelli the Prince, particularly the popular prince, masters time and space, configures them according to his own image, and overcomes the limits of reality in order to construct a new one. In Spinoza *cupiditas*, by socializing itself, changes the sign of existence and imposes generosity on egoism, love on generosity—a love that is the key itself to the world and its progressive expanding from nature toward civilization. In Marx the revolutionary process constructs the new conditions of existence, the human world, and brings nature itself back to the constituent will. Yet this formidable mixture of critical and constructive elements does not manage to avoid in a definitive manner that point of the Judeo-Christian tradition in which all experience is brought back to unity. To expropriate God of its creativity is not decisive, if we allow creativity to be defined still by the unity of the creative project. By doing so we make the divinity worldly but do not eliminate it—and constituent power will have to keep measuring itself with the universality of the project.

In this sense the standpoint of our authors (Machiavelli, Spinoza, Marx), radical as it is, does not get rid of the ultimate defining characteristic of the religious conception of creativity: it merely interprets its unitary characteristic. In this regard their standpoint remains caught in a certain finalism (residual, but not less effective) that penetrates even the most radical positions of atheism and the creativity that they themselves expressed. The strength of the multitude, for example, is always conceived here in the figure of the unity of the multitude. To claim this, however, means forgetting that the strength of the multitude is not only the strength of "much" but also the strength of "many," that is, the strength of singularities and differences. When the shadow of theological unity persists, it crushes the relation between strength and multitude because this relation withers in its progression toward unity. Unity becomes once again the assumption. This is not the teaching that the historical practice of constituent power has transmitted to us. On the contrary, in the contradiction that pits constituent power against constituted power, the former has not only the quality of creativity but also that of omniversatility. If it were not so, we could not understand why each of its results must be destroyed at the very moment when it is achieved—and the multitude, its unceasing expression of vitality, would be reduced to a unitary ghost of strength, whereas strength is really traced on the versatility of the multitude.

Wherever the possibility of a unitary imputation of all the creative acts of strength still exists, creativity is not freed from the divinity. There the category of totality, which coincides with that of unity in reducing the different and absorbing and validating the singular multiplicities, will take power again. On the contrary, what is proper to the constituent project and specific to its definition consists in this: in the essential relation that it establishes between creation and multiplicity. In this consists that crisis of the constituent project, which is proper to its concept because it cannot be referred back to the block of the temporal progression of creativity, but above all and in a much more defining way to the multitude of alternatives of creation. Atheism must prove itself on this terrain, beyond that temptation to unity that the negation of the divinity leaves as a residue.

Natural right theory is the second limit against which incurs the historical theory of constituent power that we have so far seen in action, in its creativity, and in its progression. In this case, too, it is clear that constituent power has nothing to do with natural right theory. In Machiavelli and Marx there is nothing but ironic references to it. And also in Spinoza naturalism has such an oblique and materialistically defined course that it would be grotesque to associate his thought with natural right theory. Moreover, we can even say that throughout its history constituent power presents itself as radically and continually in opposition to natural right theory since its form of dynamism runs counter to the static condition of natural right theory: creation against contract, and vitality and innovation against order and hierarchy. That said, we must stress nonetheless that in concrete human history and in the history of human ideas about life, wider and more equivocal causal series are experienced than those that can be logically proved. In this framework natural right theory, as a figure of modern rationalism, is not only a doctrine but also a context in which a series of senses and meanings of modern rationality are determined. Sometimes it is even a cage that imprisons modern rationality. Constituent power thus must always be careful and struggle in order not to be assimilated into one of the natural right families. Its creativity could always, in fact, be understood as the expression of a natural right presupposition.

Machiavelli flirts with a natural right reduction when he assumes the schema of the "return to beginnings" [*ritorno ai principii*] as motivation and articulation of the constituent principle. In Spinoza it is difficult to find any such deviation: not even his study of prophecy, which implies some element of teleology in the consideration of the historical subject, submits to such presuppositions. In Marx himself, a fierce adversary of any "pompous catalogue of the 'inalienable rights of man,'" there is a certain abstract humanism, configured above all as the ideological residue of a "primitive communism." For sure, all this has little to do with natural right theory understood as a system of thought and as a disciplinary function, but it is nonetheless relevant because it signals a perverse influence, a hard limit, opposed to the unconditioned creativity of constituent labor. Just as the Judeo-Christian tradition tries to block strength by pushing it into a unitary perspective, so the tradition of natural right tries to imprison strength within a preconceived schema. Whereas in the first case it is the multitude primarily that is attacked, in the second it is mostly strength that is under siege. In both cases the open relation between multitude and strength is blocked. But the concept and practice of constituent power consist precisely in this open relation.

The third level on which constituent power is ambushed by constituted power is the terrain of transcendentalism. It presents itself in the figure of idealism or formalism, and in both cases it tries to snare the spreading of constitutive strength, as well as the democratic and radical interweaving of *potentia* and *multitudo*. And although it is easy to recognize in transcendental idealism the direct mystification of constituent power along the theoretical line that leads from Rousseau to Hegel, the situation is more complicated when we look at formal transcendentalism. The great advantage of the formalist theories consists in the fact that they do not intervene in the reality of objects by submitting them to unitary or evolutionary (and in any case equivocal) schemata. They intervene in the conditions through which objects can be thought. We should examine them one at a time. How is constituent power thinkable?

In absolute idealism there is no problem: the conditions through which constituent power can be thought are those through which reality itself is thought. Constituent power is taken in the specificity of its concept, but at the same time diluted through a projection of its effects on the indefinite surface of reality as a whole. And since reality is a continual creative process, constituent power is nothing but the form of this process. But this continuity is flat and neutralizing: constituent power's innovative specificity is nullified and crushed in the indifference of the real. Hegel tries to make innovation circulate in the system of the real: in fact, in such a manner he cannot but sublimate innovative strength in the repetition of the real or conclude it in the hypostasis of absolute strength — that is, in absolute indifference.

Kantian formalism is much more aware of the problem posed by constituent power. What happens here to the constituent principle? All its determinations are taken into serious consideration, to the point of making strength the characteristic of the definition itself of the subject. Here the terms — either strength or multitude — do not disappear but are taken individually. And neither do the creative potentialities of the subjects disappear: they too are taken one by one. Kant tells us that the revolution is an object of our thought, that we apprehend it, and that by apprehending it we construct it and signify it.[1] From this standpoint the revolution can never end: it is the soul of ethics. The revolution is apprehended, and in this process of apprehension it affirms itself as ethical form. Now, what does all this mean? Actually, here we are dealing with a sophistic and capable figure of the negation of constituent power. In this figure, in fact, the relation between multitude and strength is interrupted and strength is resolved in the set of individuals, that is, in the category of individualism. What is lost here is the essence itself of constituent power, that historical effectiveness of constituent power that always and only presents itself as collective action. Only a pale liberal image of it is left, whereas instead the strength of constituent power is always and only democratic. Constituent power is entrusted to ethics and therefore taken away from politics — given to the individual, taken away from the collectivity. Constituent power is neutralized in individualism.

But one could object that this formal individualism is open and does not exclude taking place in the process of the imagination or connecting to the revolution as to a schematic function of reason! From this point of view, the objector could add, in Kantian formalism the two currents that in history have defined constituent power could be reunited. The individuals could transform themselves into collectivity, and individual freedom could become democracy. This, however, is not the case. The critical operation, far from operating a progressive mediation, tears apart the problematic nexus of strength and the multitude, poses its definitive figure in the preeminence of the ethical over the political, and isolates constituent power in the empty individual intentionality.

What should we say to all this? We can draw a first conclusion regarding this long history and this complex of contradictions and limits by observing that although these obstacles are fundamental when constituent power becomes constituted power, they are not at all so when constituent power expresses the strength of the critical relation that constructs it. Thus it presents itself constantly as creative principle, innovation, and prosthesis of being, and in this sense it cannot be neutralized. The second conclusion consists in observing that, beyond these limits, constituent power by continuing to live as strength and reorganize itself as multitude presents itself as the paradigm of a temporal dimension open onto the future.

This opening onto the future, this collective imagination in action, is a factual element that is always repeated and always reproposed by constituent power. On this terrain, again, it cannot be neutralized.[2] The third conclusion, and this is the most interesting one, is that if those oppositions mentioned above are effective, that is because constituent power—even though it is unimpaired by them both in its concept and its practice—has never managed to free itself fully from the progressive concept of modernity and its plot of rationality. The great tradition of materialist philosophy and democratic theory with which the history of constituent power is united has mixed and been confused with the rationalist tradition. Often it has suffered the weight of the rationalist tradition, and much more often it has reinvented it and even relaunched it. The ontological continuity of constituent thought has endured the hegemony of rationalistic thought. In Machiavelli all this is perfectly clear; in Spinoza the rupture is indicated, but the threshold of going beyond it is posed so high up that only mysticism seems to be able to achieve it; in Marx the possibility of the rupture of the rationalist horizon leans toward reality seeking a historical support, but reality is utopia.

In any case the rupture of rationalism works, for lack of an alternative, as a relaunching of rationalism and not as the resolute and definitive overcoming of it. The rupture of rationalism functions as a motor of rationalization.

This tireless impulse to overcome the rationalist limit takes constituent power from liberalism to democracy and socialism, but each time it gets lost in the impossibility of establishing the limit as absolute. The State, constituted power, and the traditional conception of sovereignty reappear each time to bring the constitutive process to an end. Therefore, our problem will be now to understand how this path of contradictions has come to its conclusion and how this destiny is by now emptied of any effectiveness. The double history of constituent power can perhaps—this at least is our problem—be definitively simplified by depriving it of that component that always led it to a mystified solution: the effectual constituted block. We must analyze how constituent power, after functioning as the motor of the development of Western rationalism, can now fold in on its own singular force and express it entirely in the fullness of its intensity.

Is it possible to consider *multitudo* and *potentia* as the index of a single productive set infinitely capable of constructive prostheses? Is it possible to construct a concept of the "political" that merges into the social and a concept of the "social" that finds in the political its own internal key of understanding and expression? That is, *simpliciter* the expression of strength?

All we have until now studied leads us to this limit of the analysis, this boundary of the problem—not simply an ideal theme but a problem raised by every insurgence of constituent power and equally by its every crisis. It is time to try to understand whether inside the continuity of these crises the radically constitutive principle of being is not already established as solidly as ever.[3]

Constitutive Disutopia

What does it mean to break the schema of modernity from the standpoint of constituent power? What does it mean to go beyond the project of rationalization that is typical of modernity in the sphere of constitutional thought? To answer these questions, we must step backward and once again consider the development of the models of constituent power in their interaction with the realized constitutional models.

In this perspective the first group of problems is raised by what we have called—after Pocock—the "Atlantic" model, that is, the constitutional forms constructed in the English and American Revolutions of the seventeenth and the eighteenth centuries (see chaps. 3, 4). Now, it seems that the specific modality in which constituent power was imprisoned in these experiences and these constitutional processes is that of the rationalization of the "political space." Constituent power is absorbed and mediated within a spatial schema.

This spatial schema constitutes an area of independence of the political and affirms its autonomy after having set in motion a double mechanism of social organization. This mechanism is, on the one hand, directed toward the horizontal representation of all the dimensions of the social, while, from another point of view, it is predisposed to their vertical mediation. Constituted power presents itself as centralized mediation, starting from a "space" that has become "political" because totally invested by the process of "representation." Constituted power is thus diluted in the representative mechanism and can only manifest itself in "political space." Here it reappears, in disguise, in the activity of the Supreme Court or in the power of initiative of other organs of the State, in any case neutralized. The division and the reciprocal control of the organs of the State, the generalization and formalization of the administrative processes consolidate and establish this system of the neutralization of constituent power.

The rationalization of the political system in this case thus consists in the stabilization of its components within a geometrical schema of controls. The possible imbalances that the living history of societies can determine must themselves be included in a mechanism of regulation or compensation and must be functional to maintaining order. Today functionalist political philosophies represent the *relais* of the contractualist and constitutionalist ones (in the sense of the ancien regime) that have preceded them.[4] Constituent power is here conceived as something extraneous or something internal to distribute in the space of the mediations, and in either case it must be neutralized when it presents itself as innovative determination. The negative evaluation of constituent power is overdetermined by the spatial conception of the political—a space traversed by a more or less formalized constitutional geometry, which is sometimes closed and sometimes open but in any case predisposed to control any innovation. Constituent power is, because of the Atlantic conceptions and the geometry of their space, always and only an accident. It is entirely obvious that from this point of view the interpretation itself of revolutionary phenomena and constituent power in action must be either eliminated from the theoretical scene of analysis of the present orders or shifted toward archaic situations in which the political space is not yet formed.[5]

What does it mean with respect to this first group of historical determinations of constituted power to go beyond and possibly against the process of constitutionalization consolidated in this way? What does it mean in these specific terms to break the schema of modernity? In the historical episodes that we have considered, Harrington and the English revolutionaries, as well as a certain Jeffersonianism, posed this problem. The solutions they gave were neither adequate nor effective, and in certain instances they even produced opposed and perverse effects. But the problem remains.

If we now consider the second group of constituent experiences and constitutional systems that we have been studying, those tied to the French and Russian Revolutions (see chaps. 5, 6), the answer to an analogous set of questions not only allows us to resolve the first problem but even complicates it. Just as in the first case constituent power was imprisoned in constituted power as in a rational schema of organization in space, so too in this second group rationalization passes through a project of organization of time. Certainly, the innovation that we witness here is enormous; not place of humans but human activity is taken into consideration, not the abstract generality of the citizens but the concreteness of labor, and not constituent power in a restricted political figure but constituent power as form of the productive force of society.

From this point of view, many of the problems that are unsolvable for spatial constitutionalism become manageable and constituent power can be reabsorbed across a wide range of possibilities. But the problem is not simply canceled for this reason. In fact, it is complicated and aggravated.

What does the rationalization of time here involve? It consists of the constitutionalization of labor, in its progressive and articulated submission to the rule of enterprise and the norm of the social reproduction of organized labor. Real temporality is broken and reconstructed as the horizon of the system. The temporal dynamic of constituent power and its capability of imposing accelerations that show the strength of the multitude become productive in all aspects and are here subordinated to the command of a constituted power as a dialectic of time. Generalized representation and spatial mediation are no longer what regulate society from the political standpoint. Time is now the seat of control and mediation. The breaking of the temporal order of development, the progress of liberties, as well as of the distribution of wealth is in any case unbearable.

Constitutions can come one after the other—each time or, rather, each historical period has its own constitution—but time must always be constitutionalized. And different times must be reduced to zero.[6] The machination of this reduction is temporal and the constitution is a temporal machine. The formal constitution is superimposed over (and at the same time precedes) a material constitution. In other words, it is an interweaving of powers and interests, limits and conditions, the establishment of norms of participation and exclusion, temporally and historically defined.[7] The temporal machine is closed, the measure of time is that of command, and the normative value is that of exchange in its relative autonomy (relative autonomy, but not less effective). A physics of preconstituted temporalities is opposed, as schema of rationalization, to spatial geometry. Their only dynamic is that of exchange value. Constituent power, as *use value*, is expelled from the scene, or liminally considered, and in any case subjected to a dialectic that must always close it down again. Even the rules of representation are themselves brought back to this dialectical schema and subjected to the concrete temporality of the norm of reproduction of the system or to the rule of enterprise. When constituent power is absorbed in the system, it is with respect to its dynamic capacities and on the condition of its constant dialectical neutralization.

In this episode, therefore, not functionalism but the dialectic becomes the theoretical key to constitutional thought. This is a dialectic of the recomposition, the continual transcending, and the continuous mediation of every constituent insurgency. From formal legitimation we go back to the productive legitimation of the system: not the legitimacy of the ancien regime, but a dynamic, productive legitimation. Legitimation invests time in order to make it administrative routine and control it within dynamic procedures, with the continual tension and care to enclose every constituent emergence within the alienated and perverted instruments of the dynamic system. Max Weber's analytic realism assumes for dialectical constitutionalism in this scenario the same positive and paradigmatic value that Thomas Hobbes's theory has had for functional constitutionalism through the centuries.

What does it mean, in the context of this second group of experiences of rationalization of constituent power, to go beyond the constitutional figure? As we have seen, in the French and Russian Revolutions the only effective answer to this problem consisted in the acceleration of time: an acceleration that insistently seeks to overcome the limits posed to constituent power. It is the active sense of "terminating the revolution"—it is permanent revolution. This insistence on time and its continuity becomes paroxysmal, and in both historical cases it degenerated into terror. But in both cases the living reflection of constituent power into the revolutionary process determines other perspectives. In this formless and accelerated time constituent power is articulated in a general way, and its claim to effectiveness is irreversibly established.

The claim to equality is the form in which the acceleration of revolutionary historical time, as manifestation of constituent power in action, consolidates itself. This is a strange paradox: equality, in this process, does not present itself anymore as the aim but as the condition. It is as if the insistence on active time and the acceleration of time against obstacles had become capable of absorbing the constitutional space and subordinating it to movement. The very concept of collectivity is modified at this point from being a totalitarian and intensive structure to being a social and extensive category. In other words, in time it assumes the characteristics of the cooperative process of individualities. On this passage and by resisting constitutionalization, the constituent power founded on temporality ingests space and poses it as the dynamic of its process, of the production of singularity.

However, this solution to the problem, as we have seen, is not actual but only possible and contingent. In fact, the liberation of the element that is simultaneously temporal and collective is anomalous, and when the project pushes the problem forward and makes it the substance of its desire, modern rationalism effectively imposes its hegemony. Terror and not liberation: this is the result that modern rationalism determines in its opposition to the ontological development of constituent power considered in this perspective. The continuous time of capitalist rationality, its linear progression, and the tendency to the reduction to zero of the world of life present themselves as an unsurpassed obstacle—this substance infiltrates the alternative process, mining it from inside, and preventing it from finding the place of reality, and thus forcing it to swing on a desperate pendulum between utopia and terror.

Disfiguring and perverse ideological representations thus latch onto the strength of a reality that does not manage to become actual. The time of constituent power, in the void of determinations to which it has been reduced, is conceived as a negative substance. It becomes time of "being for death"—the implacable perspective and totalitarian reduction of the being of the world to the negative. And there where the philosophical reflection becomes ideology, that is, where it presents itself as an interpretation and a guide for the collective praxis, constituent power is defined as "pure decision"—as a voluntary moment of emptying reality and a praxis of negating every determination, except, precisely, that of negating. The only existing determination is that of determinating. In what sense? In the sense of death. Between Heidegger and Schmitt takes place not so much the conclusive emptying of the rationality of modernity as its smug overdetermination. It is an absolute overdetermination that is absolutely opposed to the definition of constituent power. This is constituent power formally assumed and posed as the dark appearance of a will to power—certainly fully untouched by the ghosts of modernity—but at the same time absolutely inimical to any determination of the strength of the multitude.

Constituent power is taken to be terror and thus destroyed in its unresolved relation with rationality. It is emptied of any ontological constituent dimension, and it is negatively polarized in the dimension of its crisis in relation to the rationality of modernity. Fascism is this perverse conception of constituent power, pushed outside of any vitality, considered as the negativities of any *cupiditas*, and thus, in this perspective, subtracted from any possibility of a spatial or temporal alternative to the grip and destiny of modernity. The connection of Carl Schmitt's thought to Spinoza's philosophy of strength is all played in this light.[8] There where the anomaly cannot become hegemony, the alternative to utopia is reduced to the brutal act of using force—this is the cynical foundation of the fascist disfiguring of constituent power.

Let's go back to the initial question: what does it mean to break the schema of the rationality of modernity from the standpoint of constituent power? The first relevant answer to advance the research consists in stressing the actual reabsorbing of the concept of space into that of constituent time. We recognized this while analyzing the phases of the formation of the concept in the various historical instances. This absorption does not deny the specificity of the spatial determinations but sets them in a close relation with the totality of movement. Constitutive strength dislocates and transvalues space into time, sets geometry in the service of physics, and embodies topology in the tendency. This fundamental passage is not only formal—its content is in fact the inseparability of the concept of strength from that of multitude. This is all that needs to be said about this.

A second reflection is possible that takes us to the question of the continuity of the crisis of constituent power as a historical power. We need to investigate this crisis further to grasp its concept. It presents itself as the continual interruption of the constitutive rhythm and as revolutionary becoming with respect to political constructions and constituted being. This crisis is general and continual: it can be defined as a chronicle of the events and revolutionary experiences but leads us toward a negative ontology of the structural development of constituent power.[9] The clash between revolutionary becoming and political constructions does not regard only a phenomenology of the historical process but reveals the incommensurability of the expression of the strength of the multitude. It is this incommensurability that destroys in a definitive manner the modern concept of linear and progressive rationality. Yet, and this is the essential point, at the same time it indicates the crisis as activity. The crisis is a limit but it is also and, more important, an obstacle. The limit is posed against a will of strength of the multitude that is impossible to limit, and thus it becomes an obstacle. And it is by becoming deeper on this terrain of the negative that the clash and the contradictions become active: the limit does not close but liberates praxis.[10]

The third reflection must therefore bring us to the change of nature of constitutive praxis. Its definition is not given by the effectiveness of succeeding but by the effectiveness of always trying a new way of succeeding. What does not succeed is the affirmation of a will that emerges on those points of resistance that are reproduced in the points of failure. It is the revelation of an "outside" that has become an "inside" and the folding in of historical development on this omnipotence that is never actualized but always reproposed. And since this strength is the strength of the multitude, here the multitude reveals itself as subject. The conditions of realization of constituent power are given, therefore, as space led back to time, as time led to strength, and as strength led to the subject. All this in the scenario of a negative ontology. Here the utopian residue of constituent power is transformed into an operative and constitutive disutopia.

Let's read this passage again. For the first time, having come to this point of our research, we are able to see the crisis of the concept of constituent power, whose continuous history we have followed, turn into a positive opening—one that does not deny the crisis but makes it internal to the concept. This interiority of the crisis to the concept allows us to see the movement of constituent power as the ceaseless breathing of praxis; in other words, it allows us to bring the concept within the totality of spatiotemporal historical being—a critical totality that is divided and interrupted, yet still a totality. On another side it pushes us to shift the analysis from the structure to the subject and from the crisis of the concept of constituent power to the concept of constituent power as crisis. But precisely because it is crisis, constitutive strength is a radical subjective foundation of being; it is the subjectivity of creation. This is creation that is born from the crisis and therefore creation that has nothing to do with the simple linearity of modern rationality or, on the other hand, with utopia. Crisis and disutopia lead here to the establishment of constituent movement in subjectivity. The concept of constituent power recuperates its history and is conclusively formed as concept of the constitutive disutopia. Where the progressive linearity of modernity clashes with the nothingness of its effects constituent subjectivity is born, not as ultimate result of reason but as the product of its failure. This constitutive subjectivity is born from the nothingness of the determinations of modernity and on the continual, unceasing totality of the action of the multitude.

This definition brings us directly back to Machiavelli and his ability to experience radically, in its origin, the privileged historical moment of the birth of the concept. I believe that Antonio Gramsci fully grasped this fact.[11] Indeed, on the one hand he posed the Prince as element of the crisis, as the demand of a "pulverized and dispersed people" that wants, in its desperation, to organize itself and to be incited to collective action. Here is how, therefore, the crisis sets the reconstruction in motion—a strength that traverses the multitude and that in this traversing manifests and defines itself on the basis of desperation, disunion, and crisis: "The Prince is to put an end to feudal anarchy, and that is what Valentino does in Romagna, basing himself on the support of the productive classes, merchants and peasants."[12] "His 'ferocity' is turned against the residues of the feudal world, not against the progressive classes" (Gramsci, 140–41). It is important to notice that what is "progressive" here is not a future Enlightenment project but, on the contrary, the new organization of praxis, radically new and radically collective.

Machiavelli is not merely a scientist: he is a partisan, a man of powerful passions, an active politician, who wishes to create a new balance of force, and therefore cannot help concerning himself with what "ought to be" (not of course in a moralistic sense).... If one applies one's will to the creation of a new equilibrium among the forces which really exist and are operative—basing oneself on the particular force which one believes to be progressive and strengthening it to help it to victory—one still moves on the terrain of effective reality, but does so in order to dominate and transcend it (or to contribute to this). What "ought to be" is therefore concrete; indeed it is the only realistic and historicist interpretation of reality, it alone is history in the making and philosophy in the making, it alone is politics. (172)

The modern Prince, the myth-prince, cannot be a real person, a concrete individual. It can only be an organism, a complex element of society in which a collective will, which has already been recognized and has to some extent asserted itself in action, begins to take concrete form. (129)

A collective will which at least in some aspects was an original, ex novo *creation. And a definition must be given of collective will, and of political will in general, in the modern sense: will as operative awareness of historical necessity, as protagonist of a real and effective historical drama. (130)*

What a formidable image this is—the image of a new subjectivity that is born from the nothingness of any determination or preconstituted destiny and that preconstitutes collectively each determination and destiny! The notion of constituent power as crisis and strength, as multitude and subject—as constitution of strength—is affirmed here. The political form of disutopia is this completely new political form, which has neither principle nor foundation outside the strength of the multitude.

Here all the threads of our research begin to come together. As a form of disutopia constituent power shows a singular and irreducible concept of the political, but at the same time it constructs and connects a methodology, a philosophy of history, and an ethics that are equally singular. The methodology is that of the reconstruction of the object through a genealogical and radical intuition; it is the methodology of a radical inductivism that forms knowledge, its objects, and subjects on the basis of the strength of desires, and thus articulates this knowledge in the network of the multitude. This is not an ungraspable multiplicity but a multitude, the total versatility of being and its always singular multidirectionality. Not only a thousand plateaus, but a thousand directions, networks, and variables. The subject is constructed according to these dimensions. But its construction would be impossible and would belong to the category of the "bad infinity," if negativity, crisis, and resistance would not allow the multitude to recuperate the critical central determination: the point of crisis and negativity around which, within sudden, untimely events and radical discoveries of different temporalities, the multitude comes to recognize its own strength. The method is not only constitutive but also constituent. Subjectivity is a prosthesis of movement and its infinite determinations, and it arrives as an absolute event.

The philosophy of history of constituent power as the political form of disutopia is just as singular. It is properly a "nonphilosophy" of history. Since the constitutive processes of historical reality are discontinuous, burning in their unpredictability and immediacy, they are contradictory threads that only resistance, refusal, and negativity can weave together and shape positively. There is no goal—there is only the radical continuity of the discontinuous, the continual reappearance of the time of strength as alternative, but at the same time as resistance, to the "realistic" and "sovereign" dissipation of time. The relationship between multitude and strength determines the meaning of history, and this meaning is given only when it is torn away from discontinuity and connected to the multitude, constructed as the event of its absoluteness. The meaning of history is something like the photonegative of its normal lack of meaning. Certainly, the series of absolute events and insurrections of meaning are consolidated on the ontological basis of the development of consciousnesses and concepts. But this ontological background and deposit are active only in the ever new relation of strength and multitude and become effective again only upon reactivating the singular event. Constituent power describes its ontological continuity (and produces a memory) only if the absolute event activates them. Among the events there is not a flat continuity, and to tell things as they are, there is not even memory. Continuity and memory pertain only to the event. Memory is a product of constituent power in action; it is not continuity but innovation.

The ethics of constituent power, as political form of disutopia, is itself embodied, too, in the relation between strength and multitude. It is an open ethics that immediately comprehends the singularities in the conditions of realization of the multitude and of its strength. Ethical being pursues in the singularity the impossible task of realizing the substance of the disutopia. It makes of each event a testimonial and of each testimonial an act of militancy. Its waiting for the constituent event is all committed to the constitution of the event. The form of this ethics is open as much as its foundation is ontological. This ethical opening is continually tested against the concrete determinations of the multitude, its changeability, its disunion, and its antagonisms. It does not leave aside the consideration of its complexity, either of the natural one of the passions or the historical one of the institutions. It does not lose sight of the weakness of the singularities in their constituting themselves into a multitude. But it makes this proceeding toward the multitude and the will to express it as absolute strength its rule, thus preventing any other external power from coming closer or from declining the modes of strength. Disutopia is the only possibility of the expression of strength and in it are included all the critical aporias of the relations between it and the multitude. The testimonial of the process, in every moment, is ethics. Ethics consequently excludes utopia since utopia is the affirmation of alienation, or in any case presupposition of a tendency to flatten the relation between multitude and strength.

Here we reach a final point of observation. This political form of constituent power that we call disutopia and that includes its own methodological, historical-philosophical, and ethical values, we can also call "democracy." But we must specify something: here *democracy* means the omnilateral expression of the multitude, the radical immanence of strength, and the exclusion of any sign of external definition, either transcendent or transcendental and in any case external to this radical, absolute terrain of immanence. This democracy is the opposite of constitutionalism. Or better, it is the negation itself of constitutionalism as constituted power—a power made impermeable to singular modalities of space and time, and a machine predisposed not so much to exercising strength but, rather, to controlling its dynamics, its unchangeable dispositions of force. Constitutionalism is transcendence, but above all constitutionalism is the police that transcendence establishes over the wholeness of bodies in order to impose on them order and hierarchy. Constitutionalism is an apparatus that denies constituent power and democracy. It should not appear strange at this point that constitutionalism runs into paradoxes when it tries to define constituent power. It cannot accept this power as a distinct activity and consequently drowns it in sociology or otherwise grabs it by the hair and constructs formalistic definitions of it (see chap. 1). Yet the one that shipwrecks in this definitional battle is not constituent power but constitutionalism. Constituent power remains an ineluctable horizon, a massive presence, a multitude.

The question of the multitude is a thorn in the side of Western political thought, and consequently any answer avoids the existence of constituent power and leads to a malaise. However, this anguish and malaise are also ours. Our answer to the questions posed by constituent power is neither peaceful nor optimistic. It is a cautious and difficult answer that rests uneasily on the negative values of disutopia. But as much as disutopia is disenchanted, so it is open, savagely open to presence, to effectiveness, and to the desire to free it. The strength of the multitude becomes constitution of strength within this process, that is, in the unstoppable tension of the multitude to become actuality of strength.

Here our recalling Spinoza's thought will not appear strange. That process of constitution of strength that we have hitherto been defining is in fact fully illustrated in *The Ethics*. Also in Spinoza the disutopia is constituent. It situates strength among the multitude, thus accumulating in being itself the product of this collective tension. Being shows itself, first of all, as the fabric of the production of existence. This constitutive process is the same as that of life. Just as in physics it is a process that leads a multitude of atoms into configuring individuals, so too in social, ethical, and political life the multitude of individuals reinterprets the striving of strength to exist toward more and more communitarian configurations of life. The mechanisms of production of nature construct individuals; the natural individuals set in motion the processes of the construction of the social.

Here we are facing a first ontological level, on which is inscribed the progressive passage of passions, imagination, and intelligence toward higher and higher degrees of ontological density. But this process duplicates itself, and it makes us confront not only different degrees of ontological density, but also human creativity, spread out beyond the ontological limits of the process. This happens when, ethically, love and joy break the continual rhythm of the ontological process.[13] Here love constitutes the divinity, the absolute. From this union it returns to the social in order to revivify it. A second ontological level, therefore, that breaks apart the genealogical continuity of the first is no longer an accumulation of being, but one of its creative prostheses. When love intervenes and joy separates from sadness, then being has been found again. Constituent power has completely liberated itself, in its positive determination, as determination of the ontological fabric and as its creative overdetermination.

The disutopia of the relation of multitude to strength is confirmed and exalted by the act of love: collective action, cooperating human essence, and active experience of this promotion of existence beyond its limits, toward the absolute. This Spinozian trajectory corresponds to the image of constituent power that we have defined. It does so because twice it gives evidence for the creativity of the social being: first, when it considers it as conclusion of the natural process of the genealogy of the world and therefore as principle of the consolidation of its structure and as an internal ontological innovation; second, when the constituent process defines itself as a radical innovation beyond the process of structuring. One cannot but be struck by this duplicity of definitions—the first pertains to natural human history and the second determines a destiny of human liberation. Certainly, we are not dealing with the "unsurpassable aporias of pantheism," as the bigots would have it! No, the strange stupefaction and our enthusiasm stem from the fact that the break between necessity and freedom is inserted into ontology; it defines ontology and explains its permanence, progressive enrichment, and innovative strength. Once again this is a constitutive disutopia. The ontological level and its depth do not allow, in fact, to unfurl utopias and illusory declarations of overcoming. On the contrary, these conditions constitute the ground because the consciousness of the limit feeds the creative act. Constituent power is not born from an undifferentiated continuity of being but, rather, exactly from its creative differentiation and from an innovation that, after having constituted the individuals into a multitude, determines the strength of the latter.

As in Spinozian metaphysics, our history of constituent power leads us in each experience to measure the ontological degree that constituent democracy poses as the ineradicable and progressive condition, and at the same time it shows us how this first ontological dimension must be verified by a new break, a new opening of the multitude toward higher and higher figures of the constitution of strength. The disutopia is what assembles the picture. Have we perhaps come to the border of a new episode of constituent innovation today? To the possibility of a new prosthesis of the world? An absolute democracy?

Beyond Modernity

All the threads of our research lead to one conclusion: constituent power is a subject. This subject, this collective subjectivity, wrenches free from all the conditions and contradictions to which, each time, their constituent force is subjected at specific conjunctures of political and constitutional history. This subject is not progressive. On the contrary, it is the continual antithesis of any constitutional progression; its birth and also its rupture pose themselves against the constitutional process, and in no case does the constituent subject submit itself to the static and constricting permanence of constitutional life. That said, we need to specify the nature of this subjectivity and simultaneously define the rationality that distinguishes it, because clearly the fact that the constituent subject poses itself as rupture of and alternative to constituted power situates this subjectivity and its rationality beyond the usual definitions of modern rationality and adequate subjectivity. The definition of constituent power points us beyond the limits of modernity.

Now, first of all, we understand modernity as the definition and development of a totalizing thought that assumes human and collective creativity in order to insert them into the instrumental rationality of the capitalist mode of production of the world. The idealist dialectic, in the form invented by Descartes, developed in the great tradition of modern metaphysics, and concluded by Hegel, represents the schema of this totalizing process. Its political implication is celebrated in the tradition of absolutism, between Hobbes, Rousseau, and once again Hegel—a firm and steady absolutism, whose only aim is that of posing the political as transcending the multitude and power as a verification of strength.

Although constituent power and the multitude of the subjectivities unceasingly oppose this realization of power as well as the transcendental reabsorption of strength, this resistance is dissolved in the dialectic, over and over again. From the standpoint of the political, the multitude is always objectified. Its name is reduced to a curse: *vulgus*, or worse *Pöbel*. Its strength is expropriated. Nonetheless, we cannot do without the *multitudo* in social and political life—this is evident. But how can it be dominated? This is the only question that theoretical philosophy, moral philosophy, and above all political philosophy pose to themselves. The *multitudo* has to become each time either a nature that is mechanical and deprived of spirit, a nature closer to that of brutes than men, or a thing in itself, unachievable and therefore mystifiable, or a savage world of irrational passions that only the *Vernunft* will be able to unravel and control. The strength of the multitude has to become more and more the object of anguished interrogations and inflexible decisions of repression, that is, expropriation. The fear of the multitude is the strength of instrumental rationality. This savage beast must be dominated, tamed, or destroyed, overcome or sublimated. In any case, its subjectivity must be taken away from it, and rationality must be denied to it. The indestructible social determination of the multitude must be destroyed.

Modern political philosophy is born not from administration but fear. Its rationality is instrumental to the aim of order only insofar as it is so on the side of repression. Anguish is the cause and repression the effect of instrumental rationality. Modernity is therefore the negation of any possibility that the multitude may express itself as subjectivity. This can serve as a first definition of modernity. It is not strange, then, nor should it be unexpected, that no space can be allowed to constituent power. When it emerges, it must be treated as extraordinary and temporary; when it imposes itself, it must be defined as an exteriority; and when it triumphs over every inhibition, exclusion, or repression, it must be neutralized in the "Thermidore." Constituent power is this negation.

But constituent power and the collective subjectivity that gives it shape are first of all a social reality—a productive social reality that cannot be negated. Power feeds on this strength: without this strength it could not exist. To the negation of the strength of the multitude in the political must therefore correspond the enclosure of the strength of the multitude within the social. This is a second characteristic of modernity. The neutralization of the multitude in the political demands its separation in the social. This second operation implies the construction of a separate science, whether it is called political economy or sociology, whose task is the isolation of social strength from political power—even better, or more simply, of the social from the political.

The analysis, developing in the social, will have as its aim the isolation of the latter from the political. Liberal thought and anarchist thought are, on this terrain, the most perfect figurations of instrumental rationality. For both the social does not necessitate the political, and the invisible hand denies constituent power. Whether individualism and the rule of profit or anarchy and the rule of collectivism are the laws on which these representations of reality stand, in both cases the isolation of the social is the aim, an aim complementary to the transcendence of the political, whether this transcendence is invoked or critiqued. It is evident what enormous contradictions charge this tendency toward the isolation of the social: each social crisis, which inevitably touches and upsets the political, sounds as a death warning to the theories of separateness. And it serves also as a warning of modernity's difficulty or in any case its urgency in controlling the social. We are saved "in the final instance" (a final instance that always comes) through the recourse to violence and its multiple masquerades. The fear of the *multitudo* is in this case carried to the extreme, and violence is born as the synthesis of anguish and the absence of a practicable alternative.

We need to respond to this theory of violence and repropose the crucial role of constituent power as salvation from barbarism. While reconstructing the relation between multitude and strength, we referred to Machiavelli's thought, and in confronting the discourse of constitutive disutopia, we turned to the discourse of Spinoza's metaphysics. Now on this catastrophic split of the political and the social it is necessary to return once again to the Marxian standpoint. In fact, it is Marx who most strongly insists on the relation or, better, on the interiority of the social and the political within the materialist and revolutionary current of modern metaphysics. And even though he never wrote the theory of the State that he planned as part of *Capital*, he nonetheless identified, primarily in his economic writings as we have seen, the terrain of a critique of the political, starting from the social, and elaborated some fundamental prolegomena to any future science of constituent power.

The theme proposed by Marx is that of the all-expansive creativity of living labor. Living labor constitutes the world, by creatively modeling, *ex novo*, the materials that it touches. It entrusts and consolidates in nature and beyond this in a second, third, and eventually umpteenth nature the constitutive power of living labor. In this process living labor transforms itself first of all. Its projection on the world is ontological, its prostheses are ontological, and its constructions are constructions of a new being. The first result of this indefinite process is the construction of the subject. The subject is a continual oscillation of strength, a continual reconfiguring of the actual possibility of strength's becoming a world. The subject is the point on which the constitution of strength establishes itself. But the subject itself continues to take shape through the world that it itself has constructed by shaping and reshaping itself. Living labor becomes constituent power within this process. And it is within this process that the multitude is brought back to strength and discovers itself as subject. The dialectic is no longer part of this picture, nor the instrumental rationality of modernity, because there is no more teleology and because teleology is no longer theoretically definable. There is no supersession: phenomenology always wins over the science of logic, history, and any other encyclopedia of the spirit. The quantity, the materiality, and the versatility of living labor mark any rising subjectivity. It is the constituent process, the dimensions determined by the will, and the struggle and the decision on the struggle that decide the senses of being.

Far from becoming dispersive, this process is a continual determination, traversed by the concreteness of the social, by its organization, and by the continual actualization of the relation between multitude and strength. Marx brought to light a commonality of the social, the political, and being that is traversed and always newly defined by living labor, its subsidiary associations, and the subjectivities that emerge within it—in short, by constituent power. Hence the exceptional importance of Marx's teachings about the definition of constituent power and the supersession of modernity. Whereas constituent power had always been defined (in the terms of modernity) as an extraordinary power with respect to the ordinary legitimacy of the constitution, here any extraordinariness is taken away because through its reduction to the social (animated by living labor) constituent power's ordinary capability of operating in ontological terms is recognized. Constituent power is a creative strength of being, that is, of concrete figures of reality, values, institutions, and logics of the order of reality. Constituent power constitutes society and identifies the social and the political in an ontological nexus.

But one might object that from the humanistic revolution to the English Revolution, from the American Revolution to the French and Russian ones, and to all the other revolutions of the twentieth century, once the exceptional and uncontainable moment of innovation is over, constituent power seems to exhaust its effects. Now, as Marx pointed out and as we think we can continue to sustain, this is not true. This appearance of exhaustion is the effect of the mystification that the practices of constitutionalism stage in order to block the investment of the social and the political in being. Marx teaches that this endpoint is impossible, that each endpoint is not an absolute limit but an obstacle, and that beyond the endpoint constituent power continues to weave its plots on an innovative fabric. The only limits on constituent power are the limits of the world of life. Any utopian place is excluded from this perspective. But the world is larger than the actual since the political and the social intervene in the world of life, continually destabilizing it and widening it, merging together in a constitutive and radical way. Constituent power is the social and political subjectivity of this radical constitution of the world of life.

Even though Marx posed us on the terrain of subjectivity, we are beyond Marx. The political subject that constituent power reveals today not only considers the world of life limited but also already experimentally proves itself in an uninterrupted construction of new worlds. Its limits are those of its rationality. But what rationality? Beyond Marx we need to pose another fundamental question, the third to which a theory of constituent power beyond modernity points. Is the rationality of modernity in any case adequate to the subjectivity that poses itself, as constituent power, beyond and against modernity? Certainly, it cannot be. The rationality of modernity is in fact, as we have seen, a linear logic that corrals the multitude of subjects in a unity and controls its difference through the dialectic. Modern rationality is the calculation of the individual in a transcendental realm that nullifies its singular essence. It is the repetition of the individualization of what is common and therefore the colonization of its sphere, claiming to make it transcendental. We find all the effects of this rationality when modern rationality blocks the constituent process and founds modern constitutions: this obstacle is posed through the deterritorialization of subjects, the neutralization of their creativity, the fixation of their temporality, and therefore through a series of operations of normalization of movement. Transcendental formalism is the key to this rationality, the renunciation of reality and the multitude is its condition, and the construction of the command is always its effect.

Now, the theory of the constituent subject takes us beyond these determinations. The site of the new rationality is pushed and found again in ontology. We need to go and find once again the bases of the new rationality where living labor arises, that is, where the social finds its vital breadth—on the place where the sequences of acting and the creative impulses are formed. The form of rationality in the ontological site thus becomes the relation between strength and multitude. It is on the weave of this relation that rationality is formed and developed, and it is on this relation that its substantial determination finds formal validity. In other words, it finds foundation, effectiveness, and also abstract validation. The problem is not to save rationality from abstraction; this claim of vitalism and irrationalism is illusory. Abstraction is as necessary as concreteness. It is not abstraction that must be taken away but its exclusiveness and formal totalization that were affirmed from the heights of modern logic.

Abstraction must be reaffirmed from below, from the base of the processes of production where its constitutive processes are analyzed inside the ontological relation. Rationality refers to what is common and empirical, abstracted for the aim of communication. Abstraction is not a fetish but a function of communication. Yet communication is nothing but the ontological relation of multitude and strength. Here we have identified the point of departure of the new rationality—the rationality that takes us beyond modernity. Multitude and strength, in their ontological intertwining, show rationality, a new rationality, to be the key to the constitution of the world. To the social as well as the political, to individuality as well as to collective subjectivity.[14] The rational relation is therefore determined—determined not only formally from the standpoint from which it emanates, but also and above all from the substantial, ontological standpoint, from the real modality of the relation between multitude and strength, and from its subjective experiences.

What are the characteristics of the new rationality? Here it is not a matter of confronting the problem in an exhaustive manner, but only posing it from the standpoint of the theory of constituent power. And since our answer is situated at the center of a historical dynamics of alternatives and struggles, we will have to clarify and emphasize above all those characteristics of the new rationality that oppose the rationality of modernity. Let's start therefore to list these oppositions—which are as strong as the opposition between the ontological and the formal.

The first opposition is that of creativity against limit and measure. The rationality of constituent power is first of all defined by the limitlessness of its proposition. The limit is for it only an obstacle. It poses the limit only as condition of its own being, of its own expansion, and thus as condition of its own producing. Consequently, measure—this internalized limit—tends to be destroyed. Constituent power is boundless. Its only measure is the limitlessness of the multitude, the absolute versatility of its relations, and the powerful and constitutive interrelations that compose its concept and determine its real dynamic.

Measure can reappear only as the content (and not the norm) of creative relations. There is no longer measure; there exist only measures that we construct at the moment itself when we produce the reality to be measured. The "Thermidore" is measure—constituent power is beyond measure or, rather, progressive measure, the reflection of the common on itself.[15] Measure is the form of validity of the proceeding of constituent power in the moment when it makes validity itself unlimited. Measure is the relation between the outside and the inside of creative subjectivity at the moment when it is superseded. Strictly speaking, we should no longer talk of "measure," but only say, "made to measure." The measure of the new rationality is not therefore a "hard" element of the ever new creative machine, but the "soft" element that organizes its internal determinations and its software. Limits and measures, wrenched from dialectical logic, can only be considered as dynamic elements of the multiversal and critical creative continuity of constituent power.

The second opposition in the definition of the new rationality of constituent power is that of procedure/process against the deductive mechanism of substantial right and the constitutional machine. This determination does not entrap the analysis of constituent power within the juridical terrain but, rather, through a series of examples shows some concrete characteristics of the new rationality. Its movement is uninterrupted, a construction from below that traverses the singular emergences by coordinating their action. In this process general and abstract rules are not applied, but, rather, constellations of interests, agreements, and relations are continually constituted and verified. If procedural rules exist, they themselves are each time verified. Cartographies of the connections and interrelations of the relations and initiatives are constructed.[16] The frame is that of a continual expansion of "entrepreneurial" activities, cutting through the social and the political, the juridical and the institutional. Sovereignty never separates from its origin and is organized in the relation between origin and exercise. The controls are exercised as active moments of the procedure and not imputed from outside. The entire process from beginning to end is transcendental because there is no longer beginning or end. Procedure is the concrete form that each figure of subjectivity assumes in its relating to the others. It dissolves the constitutive myth of the contract, but, if we look carefully, it interprets and rationally develops its genealogical movement. In fact, the new rationality constructs itself as a genealogy that replaces the one to which the contract had mythically referred, in an interweaving of passions and institutions, interests and entrepreneurial capacities. Procedures are its open and tendential ontological fabric.[17] The genealogical method and the practice of procedures take us back to the creativity of singularities and at the same time demonstrate their always-open nature—constitutive disutopias. With this we arrive from the most abstract characteristics of the new rationality to the identification of the most concrete.

The third opposition is that of equality against privilege. It is clear how this can be logically founded. If constituent power takes roots in the relation between *multitudo* and *potentia*, if the rationality of this relation is the rationality described by the movement of creativity against the limit and measure, and continual procedure against institutional stasis, it is evident that there is no place for privilege here because it is contradictory with the constitutive movement of living labor. From this standpoint equality does not present itself as an inalienable right except in the (very fundamental) sense that equality is the condition of the constitutive process. It is a condition—not the aim, not a finality to realize, but its ontological assumption. It is a material condition—not an abstract and hypocritical declaration of a formal right, but a concrete situation. The logical nature of equality and the substantial rationality of its presenting itself as assumption consist in the fact that the multitude cannot present itself but as equality, in the fact that freedom cannot but develop among equal subjects, and finally in the fact that the relation between strength and multitude cannot but take the form of equality, of flowing without limit, without opposition or obstacle from privilege, and therefore without any block of the process.

Nor can this equality in any sense be derogatorily called uniformity, because the multitude is an infinite multiplicity of free and creative singularities. The fatal couple, equality and uniformity (cessation of freedom, slow sleep of virtue), that many reactionaries have considered as the destiny of modernity concerns only modernity. Actually, this is where a fourth opposition of the new rationality against the rationality of modernity is determined: the opposition between diversity and uniformity that logically follows from that between equality and privilege. The rationality that goes beyond modernity seizes in diversity and in the richness of equal and irreducible individualities the keystone of its every logic. Constituent power takes shape not as reduction to one of the singularities but as the place of their intertwining and their expansion. Its creative force is revealed in this unraveling of the multitude toward the richness of its infinite expressions. The new rationality will therefore represent itself in a logic of the singularities in process, in fusion, and in continual surpassing. The new rationality abhors uniformity. Once again the standpoint of constitutive disutopia helps to understand better the process because in it rationality shows itself as the impossibility of unifying the world of life at the very moment when it always reconstitutes it creatively. Uniformity, the original sin of utopia, even if it were grand and glorious, here shows once again how it is rooted in modernity and, at the same time, its definitive deficit, insofar as it participates in the rationality of modernity and therefore is a destructive element of the very conditions of becoming. On the other hand, constituent power always breaks uniformity, and its creativity seeks the different as rationality of its own ontological consistency.

The fifth and last opposition is that of cooperation against command. Here we are at the point where abstract rationality is completely inverted into the rationality of the concrete. Cooperation is in fact the living and productive pulsation of the *multitudo*. Cooperation is the articulation in which an infinite number of the singularities are composed as productive essence of the new. Cooperation is innovation, richness, and thus the basis of the creative surplus that defines the expression of the *multitudo*. Command is constructed on abstraction, alienation, and the expropriation of the cooperative creativity of the multitude. Command is privilege: the fixed and unified appropriation of constituent power. It is constituted power and constitution. The world is thus inverted: command precedes cooperation. But this reversal and the rationality and logic that exalt it are in themselves contradictory and limited because they do not possess the force of their own reproduction. Production and reproduction of the world of life reside only in the multitude, in the procedural complex of the relations of freedom and singularity, and in the result of their different and concurrent creativity. Cooperation is the form in which the singularities produce the new, the rich, and the powerful—the only form of reproduction of life. Cooperation finds an identity for its rationality in strength. On the political terrain any definition of democracy that does not assume cooperation as the interpretive key and as concrete fabric of this relation is false. Domination is this lack of truth. On the contrary, cooperation is the central value of the new rationality, its truth.

Constituent power fulfills here its ontological function, which is that of building new being and a new nature of history. A new world of life. Cooperation is life itself, insofar as it produces and reproduces itself. Rationality, beyond modernity, is the pursuing of the relations that, through cooperation, creatively install themselves in being. It is their taking shape. Its truth consists in seizing the creative moment of cooperation and in systematically orienting itself toward it. Although the new rationality is, first, critical rationality, that is, rationality that destroys any obstacle, or block, or constriction of strength that expresses itself in constitutive cooperation, nonetheless, it is, second, permanent construction of the developments of strength and the expression of the constructive tendency of cooperation. Strength is a task that is realized through the cooperation of singularities and in the uninterrupted flow of the creative determinations of being. Freedom, equality, and strength—these old formal elements become history, second nature, third, or umpteenth—they are the dynamic and agile substance of constituent power. Any definition that tears the sequence of freedom, equality, and cooperation away from its ontological foundation in strength is no longer possible: any definition that separates is in this case false. In its truth this process is that of the innovation of being. The new rationality is made to measure with the construction of the new world.

On these bases, after having proposed the theme of subjectivity and that of the new rationality, we can come back to the political definition of constituent power beyond modernity. A first observation: constituent power is the definition of any possible paradigm of the political. The political has no definition unless it takes its point of departure from the concept of constituent power. Thus, far from being an extraordinary apparition or a clandestine essence caught in the net of constituted power, constituent power is the totalizing matrix of the political. Both the traditional metaphysical definitions of the political as command over the community or the irrational definitions that imagine the political as the realm of more or less legitimated violence haplessly fall away in front of what the political actually is: *the ontological strength of a multitude of cooperating singularities.*

Both the traditional metaphysical definitions and the irrational ones clash with the definition of constituent power and cannot account for the strength of the community—an ineluctable element for any definition of the political. It must be neither of the community nor violence on the community: constituent power frees us from these definitions of the political by radically changing the terrain of its definition to the terrain of ontology, of the creation of new being. There is no preconceived community and no decisive force. In the constituent definition of the political, community is decided and reconstructed everyday, and violence is part of this decision and reconstruction. Neither community nor force is an ontological reality; they are only abstract reductions of the world of life. Ontologically, we are faced with the multitude of singularities and the creative work of strength. The political is the site of this interweaving insofar as it presents itself as creative process. It is not mediation, synthesis, or sublimation; the dialectic has fraudulently solved the problem of which it had perceived the structuring terms. Not mediation, therefore, but genealogy, coextensive and cooperating production of community and force, or better, much better, of multitude and strength. Not the dialectic, because every moment of this process opens and never closes new dimensions of being, always starting new determinations of strength. By recognizing itself and operating at every moment as constitutive disutopia.

Constituent power is the paradigm of the political because its process is metaphysically defined by necessity. There is no other manner of existence of the political: the only possibility of modifying its definition is that of dominating its productive conditions in terms of nontruth, opposing command to strength, and opposing the constitution to constituent power. But this nontruth is only the opaque screen that superimposes itself onto the permanence of the real political, that is, of constituent power in action. True political realism does not consist in recognizing oneself and satisfying oneself or in the decisive character of physical force but, on the contrary, in considering how this domination is always and indefatigably undermined by the *constituent sabotage* of the multitude. The real metaphysical approach does not consist in founding the political on its duty of being of the community but, on the contrary, on recognizing that every formation of community and its duration are the continual product of the strength of singularities. Constituent power responds to the conditions of definition of the political because it interprets the creative determination of the political and cooperation. Effectiveness and legitimacy, those truncated categories of mystification, find in strength and in the cooperation of the multitude their respective inversions—or, better, their rational substitution. The political becomes rational according to these conditions, and this is the only rationality that organizes its time. The political is brought back to the temporality of constituent movement.

We should pause on this temporality of constituent power and this definition of the political in the new rationality beyond modernity. We have seen amply how the acceleration of time represents a fundamental character of constituent power. Now, this acceleration must be not so much understood as such (in the metaphysical scenario, if we look at the creativity of the *multitudo*, this acceleration is founded on an ontological accumulation already realized) but, rather, interpreted as love of time—of time, its very singular emergencies, and the apparition of the event. The love of time is the substance of the disutopia that fills constituent power. The love of time is the indicator of the singular content of strength. The acceleration of historical time reveals the continual creativity of the ontological figure of constituent power as paradigm of the political, that is, as the matrix of an expansion of interrelations among singularities, always renewed and always open to another renewal. The love of time is nothing but the ontological expansion of the relation between constituent power and revolution. This expansion mitigates the revolutionary character of constituent power because it stretches it into the definition of the political as an arena of the transformation of interrelations and community. The love of time is the soul of constituent power because this makes of the world of life a dynamic essence, an ever renewed essence of nature and history. In this sense the concept of constituent power shows the normality of the revolution and offers a definition of being as movement of transformation. We need to reduce the dramatics associated with the concept of the revolution by making it, though constituent power, nothing but the desire of the continuous, relentless, and ontologically effective transformation of time. A continuous and unrestrainable practice. On this basis the concept of the political is taken away from the banality and the obscenity of being reduced to the spaces and times of constituted power. The political is the horizon of the revolution, not terminated but continued, always reopened by the love of time. Every human drive in search of the political consists in this: in living an ethics of transformation through a yearning for participation that is revealed as love for the time to constitute.

The dynamic, creative, continual, and procedural constitution of strength is the political. This definition is neither empty nor neutral: it is subjected to the determinations of subjectivity and tendency, that is, to the figures in which multitude and strength crisscross as figures of productive cooperation. But the expression of the multitude and the continual creation of a new world of life remain its fundamental element. To take this element away from the political means to take everything away from it; it means to reduce it to pure administrative and diplomatic mediation, to bureaucratic and police activity—that is, exactly to that against which constituent power, as origin of the political, continually struggles in order to emerge as strength. Indeed, all those activities that would like to present themselves as the nature of the political do not belong to the political but, rather, to the routine of unchanged repetition. They are effects of dead labor, perverse inversions of constituent power, and cannot be used to define the political.

We have thus inverted the frame in which the jurists and constitutionalists, as well as the sociologists and politicians, give us the definition of constituent power (see chap. 1). It does not come after the political, as in a tormented sociological pause or in a suspension of institutional reality, nor can it be reduced to an extemporaneous *blitz* of the collective will in such a way that they would have to guarantee the limitation of its effects in the constitution of the political. No, constituent power comes first, it is the definition itself of the political, and where it is repressed and excluded, the political is reduced to pure mechanical nature, to being an enemy, and a despotic power. A political power without constituent power is like an enterprise without profit, without the living labor of innovation and the enrichment of productivity. The political without constituent power is like an old property, not only languishing but also ruinous, for the workers as well as for its own owners.

Never as today are these images of past times, in which the inertia and the exhaustion of old ruling classes let their leadership get dispersed and lost in an administrative routine, which increasingly impoverished the world of life—never as today are these images valid and suggestive. A political world, many political worlds, in the West and in the East, are collapsing because they have exhausted constituent power. That notion of the political of the past, whose fabric consists solely of constituted power, reveals itself to our eyes as a decayed and at the same time fierce dimension. The time of the political seems to be absolutely opaque. Yet the continuous process of the strength of the multitude traverses it. Once in a while this movement comes to light. The metaphysical materiality of constituent power shows itself in huge fires that light up with its multitudes the squares of the dilapidated empires. Between 1968 and 1989 our generations have seen the love for time oppose any and all manifestations of being for death. The movement of the multitude has expressed its strength everywhere, with that extraordinary massive force that does not indicate its possible exceptionality but its ontological necessity.

Is what is awaiting us a history of freedom? It would be foolish to say so, confronted as we are by the horrid mutilations that constituted power continues to inflict on the ontological body of human freedoms and by the perpetual negation that the unbreakable series of the freedom, equality, and strength of the multitude posed in contrast. What awaits us is a history of liberation, disutopia in action, relentless and as painful as it is constructive. The constitution of strength is the experience itself of the liberation of the *multitudo*. The fact that in this form and with this force constituent power cannot but appear is irrefutable and that it cannot but impose itself as hegemonic in the always renewed world of life is necessary. It is our task to accelerate this strength and recognize its necessity in the love of time.

Notes

1. Constituent Power

1. Georges Burdeau, *Traité de sciences politiques*, vol. 4 (Paris: Librairie générale de droit et de jurisprudence, 1983), 171. On the terrible character of "constituent power," see Donoso Cortes, *Lecciones de Derecho politico* (1896), now in *Obras Completas*, vol. 1 (Madrid: Editorial Catolica, 1970), 390 ff.

2. On democracy as "absolute government" see Antonio Negri, *The Savage Anomaly: The Power of Spinoza's Metaphysics and Politics*, trans. Michael Hardt (Minneapolis: University of Minnesota Press, 1991). On constitutionalism as "limited democracy" in the tradition of Anglo-Saxon political science, see Nicola Matteucci, "La costituzione americana e il costituzionalismo moderno," in *Il Mulino*, 314, year 36, 6 (1987):882–901.

3. [I have translated the two Italian words *potere* and *potenza* as *power* and *strength*. Both Italian words would commonly be translated into English as *power*, but Negri's discussion rests heavily on the distinction between them. *Power*, for Negri, is always constituted power, and it often refers to the power shaped by and into existing State and political institutions. Strength, instead, is a radically democratic force that resides in the desire of the multitude and is aimed at revolutionizing the status quo through social and political change. Strength is at the core of the concept of constituent power itself as the force that produces (but cannot be contained within) power and its institutions; constituent power is fueled by strength. Negri stresses more than once here that strength, as well as constituent power, enables but is not realized in constitutionality. Trans.]

4. C. Mortati, "Appunti sul problema delle fonti del potere costituente," in *Rassegna di diritto pubblico* (1946), 1:26 ff; C. Mortati, "Costituzione," in *Enciclopedia del diritto*, vol. 11:139–231; F. Pierandrei, "La costituzione e il diritto costituente" (1946), in *Scritti di diritto constituzionale*, vol. 1 (Turin, 1965); P. Barile, "Potere costituente," in *Nuovissimo digesto italiano* (1966).

5. Emile Boutmy, *Studies in Constitutional Law: France, England, United States*, trans. E. M. Picey (London and New York: Macmillan, 1891), 250.

6. For a detailed commentary on this Napoleonic affirmation made on December 15, 1798, see Roman Schnur, *Revolution und Weltbürgerkriegm* (Berlin, 1989).

7. See chap. 5 of this book. Furthermore, besides Schnur's volume, see Reinhart Koselleck, *Critique and Crisis: Enlightenment and the Pathogenesis of Modern Society* (Cambridge: MIT Press, 1988); and *Futures Past: On the Semantics of Historical Time*, trans. Keith Tribe (Cambridge: MIT Press, 1985).

8. Once again, see Mortati. But see also P. G. Grasso, "Potere costituente," in *Enciclopedia del diritto*, vol. 34:642–70; and particularly H. Sauerwein, "Die

Omnipotenz des 'pouvoir constituant,'" in *Ein Beitrag zur Staats—und Verfassungstheorie* (Frankfurt, 1960).

9. Maurice Hauriou, *Precis de droit constitutionnel* (Paris, 1923), 10, 282.

10. Raymond Carré de Malberg, *Contribution a la theorie générale de l'Etat* (Paris: Tenin, 1922), 2:167 ff; Guillaume Bacot, *Carré de Malberg et l'origine de la destinction entre souveraineté du peuple et souveraineté nationale* (Paris: Editions CNRS, 1985); E. Fehrenbach, "Nation," in *Handbuch politisch-sozialer Grundbegriffe in Frankreich 1680–1820*, ed. Rolf Reichardt and Eberhard Schmitt, vol. 7 (Munich: Oldenbourg, 1986), 75–107.

11. See my study of Sieyès's positions (and related bibliography) in chap. 5.

12. Giovanni Sartori, *Democratic Theory* (New York: Praeger, 1965).

13. Carl J. Friedrich, *Constitutional Government and Democracy* (Waltham, Mass.: Blaisdell, 1968).

14. P. Pasquino, "Sieyès, Constant e il 'governo dei moderni.' Contributo alla storia di rappresentanza politica," *Filosofia Politica* 1, no. 1 (1987):78–98.

15. Hans Kelsen, *Vom Wesen und Wert der Demokratie* (Tübingen: J. C. B. Mohr, 1929), 47–68.

16. Georg Jellinek, *Allgemeine Staatslehere* (Berlin: Springer, 1914), 342 ff; Sauerwein, "Die Omnipotenz," 45–47.

17. Georg Jellinek, *Allgemeine Staatslehere*, 332 ff.

18. Walter Jellinek, "Revolution and Reichverfassung," in *Jahrbuch fur offentlichen Recht* (1920), 31 ff.

19. Hans Kelsen, *Der soziologische und der juristische Staatbegriff* (Tubingen, 1928), 83 ff, 98, 187; Kelsen, *Pure Theory of Law*, trans. Max Knight (Berkeley and Los Angeles: University of California Press, 1967), 193 ff.

20. Hans Kelsen, *General Theory of Norms*, trans. Michael Hartney (Oxford: Clarendon Press, 1991). In the Italian translation see the excellent introduction by Mario A. Losano. On Kelsen's interpretation of the principle of effectiveness, see G. Piovani, *Il significato del principio di effettivita* (Milan, 1953). See also L. G. Guerrero Perez, *Poder constituyente y Control jurisdiccional* (Bogotá, 1985).

21. John Rawls, *A Theory of Justice* (Cambridge, Mass.: Harvard/Belknap, 1971), 152 ff.

22. See the end of chap. 3 of this book. But see also Philip Pettit, *Judging Justice* (London: RKP, 1980), 143 ff; and Antonio Negri, "Rawls: Un formalisme fort dans la pensée molle," in *Futur Anterieur* suppl. 1 (1991).

23. Ferdinand Lassalle, *Uber Verfassungswesen* (Berlin, 1862); see also E. Beling, *Revolution und Recht* (Augsburg, 1923).

24. Hermann Heller, *Staatslehre* (Leiden: Sijthoff, 1934); "Die Krisis de Staatslehre," *Archiv fur soziale Wissenschaft und Sozialpolitik* (1926).

25. Rudolf Smend, "Verfassung und Verfassungrecht" (1928), in *Staatrechliche Abhandlungen* (Berlin: 1955), 119–276.

26. Max Weber, "Parliament and Government in Germany under a New Political Order," in *Weber: Political Writings*, ed. Peter Lassman and Ronald Speirs (Cambridge: Cambridge University Press, 1994), 209–33. See also *Economy and Society*, ed. Guenther Roth and Claus Wittich (Berkeley and Los Angeles: University of California Press, 1978).

27. Max Weber, *The Russian Revolutions*, trans. and ed. Gordon G. Wells and Peter Baehr (Ithaca, N.Y.: Cornell University Press, 1995); *Socialism*, trans. H. F. Dickie-Clark (Durban: South Africa Institute for Social Research, University of Natal, 1967).

28. Carl Schmitt, *Verfassunglehre* (Munich and Leipzig, 1928).

29. P. Pasquino, "Die Lehre vom 'pouvoir constituant' bei Emmanuel Sieyès und Carl Schmitt," in *Complexio oppositorum: Uber Carl Schmitt* (Berlin, 1988). Above all, note in that work the opposition to Udo Steiner, *Verfassunggebung und verfassunggebende Gewalt des Volkes* (Berlin: Duncker & Humblot, 1966), which purports to counterpose the French tradition to the German one in the juridical conception of constituent power, and in particular Sieyès's concept of "nation" and Schmitt's notion of "decision."

30. Sauerwein, "Die Omnipotenz," 57–77.

31. C. Mortati, "Costituzione"; see in particular 158–61, where the perspectives of French, Italian, and German constitutionalism are each followed in order to define *constitution* and *constituent power*.

32. C. Mortati, *La costituzione in senso materiale* (Milan, 1940); F. Pierandrei, "La constituzione."

33. S. Romano, *Principi di diritto costituzionale generale* (Milan, 1954), and "L'istaurazione di fatto di un ordinamento costituzionale e sua legittimazione," in *Scritti Minori.*.

34. C. Schmitt, *Verfassungslehre*.

35. Maurice Hauriou, *La théorie de l'institution et de la fondation* (Paris: 1925); Leon Duguit, *Traité de droit constitutionnel* (Paris: Editions du Boccard, 1927). It is well known how prominent the motifs of Christian personality in Hauriou are, and in Duguit those of Proudhonian solidarity.

36. Mortati, "Costituzione," 145. Besides the other cited works by Mortati, see also on this question S. Romano, *L'ordinamento giuridico* (Milan, 1945).

37. Ernst Forsthoff, *Rechtsstaat im Wandel* (Stuttgart, 1964).

38. Besides the book by Carl Friedrich already mentioned, see Charles Howard McIlwain, *Constitutionalism, Ancient and Modern* (Ithaca, N.Y.: Great Seal, 1958); Harold J. Laski, *Reflections on Constitution* (Manchester: Manchester University Press, 1962); J. Agnoli, *Trasformazioni della democrazia* (Milan, 1969).

39. Nicola Matteucci, "La costituzione americana," 892.

40. Here it is not inappropriate to point out that the notion of "the limits of democracy" received a great deal of attention during the decade from 1975 to 1985, at the beginning of the neoliberal phase of modern ideology, which we are now perhaps coming out of. We should situate at the root of the reprise of that antidemocratic theme the 1975 Trilateral Commission Report.

41. A. de Tocqueville, *Democracy in America*, trans. Henry Reeve, F. Bowen, and P. Bradley (New York: Knopf, 1945), vol. 2, bk. 4, chap. 8:331.

42. E. W. Böckenförde, *Die Verfassunggebende Gewalt des Volkes: Eine Grenzbegriff der Verfassungsrechts* (Frankfurt, 1986).

43. For a bibliography on the relationship of "constituent power to revolution" see Mortati, "Costituzione," 232. See also the works cited by Reinhart Koselleck. I will discuss these themes often in the rest of this work.

44. Elise Marienstras, *Nous, le peuple: Les origines du nationalisme américain* (Paris: Gallimard, 1988), particularly 424, on the multiple clashes between constitutionalism and constituent power in the American Revolution.

45. This problematic is developed in the work of Carl Schmitt, most broadly in his *Verfassunglehre*. See Genaro Carriò's linguistic-juridical analyses, *Sobra los limites del lenguajo normative* (Buenos Aires, 1973), 34 ff; and also Mario Cattaneo, *Il concetto di rivoluzione nella scienza del diritto* (Milan: Istituto editoriale cisalpino, 1960).

46. On this question see Carl Friedrich's position in *Constitutional Government*. Against this position see Wilhelm Henke, *Straatsrecht, Politik und vergassunggebende Gewalt*, in *Der Staat* (1980):207 ff. Also on this topic see Egon Zweig, *Die Lehre vom Pouvoir Constituant: Ein Beitrag zum Staatrecht der französischen Revolution* (Tübingen: J. C. B. Mohr, 1909).

47. Karl Loewenstein, *Volk und Parlament nach der Staatstheorie der franzosischen Nationalversammlung von 1789* (Munich: Drei Masken Verlag, 1922).

48. It is on this point that notions of the "material constitution" swerve dangerously toward the continuist historical conception of the State and fail in their attempt to renew the theory. I discuss the contemporary state of constitutional theory in my book *La forma Stato* (Milan: Feltrinelli, 1977).

49. I consider Michel Foucault's historiographic methodology from this point of view, exemplary. See Gilles Deleuze, *Foucault*, trans. and ed. Sean Hand (Minneapolis: University of Minnesota Press, 1988).

50. A large current of contemporary philosophy is being redefined on this terrain. See N. Terullian, "De Schelling à Marx: Le dernier Schelling et sa posterité," *Archives de Philosophie* 50 (1987):621–41. See also my book *Fabbriche del soggetto* (Livorno, 1987). In general, see Giorgio Agamben's work.

51. Antonio Negri, *The Savage Anomaly*.

52. See Louis Althusser, "Machiavelli's Solitude," *Economy and Society* 17, no. 4 (1988):468–79.

53. Hannah Arendt, *On Revolution* (New York: Viking Press, 1963).

54. Friedrich von Gentz, *Betrachtungen über die französischen Revolution, nach dem Englischen des Herrn Burke neu bearbeitet mit einer Einleitung* (Hohenzollern, 1793). On von Gentz see Antonio Negri, *Alle origini del formalismo giuridico* (Padua: CEDAM, 1962), 341 ff.

55. John Quincy Adams translated von Gentz's essay during the presidential campaign of 1800, which his father, John Adams, lost to Jefferson. On this translation, and in general on the American view of the French Revolution, see Richard Buel, *Securing the Revolution: Ideology in American Politics 1789–1815* (Ithaca, N.Y.: Cornell University Press, 1972).

56. Hannah Arendt, *On Revolution*, 21–22.

57. Ibid., 66–110. These are the famous passages in which Arendt establishes a direct connection between compassion, equality, and terror.

58. In her work Arendt generally shows a sort of democratic Luxemburgism, strongly valorizing spontaneity and councils as political structures. The discussions of the coherence of this attitude and of her judgment on the French Revolution (not to mention the construction of the categories of "totalitarianism") are certainly not closed.

59. Here I am following some of the theses proposed by Jürgen Habermas, "Die Geschichte con den zwei Revolutionen," *Merkur* 218 (1966):479 ff and "Natural Law and Revolution," in *Theory and Practice*, trans. John Viertel (Boston: Beacon Press, 1973), 82–120. I will return to the polemic between Arendt and Habermas, particularly in chaps. 4 and 5.

60. This is not the place to propose an analysis of the relationship between "Atlantic political sociology" and Arendt's thought; it is enough to stress once again how contradictory and equivocal this thought is.

61. This is particularly true of contemporary institutionalism, which, during the years of the neoliberal reaction in France, has been represented above all by the work of Claude Lefort and Cornelius Castoriadis.

62. The relationship between Arendt and Heidegger is well known. Arendt's thought has been dealt with on the terrain of "weak" Heideggerian interpretation, above all, by its postmodern critics.

63. Myriam Revault d'Allones, "Lectures de la modernité: Heidegger, C. Schmitt, H. Arendt," *Les Temps Modernes* 45, no. 523 (1990):89–108.

64. Here we are referring to the essays by Habermas cited in n. 59.

65. In this perspective Habermas refers to the theses proposed by E. Topisch, *Sozialphilosophie zwischen Ideologie und Wissenschaft* (Neuwild: 1967).

66. See the first section of this chapter for a discussion of constitutional thought in Max Weber and Carl Schmitt.

67. Carl Schmitt, *Die Diktatur* (Munich and Leipzig: Duncker & Humblot, 1928); *The Concept of the Political*, trans. George Schwab (Chicago: University of Chicago Press, 1996).

68. This is true, too, of Schelling's late work. See Terullian, "De Schelling à Marx."

69. Schmitt, *The Concept of the Political.*

70. Arendt's position on this has been taken up by the followers of that current of thought that, in France, had most effectively represented critical Marxism in the 1960s, *Socialisme ou Barbarie.* My impression is that, when critical materialism became diluted, and because of the infiltration of a generic psychoanalytical discourse into this type of critique, here the strength of Arendt's intuition has become completely dispersed in favor of ideological options that are politically superficial.

71. See chap. 4 of this book.

72. H. Arendt, "Ziviler Ungehorsam," in *Zur Zeit, Politische Essays* (Berlin, 1987), 137–38. On the relationship between Schmitt and Calhoun, see M. Surdi, "Introduzione" to J. C. Calhoun, *Disquisizione sul governo* (Rome, 1986), 44 ff.

73. Hannah Arendt, citing Saint-Just, in *On Revolution*, 87.

74. Claude Lefort, *L'invention democratique* (Paris: Fayard, 1981); Richard Rorty, "The Priority of Democracy to Philosophy," in *Philosophical Papers, vol. 1: Objectivity, relativism and truth* (Cambridge: Cambridge University Press, 1991); Gianni Vattimo, *La secularisation de la philosophie* (Paris, 1988).

75. A certain Bergsonism is present, in latent or self-conscious form, in the tradition of French institutionalism. See for instance M. Leroy, *La loi: Essai sur la theorie de l'authorité dans la démocratie* (Paris, 1908); or, at the end of an era, Georges Burdeau, "Essai sur l'evolution de la notion de loi en droit francais," *Archives de Philosophie du droit et de la Sociologie juridique* 9 (1939):7 ff.

76. The influence of Giovanni Gentile's neoidealist philosophy is very strong in the field of Italian constitutional law. See W. Cesarini Sforza, "Il potere costituente nella Repubblica Italiana," in *Studi sulla costituzione* (Milan, 1958), 121 ff.

77. Jean-Paul Sartre, *Critique of Dialectical Reason*, vol. 2, *The Intelligibility of History*, trans. Quintin Hoare (London: Verso, 1991).

78. Here our reference is clearly to Georges Bataille and his mysterious and extremely powerful essay "On Sovereignty," in his *Visions of Excess: Selected Writings 1927–1939*, ed. Allan Stoekl, trans. Allan Stoekl, Carl Lovitt, and Donald M. Leslie (Minneapolis: University of Minnesota Press, 1985).

79. Maurice Blanchot, *The Unavowable Community*, trans. Pierre Joris (Barrytown, N.Y.: Station Hill Press, 1988); Jean-Luc Nancy, *The Inoperative Community*, ed. Peter Connor, trans. Peter Connor, Lisa Garbus, Michael Holland, and Simone Sawhney (Minneapolis: University of Minnesota Press, 1991).

80. Aristotle, *Metaphysics*, in *Basic Works of Aristotle*, ed. Richard McKeon (New York: Random House, 1941), bk. 9:820 ff.

81. Elise Marienstras, *Nous, le peuple*, 299–301.

82. Reinhart Koselleck, *Futures Past*, 39–54. Koselleck makes a crucial reference to Immanuel Kant, *The Conflict of the Faculties*, trans. Mary J. Gregor (New York: Abaris Books, 1979), where the right to revolution is interpreted as historical and revolutionary *Bildung*, as capacity of historical transformation.

83. Hobbes, *Behemoth*, quoted in Koselleck, *Futures Past.* On this theme see Antonio Negri, *Macchina Tempo* (Milan: Feltrinelli, 1982).

84. The French citation is from an obscure social critic of the eighteenth century, quoted in Koselleck, *Futures Past*, 46. On the new notion of "constituted" history, see again Reinhart Koselleck, *Critique and Crisis*, 49–50, 127–30, 181–83.

85. Reinhart Koselleck, *Critique and Crisis*, 187–89; see also E. Rosenstock, "Revolution als politischer Begriff der Neuzeit," in *Festschrift für Heilborn* (Breslau, 1931);

K. Griewank, *Der neuzeitliche Revolutionsbegriff* (Frankfurt: Eurapaeische Verlaganst, 1955).

86. S. Rohatyn, "Die juristische Theorie der revolution," *Internationale Zeitschrift für Theorie des Rechts* 4 (1929–1930):193–227. On this topic C. Cesa's introduction to the Italian translation of Griewank's book is key.

87. Condorcet, "Sur le sens du mot révolutionnaire," in *Oeuvres complètes* (Brunswick, 1801), 18:3 ff.

88. Christine Fauré, "Presentation," in *Les déclarations des droits de l' homme de 1793*, ed. Christine Fauré (Paris: Payot, 1988), 15–36. This book provides an exhaustive bibliography on the singular and unique historical experience of revolution of 1793.

89. D. A. F. Sade, *Francaises, encore un effort, si vous voulez être republicains* (Paris, 1989).

90. Kant, *Conflict of the Faculties.*

91. Carl Schmitt, *Die Diktatur; Verfassunglehre*; *The Crisis of Parliamentary Democracy*, trans. Ellen Kennedy (Cambridge: MIT Press, 1986); *Political Theology: Four Chapters on the Concept of Sovereignty*, trans. George Schwab (Cambridge: MIT Press, 1985). Everywhere in these texts we are referred to Spinoza for a fundamental definition of *constituent power*. For an analysis of these texts, see Manfred Walther, "Schmitt und B. Spinoza, oder Irritationen im Begriff des Politischen," presented at a conference at the Sorbonne, Paris, 1990. Carriò agrees in *Sobra los limites*, 44 ff; Hermann Heller disagrees in *Staatslehre*, 279 ff.

92. Louis Althusser, *Elements d'autocritique* (Paris, 1974), 81.

93. H. Sauerwein, "Die Omnipotenz," chap. 5. The limitations of this author's discourse lie in his referring the thematic of subjectivity to the currents of neonatural law in the 1950s.

94. On the continuity of the "national" tradition as foundation of constituent power, see also Tosch, *Die Bindung des verfassungsändernden Gesetzgebers an den Willen des historischen Verfassungsgebers* (Berlin: Duncker & Humblot, 1979). In general, on Sieyès and the tradition connected to him, see chap. 5 of this book.

95. Etienne Balibar and Immanuel Wallerstein, *Race, Nation, Class: Ambiguous Identities*, trans. Chris Turner (London and New York: Verso, 1991).

96. Hans Kohn, *The Idea of Nationalism: A Study in Its Origins and Background* (New York: Macmillan, 1967); Hannah Arendt, *The Origins of Totalitarianism* (New York: Harcourt Brace, 1951).

97. It is Carl Schmitt in *Verfassungslehre* who, outside of the ambiguous Anglo-Saxon constitutionalist tradition, offers the most accomplished conceptual construction of "the people" as constitutional foundation. But see also D. Schindler, *Verfassungsrecht und soziale Struktur* (Zurich: Schulthess, 1950).

98. L. Taparelli d'Azeglio, *Saggio teoretico di diritto naturale appoggiato sul fatto* (Rome: 1949), 2:28.

99. See S. Romano, "Mitologia giuridica," in *Frammenti di un dizionario giuridico* (Milan, 1953), 131 ff, 126 ff; G. Sartori, *Democratic Theory.*

100. See the first section of this chapter.

101. S. Romano, *Frammenti*, 223 ff; C. Mortati, *La costituzione in senso materiale.* Ernst Forsthoff, "Zur heutigen Situation einer Verfassungslehre," in *Fetsgabe fur C. Schmitt* (Berlin: Duncker & Humblot, 1968), 1:185 ff.

102. Michael Theunissen, *Hegels Lehre vom absolutem Geist als theologischen-politischer Traktat* (Berlin: de Gruyter, 1970); *Sein und Schein: Die kritische Funktion der Hegelschen Logik* (Frankfurt: Suhrkamp, 1980).

103. The reference is obviously to the "second" Foucault, the author of *History of Sexuality*, vol. 1, of *The Uses of Pleasure*, of *The Care of the Self*, trans. Robert Hurley (New York: Random House, 1978–1986). On the "first" Foucault, see my "Sul metodo della critica della politica," in *Macchina tempo*, 70–84.

104. Gilles Deleuze, *Foucault.*

105. Foucault developed these positions in the lectures he gave in the 1970s.

106. Gilles Deleuze, *Expressionism in Philosophy: Spinoza*, trans. Martin Joughin (New York: Zone, 1990).

107. From this perspective Foucault's position is opposed, on metaphysical and sociological terrain, to Habermas's theory of the "public sphere." In my view, however, Foucault interprets the lessons of the Frankfurt School more faithfully than do its direct descendants.

108. On the impossibility of considering the social in purely political terms, and thus of redirecting it toward "totalitarianism" (as Arendt does), as well as on the abstract emptiness and purely polemical use (in the worst ideological sense) of the concept of "totalitarianism," see Karl Polyani, *The Great Transformation: The Political and Economic Origins of Our Time* (Boston: Beacon Press, 1957). See also Richard Bernstein, *The Restructuring of Social and Political Theory* (Oxford: Oxford University Press, 1976).

109. Arendt's *The Origins of Totalitarianism* (New York: Harcourt Brace, 1966), in which she explores the theme of totalitarianism in its full range, is certainly her worst book. The categories of the so-called Cold War are deeply imbricated in her argument at all turns. The great social movements that brought about the destruction of the system of "real socialism" have demonstrated how false and heuristically dangerous these categories were.

110. On the tradition of contractualism as the ground for the definition of the transcendence of power, see my book *The Savage Anomaly.*

111. Foucault introduced the analysis of the concept of democracy onto the terrain of the "forms of governability" or "government."

112. Karl Marx, *Critique of Hegel's Doctrine of the State,* in Marx, *Early Writings,* trans. Rodney Livingstone (Harmondsworth: Penguin, 1975), 87.

113. Heidegger maintains this position in the 1927 Marburg seminar and also in section 3 of Part 1 of *Being and Time,* which he never saw published and which has appeared in print only recently.

114. On Marx's theorization of time, we should keep in mind in addition to the famous passages from the *Grundrisse,* about which see my book *Marx beyond Marx: Lessons on the Grundrisse,* trans. Harry Cleaver, Michael Ryan, and Maurizio Viano, ed. Ian Fleming (South Hadley, Mass.: Burgin and Savey, 1984); *The Poverty of Philosophy* (New York: International Publishers, n.d.); and *Letter to Annenkov,* English translation in Karl Marx and Friedrich Engels, *Selected Correspondence* (Moscow: Progress Publishers, 1975), 29–39. We will return to this topic later in the course of this book. On the prehistory of the category of time in Marx, see Eric Alliez, *Capital Times: Tales from the Conquest of Time,* trans. Georges Van Den Abbeele (Minneapolis: University of Minnesota Press, 1996).

115. See Jean-Marie Vincent, *Abstract Labor: A Critique,* trans. Jim Cohen (New York: St. Martin's Press, 1991).

116. Karl Marx, *The Holy Family,* trans. R. Dixon (Moscow: Foreign Languages Publishing House, 1956), chap. 4.

117. Karl Marx, "On The Jewish Question," in *Early Writings* (New York: Penguin, 1975), 211–41. As we will see later, in the polemic that divides them concerning the problem of the "two revolutions," Jürgen Habermas rightly reproaches Arendt for treating the Marxian theme of the emancipation of the political in purely formal terms, or, better, for having exalted as positive what Marx criticized from the point of view of social liberation. If she maintained this style of argumentation but changed its sense and referents, Arendt would produce, according to Habermas, a classical sophism.

118. Karl Marx, *The German Ideology,* pt. 1, ed. C. J. Arthur (New York: International Publishers, 1991), A4:56–57.

119. Ibid., D2:92–93.

120. Karl Marx, *Revolution and Counter-Revolution,* ed. Eleanor Aveling Marx (London: Unwin, 1971), chap. 18.

121. Karl Marx, *The Civil War in France,* in *The First International and After,* ed. David Sternbach (New York: Penguin, 1974), 213, 217.

122. Karl Marx, *Letter to Bolte,* in Marx and Engels, *Selected Correspondence,* 253–55.

123. Once again allow me to refer the reader to my *Marx beyond Marx.* For the passages from Marx quoted up to this point, see chaps. 5 and 6 of this book, where they are discussed in detail.

124. E. P. Thompson, *The Making of English Working Class* (London: Gollancz, 1968).

125. On this question, permit me to refer the reader once again to my *Fabbriche del soggetto.*

126. Antonio Negri, *The Politics of Subversion* (Cambridge: Polity Press, 1989), part 1.

127. Gilles Deleuze and Félix Guattari, *A Thousand Plateaus: Capitalism and Schizophrenia,* trans. Brian Massumi (Minneapolis: University of Minnesota Press, 1987).

2. Virtue and Fortune

1. *Decennale Primo,* in *Opere,* 1:790. All the quotations from Machiavelli come from Antonio Panella's edition, *Niccolo' Machiavelli: Opere,* 2 vols. (Milan: Rizzoli Editore, 1939). English translation, *First Decennale, Machiavelli: The Chief Works and Others,* 3 vols., trans. Allan Gilbert (Durham, N.C.: Duke University Press, 1965), 3:1445. On 1484 and the descent of Charles VIII, see A. Denis, *Charles VIII et les italiens: Histoire et mythe* (Geneva, 1979).

2. *Opere,* 1:803; *Chief Works,* 1455.

3. *Opere,* 2:768; English translation "Letter to Giovanni Ridolfi 1/6/1504," in *Machiavelli and His Friends: Their Personal Correspondence* (DeKalb: Northern Illinois University Press, 1966), 102–103.

4. *Opere,* 2:769, 773; English translation, "Letter to Giovanni Ridolfi, 12/6/1506," in ibid., 124–27.

5. *Opere,* 2:766–68.

6. Written in 1503, before August (*Opere,* 2:679–84); *Chief Works,* 2:1439–44.

7. *Opere,* 1:608; *Chief Works,* vol. 3, *Decennale Primo,* 1457.

8. On Renaissance naturalism see N. Badaloni, *Storia della filosofia,* ed. Mario Dal Pra' (Milan: Vallardi, 1975–76), 7:173–274.

9. From January 17 to June 14, 1508. See *Opere,* 2:1020–27.

10. See *Opere,* 734–49; *Chief Works,* 1:101–16.

11. From October 1502 to January 1503. See *Opere*, 2:911–57.

12. *Prima Legazione alla Corte di Francia* (August–November 1500), in *Opere*, 2:863–910.

13. *Opere*, 2:934; *Legation 11. An Official Mission to Duke Valentino [Cesare Borgia] in Romagna*, in *Chief Works*, 2:128.

14. The pamphlet is perhaps from 1503. See *Opere*, 1:729–36; *Chief Works*, 1:163.

15. Jacob Burckhardt, *The Civilization of the Renaissance in Italy*, trans. S. G. C. Middleman (New York: Macmillan, 1921).

16. See the *Legation* cited in n. 12. In general, see Johan Huizinga, *The Autumn of the Middle Ages*, trans. R. J. Payton and U. Mammitzsch (Chicago: University of Chicago Press, 1996).

17. Eduardo Sanguineti, "Presentazione Critica," to Ludovico Ariosto, *Orlando Furioso* (Milan: Garzanti, 1974), 1:55 ff.

18. *Opere*, 2:674–79; *Chief Works*, 1:161–63.

19. We have already mentioned the *Prima Legazione alla Corte di Francia. La seconda* and *La terza* take place between January 22 and February 25, 1504 (*Opere*, 2:958–62), and between July 7 and September 10, 1510 (ibid., 1028–82), respectively.

20. *Opere*, 1:739–54. See also *De natura Gallorum*, in ibid., 737–38.

21. In *Opere*, 2:958 ff, Machiavelli's annotations on the "barbarian" are interesting.

22. Machiavelli considers as Savonarolian those themes that, in the Council of Tours, are clearly pre-Reformation.

23. Letter to Alfonsina Orsini de' Medici, September 1512 (*Opere*, 2:773–78); *Chief Works*, 2:894.

24. Letter to the cardinal Giulio de' Medici, September 1512 (*Opere* 2:778–79). Cf. J. N. Stephens, *The Fall of the Florentine Republic, 1512–1530* (Oxford: Oxford University Press, 1983).

25. For this question and what follows, concerning Machiavelli's biography and the vicissitudes of the composition of *The Prince* and *Discourses*, see Sergio Bertelli's "Note Introduttive" to the Feltrinelli edition of Niccolò Machiavelli, *Il principe* and *I discorsi*, ed. G. Procacci (Milan, 1960), 3–11, 109–19. This edition also contains the most important bibliography, which is adequately discussed.

26. See Paul Larivaille, *La pensée politique de Machiavel* (Nancy: Presses Universitaire de Nancy, 1982).

27. The conclusions of Larivaille on *Princedoms* seem to assume a continuity with the drafting of *The Prince*, which to us appears more confused and incoherent.

28. To Vettori, March 13, 1513 (*Opere*, 1:908); *Chief Works*, 2:898.

29. To Vettori, March 18, 1513 (*Opere*, 1:908–10); *Chief Works*, 2:898.

30. To Vettori, April 16, 1513 (*Opere*, 1:911–13); *Chief Works*, 2:902.

31. To Vernacci, June 26 and August 4, 1513 (*Opere*, 1:914–15); *Chief Works*, 2:914.

32. To Vettori, April 9, 1513 (*Opere*, 1:910–11); *Chief Works*, 2:900.

33. The following quotation is in *Chief Works*, 1:240. For the construction of the critical question see G. Lisio, "Introduction" to *Il principe* (Carabba Firenze, 1899); Federico Chabod, *Machiavelli and the Renaissance*, trans. David Moore (Cambridge, Mass.: Harvard University Press, 1960); Roberto Ridolfi, *The Life of Niccolò Machiavelli*, trans. Cecil Grayson (Chicago: University of Chicago Press, 1963); Genaro Sasso, *N. Machiavelli. Storia del suo pensiero politico* (Naples: Ricciardi, 1958).

34. To Vettori, April 9, 1513.

35. On Machiavelli's terminology, see O. Condorelli, *Per la storia del nome dello Stato* (Modena, 1923); F. Chiappelli, *Studi sul linguaggio di Machiavelli* (Florence: Le Monnier, 1952).

36. Hans de Vries, *Essai sur la terminologie constitutionelle chez Machiavel (Il principe)* (Amsterdam: These, Faculte de Droit, 1957).

37. To Vettori, December 10, 1513 (*Opere*, 1:916–20); *Chief Works*, 2:929.

38. To Vettori, various letters (*Opere*, 2:782–806); *Chief Works*, 2:900–38.

39. *Opere*, 2:779–82; *Chief Works*, 2:895–98.

40. Chabod, *Machiavelli and the Renaissance*, appropriately speaks of "furor politicus" that is at the basis of the formation of the text of *Il principe*.

41. Louis Althusser, "Machiavelli's Solitude."

42. Besides the edition to which we refer, see also Federico Chabod's (Torino, 1944), and M. Bonfantini's (Milan and Naples, 1954), as well as the already cited Sergio Bertelli's; *The Prince*, in *Chief Works*, 1:5–97.

43. *The Prince*, in *Chief Works*, 2:11.

44. By "prolix order," we are referring here to Spinoza, *The Ethics*, in *A Spinoza Reader*, ed. Edwin Curley, pt. 4 (Princeton, N.J.: Princeton University Press, 1994), appendix, intro., 239.

45. See on this point S. Bertelli's "Note Introduttive," 10, 109 ff.

46. Bertelli rightly sees a reference to these questions in *The Art of War*, written between 1519 and 1520.

47. For the date of the "dedication," see Ridolfi, *The Life of Niccolò Machiavelli*, 400 ff.

48. *Opere*, 2:10; *Chief Works*, *The Prince*, "Dedication," 10–11.

49. Chabod's interpretation of *Il principe*, philologically correct and politically impassioned, is in any case indicative of a certain anachronism (Machiavelli's nationalism), nourished variously by the entire Risorgimento school, from De Sanctis to Ercole to Gramsci.

50. It is known that the opposite interpretation (that *The Prince* was not written at once but in a meditated manner, and certainly on two distinct occasions; furthermore, it is articulated in two groups of chapters—the first, chaps. I–IX, and the second the next fifteen chapters) was sustained by Friedrich Meinecke, *Machiavellism: The Doctrine of Raison D'etat and Its Place in Modern History*, trans. Douglas Scott (London: Routledge and Kegan Paul, 1978). Chabod reacts against Meinecke.

51. Félix Gilbert, "The Humanistic Concept of the Prince and 'The Prince' of Machiavelli," *Journal of Modern History* 11 (1939):481 ff.

52. J. G. A. Pocock, *The Machiavellian Moment* (Princeton, N.J.: Princeton University Press, 1975), 198.

53. See Sergio Bertelli, "Note," 109–18. Keep also in mind L. J. Walker, introduction to the English translation of *Discourses*, pt. I (London, 1950), 210 ff.

54. See n. 49. Recent interpreters also contribute to this apology for autonomous primacy, from Sasso to Tronti (*Il politico: Da Machiavelli a Cromwell* [Milan, 1980]); they transform the apology for the "political-national" (so important for the interpreters of the time of the Risorgimento) into an apology for the political *tout court*, that is, an apology for the political of the contemporaries' political science.

55. Félix Gilbert, "The Composition and Structure of Machiavelli's Discorsi," *Journal of History of Ideas* 14 (1953):136–56; J. H. Hexter, "Seyssel, Machiavelli and Polibius VI: The Mystery of the Missing Translation," *Studies in the Renaissance* 3 (1956):75–96; H. Baron, "The Principe and the Puzzle of the Date of the Discorsi," *Bibliothèque d'Humanisme et de la Renaissance* 18 (1956):405–28; as well as Walker's introduction to *Discourses*; and Pocock, *Machiavellian Moment.*

56. Benedict de Spinoza, chap. 5 of the *Political Treatise*, in *Chief Works of Spinoza* ed. R. H. M. Elwes, vol. 1 (Dover, 1951).

57. *Discourses on the First Decade of Titus Livius*, in *Chief Works*, preface, 1:190–91.

58. See the reference to the ancients in *Del modo di trattare i popoli della Valdichiana ribellati, On the Method of Dealing with the Rebellious Peoples of the Valdichiana*. See R. T. Ridley, "Machiavelli and Roman History in the *Discourses*," *Quaderni di Storia* 9 (1983):18.

59. *Discourses on the First Decade of Titus Livius*, I.2:199.

60. To Vettori, January 13, 1515 (*Opere*, 2:823–26); *Chief Works*, 2:961.

61. On Polybius and book I of his work, see Kurt von Fritz, *The Theory of the Mixed Constitution in Antiquity: A Critical Analysis of Polybius' Political Ideas* (New York: Arno Press, 1954); Elpidio Mioni, *Polibio* (Padua, 1949); F. W. Walbank, *A Historical Commentary on Polybius*, vol. 3 (Oxford: Oxford University Press: 1957–1979); Paul Pedech, *Le methode historique de Polybe* (Paris: Societe d'edition "Les Belles Lettres," 1964).

62. See Sergio Bertelli's reflections in the cited *Introduction*, as well as the bibliography that he presents on the discussions concerning the Greek influences on Machiavelli. In general, see Sergio Bertelli and Piero Innocenti, *Bibliografia Machiavelliana* (Verona: Edizioni Valdonega, 1979).

63. A. Momigliano, "La découverte de Polybe en Europe Occidentale" (1973), in *Problèmes d'historiographie ancienne et moderne* (Paris, 1983), 186–209.

64. C. Vivanti, "Sur Machiavel," *Annales ESC* 42, no. 2 (1987):303–12.

65. To Vettori, January 31, 1515.

66. It is entirely obvious that this conception of subjectivity, even in its democratic implication, is still equivocal. On the one hand, we have a possible "Gramscian" reading of this subjectivity, that is, one meant to foreground the popular determinations, strictly "democratic"; on the other, we have a possible "republican" reading (à la Pocock, on the basis of the Anglo-Saxon tradition of the interpretation of Machiavelli), that is, one meant to characterize the democratic determination as a simple emanation of the "civil" ideology. As we will see, for us the only solution to this equivocity lies not in reducing, but in exalting it: in assuming the importance of subjectivity as a problematic aspect and as an open tendency in Machiavellian thought, both for him and for the coming centuries in the *translatio* of his thought across the Atlantic.

67. On this question see *The Treatise on Tyranny* by Xenophon, trans. L. Strauss, in *On Tyranny* (Ithaca, N.Y.: Cornell University Press, 1975). Here Strauss affirms that Machiavelli made no distinction between sovereign and tyrant. The same volume contains a sharp intervention by Alexandre Kojève. Strauss's disputable theses had a follow-up in his *Thoughts on Machiavelli* (Chicago: University of Chicago Press, 1978), one of the least fortunate essays by this otherwise prodigious historian of political thought.

68. *Discorso dell'ordinare lo stato di Firenze alle armi* (*Opere*, 2:684–90), A. Gilbert, *A Discourse on Remodeling the Government of Florence*, 101–15; *Discorso sopra l'ordinanza e milizia fiorentina* (*Opere*, 2:690–94); *Provisioni della repubblica di Firenze per istituire il Magistrato de' Nove ufficiali dell'Ordinanza e Milizia fiorentina. Dettata da Niccolò Machiavelli, Provvisione Prima per le Fanterie, del 6 dicembre 1506* (*Opere*, 2:694–708); *A Provision for Infantry*, in Gilbert, *A Discourse on Remodeling*, 3–5. These writings precede and follow the creation of a delegated administration of the Florentine militia, of which Machiavelli becomes chancellor in December 1506. Analogous ordinances for the Florentine cavalry will be drafted by Machiavelli in 1512: *Provvisione seconda per le Milizie a cavallo, del 30 marzo del 1512* (*Opere*, 2:708–15).

69. In *The Prince*, see sect. 1 of this chapter.

70. *Ritratto delle cose della Magna* (*Opere*, 1:755–61).

71. As we have seen above, and in particular with regard to the writings of 1503, Machiavelli has already developed a perspective fully opposed to any theory of the legitimation of the State in contractual or customary terms. It is mutation that makes power, charisma that renovates the institution: with respect to this fundamental declaration here, there are no reservations but only further proofs.

72. In this book Machiavelli's argument reaches its acme: it seems that, in general, the Machiavellian reading turns on this affirmation.

73. From this point of view all the positions that, in modern thought, consider the secularization of religion and the desacralization of civil life as homogeneous are dubious. They are dubious from the historiographic point of view, and certainly false from the point of view of a phenomenology of the political that wants to follow the development and the crisis of modernity, avoiding postmodern illusions. A perfect example of this lack of understanding is Giacomo Marramao's *Potere e secolarizzazione* (Rome: Editori Riuniti, 1985).

74. Antonio Negri, "Problemi di storia dello Stato moderno: Francia 1610–1650," *Rivista critica di storia della filosofia* 2 (1967):182–220.

75. Concerning the reform of the Renaissance, others (in particularly Hiram Collins Haydn in his classic *The Counter-Renaissance* [New York, 1950]) after Benedetto Croce have noticed the points of contact of Machiavelli's thought with that of religious reformers such as Luther and Calvin. This is a fundamental passage of the reform of the Renaissance. Machiavelli, however, in contrast to the religious reformers, conducts this operation in extremely modern, contemporary terms. With Machiavelli the other path of modern metaphysics begins, which leads "beyond" modernity in either its religious or idealist form and in either case beyond the production of capitalism.

76. Letter to Ricciardo Bechi, March 8, 1497 (*Opere*, 2:759–62); *Chief Works*, 2:886.

77. "Prudence . . . prescribes the end for all the moral virtues. . . . prudence musters and commands the other moral virtues. And therefore fixes their end." Saint Thomas Aquinas, *Summa Theologiae: Prudence*, ed. and trans. Thomas Gilby, 2a2ae, questions 47–56 (New York: McGraw-Hill, 1964), 36:21–23. As we will see later, particularly with reference to the writings of 1500, Machiavelli has completely modified his conception of prudence, understood by him as immanent virtue of the order of things.

78. *Ragguaglio delle cose fatte dalla Repubblica fiorentina per quietare le parti di Pistoia*, 1500 or 1501 (*Opere*, 2:671–74): three times in the course of 1500, Machiavelli had been sent to Pistoia by the Signoria.

79. *Prima Legazione alla Corte di Francia* (First Legation to France).

80. Here it must be stressed how in Machiavelli we can read the origin of that theory of the "apparatus": that if we isolate the extreme range of its epistemological impact between Nietzsche and Heidegger, Foucault and Deleuze, we find in the "alternative" currents of modern metaphysics (Spinoza and Marx) its constitutive process. This epistemological annotation is fundamental to the construction of the concept of "constituent power."

81. *Opere*, 2:676: "I have heard that history is the teacher of our actions, and above all of the princes, and that the world has always been inhabited by men who have always had the same passions, and there have always existed those who serve and those who command; and those who serve unwillingly and those who serve willingly; those who rebel themselves and those who are reproached" (from *Del modo di trattare*).

82. Delio Cantimori, "Rhetoric and Politics in Italian Humanism," *Journal of the Warburg and Courtauld Institute* 1 (1937–1938):82–102; Félix Gilbert, "Bernardo Rucellai and the Orti Oricellari: A Study on the Origins of Modern Political Thought," *Journal of the Warburg and Courtauld Institute* 12 (1949):101–31, as well as "Political Florentine Assumptions in the Period of Savonarola and Soderini," *Journal of the Warburg and Courtauld Institute* 20 (1957):187–214. In general for Félix Gilbert, see *Machiavelli and Guicciardini: Politics and History in Sixteenth Century Florence* (Princeton, N.J.: Princeton University Press, 1965).

83. To Vettori, December 20, 1514 (*Opere*, 2:808–22); *Chief Works*, 2:948.

84. *History of Florence*, composed between 1521 and 1525. The commission to write the *History* dates from

November 5, 1520, by Cardinal Giulio de' Medici; in *Chief Works*, 3:1029–435.

85. Ibid., *Preface*, 3:1031.

86. To Francesco del Nero, November 1520 (*Opere*, 1:946); *Chief Works*, 2:971. But on this question see R. Ridolfi, *Vita di N. Machiavelli.*

87. *History of Florence*, Book V: "Dal ritorno di Cosimo de' Medici dall'esilio alla morte di Rinaldo degli Albizzi"; "The government of Cosimo until the Battle of Anghiari, 1434–1440."

88. So far we have spoken inprecisely of the first four books. In fact, there is also the problem of understanding the placement of Book I ("Italy from the Fall of the Roman Emire to 1434"), the most general and approximate of the series. From a logical point of view—that is, if we follow the topics so far presented—it could be inserted either in the first or in the second group. From the stylistic point of view, nothing in fact prevents us from situating Book I anywhere, considering the quality of the writing and the intensity of the project. Only one interesting point: the denunciation of the papacy, as a "practico-inert" that runs through all the *History* but that here is elaborated with singular force as the fundamental plot of the political reading of the history of Italy. Suspending this motif, and for expositional convenience, we will consider Book I of the *History* together with II, III, and IV.

89. Félix Gilbert, "Bernardo Rucellai." But see also Vasari, *Vite, ragionamenti, etc*..., ed. Milanesi (1878–85), 7:221; and E. H. Gombrich, "Renaissance and Golden Age," *Journal of the Warburg and Courtauld Institute* 24 (1961):306–9.

90. On this question, see the many letters written by Machiavelli between 1520 and 1525.

91. On this point we must once again remember the fundamental contributions of D. Cantimori and F. Gilbert: constituent strength is the synthesis of will and myth, of apparatus and project. The substratum of this Machiavellian attitude lies in the special and extraordinary nature of Renaissance naturalism: see again N. Badaloni, *Storia della filosofia.* But the fact that Machiavelli has, nonetheless, absorbed this naturalism is beyond this synthesis.

92. On the question of laughter, see Antonio Negri, *Il lavoro di Giobbe* (Milan: Sugar, 1990), n. C and bibliographical notes.

93. See Eduardo Sanguineti, "Presentazione Critica."

94. To Ludovico Alemanni, December 17, 1517 (*Opere*, 1:941–43); *Chief Works*, 2:941–43.

95. *Legazione al capitolo dei frati minori a Carpi*, 1521 (*Opere*, 2:1085–88).

96. From 1521 onward in Machiavelli's epistolary appear letters to Francesco Guicciardini, the son of Luigi, already friend and correspondent of Machiavelli. See in particular the 1521 letters (*Opere*, 1:946–52). In general, see F. Gilbert, *Machiavelli e Guicciardini* (Turin, 1970).

97. *Capitoli per una compagnia di piacere* (*Opere*, 1:767–71); (*Articles for a Pleasure Company*, in *Chief Works*, 2:865), certainly composed in San Casciano after 1514.

98. *Il demonio che prese moglie, ovvero Belfagor* was written after 1514 (*Opere*, 1:701–11); *Belfagor, the Devil Who Married*, in *Chief Works*, 2:869–78; *L'Asino d'oro* (*The Golden Ass*, in *Chief Works*, 2:750–73) is probably from 1517, eight chapters that tell of an adventure in the forest and in the castle-grotto of Circe the witch. See Gian Mario Anselmi and Paolo Fazion, *Machiavelli, l'Asino e le bestie* (Bologna: CLEUB, 1984). Take also into consideration the *Canti carnascialeschi* (*Opere*, 1:871–79); *Carnival Songs*, in *Chief Works*, 2:878–83, which Machiavelli drafted between 1514 and 1524: these are short compositions, centered on an invitation to love, the uncertainty of tomorrow, and the enjoyment of today: "Low knowledge" par excellence, but Florentine, extremely witty and elegant.

99. The obvious reference, as far as the text tells us, is to the analysis of Mikhail Bakhtin, in particular the introduction and chap. 1 of *Rabelais and His World*, trans. Helene Iswolsky (Bloomington: Indiana University Press, 1984).

100. *Capitoli in terza rima: Di Fortuna a Giovan Battista Soderini* (*Opere*, 1:857–62); *Tercets on Fortune to Giovan Battista Soderini*, in *Chief Works*, 2:745–50, composed after 1514, until 1517. Among the other *Tercets*, *On Fortune* is particularly important in the theoretical thematics that Machiavelli proposes in good academic language. On the humanistic distinction of virtue and fortune, see Croce, *Theory and History of Historiography*, trans. Douglas Ainslie (London: Harrap, 1921), 233 ff. From the iconographic point of view, the two articles by Rudolf Wittkower in *Journal of the Warburg and Courtauld Institute* 1 (1937–38), 171–77, 313–21, are fundamental.

101. *Clizia*, a comedy in five acts, 1525 (*Opere*, 1:601–50); *Chief Works*, 2:822–65.

102. To Luigi Guicciardini, November 20, 1509 (*Opere*, 1:549–600); *Chief Works*, 2:889.

103. To Francesco Vettori, especially in the letters of 1514.

104. To Francesco Vettori, August 3, 1514 (*Opere*, 1:935–36); *Chief Works*, 2:946.

105. *Andria*, a comedy in five acts, probably completed before 1518 (*Opere*, 1:651–98). *La Mandragola*, a comedy in five acts, 1518, (*Opere*, 1:549–600); *Chief Works*, 2:776–822.

106. *Dell'Arte della guerra*, 1520 (*Opere*, 2:471–664), "Proemio di Niccolò Machiavegli, cittadino e segretario fiorentino, sopr'al Libro dell'Arte della Guerra, a Lorenzo di Filippo Strozzi, patrizio fiorentino"; *The Art of War*, in *Chief Works*, 2:561–726, "Preface by Niccolò Machiavelli Florentine secretary and citizen, for the book of the art of war, to Lorenzo di Filippo Strozzi, Florentine patrician." The dialogue takes place in the Orti of Cosimo Rucellai, who is praised; the protagonist is Fabrizio Colonna, General of the Catholic King; present are Zanobi Buondelmonte, Battista dall Palla, Luigi Alamanni.

107. *Parole da dirle sopra la provisione del denario* (*Opere*, 2:679–84); *Chief Works*, 2:1439–44. See n. 68 of this chapter for these three important writings.

108. See in particular the letter to Johannes de Rodulfis, June 12, 1506 (*Opere*, 2:769–73).

109. See in particular the letter to Francesco Vettori of August 26, 1513 (*Opere*, 2:800–805; *Chief Works*, 2:922–26).

110. *Relazione di una visita fatta per fortificare Firenze*, 1526 (*Opere*, 2:749–56); *The Account of a Visit Made to Fortify Florence*, in *Chief Works*, 2:727–35.

111. Letter to Francesco Guicciardini in 1526 (*Opere*, 2:826–38; *Chief Works*, 2:1002); *Prima legazione a Francesco Guicciardini, luogotenente del Papa*, December 1526 (*Opere*, 2:1089–93), *Seconda legazione* (*Opere*, 2:1094–106), in February, March, April 1627.

112. *The Art of War*, VII:726.

113. Ibid., 724.

114. R. W. and A. J. Carlyle, *A History of Medieval Political Theory in the West* (New York: Barnes and Noble, 1964).

115. From this point of view it is very difficult (we will see this later) to approve of Pocock's argumentation in *The Machiavellian Moment*, as well as the general Anglo-Saxon discussions of Machiavellian thought, when they propose the Atlantic (constitutional) continuity of his thought.

116. In reference to note 36 of this chapter, we can now say that Hans de Vries's approach is correct, when he refuses to link the terminology of *The Prince* and Machiavelli's terminology in general strictly to the schemata of the constitutional tradition. He links back, instead, to a very fundamental conception of strength.

117. We refer here to the plot that took place in 1522 against the Medici. The literary interlocutors of *The Art of War* are involved in the plot and in its repression: Buondelmonti, Alamanni, and della Palla.

118. *La vita di Castruccio Castracani da Lucca, descritta da Niccolò Machiavelli e mandata a Zanobi Buondelmonte e a Luigi Alamnni, suoi amici*, 1520 (*Opere*, 1:516–64); *The Life of Castruccio Castracani of Lucca, Written by Niccolò Machiavelli and Sent to Zanobi Buondelmonti and Luigi Alamanni, His Very Dear Friends*, in *Chief Works*, 2:533–61.

119. The dialogue on language (*Discorso o dialogo intorno alla nostra lingua*, written in the period of San Casciano, now in *Opere*, 1:713–27) must be referred to Machiavelli's metaphysical positions more than to the traditional dispute on the language. It expresses a conception of the language as strength, as a creative moment on the natural and historical horizon. The apologia for the Florentine language is the refusal of any proposal of a curial, purist, artificial language: it is popular creativity in history.

120. See again the two *Legazioni a Francesco Guicciardini.*

121. To Francesco Vettori, April 14 and 16, 1527 (*Opere*, 2:845–47); *Chief Works*, 2:1009–10.

122. To his son Guido Machiavelli, April 2, 1527 (*Opere*, 2:845–47); *Machiavelli and His Friends: Their Personal Correspondence*, 413.

123. Louis Althusser, "Machiavelli's Solitude."

3. The Atlantic Model and the Theory of Counterpower

1. Félix Gilbert, "Bernardo Rucellai," 128 ff. But before this, see Giuseppe Toffanin, *Machiavelli e il tacitismo* (Padua: Draghi, 1921).

2. Here I am referring above all to L. Burdach, "Sinn und Ursprung der Worte Renaissance und Reformation," in *Sitzungberichte der preussischen Akademie der Wissenschaften* 32 (1910):594–646. On this essay and on the fundamental works by Burdach, as well as the debate about this question between Toffanin and Cantimori, see W. K. Ferguson, *The Renaissance in Historical Thought* (Cambridge: Riverside Press, 1948), 306 ff.

3. Marjorie Reeves, *The Influence of Prophecy in Later Middle Ages: A Study in Joachiminism* (Oxford: Clarendon Press, 1969), 345 ff, 354 ff, 359–74. See also G. Tognetti, "Note sul profetismo nel Rinascimento e la letteratura relativa," *Bollettino Archivio Muratoriano* 82 (1970). Last, see two interesting notes that appeared in the *Journal of the Warburg and Courtauld Institute*, A. Linder, "An Unpublished 'Pronostication' on the Return of Charles VIII to Italy" (47:200–203); and J. Britnell and D. Stubbs, "The Mirabilis Liber: Its Composition and Influence" (49:126–49).

4. Donald Weinstein, *Savonarola and Florence: Prophecy and Patriotism in the Renaissance* (Princeton, N.J.: Princeton University Press, 1970). This fundamental text must be integrated, through the contributions of D. Cantimori (1932), G. Spini (1948), J. H. Whitfield (1949), R. De Mattei (1956), into the study of the thought and the civic value of Savonarola, as well as through the reading that Félix Gilbert, "Bernardo Rucellai," and R. von Albertini, *Firenze dalla repubblica al principato* (Turin, 1970) propose of those years of Florentine history.

5. See Marjorie Reeves, "The Originality and Influence of Joachim da Fiore," *Traditio* 36 (1980): 269–316.

6. Donald Weinstein, "Critical Issues in the Study of Civic Religion in Renaissance Florence," in *The Pursuit of Holiness in Late Medieval and Renaissance Religion*, ed. C. Trinkas (Leiden, 1974), 265–70; Nicolai Rubenstein, "The Beginning of Political Thought in Florence: A Study in Medieval Historiography," *Journal of the Warburg and Courtauld Institute* 5 (1942):198–227.

7. "A Francesco Vettori," December 19, 1513 (*Opere*, 1:921–24); *Chief Works*, 2:933.

8. It would be worthwhile, here, to follow the studies by the Warburg School (in particular F. Saxl and E. H. Gombrich) of the prophetic symbologies in great Florentine painting; see for instance Marjorie Reeves, "The Originality," 434ff, where she sums up Botticelli's problematics.

9. The reference is again to Weinstein, "Critical Issues," and Rubenstein, "The Beginning of Political Thought."

10. See the references to the works of Vasari, Gombrich, and Gilbert cited in n. 89 of chap. 2.

11. J. G. A. Pocock, *The Machiavellian Moment*; as its subtitle indicates, *Florentine Political Thought and the Atlantic Republican Tradition*, the volume is dedicated to the demonstration of this thesis.

12. R. von Albertini, *Firenze dalla repubblica*, and in general W. K. Ferguson, *The Renaissance*.

13. J. Roger Charbonnel, *La pensee italienne au XVIe siecle et le courant libertin* (Paris: Champion, 1919); Albert Cherel, *La pensee de Machiavel en France* (Paris: Artisan du livre, 1935); G. Benoist, *Le Machiavelism apres Machiavel* (Paris, 1936).

14. For the literature on this subject see the *Bibliographie internationale de l'Humanisme et de la Renaissance*, regularly published by Droz Press (Geneva).

15. E. B. Beame, "French Adaptation of Machiavelli (1500–1598)," "The Use and Abuse of Machiavelli," *Journal of the History of Ideas* 43, no. 3 (1982):396–416.

16. Antonio Negri, *Problemi*; Antonio Negri, *Descartes Politico o della ragionevole ideologia* (Milan: Feltrinelli, 1970).

17. Felix Raab, *The English Face of Machiavelli* (London and Toronto: RKP, 1964). See also the review of Raab's work by J. G. A. Pocock, "'The Onely Politician': Machiavelli, Harrington and Felix Raab," *Historical Studies: Australia and New Zealand* 3 (1966).

18. In two important articles in the *Journal of the Warburg and Courtauld Institute*, respectively (1937–38):166–69, and (1946):122–34, as well as in *Bacone e Machiavelli* (Genoa, 1936), and in the collection *Studi sul Rinascimento italiano in Inghilterra*, M. Orsini has worked extensively on these problems. See also Frances Yates, "Italian Teachers in Elisabethan England," *Journal of the Warburg and Courtauld Institute* (1937–38):103–16.

19. T. S. R. Boase, "The Medici in Elisabethan and Jacobean Drama," *Journal of the Warburg and Courtauld Institute* (1974):373–78. See also the old but still important study by Edward Meyer, *Machiavelli and the Elisabethan Drama* (Weimar: Felber, 1897). On the continuity of the Machiavellian and Florentine tradition, see John M. Steadman, "Heroic Virtue and the Divine Image in *Paradise Lost*," *Journal of the Warburg and Courtauld Institute* (1959):88–105.

20. Richard H. Popkin, *The History of Scepticism from Erasmus to Descartes* (Assen: Van Gorcum, 1964).

21. On this set of problems in general, besides the texts on English Protestantism that I will discuss later, let's keep in mind the particular modalities through which humanistic and Renaissance thought was absorbed into English culture, as they are presented by Hiram Haydn, who opens and closes his *The Counter-Renaissance* with two chapters dedicated to the encounter of Elizabethan culture with the Italian Renaissance.

22. See the articles by Wittkower cited in n. 100 of chap. 2.

23. The reference is again to Benedetto Croce, *Theory and History of Historiography*; to Hiram Haydn, *The Counter-Renaissance*; and to the theses of Félix Gilbert, who in studying the relationship of Machiavelli and Guicciardini grasps the distinctive character of the former's thought in its scientific "Romanism," that is, in the rational notion of historical development, beyond and through the accidents of praxis, within the fabric of Roman history.

24. E. Gilbert, *Florentine Political Assumptions*.

25. D. Cantimori's analysis of Antonio Brucioli's "Dialoghi" in *Rhetorics and Politics* is excellent because it discovers and celebrates revolutionary humanism. Hans Baron writes his *The Crisis of the Early Italian Renaissance* (Princeton, N.J.: Princeton University Press, 1967) with the same strong sense of this *humanitas*.

26. Félix Gilbert, "Bernardo Rucellai."

27. J. G. A. Pocock, "Historical Introduction," in *The Political Works of James Harrington* (Cambridge:

Cambridge University Press, 1977), 15. This edition of Harrington's political works is fundamental, and it will be our point of reference. There was also a 1699–1700 edition of Harrington's complete works by John Toland. There were new editions in 1737 and 1758, and others throughout the eighteenth century. James Harrington lived between 1611 and 1677. He took part in the civil war and was one of the gentlemen who, between 1647 and 1649, controlled the imprisoned King Charles. Harrington's entire production is concentrated between 1656 and 1661 (except for a short text, left incomplete, on *The Mechanics of Nature*, which he wrote later). On December 18, 1661, Harrington was arrested for plotting. After his liberation from the Tower of London, he fell prey to a serious psychological crisis that lasted the rest of his life.

28. Ibid., 43 ff, with a reference to Francis Bacon and Walter Raleigh. On the first one see Mary Sturt, *Francis Bacon: A Biography* (London: Kegan Paul/Trench Trubner, 1932); on the second see Pierre Lefranc, *Sir Walter Raleigh, ecrivain, l'oeuvre et les idees* (Quebec: Presses de l'Universite Laval, 1968). On this topic see above all Christopher Hill, *The Intellectual Origins of the English Revolution* (Oxford, 1965), and, on Hill's interpretation, M. Cuaz, "Hill e la interpretazione marxiste della rivoluzione inglese," *Studi storici* 3 (1985):635–65.

29. Pocock, "Historical Introduction," 16. See also Charles Blitzer, *An Immortal Commonwealth: The Political Thought of James Harrington* (New Haven, Conn.: Yale University Press, 1960).

30. *His Majesty's Answer to the Nineteen Propositions of Parliament* (of June 1642, drafted by Falkland and Colepeper upon Charles I's order), is now published by Corinne Weston, *English Constitutional Theory and the House of Lords, 1556–1832* (New York and London: RKP, 1965), 261–65. In Weston's volume, besides other materials on the constitutional debate of the time, see also a debate redefined by the new formulation of the theory of the "mixed constitution" proposed by Charles I, as well as the analysis and the narration of the vicissitudes of this type of constitution. For the first period, which is the period we are concerned with, see 9–43, 44–86. But this volume is important also for our discussion in chaps. 4 and 5. Again, in general, on the "mixed constitution" see the work of Charles Howard McIlwain; and Wilfried Nippel, *Mischenverfassungstheorie und Verfassungrealitat in Antike und fruher Neuzeit* (Stuttgart, 1980).

31. In James Harrington, *Political Works*, 155–359.

32. On the fortunes of this phrase, see C. Weston, *English Constitutional Theory*, 71, who attributes it first to John Adams.

33. Although it could be critiqued on political grounds, Pocock's work, both in *The Machiavellian Moment* and the "Historical Introduction," is philologically faultless, particularly on this topic.

34. Ernest Tuveson, *Millennium and Utopia: A Study in the Background of the Idea of Progress* (Berkeley and Los Angeles: University of California Press, 1949); N. Cohn, *The Pursuit of the Millennium*, 2nd ed. (New York, 1961); Michael Walzer, *The Revolution of the Saints: A Study in the Origins of Radical Politics* (Cambridge, Mass: Cambridge University Press, 1965); and also by Walzer, "Exodus 32 and the Theory of Holy War: The History of a Citation," *Harvard Theological Review* 61, no. 1 (1968):1–14, and *Exodus and Revolution* (New York, 1984).

35. Pocock, "Historical Introduction," 15–42. This is more extensively discussed in *The Machiavellian Moment.*

36. See nn. 61 and 63 in chap. 2. Furthermore, for a discussion of Polybius's fortune, see J. de Romilly, "Le classement des Constitutions de Herodote à Aristote," *Revue Etudes Greques* 72 (1959):81 ff; Raymond Weil, *Aristote et l'histoire* (Paris: Klincksieck, 1960); T. Cole, "The Sources and Composition of Polybius VI," *Historia* 13 (1964):440 ff; G. J. A. Aalders, *Die Theorie der gemischten Verfassung im Altertum* (Amsterdam: de Gruyter, 1968); Paul Moraux, *Der Aristotelismus bei den Griechen*, vol. 1 (Berlin, 1973). We must also take into consideration the contributions to the *IX Congres de l'Association G. Bude.*

37. Polybius, *The Histories*, trans. F. Hultsch (Bloomington: Indiana University Press, 1962).

38. Ibid., VI.9, 10:466.

39. Ibid., VI.9, 12–13.

40. Ibid., VI.10, 12–14:467.

41. Ibid., VI.11–18.

42. George Holland Sabine, *A History of Political Theory* (New York: Holt, Rinehart & Winston, 1951).

43. For the biological argument see Raymond Weil, *Notice* to the French edition (ed. and trans. R. Weil and C. Nicolet [Paris, 1977]) of Polybius's Book VI:50 ff; for the interpretation à la Thucydides see F. G. Wallbank, *A Historical Commentary*, 1:16–26. We don't need to add that the two interpretations may be perfectly compatible.

44. Above all, it is von Fritz, *Theory of the Mixed Constitution*, 60–95, 388–97, who bends the interpretation of Polybius in this direction. In the *Addenda* to his *Historical Commentary*, 3:774–76, Wallbank tries to mediate his positions vis-à-vis those of von Fritz: he proposes an interpretation in terms of a vague Polybian hylozoism.

45. Pocock, "Historical Introduction," agrees on this point, on this moment of the evolution of Harrington's thought.

46. Hobbes, *Leviathan*, chaps. 17, 19, 20, 26, 29. The attack on the constitution of the Roman republic is conducted by Hobbes in essential terms, since this constitution is interpreted by Hobbes according to the Polybian description of the "mixed constitution." Hobbes completely avoids the fundamental problem of Polybius: that of the birth and the corruption of the republic.

47. C. B. Macpherson, *The Political Theory of Possessive Individualism* (Oxford: Oxford University Press, 1962). [The Italian translation (Milan, 1973), includes an introduction by Antonio Negri. Trans.]

48. Gerard Colonna d'Istria and Roland Frapet, *L'art politique chez Machiavel* (Paris: Vrin, 1980), chap. 3, "Machiavel lecteur de Polybe," 135–205. The authors situate the problem correctly, but their argument is at times rather extreme.

49. Wallbank, *Historical Commentary*, has stressed the Neoplatonic subtext of the entire Polybian tradition. As for the importance of Neoplatonism in the development of English thought, it is almost one of its constants, continually present and continually critical. See Ernst Cassirer, *The Platonic Renaissance in England*, trans. James P. Pettegrove (Austin: University of Texas Press, 1953).

50. The way Pocock reads this passage is completely wrong and a clear apology for an American republican ideal that sounds very trendy. Cf. C. Vasoli, "The Machiavellian Moment: A Grand Ideological Synthesis," *Journal of Modern History* 49, no. 4 (1977):661–70. Pocock has written a long introduction to the Italian translation of his own work (also published in *Journal of Modern History* 53 [1981]:49 ff), in which he defends himself, none too convincingly, from this and other strong criticisms, all centered on an essential fact: the ideal linearity of the dialectic of historical positions expressed in his work.

51. Christopher Hill, *The World Turned Upside Down* (London: Temple Smith, 1972); but above all, "A Bourgeois Revolution?" in *Three British Revolutions, 1641, 1688, 1776*, ed. J. G. A. Pocock (Princeton, N.J: Princeton University Press, 1980), 109–39.

52. Pocock very pointedly insists on this point in "Historical Introduction," 70 ff, and in *The Machiavellian Moment*, 317, 390. The non-Platonic but rather "modern" utopian character of Harrington's work is proved by the modern references of his theory, of his "models"—the Florentine civic tradition, Bacon's and Raleigh's thought—and finally his taking up the Venetian model (on this point see the notes to the third section of this chapter).

53. The utopia of *Oceana* is, as Pocock again observes ("Historical Introduction," 72 ff), more millenarian and messianic than idealist and transcendental. Cf. Christopher Hill, *Intellectual Origins*; and Donald Weinstein, *Savonarola and Florence*.

54. See n. 28 of this chapter.

55. Christopher Hill, *Society and Puritanism in Pre-Revolutionary England* (London: Secker & Warburg, 1964); and *Intellectual Origins of the English Revolution*. Hill's work, particularly in the sixties, is very important for clarifying the intellectual position within which Harrington operates: this position is certainly the result of a precedent culture, but nonetheless also, and above all, the result of a concrete and mass "praxis" that does not let itself be contained within purely intellectual filiations. On the polemics provoked by Hill's analysis, and on the profound continuity of his thought, from the "classical Marxism" of the forties to these positions strongly insisting on the "primacy of praxis," cf. M. Cuaz's article, "Hill e la interpretazione marxiste" (which nonetheless at times seems to underline the evolution and revisionism of Hill's thought in purely methodological terms).

56. Pocock, "Historical Introduction," 43–76; see also *The Machiavellian Moment*.

57. Pocock, "Historical Introduction," 56 ff (against Tawney's, Macpherson's, and Hill's interpretations). See also *The Machiavellian Moment*, 369–98.

58. *Oceana*, 161 ff. Hereafter the citations from Harrington's work will be from J. G. A. Pocock's cited edition and in most cases will appear parenthetically in the text.

59. Christopher Hill, *Society and Puritanism*, and *Intellectual Origins*.

60. The interpretation that Macpherson, *Political Theory of Possessive Individualism*, 160–93, gives of Harrington's thought is from this point of view in many ways acceptable. In any case we will discuss this reading in the text.

61. It seems to us that in his reading of Harrington's work in *The Machiavellian Moment* and in the "Historical Introduction," Pocock yields to this interpretative danger, which is perhaps partially corrected in his essay *Three British Revolutions*.

62. Matthew Wren, *Considerations upon Oceana* (London: Gellibrand, 1657). Pocock, "Historical Introduction," 77 ff, deploys Wren's work, against the lucidity of this author who wants an absolute monarchy allowing the security of the contracts and guaranteeing the solution of the conflicts of interest, to show Harrington's backwardness as an ideologue of classical constitutional relations. The argument here is used particularly against Macpherson. See also Pocock's *The Machiavellian Moment*, 31 ff.

63. Christopher Hill, *Society and Puritanism*, and *Intellectual Origins*. Pocock himself, in *Three English Revolutions*, is forced to leave space for this hypothesis.

64. It is the methodology of Hill's latest period, that of "the world upside down," that we must assume here. We don't need to mention how much this methodology owes to the innovation introduced by E. P. Thompson, *The Making of the English Working Class.* On the subjective point of view, in the history of social movements and popular struggles, that is, on pluralistic induction and the methodology of the assemblages, see Antonio Negri, *Macchina tempo*, chap. 5, "Sul metodo della critica storica."

65. *The Art of Lawgiving*, 599–704.

66. *A System of Politics*, 833–54. Pocock, "Historical Introduction," 121, 120.

67. Such is the creative naturalism showed by *The Mechanics of Nature*, a text written by Harrington after his imprisonment, and probably after the psychic crisis that struck him. It's not necessary to give precise references here: it is enough to refer in general to the influences of Renaissance naturalism, as we have seen it impact upon Machiavelli and other authors.

68. *Oceana*, 165. This passage would be enough to make us understand how "agrarian law," far from being connected to the old classist schemata of pre-Renaissance constitutionalism, fully introduces us into the age of possessive individualism and thus upsets Pocock's polemics against Macpherson.

69. *Oceana: The Preliminaries, Showing the Principles of Government*, 161–63.

70. The term *superstructure* is used by Harrington to indicate the complex of the juridical-institutional apparatus. The "structure" seems to be the natural foundation of the balance of property, that is, the constituent foundation of the agrarian law, though with many lexical ambiguities and imprecisions. Also the terms *overbalance* and *overpower* are at times used in an equivocal way, but in general they indicate the effect of the preponderance of aristocratic power, in the mechanism of representation and in that of property, respectively.

71. In general, see *The Second Part of Preliminaries*, 188–207.

72. Cf. Pocock, *The Machiavellian Moment*, 26–27.

73. See also *The Art of Lawgiving.*

74. On the theme of imagination in seventeenth-century philosophy, and in particular on the imagination of that contemporary of Harrington, Spinoza, cf. Antonio Negri, *The Savage Anomaly.*

75. *Pian Piano. Or Intercourse, between H. Ferne, Doctor in Divinity, and J. Harrington, Esq. upon occasion of the Doctor's Cansue of the Commonwealth of Oceana*, 369–87. We will return to this topic later. Let's keep in mind, in any case, its defensive character, which is not without theoretical consequences.

76. Notice that, in his reading of Harrington's work, Pocock says exactly the opposite.

77. When he deals with the theme of the electoral laws, Harrington is inspired by those of the Republic of Venice. Cf. his short text *The Manner and Use of the Ballot*, 361–67, of 1656, the direct correlative of *Oceana*, where the Venetian method of election and selection of magistrates is described. On Harrington's relation to the "Venetian myth" in general see Nicola Matteucci, "Machiavelli, Harrington, Montesquieu e gli 'Ordini' di Venezia," *Il pensiero politico* 3, no. 3 (1970):337–69; Pocock, "Historical Introduction," 68–69; *The Machiavellian Moment*, 285, 300–303; R. Pecchioli, *Dal mito di Venezia all'ideologia americana* (Venice, 1983). On the importance of the Venetian model see, the third section of this chapter.

78. Machiavelli, *Discorsi*, 1.58. See chap. 2, sect. 2.

79. In *Oceana*, 169–72, see the discussions that lead into the theory of the body and the soul, and of their symbiosis, in political institutions. It has been noticed that the assumption of these positions pushes Harrington toward a rather naive naturalism and situates him in the tradition of natural right theory. This reading seems to forget the strongly constructive character of Harrington's naturalism, a character that is connected to ancient and Renaissance philosophy rather than to the pale figure of the natural right tradition.

80. See Pocock, "Historical Introduction," 77–99, 128 ff.

81. Again, on this point Pocock's interpretation must be refused because it blurs Renaissance naturalism and Harrington's realism with the tradition of natural right.

82. *The Second Book, or a Political Discourse concerning Ordination, against Dr. H. Hammond and Dr. L. Seaman, and the Authors They Follow* is published separately from, even though within, the framework laid out by the dedication and by the introduction of Book I of *The Prerogative.* On the works of Hammond and Seaman, cf. Pocock's notes, 480n.

83. *Brief Directions Showing How a Fit and Perfect Model of Popular Government May Be Made, Found or Understood*, 579–81.

84. Besides *The Art of Lawgiving* (599–704), *Politicaster* (705–25), again against Wren; *Pour Enclouer le Canon* (727–33); two *Discourses* in defense of the freedom of conscience (735–45, 748–53); another polemical text against Mr. Rogers, on oligarchy (755–60); and finally *Aphorisms Political* (761–79), a collection of 120 aphorisms (in the second edition; the first included only 76) that reduce to a simple form all the themes that

Harrington had been developing in 1659. See Pocock's historical notes.

85. J. Cotton, "J. Harrington and T. Hobbes," *Journal of the History of the Ideas* 42, no. 3 (1981):407–21, brilliantly sums up the theme of the clash between the two authors, insisting in particular on the superiority of the Harringtonian philosophy of the "body," vis-à-vis Hobbes's mechanicism. It is on this constructive, Harveyan naturalism that the philosophy of the *Commonwealth of Oceana* is founded.

86. *The Prerogative*, 423.

87. See n. 50 of this chapter.

88. *The Prerogative of Popular Government* is aimed (*Epistle dedicatory*, 390, but see also 309–93) at the confutation of the critics and the irony of the "good Companies" behind which Wren hides. Good Companies: perhaps the "circle of virtuosi" of Oxford, the budding Royal Society, where Harrington's *Commonwealth* seems to have provoked impertinent criticisms, insinuations, and so forth.

89. Spinoza, *The Letters*, trans. Samuel Shirley (Indianapolis: Hackett, 1995). See my *Savage Anomaly*; Henry Oldenburg, Spinoza's addressee, belongs to these circles.

90. I am referring to the fundamental theses of my *Savage Anomaly*. There's no need to repeat that I consider this book on "constituent power" as a sort of extension of the studies done in that book on the development of modern political metaphysics.

91. George Holland Sabine, *History of Political Theory*, 399–408.

92. For example, *Oceana*, 281–332 (*de judiciis*, 281–87; on the budgets of the nation, 287–300; on raising youths, 300–17; on the organization of the provinces, 317–32); *The Prerogative*, passim.

93. *The Manner and the Use of the Ballot.*

94. Pocock, "Historical Introduction," 68–69. But see in general the works cited in n. 77 of this chapter. Also see William James Bouwsma, *Venice and the Defense of Republican Liberty: Renaissance Values in the Age of Counter-Reformation* (Berkeley and Los Angeles: University of California Press, 1968) and R. Pecchioli's review in *Studi Veneziani* 13 (1971):693–708; Sergio Bertelli, Nicolai Rubenstein, and Craig Hugh Smith, *Florence and Venice: Comparisons and Relations*, vols. 1 and 2 (Florence: La nuova Italia, 1979); Robert Finlay, *Politics in Renaissance Venice* (New Brunswick, N.J.: Rutgers University Press, 1980); P. Braunstein and C. Klapisch-Zuber, "Florence et Venise, les rituels publics a l'epoque de la Renaissance," *Annales ESC* 38, no. 5 (1983):1110 ff.

95. Above all, Josef Bohatec, *England und die Geschichte der Menschen—und Burgerrechte* (Munich, 1956), 117 ff; *James Harrington: Eine Beitrag zum dem Einfluss von Aristoteles auf die englische Publizistik der Menschenrechte.* Indeed, in *The Prerogative* there are lots of references to Aristotle in the course of a discussion that tends to fix the transcendental rules of the functioning of "agrarian law." Harrington answers this question positively in this way: if there is no expressed agrarian law, is there something analogous that functions in each political regime? But this way of arguing, far from implying a formalization of agrarian law in terms of Aristotelian naturalism, is simply a logical support for the affirmation of the historical determinacy of modern prudence. And we cannot be deceived by the Aristotelian reference vis-à-vis the constancy of Harrington's historical reasoning.

96. Josef Bohatec, ibid., nonetheless has the merit of having grasped with great precision other points of Harrington's thought, and in particular of having clearly defined the relation of structure to superstructure and the naturalistic component (à la Harvey) of his naturalism.

97. All in all, this is Pocock's fundamental thesis. This interpretation seems to be fully part of Pocock's method, along with that hermeneutical deconstruction that is at the basis of his work as well as that of Quentin Skinner. We must obviously remember the two volumes of the *Foundations of Modern Political Thought* (Cambridge: Cambridge University Press, 1978), and *Machiavelli* (Oxford: Oxford University Press, 1981) by Skinner. On the interpenetration of method and research, of theoretical approach and ideological direction, Pocock gives explicit proof in his introduction to the Italian translation of *The Machiavellian Moment*, 17, 43. For the discussion of Skinner's thesis, and in general on the methodological direction of his school, see *Meaning and Context: Q. Skinner and His Critics*, ed. James Tully (Cambridge: Cambridge University Press, 1988). An intelligent critical stance toward the method and the results of Pocock's research is found in F. Fagiani's "La storia del 'discorso' politico inglese dei secoli XVII e XVIII fra 'virtu' e 'diritti,'" *Rivista di storia della filosofia* 3 (1987):481–98. The conservative text on which all the future developments of Pocock's thought are inscribed is *The Ancient Constitution and the Feudal Law: English Historical Thought in the XVII century* (Cambridge: Cambridge University Press, 1957). Here on Harrington, in essential terms, see 128 ff.

98. See Josef Bohatec, *England und die Geschichte*, 117 ff.

99. C. B. Macpherson, *Political Theory of Possessive Individualism*, in particular 161 ff, 165, 174 ff, 181 ff, 191 ff. We do not need to refer here to the general bibliography on the English Revolution, from Tawney to Hill, from Trevor Roper to Stone, which we consider well known. On the Marxist interpretation, see Bruno Bongiovanni, "Tra storia e storiografia, K. Marx e la rivoluzione inglese," *Quaderni di storia* 9, no. 18 (1983): 85–119. On various aspects of the revolutionary and institutional movement, with reference to the most recent bibliography, see C. S. L. Devies, "Les Révoltes populaires en Angleterre (1500–1700)," *Annales ESC* 24, no. 1 (1969):24–60; L. Stone, "L'Angleterre de 1540 a 1880. Pays de noblesse ouverte," *Annales ESC* 40, no. 1 (1985):71–94; B. Cottret, "Le Roi, les Lords, et les Communes. Monarchie miste et etats de Royaume en Angleterre (XVI–XVIIe siecles)," *Annales ESC* 41, no. 1 (1986):127–50.

100. P. G. M. Dickson, *The Financial Revolution in England: A Study in Development of Public Credit, 1688–1756* (London: Macmillan, 1967); J. H. Plumb, *The Growth of Political Stability in England, 1660–1730* (London: Macmillan, 1967).

101. See n. 7 of this chapter.

102. J. G. A. Pocock, "Historical Introduction," 100 ff.

103. Ibid., 128 ff.

104. C. B. Macpherson, *Political Theory*, passages cited in n. 99.

105. Extremely important are Pocock's annotations on this point: *Politics, Language and Time: Essays in Political Thought and History* (New York: Atheneum, 1971). See in this text the important bibliography on the modification of the notion of time that the financial revolution determines.

106. Pocock, "Historical Introduction," 133.

107. C. Hill, *Intellectual Origins*, and in general the literature on the "revolution of the Saints" that we have mentioned. As for the Harringtonian legacy in America, see T. W. Dwight, "Harrington and his Influence upon American Political Institutions," *Political Science Quarterly* 2 (1987):1 ff; as well as the classic Zera Silver Fink, *The Classical Republicans* (Evanston, Ill.: Northwestern University Press, 1945); Caroline Robbins, *The Eighteenth Century Commonwealthman* (Cambridge, Mass.: Harvard University Press, 1959); J. R. Pole, *Political Representation in England and the Origins of the American Republic* (London: Macmillan, 1966).

108. *The Rota, or a Model of a Free State or Equal Commonwealth*, 807–21; *The Ways and the Means, Whereby an Equal and Lasting Commonwealth May Be Suddenly Introduced and Perfectly Founded*, 823–31. Also in 1660 Harrington publishes *A Letter unto Mr. Stubbe*, in defense of *Oceana* (827–31).

109. See *The Examination of James Harrington*, 855–59. This probably dates from 1661. It is the reconstruction of the interrogations (done directly by Harrington himself) to which the author had been subjected in the Tower of London. Harrington defends himself from the accusation of plotting.

110. For an introduction to the problems of the militia, see John R. Western, *The English Militia in the XVIIIth Century: The Story of a Political Issue* (London: RKP, 1965).

111. Pocock, "Historical Introduction," 100–27.

112. See the writings cited earlier in n. 84 of this chapter, to which we should add the short polemical text *Valerius and Publicola*, dedicated to the polemic against Stubbe.

113. *A System of Politics, Delineated in Short and Easy Aphorisms, Published from the Author's Own Manuscript* (perhaps 1661), 833–54.

114. Even though Machiavelli is now considered more a "physician" than a "prince": "Corruption in government is to be read and considered in Machiavel, as diseases in body are to be read and considered in Hyppocrates" (854).

115. Pocock, "Historical Introduction," 128–58; *The Machiavellian Moment.*

116. Christopher Hill, *The Experience of Defeat: Milton and Some Contemporaries* (London, 1984).

117. Pocock, *The Machiavellian Moment*: on Shaftesbury, 406–20; on Marvell, 408–20; on Nedham, 379–84; on Neville, 417–21.

118. Alfred Sohn-Rethel, *Manual and Intellectual Labor: A Critique of Epistemology* (Atlantic Highlands, N.J.: Humanities Press, 1978).

119. On the "standing army controversy," see Pocock, "Historical Introduction," 138 ff. But see, besides Western's work cited in n. 110, Lois F. Schwoerer, *No Standing Armies: The Anti-Army Controversy in XVII Century England* (Baltimore: Johns Hopkins University Press, 1972); L. D. Cress, "Radical Whiggery on the Role of the Military: Ideological Roots of the American Revolutionary Militia," *Journal of the History of Ideas* 40, no. 1 (1979).

120. George Holland Sabine, *History of Political Theory*, 408 ff; J. Connif, "Reason and History in Early Whig Thought," *Journal of the History of Ideas* 43, no. 3 (1982):397–416.; Paulette Carrive, *La pensee politique de A. Sidney* (Paris, 1989); and obviously Christopher Hill, *Milton and the English Revolution* (London, 1977).

121. Christopher Hill, *A Bourgeois Revolution?*, 109–39.

122. See n. 30 of this chapter.

123. Corinne Weston, *English Constitutional Theory*, 9–43, 44–86.

124. Christopher Hill, *The English Revolution 1640: An Essay* (London: Lawrence & Wishart, 1955).

125. Pocock, "Historical Introduction," 145.

126. L. Stone's "The Results of the English Revolution in the XVIIth Century," in *Three British Revolutions*, 23–108, clearly denounces these directions of research, while exalting the power of the American appropriation of the revolutionary thematics.

127. See, on the one hand, the essays collected in *Il contratto sociale nella filosofia politica moderna*, ed. Giuseppe Duso (Bologna, 1987); on the other, I take the liberty once again to refer you to my *Savage Anomaly*, particularly to those parts where the contradiction between the idea of contract and the metaphysical-ontological substratum of Spinoza's philosophy is foregrounded.

128. See the introduction by P. Laslett to the edition of John Locke, *Two Treatises of Government*, 2nd ed. (Cambridge: Cambridge University Press, 1967). For other reasons consider also M. J. C. Vile, *Constitutionalism and the Separation of Powers* (Oxford: Clarendon Press, 1967).

4. Political Emancipation in the American Constitution

1. Edmund Burke, "Speech on Conciliation with America," in *Writings and Speeches of Edmund Burke*, vol. 3, ed. Warren M. Elofson (Oxford, 1996), 129.

2. Edmund Burke, *A Philosophical Inquiry into the Origins of Our Ideas of the Sublime and the Beautiful*, ed. James T. Boulton (Oxford, 1987).

3. Gordon S. Wood, *The Creation of the American Republic, 1776–1787* (Chapel Hill: University of North Carolina Press, 1969), 562–615; Pocock, *The Machiavellian Moment*, 523 ff. From this point of view, Bernard Bailyn's work, *The Ideological Origins of the American Revolution* (Cambridge, Mass.: Harvard/Belknap, 1967), and *The Origins of American Politics* (New York: Vintage, 1970), is fundamental.

4. We will return to Tocqueville's and Arendt's interpretations of the American Revolution later in the course of this chapter.

5. See Michael Kammen, "The Meaning of Colonization in American Revolutionary Thought," *Journal of the History of Ideas* 31 (1971):337–58. Also by Michael Kammen see *An Inquiry Concerning the Origins of American Civilization* (New York, 1980), and above all, *A Machine That Would Go of Itself: The Constitution in American Culture* (New York, 1987); in our research we have particularly kept this text in mind.

6. Elise Marienstras, *Nous, le peuple*, 142–46, 203–7. By Marienstras see also *Les Mythes fondateurs de la nation Americaine: Essai sur le discours idéologique aux Etats-Unis à l'époque de l'Independence, 1763–1800* (Paris: Maspero, 1976). On the development of radical thought and practices in the course of the American Revolution see Alfred Fabian Young, *Dissent: Explorations in the History of American Revolution* (Chicago, 1968); Pauline Maier, *From Resistance to Revolution: Colonial Radicals and the Development of American Opposition to Britain* (New York: Knopf, 1972); John Shy, *A People Numerous and Armed: Military Struggle for American Independence* (London and New York: Oxford University Press, 1976); John M. Murrin, "A Roof without Walls: The Dilemma of National Identity," in *Beyond Confederation* (Chapel Hill: University of North Carolina Press, 1987).

7. Roderick Nash, *Wilderness and the American Mind*, 3rd ed. (New Haven, Conn.: Yale University Press, 1982). See Marienstras, *Nous le peuple*, 345–50 for an extensive bibliography.

8. Gordon S. Wood, *Creation*, 567.

9. *Thoughts on Government*, in *The Works of John Adams*, ed. Charles F. Adams, 4:193–200 (Boston, 1853).

10. *Ibid.*, vols. 4–6. The complete title of the work is *A Defence of the Constitutions of the Government of the United States of America, against the Attack of M. Rurgot, in His Letter to Dr. Price, Dated 22. March. 1778, in Three Volumes.* See John R. Howe Jr., *The Changing Political Thought of J. Adams* (Princeton, N.J.: Princeton University Press, 1966).

11. Wood, *Creation*, 567–92; Richard Buel, *Securing the Revolution, 1789–1815* (Ithaca, N.Y.: Cornell University Press, 1972); Dick Howard, *The Birth of American Political Thought 1763–1787*, trans. David Ames Curtis (Minneapolis: University of Minnesota Press, 1989), 99–105.

12. *Massachusetts, Colony to Commonwealth: Documents of the Formation of Its Constitution, 1775–1780*, ed. Robert Joseph Taylor (New York, 1961).

13. See Wood, *Creation*; Howe, *Changing Political Thought*; Howard, *Birth*.

14. For the origins of the concept of "virtual representation" and for the quotations from Burke, see J. R. Pole, *Political Representation in England and the Origins of the American Republic* (Berkeley and Los Angeles: University of California Press, 1971), 441.

15. For the American discussion, see ibid., and Marienstras, *Nous, le peuple*, 163 ff; Howard, *Birth*, 76 ff.

16. Giovanni Sartori, *Democrazia e definizioni.*

17. Lewis Hinchman, *Hegel's Critique of the Enlightenment* (Gainesville: University Press of Florida, 1987), 258–63.

18. W. P. Adams, *The First American Constitution* (Chapel Hill: University of North Carolina Press, 1980), 65.

19. Marienstras, *Nous, le peuple*, 240.

20. See the works mentioned in n. 6 of this chapter. Particularly important is Pauline Maier's work concerning the function of the mobs/*comitia*.

21. See Marienstras, *Nous, le peuple,* 299–301.

22. Thomas Paine, *Common Sense,* in *Collected Writings* (New York: Library of America, 1995), 36.

23. Howard, *Birth,* 107–13. See Eric Foner's reading of the constitution of Pennsylvania in *Tom Paine and Revolutionary America* (Oxford: Oxford University Press, 1976), which is radically different.

24. In *The Papers of Thomas Jefferson,* ed. J. P. Boyd (Princeton, N.J.: Princeton University Press, 1950), 1:121–34.

25. John M. Head, *A Time to Rend: An Essay on the Decision for American Independence* (Madison: State Historical Society of Wisconsin, 1968).

26. Carl Lotus Becker, *The Declaration of Independence,* rev. ed. (New York: Vintage, 1956); Lance Banning, *The Jeffersonian Persuasion* (Ithaca, N.Y.: Cornell University Press, 1977); Garry Wills, *Inventing America: Jefferson's Declaration of Independence* (Garden City, N.J.: Doubleday, 1978); Joyce Appleby, *Capitalism and a New Social Order: The Republican Vision of the 1790s* (New York: New York University Press, 1984).

27. *The Declaration of Independence,* in *American State Papers,* ed. Mortimer J. Adler (Chicago, 1990), 1. Once again, the reference is above all to C. L. Becker. Not by chance is Becker, besides being a formidable interpreter of the *Declaration of Independence,* the instigator of the "progressive" school in the historiography of the American Revolution and constitution. Subsequent citations will come from this edition and will appear parenthetically in the text.

28. Staughton Lynd, in *Intellectual Origins of American Radicalism* (Cambridge, Mass.: Harvard University Press, 1982), nonetheless illuminates the different meanings of "Lockeanism" in the American Revolution.

29. Elise Marienstras, *Nous, le peuple,* 294 ff.

30. Samuel Bowles and Herbert Gintis, *Democracy and Capitalism: Property, Community and the Contradictions of Modern Social Thought* (New York, Basic Books, 1987), 47 ff.

31. Frederick Jackson Turner, *The Frontier in American History,* rev. ed. (New York: Holt, 1947); Henry Nash Smith, *Virgin Land: The American West as Symbol and Myth* (Cambridge, Mass.: Harvard University Press, 1950); William Henry McNeill, *The Great Frontier: Freedom and Hierarchy in Modern Times* (Princeton, N.J.: Princeton University Press, 1983).

32. For the progressive school, see the seminal work of Charles Beard, *An Economic Interpretation of the Constitution* (New York: Macmillan, 1913), and see the numerous editions of this work, in particular the 1960 edition, which we use here. F. MacDonald, *We the People: The Economic Origins of the Constitution* (Chicago and London, 1958) offers a strong critique of this work and sums up, around some contemporary phenomena, the antiradical and counterrevolutionary spirit determined at that time by the culture of the Cold War. The characterization of the American Revolution in Hannah Arendt's *On Revolution* is tied to this climate. For a systematic attack, of a historical and factual order, against MacDonald see Staughton Lynd, *Class Conflict, Slavery and the U.S. Constitution* (Indianapolis: Bobbs-Merrill, 1967). We will return later to the questions of "American exceptionalism" and the "new republican synthesis."

33. Elise Marienstras, *Nous, le peuple,* 202–6.

34. Reinhart Koselleck, *Critique and Crisis,* 138 ff, 181–83.

35. Karl Marx, *Grundrisse: Foundations of the Critique of Political Economy,* trans. Martin Nicolaus (New York, 1973), *Bastiat and Carey,* 884.

36. Ibid., 884–85, 888.

37. Edward S. Corwin, "The Progress of Constitutional Theory between the Declaration of Independence and the Meeting of Philadelphia Convention," *American Historical Review* 30 (1925): 511–36; Merrill Jensen, *The Articles of Confederation* (Madison: University of Wisconsin Press, 1963); Jackson Turner Main, *Political Parties before the Constitution* (New York, 1972); Jack N. Rakove, *The Beginnings of National Politics* (New York: Knopf, 1979). See also Andre Kaspi, *Revolution ou guerre d'indépendence? La naissance des Etats-Unis* (Paris, 1972).

38. But also numbers 6–8, 21. We are citing *The Federalist Papers* in the edition of Clinton Rossiter (New York: Mentor, 1961). See, in the Italian translation of *The Federalist,* edited by G. Ambrosini (Pisa, 1955), the fundamental bibliography, as well as the annotations regarding the attribution of the essays. Further citations to this work will refer to the Rossiter edition, and they will appear parenthetically in the text.

39. In *The Writings of J. Madison,* ed. G. Hunt, vol. 3 (New York, 1913).

40. Lance G. Banning, *The Quarrel with Federalism: A Study in the Origins and Character of Republican Thought,* Ph.D., diss., Washington, D.C., 1972; Morton White, *The Philosophy of American Revolution* (Oxford: Oxford University Press, 1978); Garry Wills, *Explaining America: The Federalist* (Garden City, N.J.: Doubleday, 1981).

41. On this question, our reference is to Bailyn, *Ideological Origins*; Wood, *Creation*; and Pockock, *Machiavellian Moment.*

42. On the polemic that has developed around Pocock's positions, see the introduction to the Italian edition of *The Machiavellian Moment.* See also Jack H. Hexter, "The Political Universe of J. G. A. Pocock," in *The Historians* (Cambridge, Mass., 1979).

43. "Neither the Federalists nor their critics employed Rousseau as a tool of analysis," Pocock, *Machiavellian Moment*, 520. See also P. M. Sperlin, *Rousseau in America, 1760–1809* (Alabama, 1969).

44. Here I refer you to Vasoli's critiques of Pocock's work, already mentioned.

45. Charles A. Beard's thesis in *An Economic Interpretation of the Constitution* remains here fundamentally valid. As a confirmation see in particular Jackson Turner Main, *Political Parties before the Constitution*.

46. Again, on *The Federalist*, besides the texts mentioned in the nn. 38, 40 of this chapter, see George Mace, *Locke, Hobbes and the Federalist Papers* (Carbondale: Southern Illinois University Press, 1979).

47. *The Writings of T. Jefferson*, 8:31–32.

48. The distinction between republic as indirect, representative democracy and democracy as direct democracy and power of the people is radically affirmed first by Hamilton in nos. 1 and 9, and then by Madison, nos. 10 and 37; finally the distinction is taken up by Hamilton in no. 70. For more on this distinction see also Madison, no. 14.

49. See also nos. 12, 21 on the direct tax.

50. In this regard, Gerlad Stourzh, *A. Hamilton and the Idea of Republican Government* (Stanford, Calif.: Stanford University Press, 1970), is fundamental. See also Albert Furtwangler, *The Authority of Publius: A Reading of the Federalist Papers* (Ithaca, N.Y.: Cornell University Press, 1984).

51. To clarify the problem of Montesquieu's influence, besides Garry Wills, *Explaining America*, see the fundamental work of William B. Gwyn, *The Meaning of the Separation of Powers: An Analysis of the Doctrine from Its Origin to the Adoption of the U.S. Constitution* (New Orleans: Tulane University Press, 1965).

52. Hannah Arendt, *On Revolution*, 13–53. The Arendtism of our contemporaries can be measured, first of all, in the literature on "the rights of man," which, particularly in France, has dominated the years of neoliberalism.

53. Ibid., 121.

54. See the essays by Habermas that we have already mentioned.

55. In particular see the essay "Die Geschichte von den zwei Revolutionen."

56. On this question see Buel's work, *Securing the Revolution*.

57. Before the cases *MacCulloch versus Maryland* (1819) and *Gibbons versus Ogden* (1824), which affirm and develop the theory of "multiple powers" attributed to the federal government. See also A. Levi, "La teoria hamiltoniana degli 'implied powers' della Costituzione," *Rendiconti dell'Accademia dei Lincei* 8, nos. 11–12 (1951):492 ff.

58. On this question see in particular Douglass Adair, *Fame and the Founding Fathers* (New York: W. W. Norton, 1974); Garry Wills, *Explaining America*; and, obviously, Bailyn's and Wold's positions that we have already mentioned. Adair and Wills insist on the influence of Scottish philosophy, against the positions that consider important only the reference to the Atlantic tradition of the Country Party. Useful, on the whole polemic, is Herbert J. Storing, *What the Anti-Federalists Were For* (Chicago: University of Chicago Press, 1981). For classical texts on Scottish thought and its influences see Istvan Hont and Michael Ignatieff, eds., *Wealth and Virtue: The Shaping of Political Economy in the Scottish Enlightenment* (Cambridge: Cambridge University Press, 1983).

59. On this question see, besides the works on Hamilton's and Madison's thought that we have already cited, Richard C. Hofstadter, *The Idea of a Party System* (Berkeley and Los Angeles: University of California Press, 1966); William Chambers, *Political Parties in a New Nation* (Oxford: Oxford University Press, 1963).

60. Richard Buel, *Securing the Revolution*.

61. According to the alternative proposed by both Arendt and Pocock.

62. Besides the texts by Turner and Marienstras already so often quoted, see Félix Gilbert, *To the Farewell Address: Ideas of American Foreign Policy*, 2nd ed. (Princeton, N.J.: Princeton University Press, 1970); Lloyd C. Gardner, *A Different Frontier* (Chicago: Quadrangle, 1966).

63. Besides Nicola Matteucci's text, "La costituzione americana," which constitutes its extremist caricature, we refer the reader to the medieval-constitutionalist tradition represented by the works of C. H. McIlwain, Edward S. Corwin, B. Fletcher Right, Carl J. Friedrich, F. A. Hayek, Giovanni Sartori.

64. Samuel Bowles and Herbert Gintis, in the cited *Democracy and Capitalism*, have broadly illustrated the alternatives to the American constitutional model with regard to the themes of participation.

65. Jürgen Habermas, "Natural Right and Revolution," and E. Topich, *Sozialphilosophie zwischen Ideologie und Wissenschaft*, are certainly the authors who have best approached this concept.

66. Alexis de Tocqueville, *Democracy in America*, trans. Henry Reeve with Francis Bowen and Phillips Bradley (New York: Knopf, 1966), 1:6–7. Hereafter, this source is cited parenthetically in the text.

67. The opposite of what François Furet affirms in "Tocqueville. De la democratie en Amerique," in *Dictionnaire des oeuvres politiques*, 821–33.

68. Alexis de Tocqueville, *Souvenirs* (Paris, 1964), part II, particularly in the pages dedicated to the revolution of June 1848.

69. John C. Calhoun, *A Disquisition on Government, and A Discourse on the Constitution and Government of the United States*, ed. Richard Cralle (New York: P. Smith, 1943). These texts are drafted by Calhoun between 1845 and 1850. On Calhoun, besides the important *Introduzione* by M. Surdi, in John C. Calhoun, *Disquisizione sul governo* and *Discorso sul governo e la Costituzione degli Stati Uniti*, trans. M. Surdi (Rome, 1986), to which we will often refer in the following pages, see the biography by Charles Maurice Wiltse, *John C. Calhoun* (New York: Russell & Russell, 1968), 3 vols.

70. Richard Hofstadter, *The American Political Tradition* (New York: Knopf, 1948), 67–91; Eugene D. Genovese, *The World the Slaveholders Made* (New York: Pantheon, 1971), 136, 182.

71. M. Surdi, "Introduzione," 7. Citations hereafter appear parenthetically in the text.

72. Ibid., 13.

73. L. Hartz, *The Liberal Tradition in America* (New York: Harcourt Brace, 1955), 159.

74. Besides *Les Mythes fondateurs de la nation américaine*, by Elise Marienstras (Paris: Maspero, 1976), see Staughton Lynd, *Class Conflict, Slavery and the U.S. Constitution*; and William M. Wiecek, *The Sources of Antislavery Constitutionalism in America, 1760–1848* (Ithaca, N.Y.: Cornell University Press, 1977).

75. In this sense we must always remember Michael Kammen's *A Machine That Would Go of Itself.*

76. Lewis Hinchman, *Hegel's Critique of Enlightenment* (Gainesville: University of Florida Press, 1984), 258–63.

77. The simplest reference here is to the Hegelian study of the Reform Bill of 1831; see G. W. F. Hegel, *Hegel's Political Writings*, trans. T. M. Knox (Oxford: Clarendon/Oxford University Press, 1964), 295 ff. It is here, in fact, that the *Elements of the Philosophy of Right* (Cambridge: Cambridge University Press, 1964) is compared to the English constitutional model and to its democratic reform, to show its capacity to absorb both.

78. For a bibliography of these thematics in Max Weber see my "Studi su Max Weber," in *Annuario bibliografico di filosofia del diritto* (Milan, 1967), 427–59.

79. Olivier Zunz, "Genèse du pluralism americain," *Annales ESC* 42, no. 2 (1987):429–44.

80. Allow me to refer you once again to my *Savage Anomaly*, in which I emphasize the terrific and paradigmatic innovation that Spinoza introduces into the history of the concept of democracy.

81. See n. 74 of this chapter.

5. The Revolution and the Constitution of Labor

1. Olivier Betourne and Aglaia Hartig, *Penser l'histoire de la révolution francaise* (Paris: La Découverte, 1989), 83 ff.

2. See what I say about the reception of Machiavelli in the French thought of the Renaissance of the seventeenth century in my *Descartes Politico*, 164–65, with reference to works by Procacci, Garin, Busson, Lenoble, Meinecke, Von Albertini, and others. For an update of the bibliography, which, nonetheless, does not modify our judgment, see Innocent Gentillet's edition of *Discours contre Machiavel*, ed. A. d'Andrea and P. D. Stewart (Florence, 1974); as well as the articles of specialists such as K. T. Butler, H. Ingman, and L. A. McKenzie in *Journal of Warburg and Courtauld Institute*, *Bibliothèque d'Humanisme et Renaissance*, and *Journal of the History of Ideas.*

3. Alexis de Tocqueville, *Democracy in America*, vol. 2, Book IV, chap. 8, 331.

4. René Char, quoted by Hannah Arendt in *On Revolution*, 217.

5. Albert Soboul, *Précis d'histoire de la révolution française* (Paris: Editions Sociales, 1962). On Soboul and the movements of the masses in the revolution, see the always accurate annotations of Betourne and Hartig, *Penser l'histoire.* See also Soboul, "Classes populaires et rousseauisme sous la Révolution," *Annales historiques de la révolution française* 5 (1963), special issue. We will discuss this article more later.

6. Georges Lefebvre, "Foules révolutionaires," in *Etudes sur la révolution française* (Paris: Presses Universitaires de France, 1963), 371–92.

7. On this point such extremely different positions as those of Daniel Guerin, in *La lutte des classes sous la première république 1793–1797*, 2nd ed. (Paris: Gallimard, 1969), 2 vols.; and Bronislaw Baczko, in *Ending the Terror: The French Revolution after Robespierre*, trans. M. Petheram (Cambridge: Cambridge University Press, 1994), in particular 231 ff, agree. See also Guerin's *La révolution française et nous* (Brussels: Editions la Taupe, 1969).

8. On the basis of François Furet, *Interpreting the French Revolution*, trans. Elborg Forster (Cambridge: Cambridge University Press, 1981).

9. Baczko, *Ending the Terror*, 193.

10. Mallet du Pan, *Considérations sur la nature de la révolution française* (London: Emmanuel Flon, 1793). On Mallet du Pan see the work of Nicola Matteucci, *Jacques Mallet du Pan* (Naples: Nella sede dell'Istituto, 1957).

11. Fundamental on this question is Evgenii Tarle, *Germinal et Prairial* (Moscow: Editions en langues étrangères, 1959). Finally, see George Rudé, *The Crowd in the French Revolution* (London: Oxford University Press, 1972).

12. Quoted by Baczko, *Ending the Terror*, 240.

13. Such a conclusion is strongly supported, through an analysis of the difficulties of the interpretations, in Betourne and Hartig, *Penser l'histoire*.

14. D. Mornet, *Les origines intellectuelles de la révolution française 1715–1787*, 4th ed. (Paris: A. Colin, 1947). There are useful annotations in "Rousseau et la philosophie politique," *Annales de la philosophie politiques* 5 (1965), particularly in the articles by H. Barth and I. Fetscher. The contribution of A. Soboul, to which we will return soon, is also fundamental. See also François Furet and Denis Richet, *The French Revolution*, trans. S. Hardman (London: Weidenfeld & Nicolson, 1970), x ff; Bronislaw Baczko, "Lumières et utopies," *Annales ESC* 26 (1971):355–86; and, by the same author, "Le contrat social des françaises: Sieyès et Rousseau," in *The French Revolution and the Creation of the Modern Political Culture*, ed. Keith M. Baker (Oxford: Oxford University Press, 1987), 1:493–513. On Rousseau's political thought in general Judith Shklar's reading in *Men and Citizens: A Study of Rousseau's Social Theory* (Cambridge: Cambridge University Press, 1969) is always useful.

15. Albert Soboul, "L'audience des lumières sous la révolution, J.-J. Rousseau et les classes populaires," in *Utopie et institutions au XVIIIeme siècle*, ed. Pierre Francastel (Paris-La Haye: Mouton, 1963), 298–303.

16. Ibid., 294.

17. Baczko, *Ending the Terror*, 110 ff.

18. On the relations between notions and practices of time, and the antagonistic consciousness, allow me to refer you to my "La costituzione del tempo: Prolegomeni," in *Macchina tempo* (Milan: Feltrinelli, 1982), 253 ff. From another point of view see S. Breuer's discussion in "Oltre Foucault: Verso una teoria della societa disciplinare," *Rivista italiana di sociologica* 28, no. 4 (1987):259 ff.

19. B. Bongiovanni, *Tra storia e storiografia: Marx e la rivoluzione inglese*, 93 ff offers good observations on this point.

20. We consider it obvious that the classical interpretations of historical materialism (à la Borkenau, etc.), which keep the revolutionary renovation of the critique of time within parameters of objective transformation (in this case, monetaristic parameters), are completely inadequate. The time discovered by the revolutionary movement is not a form of modernization, but a form of insubordination and revolt. The sharpest critiques of historical materialism (and the efforts to neutralize its subversive potential), which we find today in the various Peacocks or Elsters, will turn then, not by chance, to the classical materialist interpretations.

21. Here we will be referring to the Alan Ritter and Julia C. Bondanella edition of J.-J. Rousseau's *On Social Contract*, in *Rousseau's Political Writings* (New York: Norton, 1988), trans. Julia Bondanella, hereafter cited parenthetically in the text.

22. Robert Derathe, "Les rapports de l'exécutif et du legislatif chez Rousseau," in *Annales de philosophie politique*, 153–69. On this question see also Rousseau's entry "Discourse on Political Economy," in the *Grande Encyclopedie* (translated by Julia Bondanella in *Rousseau's Political Writings*, 58–83).

23. Derathe, "Les rapports," 166.

24. See P. Comanducci, ed., *L'illuminismo guiridico* (Bologna, 1989), 89 and following.

25. Irving Fetscher, in *Annales de philosophie politique*, 62–63.

26. Benjamin Constant, *Reflexions sur les constitutions et les guaranties* (1818), appendices.

27. Bernard Rousset, "La philosophie de Rousseau et la question de la directivité," in *Cahiers des Archives de philosophie* (Paris, 1980), 152–53.

28. Louis Althusser, *Politics and History: Montesquieu, Rousseau, Hegel and Marx*, trans. Ben Brewster (London: New Left Books, 1972), 106.

29. G. Eisenman, "L'Esprit des Lois et la séparation des pouvoirs," in *Mélanges Carre de Malberg* (Paris, 1933), 190 ff; and "La pensée constitutionelle de Montesquieu," in *Recueil Sirey: Bicentenaire de l'Esprit des Lois* (Paris, 1952), 133–60.

30. If, in Montesquieu, the principle of the separation of powers is a "purely negative principle," obviously it is not so in the revolutionary constitutional situation, despite what Michel Troper affirms in *La séparation des pouvoirs et l'histoire constitutionelle française* (Paris: Librairie générale de droit et de jurisprudence, 1980). "It is necessary from the very nature of things that power should be a check to power," said Montesquieu in *Spirit of the Laws*, in "Great Books of the Western World" (Chicago: Encyclopedia Britannica, 1990), trans. Thomas Nugent with J. V. Pritchard, XI.4.69.

31. All references to the 1789 *Declaration of the Rights of Man and of the Citizen* are made by article number to the version in Norman L. Torrey, ed., *Les Philosophes*

(New York: Capricorn, 1960), 284–87; references to later revisions of the *Declaration* have been translated directly from the French edition, *La declarations des droits de l'homme de 1789*, ed. Christine Fauré (Paris, 1988). On the question we are discussing, the fundamental reference is to Robert Redslob, *Die Staatstheorie der französischen Nationalversammlung von 1789* (Berlin, 1912), 110ff.

32. Paul Bastid, *B. Constant et sa doctrine*, vol. 2 (Paris: A. Colin, 1966); P. Pasquino, "Sieyès, Constant e il governo dei moderni: Contributo alla storia del concetto di rappresentanza politica," *Filosofia politica* 1, no. 1 (1987):77–98.

33. Joachim Ritter, *Hegel and the French Revolution*, trans. R. D. Winfield (Cambridge: MIT Press, 1982). I have discussed extensively the relation between Rousseauism and German thought in the genesis of the philosophy of absolute idealism in my *Stato e diritto nel giovane Hegel* (Padua: CEDAM, 1958).

34. Christine Fauré, "Presentation," in *La declarations des droits de l'homme de 1789*, 35.

35. See in particular *Théorie des actes et langage: Ethique et droit*, ed. Paul Anselek (Paris: Presses universitaires de France, 1986).

36. For the essential bibliography on this question, from Georg Jellinek to Emile Boutmy by way of Carre de Malberg, besides the texts already cited in the notes of chap. 1 of this book, see G. Bacot, *Carre de Malberg et l'origine de la distinction entre souveraineté du peuple et souveraineté nationale* (Paris: Editions Centre Nationale de Recherche Scientifique, 1985).

37. For the more general juridical problematic, see Antonio Negri, "Il lavoro nella costituzione," chap. 2 in *La forma Stato*.

38. Arendt, *On Revolution*.

39. See 1789 "Declaration," sects. 13–17; 1793 version, sects. 20 and 24; 1795 version, sects. 10–14, 16.

40. See Fauré, "Presentation," 37–41, 305–7.

41. Georges Labica, *Robespierre: Une politique de la philosophie* (Paris: Presses universitaires de France, 1990), 35ff; M. Abensour, "Saint-Just," in *Dictionnaire des oeuvres politiques*, 711–25.

42. Maximilien Robespierre, "Discours du 18 Floreal An II," in *Textes choisis* (Paris, 1974), 1:160.

43. Furet, *Interpreting the French Revolution*, 50. In general on Furet, see Roger Chartier, "Une relecture politique de la révolution française," *Critique* 382 (1979):261–72; but also the critical anticipations against his methodology in M. Vovelle, "L'Elite ou la mensonge des mots," *Annales ESC* (1974):49–72.

44. Emmanuel Sieyès, *What Is the Third Estate*?, trans. M. Blondel and ed. S. E. Finer (London: Pall Mall Press, 1963), hereafter cited parenthetically in the text. On Sieyès, besides the already cited texts by P. Pasquino, and keeping in the background the seminal work of P. Bastid, *Sieyès et sa pensée* (Paris: Hachette, 1939; rev. ed., 1970), keep the following in mind: R. Mozo, "L'arte sociale e l'idea di societa nel pensiero politico di Sieyès," *Rivista internazionale di filosofia del diritto* 54 (1968):226–66; C. Clavreul, "L'influence de la théorie de E. Sieyès sur les origines de la représentation en droit public," thesis, Paris, 1982; S. Breuer, "Nationalstaat und 'Pouvoir constituant' bei Sieyès und Carl Schmitt," *Archiv für Rechts—und Sozialphilosophie* (1984):495–517; Jean-Denis Bredin, *Sieyès* (Paris: Editions de Fallois, 1988). Important references to Sieyès are also found in R. Reichardt, ed., *Handbuch politisch-sozialer grundbegriffe in Frankreich 1680–1820* (Munich: Oldenbourg, 1985).

45. P. Pasquino, "Sieyès, Constant e il governo dei moderni"; C. Clavreul, "Sieyès," in *Dictionnaire des oeuvres politiques*, 747–57.

46. Roberto Zapperi, "Introduction," in *Qu'est-ce que le Tiers état?* (Paris: Plon, 1970), 19. As a useful complement to this introduction, see Zapperi's *Per la critica del concetto di rivoluzione borghese* (Bari, 1978).

47. Pasquino, "Sieyès, Constant."

48. Bredin, *Sieyès*, 81ff.

49. Pierre Macherey, "Une nouvelle problematique du droit: Sieyès," *Futur Antérieur* 4 (1990):29ff.

50. Zapperi, "Introduction," 10.

51. Ibid., 38, 41, 43.

52. Ibid., 63.

53. Pasquino, "Sieyès, Constant"; Clavreul, "Sieyès."

54. Pasquino, "Sieyès, Constant."

55. Zapperi, "Introduction," 44–81.

56. Ibid.

57. P. Pasquino, *Il concetto di nazione e i fondamenti del diritto pubblico della rivoluzione: E.-J. Sieyès*, manuscript. On these themes we refer the reader to the discussion developed in chapter I of this book. In general, on the themes recalled here, see, besides Karl Loewenstein's classic *Volk und Parlament*: U. Steiner, *Verfassunggebung und verfassunggebende Gewalt des Volkes* (Berlin, 1966); P. Haberle, "Die verfassunggebende Gewalt des Volkes im Verfassunstaat," *Archiv für offentliche Recht* 112 (1987): 54–92.

58. Egon Zweig, *Die Lehre vom "pouvoir constituant": Ein Beitrag zum Staatslehre der französischen Revolution* (Tübingen: J. C. B. Mohr, 1909), 4.

59. See also the works of Bastid, *B. Constant*; Bredin, *Sieyès*; Baczko, *Ending the Terror*.

60. Baczko, *Ending the Terror*, 252.

61. See Bastid, *B. Constant*; Bredin, *Sieyès*; Baczko, *Ending the Terror*.

62. In 1789, in London and Paris, a pamphlet titled "Examen du gouvernment d'Angleterre compare aux Constitutions des Etats-Unis . . . ," attributed to the American W. Livingston, was published; it contains ample and numerous texts by Condorcet, du Pont de Nemours, Ganvin Gallois, all criticizing the pro-English point of view maintained by the monarchists.

63. Jean Louis de Lolme, *Constitution of England; or, An Account of the English Government*, ed. W. H. Hughes (London: Hatchard & Son, 1834) in numerous other editions. See the article by P. L. Assoun on de Lolme in *Dictionnaire des oeuvres politiques*, 472–77.

64. G. W. F. Hegel, *Phenomenology of Spirit*, trans. A. V. Miller (New York: Oxford University Press, 1977), 111–14.

65. F. Furet, *Marx and the French Revolution*, trans. D. K. Furet (Chicago: University of Chicago Press, 1988), 90–91.

66. Ibid., 92.

67. Furet's reading is ambiguous; in fact, his proposal for reading Marx's interpretation, in different periods, according to different "modes" does not contradict the fundamental and linear interpretation of Marx.

68. Furet, *Marx*, 44–46, 56–59. But see above what we say about this question when we analyze the Marxian relation to the English Revolution in chap. 3 of this volume.

69. Karl Marx and Friedrich Engels, *The Holy Family*, trans. R. Dixon (Moscow: Foreign Languages Publishing House, 1956), chaps. 4 and 6.

70. For how to think the "critical caesura" and Marx's passage to the maturity of his thought, allow me to refer you to my *Marx beyond Marx*, trans. H. Cleaver, M. Ryan, and M. Viano, ed. J. Fleming (Brooklyn: Autonomedia, 1991).

71. Karl Marx and Friedrich Engels, *The German Ideology* (1845–1846) (New York: International Publishers, 1947), chap. IA, 56–57 (hereafter cited parenthetically in the text).

72. Karl Marx, *The Poverty of Philosophy* (1847) (New York: International Publishers, n.d.), chap. 2, 145–47.

73. Karl Marx, *Revolution and Counter-Revolution*, ed. Eleanor Marx Aveling (London: Unwin, 1971), 6.

74. Ibid., chap. 5, 31.

75. B. Bongiovanni, *Fra storia e storiografia*; see also Bongiovanni's "K. Marx e il giacobinismo," *Annuali del mondo contemporaneo* 1 (1984).

76. Karl Marx, *The Eighteenth Brumaire of Louis Bonaparte* (1852), in *Surveys from Exile: Political Writings*, vol. 2 (New York: Penguin, 1973), 150 (hereafter cited parenthetically in the text).

77. See n. 67.

78. Karl Marx, *The Civil War in France*, in *The First International and After: Political Writings*, vol. 3 (New York: Penguin, 1974), 187–268; "Address of the General Council," 206.

79. Friedrich Engels, "Introduction" to Marx, *The Civil War in France*, in Marx and Engels, *Selected Works*, vol. 1 (Moscow: Foreign Languages Publishing House, 1962), 483.

80. Marx, *Civil War in France*, 208–9 (hereafter cited parenthetically in the text).

81. Karl Marx, letter to Friedrich Bolte, Nov. 23, 1871, in Marx and Friedrich Engels, *Selected Correspondence*, 3rd rev. ed. (Moscow: Progress Publishers, 1975), 254.

82. Guerin, *La lutte des classes*, 2:379, 568.

83. In Baczko, *Ending the Terror*, 224 (quoting Madame de Staël, from *Des circomstances actuelles qui peuvent terminer la révolution* [Geneva, 1979]).

84. Bastid, *B. Constant et sa doctrine*, 2:702.

85. Again, concerning these alternatives of the constitutive process of historical time, allow me to refer you to my *Macchina tempo*, chap. 13.

86. The reference to Alexandre Kojève's classic reading is in order here.

87. We will refer to Edmund Burke, *Reflections on the Revolution in France and on the Proceedings in Certain Societies in London Relative to that Event; in a Letter Intended to Have Been Sent to a Gentleman in Paris* (1790) (New York: Penguin, 1968), ed. Conor Cruise O'Brien, in the following discussion (cited parenthetically in the text). See also *An Appeal from the New to the Old Whigs: In Consequence of Some Late Discussions in Parliament, Relative to the Reflections on the French Revolution* (London: J. Dodsley, 1791). On Burke's thought in general, besides the texts that we will cite later, see Carl B. Cone, *Burke and the Nature of Politics* (Lexington: University of Kentucky Press, 1964), vol. 2; M. Ganrin, *La pensée politique d'Edmund Burke* (Paris, 1972); Marilyn Butler, ed., *Burke, Paine, Godwin and the Revolution Controversy* (Cambridge: Cambridge University Press, 1984).

88. Is this a return to the Aristotelian tradition, as Peter J. Stanlis claims in *Edmund Burke and the Natural*

Law (Ann Arbor: University of Michigan Press, 1958)? And to the school of natural rights in scholastic terms? Or isn't it, rather, a variation on the theme of that profound Neoplatonism of the English cultivated classes, so characteristic of nonacademic thought? If we could investigate this problem more extensively here, I would like to proceed in this direction. In any case, Burke breaks decisively with the political thought of the triumphant bourgeoisie and moves against its two variants, the Hobbesian and the Lockean ones.

89. C. B. Macpherson, in *Burke* (Oxford: Oxford University Press, 1980), has affirmed, and I believe with good reason, that the hierarchical conception of society expressed in *Reflections* coexists with an individualistic conception of market relations that is expressed in his interventions on social politics. This means that, regarding the control of the rising working class, Burke wants to rely on the forces of history rather than on the intervention of the state.

90. Novalis, *Fragmente 1798*, in J. Baxa, *Gesellschaft und Staat im Spiegel der deutschen Romantik* (Jena, 1927), 184.

91. As is well known, this is the thesis expressed by Friedrich Meinecke in his *Historicism: The Rise of a New Historical Outlook*, trans. J. E. Anderson (London: RKP, 1972), about which see my *Saggi sulla storicismo tedesco, Dilthey e Meinecke* (Milan: Feltrinelli, 1959). See also Roger Ayrault, *La genese du romantisme allemand* (Paris: Aubier, 1961).

92. Leo Strauss, *Natural Right and History* (Chicago: University of Chicago Press, 1953), 319.

93. Thomas Paine, *Rights of Man* in Paine, *Collected Writings* (Library of America, 1995). On Paine, see chap. 4 of this book.

94. On this polemic, see the collection cited by Marilyn Butler, *Burke, Paine, Godwin*. See also Patrick Thierry, "De la révolution américaine à la révolution française: Paine, Burke et les droits de l'homme," *Critique* 481–482 (1987):476–505.

95. I have studied these translations and von Gentz's positions carefully in my *Alle origini del formalismo giuridico: Studio sul problema della forma in Kant e nei guiristi kantiani fra il 1789 e il 1802* (Padua: CEDAM, 1962), 341–46.

96. Ibid., 329 ff; Antonio Negri, *Stato e diritto del giovane Hegel* (Padua: CEDAM, 1958), 188 ff.

97. This is a fundamental point in the genesis of Romantic historicism, according to Friedrich Meinecke's intuition (about whom see my aforementioned work). And this is the point at which, in Germany, Enlightenment currents intersect with modernity and open up to the specificity of early nineteenth-century German philosophy.

98. Antonio Negri, *Alle origini del formalismo giuridico*, 345 ff; here I have reconstructed the sense of von Gentz's experience for contemporary German thought by recalling the fundamental aspects of his reception.

99. Antonio Negri, "Rileggendo Hegel, filosofo del diritto," *Incidenza di Hegel*, ed. Fulvio Tessitore (Naples: Morano, 1970), 251–70.

100. G. W. F. Hegel, *Jenenser Philosophie*, vol. 1 (Leipzig, 1932), 239.

101. G. W. F. Hegel, *Hegel's Philosophy of Right*, trans. T. M. Knox (New York: Oxford University Press, 1952), 161.

102. G. W. F. Hegel, *Lectures on the History of Philosophy* (1840) (Lincoln: University of Nebraska Press, 1995), trans. E. S. Haldane and Frances H. Simpson, 2:98.

103. Alexis de Tocqueville, *The Old Regime and the French Revolution*, trans. S. Gilbert (Garden City, N.J.: Doubleday, 1955).

104. Raymond Aron, *Main Currents in Sociological Thought*, trans. R. Howard and H. Weaver (Harmondsworth: Penguin, 1968–1970), 2 vols.

105. Tocqueville's procedure recalls the Machiavellian procedure of the *Rapporto sulle cose di Francia* (see chap. 2).

106. Tocqueville, "Foreword," xiii.

107. All of contemporary French historiography, under the aegis of or influenced by F. Furet's positions and by the line that presently dominates in the *Annales* school, moves in this direction. An intelligent critical position is expressed by Denis Berger and Michèle Riot-Sarcey in "Le gai renoncement," in *Futur antérieur* suppl. 1 (1991).

108. A Nietzschean version of Tocqueville's history of democracy and revolution hasn't been written yet; nonetheless the history of contemporary historiography would find in this reference a sure handhold for clarifying how deeply the critique of modernity has traversed modern historiography. We are certainly not taking a "destruction of historiography" [*Zerstorung der Historiographie*] perspective, in imitation of Lukács's "destruction of reason"; on the contrary, we are thinking of a reconsideration capable of making a constructive sense of modern disutopia, as constitutive of capitalist progress, emerge.

109. Alexis de Tocqueville, *The European Revolution and Correspondence with Gobineau*, ed. J. Lukacs (Gloucester: Peter Smith, 1968).

110. Ernst Cassirer, *The Myth of the State* (New Haven, Conn.: Yale University Press, 1946), 244; P. Raynaud, "Gobineau: Essai sur l'inegalité des races humaines," in *Dictionnaire des oeuvres politiques*, 278–82.

111. In different ways, the positions expressed in the following works are entirely unsatisfying: J. P. Meyer in

Tocqueville (Paris, 1948); François Furet in "Tocqueville est-il un historien de la révolution française?" and "Naissance d'un paradigme: Tocqueville et le voyage en Amerique," published in *Annales ESC* 25 (1970):434–51 and 39 (1984):225 ff; and Pierre Rosanvallon in *Le moment Guizot* (Paris: Gallimard, 1985).

6. Communist Desire and the Dialectic Restored

1. Karl Marx, *Capital*, vol. 1, trans. Ben Fowkes (New York: Vintage, 1977), 874 (hereafter cited parenthetically in the text).

2. See Karl Marx, *Capital*, vol. 3, trans. David Fernbach (London: Penguin, 1981), chaps. 22 and 23, 480–51. (Citations to this volume hereafter appear in the text.)

3. Karl Marx, *Capital*, vol. 2, trans. David Fernbach (London: Penguin, 1978), 201. (Citations hereafter appear in the text.)

4. In this regard see my *La forma Stato*, 306–16.

5. Karl Marx, *Grundrisse*, trans. Martin Nicolaus (New York: Vintage, 1973), 676 (emphasis in the original). (Citations will hereafter appear in the text.) In general on Marx's *Grundrisse* see my *Marx beyond Marx*.

6. On the concept of crisis in Marx see my essay "Marx on Cycle and Crisis," in *Revolution Retrieved* (London: Red Notes, 1988), 43–90. In this text I analyze Marx's positions on the concept of crisis with a particular attention to its relation to the rise and fall of the rate of profit.

7. Karl Marx, *The Eighteenth Brumaire of Louis Bonaparte*, 238.

8. Karl Marx, *The German Ideology*, 56–57.

9. It seems to me that the theoretical work of the Communist Left of the Thirties, primarily that of Georg Lukács and Karl Korsch, falls into this trap.

10. I am referring again to E. P. Thompson, *The Making of the English Working Class.*

11. A. Negri, *La fabbrica della strategia. 33 lezioni su Lenin* (Milan and Padua, 1976).

12. See Karl Marx, *The Class Struggles in France: 1848 to 1850*, in *Surveys from Exile, Political Writings*, vol. 2, ed. David Fernbach (London: Penguin, 1992), 44–47.

13. Karl Marx and Frederick Engels, "Address to the Central Committee of the Communist League," in Marx and Engels, *Selected Works*, 1:110.

14. Marx, *The Civil War in France*, 212.

15. V. I. Lenin, "Lecture on the 1905 Revolution," in *Collective Works*, vol. 19 (New York: International Publishers, 1942), 389–90.

16. Lenin, "Preface to the Second Edition," of *The Development of Capitalism in Russia* (Moscow: Foreign Languages Publishing House, 1956), 6–10. See also Lenin's polemical writings and interventions in internal party struggles before the explosion of the first Russian Revolution: *The Tasks of the Russian Social Democrats* (1898); *What Is to Be Done? Burning Questions of Our Movement* (1902); *One Step Forward, Two Steps Back (The Crisis of Our Party)* (1904)—all included in Lenin, *Selected Works*, vol. 1 (London: Lawrence & Wishart, 1947).

17. Lenin, *The Proletarian Revolution and the Renegade Kautsky*, in *Selected Works*, vol. 2 (London: Lawrence & Wishart, 1947), 381 ff.

18. R. Luxemburg, *Massenstreik, Partei und Gewerkschaften* (Hamburg: E. Debber, 1906), 32.

19. Leon Trotsky, *1905*, trans. Anya Bostock (New York: Random House, 1971), 104.

20. The best recent study on the "soviets" is certainly A. Anweiler, "Die Ratebewegung in Russland, 1905–1931," in *Studien zur Geschichte Osteuropas*, vol. 5 (E. J. Brill, 1958). I have relied on this study in the following argument.

21. J. Martow and T. Dan, *Geschichte der russischen Sozialdemokratie* (Berlin, 1926), 110 ff.

22. Lenin, "Lecture on the 1905 Revolution," 399 ff.

23. Lenin, "The Boycott of the Bulygin Duma, and Insurrection," in *Collected Works*, vol. 9 (London: Lawrence & Wishart, 1962), 184–85.

24. Lenin, "Socialism and Anarchism," in *Selected Works*, vol. 3.

25. Lenin, "Should We Boycott the State Duma? The Platform of the 'Majority,'" in *Selected Works*, vol. 3.

26. See Lenin, "Our Tasks and the Soviet of Workers' Deputies: Letter to the Editorial Board." See also Lenin, "Lecture on the 1905 Revolution," 399.

27. Lenin, "The Dissolution of the Duma and the Tasks of the Proletariat," in *Selected Works*, vol. 3, 371.

28. Ibid., 378–79 (emphasis in original).

29. See Lenin, "Ueber die parteilosen Arbeiterorganisation im Zusammenhang mit den anarcho-syndakalistichen Stromungen im Proletariat," in *Samtliche Werke* (Moscow, 1927–1941), 10:552 ff. On this complex of problems see A. G. Mayer, *Leninism* (Cambridge, Mass.: Harvard University Press, 1957).

30. See Lenin, "A Few Theses, Proposed by the Editors," in *Selected Works*, vol. 5 (New York: International Publishers, 1934), 155–57.

31. Lenin, *Samtliche Werke*, 8:248, 572.

32. Rosa Luxemburg, *Massenstreik, Partei und Gewerschaften*, 42.

33. Leon Trotsky, "Discours devant le tribunale, 19 septembre 1906," in P. Boue, *Le parti bolscevique* (Paris: Editions de Minuit, 1963), 74.

34. See Leon Trotsky, "Der Arbeiterdeputiertenrat und die Revolution," *Die Neue Zeit* 25, no. 2 (1906–7):76–86.

35. Lenin, *The Proletarian Revolution*, 392.

36. Lenin, *Samtliche Werke*, 20:322.

37. Lenin, "Plans of Chapter VII (Unwritten)," in *Marxism on the State: Preparatory Material for the Book The State and Revolution* (Moscow: Progress Publishers, 1972), 94.

38. Lenin, "First Letter from Afar," in *Selected Works*, 1:737–40.

39. See Lenin, "A Few Theses, Proposed by the Editors."

40. Such program is already defined in the "First Letter from Afar."

41. Lenin, *What Is to Be Done?*, in *Selected Works*, 1:166 ff.

42. Lenin, "The Tasks of the Proletariat in the Present Revolution," in *Selected Works*, vol. 2 (New York: International Publishers, 1934), 17–21.

43. On the polemic of April 1917 between Lenin and Kamenev, see Anweiler, "Die Ratebewegung," 193 ff.

44. See Leon Trotsky, *The History of the Russian Revolution*, trans. Max Eastman, vol. 1 (New York: Simon & Schuster, 1932), 166 ff. See also Lenin, "Lessons of the Revolution," in *Selected Works*, 2:77–79.

45. For Lenin's analysis of the struggle in the countryside in this period, see *Selected Works*, vol. 2.

46. See Lenin, "On Slogans," in *Selected Works*, 2:67, 71.

47. Ibid., 69, 72.

48. Lenin, *State and Revolution: The Marxist Doctrine of the State and the Tasks of the Proletariat in the Revolution*, in *Selected Works*, 2:141–225.

49. See Lenin's draft *Marxism and the State.* This volume provides references to the Kautsky texts that Lenin read. See also Anton Pannekoek, "Massenaktion und Revolution," *Die Neue Zeit* 30 (1911–1912):541–50, 585–93, 609–16; and N. Bucharin, "Der imperialistiche Raubstaat," *Die Jugendinternationale*, no. 6, December 1, 1916.

50. Lenin quotes the entire extended passage in which this sentence appears: "But the revolution is thorough. It is still on its journey through purgatory. It goes about its business methodically. By 2 December 1851 [the date of Louis Bonaparte's coup d'état] it had completed one half of its preparatory work; it is now completing the other half. First of all it perfected the parliamentary power, in order to be able to overthrow it. Now, having attained this, it is perfecting the *executive power*, reducing it to its purest object of attack, in order *to concentrate all its forces of destruction against it* [emphasis added]. And when it has completed this, the second half of its preliminary work, Europe will leap from its seat and exultantly exclaim: 'Well worked, old mole!' The executive power possesses an immense bureaucratic and military organization, an ingenious and broadly based state machinery, and an army of half a million officials alongside the actual army, which numbers a further half million. This frightful parasitic body, which surrounds the body of French society like a caul and stops up all its pores, arose in the time of the absolute monarchy, with the decay of the feudal system, which it helped to accelerate." The first French Revolution carried centralization further, "but at the same time it had to develop the extent, the attributes and the number of underlings of the governmental power. Napoleon perfected this state machinery. The Legitimist and July monarchies only added a greater division of labour. . . . Finally, the parliamentary republic was compelled in its struggle against the revolution to strengthen by means of repressive measures the resources and centralization of governmental power. *All political upheavals perfected this machine instead of smashing it* [emphasis added]. The parties that strove in turn for mastery regarded possession of this immense state edifice as the main booty for the victor" (*The Eighteenth Brumaire*, 236–38).

51. See Lenin, "First All-Russian Congress of Soviets of Workers' and Soldiers' Deputies," in *Selected Works*, 2:57–60.

52. In Lenin, *Samtliche Werke*, 20:43.

53. Lenin, "The Tasks of the Proletariat in the Present Revolution"; and "A Dual Power," in *Selected Works*, 2:17–24.

54. See Lenin, "The Immediate Tasks of the Soviet Government," in *Selected Works*, 2:337 ff.

55. See, for example, Hans Kelsen, "Interno alla natura e al valore della democrazia," in *Lineamenti di una teoria generale dello Stato* (Rome: A. R. E., 1932), 71 ff.

56. Lenin, "Immediate Tasks," 337.

57. Lenin, "Excerpt from a Speech Delivered at the VIIth Congress of the Communist Party of Russia, on the Revision of the Program and the Name of the Party," in *The Paris Commune* (New York: International Publishers, 1931), 51.

58. See primarily "Immediate Tasks."

59. See Lenin, *L'internazionale comunista* (Rome: Edizioni Rinascita, 1950).

60. Max Weber, *The Russian Revolutions*, trans. Gordon C. Wells and Peter Baehr (Ithaca, N.Y.: Cornell

University Press, 1995). This volume contains Weber's writings on both Russian revolutions.

61. Claude Sergio Ingerflom, in *Le citoyen impossible: Les racines sociales du leninisme* (Paris: Payot, 1988), has provided a realistic picture of these conditions and of the (necessary?) processes determined by them.

62. I am essentially referring to the following writings by Rosa Luxemburg, *La rivoluzione in Russia* (1905), *Sciopero di massa, Partiti e sindacati* (1906), *La tragedia russa* (1918), *La rivoluzione russa. Un esame critico* (1918). I am reading them in the translation by L. Amodio of Luxemburg's *Scritti scelti* (Milan, 1963), respectively, at 268 ff, 282 ff, 547 ff, 562 ff. Further citations of *Scritti scelti* will appear in the text.

63. J-P. Sartre, *The Critique of Dialectical Reason*, vol. 2: *The Intelligibility of History*, trans. Quintin Hoare (New York: Verso, 1991).

64. From our point of view Sartre's discourse, although blocked by contemporary political demands, offers an exceptional perspective on developments in the world of "real Socialism." Obviously, this question has not yet received a sufficient critical answer.

65. Moshe Lewin, *La formation du système sovietique*, Paris 1987.

66. See the many useful reflections on this problem in Hans-Jürgen Krahl, *Konstitution und Klassenkampf: Zur historischen Dialektik von Bürgerlicher Emanzipation und proletarischer Revolution* (Frankfurt: Verlag Neue Kritik, 1971).

67. See the interesting references in Cavazzutti, *La teoria dell'impresa* (Bologna, 1974).

68. See on this question my essay "Keynes and the Capitalist Theory of the State," in Michael Hardt and Antonio Negri, *Labor of Dionysus* (Minneapolis: University of Minnesota Press, 1994), 23–51.

7. The Constitution of Strength

1. Reinhart Koselleck, in *Futures Past*, see "Historical Criteria of the Modern Concept of Revolution," 39–54, above all the commentary on the *Conflict of the Faculties* by Immanuel Kant.

2. It seems to us that we have clarified this concept by studying in chap. 1 the openings that the concept of constituent power determines against all the dogmatic closures, in the concrete work of the jurists. Hermann Heller's work in particular should be kept in mind here.

3. See my "Prolegomeni sul tempo," in *Macchina tempo.*

4. And even more so the systemic ones, as is evident in Niklas Luhmann's work.

5. From this point of view Theda Skocpol's work is absolutely characteristic. In order to allow the emergence of the autonomy of the State, and therefore the invalidation of constituent power, her comparative work on the concept of revolution always implies the reference to archaic revolutionary societies in the social structure. When Skocpol's discourse tries to move into the present, this sequence undoubtedly becomes grotesque. See the two fundamental works by Skocpol, *States and Social Revolutions: A Comparative Analysis of France, Russia and China* (Cambridge: Cambridge University Press, 1979), and *Bringing the State back In* (Cambridge: Cambridge University Press, 1985).

6. Negri, *Macchina tempo*, "Prolegomeni," 253–334.

7. On the concept of "material constitution," see the passages in chap. 1 where I discuss the work of Mortati and Forstoff. See also my own *La forma Stato.*

8. At the conference "Spinoza in the Twentieth Century," organized by Olivier Bloch at the Sorbonne (Paris) in 1990, Manfred Walther presented a very suggestive paper on Schmitt's use of Spinoza's work.

9. Gilles Deleuze, "Control and Becoming," in *Negotiations 1972–1990* (New York: Columbia University Press, 1995), 169 ff.

10. Giorgio Agamben, *The Coming Community*, trans. Michael Hardt (Minneapolis: University of Minnesota Press, 1993).

11. Antonio Gramsci, *Note sul Machiavelli, sulla politica e sullo Stato moderno* (Turin, 1953), 3–94. But see also Louis Althusser, "Machiavelli's Solitude," from which the following citations come.

12. Antonio Gramsci, *The Modern Prince*, in *Selections from Prison Notebooks*, ed. and trans. Quintin Hoare and Geoffrey Nowell Smith (New York: International Publishers, 1971), 141. (Citations hereafter appear in the text.)

13. Benedict de Spinoza, *The Ethics*, in *A Spinoza Reader*, ed. Edwin Curley (Princeton, N.J.: Princeton University Press, 1994), pt. IV, prop. 40 ff, 222 ff.

14. Here we are referring to Michel Foucault's work, and in particular to his lectures of the 1970s.

15. On this question, that is, on the problem of measure and limitlessness, I take the liberty of referring the reader to my work *Il lavoro di Giobbe* (Milan: Sugar Co., 1990).

16. Gilles Deleuze and Félix Guattari, *A Thousand Plateaus: Capitalism and Schizophrenia*, trans. Brian Massumi (Minneapolis: University of Minnesota Press, 1987).

17. Here the reference is again to Foucault.

Index

Created by Eileen Quam

Antonio (Toni) Negri, a political exile in France for many years and the emblematic figure of the Italian radical Left, was a professor at the Collège International de Philosophie and the University of Paris VIII (Saint-Denis). He is the author of numerous articles and books, including *The Savage Anomaly: The Power of Spinoza's Metaphysics and Politics* (Minnesota, 1991); *Communists Like Us: New Spaces of Liberty, New Lines of Alliance,* written in collaboration with Félix Guattari; *Labor of Dionysus: A Critique of the State-Form,* written in collaboration with Michael Hardt (Minnesota, 1994); and *The Politics of Subversion: A Manifesto for the Twenty-First Century.* An ardent activist, Negri has been imprisoned in Rome since July 1, 1997, when he voluntarily returned to Italy.

Maurizia Boscagli is associate professor of English at the University of California at Santa Barbara. She is the author of *The Eye on the Flesh: Fashions of Masculinity in the Early Twentieth Century.*